The Jews and
British Romanticism

THE JEWS AND BRITISH ROMANTICISM

POLITICS, RELIGION, CULTURE

Edited by

Sheila A. Spector

THE JEWS AND BRITISH ROMANTICISM
© Sheila A. Spector, 2005.

First published in 2005 by
PALGRAVE MACMILLAN™
175 Fifth Avenue, New York, N.Y. 10010 and
Houndmills, Basingstoke, Hampshire, England RG21 6XS
Companies and representatives throughout the world.

PALGRAVE MACMILLAN is the global academic imprint of the Palgrave
Macmillan division of St. Martin's Press, LLC and of Palgrave Macmillan Ltd.
Macmillan® is a registered trademark in the United States, United Kingdom
and other countries. Palgrave is a registered trademark in the European
Union and other countries.

Library of Congress Cataloging-in-Publication Data

The Jews and British romanticism: politics, religion, culture / edited by
Sheila A. Spector.
p. cm.
Includes bibliographical references and index.
ISBN 1–4039–6454–8 (alk. paper)
1. Jews—Great Britain—History. 2. Judaism and literature—Great Britain.
3. Judaism in literature. 4. Jews in literature. 5. Romanticism—Great Britain.
6. English literature—History and criticism. 7. Great Britain–Ethnic relations.
8. Coleridge, Samuel Taylor, 1772–1834—Criticism and interpretation.
I. Spector, Sheila A., 1946–

DS135.E5J445 2004
305.892'4041—dc22   2004052795

A catalogue record for this book is available from the British Library.

Design by Newgen Imaging Systems (P) Ltd., Chennai, India.

First edition: January 2005

10 9 8 7 6 5 4 3 2 1

Printed in the United States of America.

For the next generation—

Miriam, Benjamin, Hanan
Avra
Aiyana, Sophia, Zohara

CONTENTS

ILLUSTRATIONS

CONTRIBUTORS

Frederick Burwick, Professor of English and Comparative Literature at the University of California at Los Angeles, held visiting positions in Germany at the Universities of Würzburg, Siegen, Göttingen, and Bamberg. He has also lectured at the Universities of Heidelberg, Köln, Giessen, Leipzig, and Jena in Germany, as well as Oxford and Cambridge in England. With an interdisciplinary approach to literature, he has explored the interactions of literature with art, science, music, and theater. Author and editor of twenty books and close to a hundred articles, his research is dedicated to problems of perception, illusion, and delusion in literary representation and theatrical performance. With Paul Douglass, he edited *A Selection of Hebrew Melodies, Ancient and Modern* of Lord Byron and Isaac Nathan (Tuscaloosa: University of Alabama Press, 1988), which was marketed with a recording of the songs. He has been named Distinguished Scholar by both the British Academy (1992) and the Keats-Shelley Association (1998).

Lloyd Guy Davies received his Ph.D. in Literature from Duke University's Graduate Program in Literature. He is Professor of English Literature at Western Kentucky University with research interests in Romanticism, literary theory, and Jewish studies. He has published articles on Romanticism and on traditional Judaic textual study as a theoretical model for contemporary literary criticism, and is currently completing a book, inspired by the work of Harold Fisch, entitled *Romantic Hebraism: A Covenantal Reading of English Romanticism*.

Frank Felsenstein's book, *Anti-Semitic Stereotypes: A Paradigm of Otherness in English Popular Culture, 1666–1938* (Baltimore: The Johns Hopkins University Press, 1995), examined the representation of the Jews in English popular culture from 1660 to 1830. He is at present working on a parallel study of depictions of the Jews during the Victorian era. Felsenstein is Reed D. Voran Honors Distinguished Professor of Humanities at Ball State University.

Diane Long Hoeveler is Professor of English and Coordinator of Women's Studies at Marquette University, Milwaukee, Wisconsin. She is author of *Romantic Androgyny: The Women Within* (University Park, PA: Pennsylvania State University Press, 1990) and *Gothic Feminism: The Professionalization of Gender from Charlotte Smith to the Brontës* (University Park, PA: Pennsylvania

State University Press, 1998), and coauthor of *Charlotte Brontë* (New York: Twayne Publishers, 1997) and the *Historical Dictionary of Feminism* (Lanham, MD: Scarecrow Press, 1996; 2004). Edited or coedited works include *Comparative Romanticisms: Power, Gender, Subjectivity* (Columbia, SC: Camden House, 1998), *Women of Color: Defining the Issues, Hearing the Voices* (Westport, CN: Greenwood Press, 2001), *Approaches to Teaching "Jane Eyre"* (New York: Modern Language Association, 1993), *Approaches to Teaching Gothic Fiction: The British and American Traditions* (New York: Modern Language Association, 2003), *Wuthering Heights: Complete Text with Introduction, Contexts, Critical Essays* (Boston: Houghton Mifflin, 2001) and *Written on the Bodily Text: Gender and Creativity Across Cultures* (forthcoming 2005). In addition, she has published over thirty-five articles on a variety of topics, including the gothic, melodrama, women writers, romanticism, and gender. She is past President of the International Conference on Romanticism (2001–2003), and serves on the editorial board of a number of journals in the field of Romanticism.

Lilach Lachman teaches in the Comparative Literature Department of Tel Aviv University. She has published essays on the poetics of witnessing in Poussin, John Keats, Emily Dickinson, Paul Celan, and Avot Yeshurun. She is the editor of an anthology of Hebrew, Yiddish, and Arabic lullabies, *Even Hoshen* (forthcoming), and she is currently completing a book on the seminal but neglected Israeli poet, Avot Yeshurun.

Judith W. Page teaches in the English Department and the Center for Jewish Studies at the University of Florida. She is the author of *Wordsworth and the Cultivation of Women* (Berkeley: University of California Press, 1994) and of *Imperfect Sympathies: Jews and Judaism in British Romantic Literature and Culture* (New York: Palgrave/Macmillan, 2004). In addition, she has written numerous articles and reviews on Romanticism, including a contribution to the first volume that Sheila Spector edited on British Romanticism and the Jews.

Stuart Peterfreund is Professor of English and Graduate Coordinator at Northeastern University, where he has taught since 1978. The author of three books of poetry, books on Blake and Shelley, and the editor of several collections of essays, Peterfreund has been at work recently on a number of essays that explore the discourses of racial and cultural difference in the late eighteenth and early nineteenth centuries. These essays include "Not for 'Antiquaries,' but for 'Philosophers': Isaac D'Israeli's Talmudic Critique and His Talmudical Way with Literature," which appeared in *British Romanticism and the Jews: History, Culture, Literature*, as well as forthcoming essays on Mary Wollstonecraft and Orientalism, and on Isaac D'Israeli's response to the theories of the eighteenth-century Dutch physician, physiognomist, and artist, Petrus Camper.

Michael Ragussis is Professor of English at Georgetown University. He is the author of *Figures of Conversion: "The Jewish Question" and English*

National Identity (Durham: Duke University Press, 1995), and is currently working on a book-length project entitled *Jews and Other "Outlandish Englishmen": Ethnic Performance and National Identity in Georgian England and Beyond.*

Marsha Keith Schuchard, an independent scholar from Atlanta, Georgia, received her Ph.D. in English from the University of Texas at Austin. She investigates the influence of esoteric movements on British culture and politics, with special attention to Sabbatian Kabbalism, Illuminist Freemasonry, and Swedenborgianism. Schuchard's essays have appeared in *Blake: An Illustrated Quarterly, Studies in Eighteenth-Century Culture, British Journal of Eighteenth-Century Studies, Consortium on Revolutionary Europe*, and *Esoterica*, as well as anthologies such as *Secret Texts: The Literature of Secret Societies*, ed. Marie Mulvey Roberts and Hugh Ormsby-Lennon (New York: AMS Press, 1995); *Leibniz, Mysticism, and Religion*, ed. Allison P. Coudert, Richard H. Popkin, and Gordon M. Weiner (Boston: Kluwer Academic Publishers, 1998); *Blake, Politics, and History*, ed. Jackie DiSalvo, G. A. Rosso, and Christopher Z. Hobson (New York: Garland, 1998); *Blake in the Nineties*, ed. Steve Clark and David Worrall (New York: St. Martin's Press, 1999). She recently published *Restoring the Temple of Vision: Cabalistic Freemasonry and Stuart Culture* (Leiden: Brill, 2002), and has a new book, *William Blake and the Sexual Basis of Spiritual Vision*, forthcoming from London: Random House.

Michael Scrivener is the author of three books on Romanticism and politics, the most recent of which is *Seditious Allegories: John Thelwall and Jacobin Writing* (University Park, PA: Pennsylvania State University Press, 2001). Scrivener currently is working on a study of modernity and Jewish representations in nineteenth-century literature and culture.

Reeva Spector Simon is a Research Scholar at the Middle East Institute, Columbia University. She is the author of *Iraq Between the Two World Wars: The Militarist Origins of Tyranny* (updated ed., New York: Columbia University Press, 2004), and *The Middle East in Crime Fiction: Mysteries, Spy Novels, and Thrillers from 1916 to the 1980s* (New York: L. Barber Press, 1989); and she is coeditor of *The Jews of the Middle East and North Africa in Modern Times* (New York: Columbia University Press, 2003), and the forthcoming *The Creation of Iraq 1914–1921.*

Sheila A. Spector, an independent scholar, has devoted her career to studying the intersection between British culture and Judaica. In addition to compiling *Jewish Mysticism: An Annotated Bibliography on the Kabbalah in English* (New York: Garland, 1984), she has written two books on Blake— *"Glorious incomprehensible": The Development of Blake's Kabbalistic Language* and *"Wonders Divine": The Development of Blake's Kabbalistic Myth* (both published by Lewisburg, PA: Bucknell University Press, 2001); and she edited *British Romanticism and the Jews: History, Culture, Literature* (New York: Palgrave/Macmillan, 2002).

Stanley J. Spector, who received the Ph.D. in Philosophy from the University of Colorado, specializes in twentieth-century European thought, including phenomenology, transcendental philosophy, existential philosophy and hermeneutics. He has presented several essays at the *Southwest Texas Popular Culture Association*, including "Bound to Cover Just a Little More Ground: A Heideggerian Reflection on the Grateful Dead," and "Who is Dionysos, and Why Does He Keep Following Me Everywhere?," published in *Dead Letters*, volume II. His "Dionysus and the Dead: A Nietschean Perspective," will be included in N. Merriweather's *It All Rolls Into One: Rapture, Dionysus, Nietzsche and the Grateful Dead* (Berkeley: University of California Press, forthcoming).

R. Paul Yoder is Associate Professor of English at the University of Arkansas at Little Rock. He is the coeditor (with Wallace Jackson) of *Approaches to Teaching Pope's Poetry* (New York: Modern Language Association, 1993), and *Critical Essays on Alexander Pope* (New York: G. K. Hall, Toronto: Maxwell Macmillan Canada, and New York: Maxwell Macmillan International, 1993). He has also published essays on Milton, Pope, Thomas Gray, Samuel Richardson, Blake, and Wordsworth.

INTRODUCTION: THE POLITICS OF RELIGION

Sheila A. Spector

We are only now beginning to recognize the full ramifications of the relationship between Christians and Jews during the European Romantic Movement.[1] Before the Enlightenment, the Jews were a despised, though protected, minority in Europe.[2] As the purported Christ killers, the Jews were condemned, so Christians believed, to wander throughout the world bearing witness to the new dispensation. Yet, because a cornerstone of much Christian eschatology was the conversion of the Jews, who were prophesied first to be dispersed throughout the four corners of the universe, Europeans permitted small Jewish communities to survive in their midst, though as separate *nations* within the larger geographical entities that comprised the Continent.[3] As a result of Enlightenment rationality, however, Europeans were compelled to reconsider the morality, not to mention practicality, of retaining separate, though decidedly unequal communities within their nominal bounds. As the West grew progressively more secularized, with Christians defining themselves primarily as moral and rational creatures, it became less and less acceptable to maintain separate ethnic communities whose members were tolerated, though denied the rights of citizenship. Instead, as part of the process by which the modern nation-states were consolidated, Europeans were forced to reconfigure their own self-identities, very often by contrasting themselves with the *others* who presumably threw into relief those characteristics by which each group defined itself.

At the same time that the dominant community was becoming modernized, the European Jewish communities were experiencing their own Enlightenment, the *Haskalah*.[4] In part influenced by the corresponding European movement, the *Haskalah* was a secularizing force in which the Jews, under the leadership of Moses Mendelssohn (1729–1786), sought ways to assimilate economically and culturally, though without compromising their religious and ethnic identity. This process of acculturation entailed a vocational education in the vernacular, so that Jews would learn how to work and speak with others within the labor force. Beyond that, the Reform Movement advocated a relaxation of Jewish law to permit outward assimilation, and the substitution for a literal return to Zion a metaphorical transfer of the values of Zionism to the host country.[5] In this way, Western Jews hoped to make themselves eligible for citizenship through an intellectual process comparable to that which Christians were experiencing during the same time.

As is so often the case, the process was even more complex in Great Britain.[6] Having already begun annexing various regions of the expanding empire, the British required a national policy that would facilitate assimilating members of different ethnic groups, while still retaining a national identity that was at least nominally Anglo-Saxon Protestant. At the same time that the British were reconciling their self-identity to their new imperial reality, English Jews were experiencing their own form of *Haskalah*, in which they established the kinds of educational and cultural institutions that would permit a degree of assimilation, while externally, defending themselves against the theological polemics of anti-Semites, and conversionist efforts of so-called philo-Semites. Not coincidentally, the efforts of the two communities coalesced during the romantic long century, the interim between the 1750s and 1850s. Specifically, the passage and immediate repeal of the Jewish Naturalization Bill of 1753 serves as an atavistic reminder of the older prejudices that both communities had to overcome before Emancipation;[7] while in 1858, Baron Lionel de Rothschild's assumption of his seat in Parliament, without first being required to swear an oath as a Christian, signals the integration of the two nations within the larger British Empire.

"No Jews! No wooden shoes!"

This slogan, shouted by the mob in response to the passage of the "Jew Bill," indicates just how important myth is to national consciousness. Actually, there is no connection between the Jews and wooden shoes, the footwear being associated with the French, the historical antagonists of the English, not least because of religious differences. In this exclamation, the irrational mob combined the two enemies of English Protestants—the Pope and the Jews—both having been, under various circumstances, identified as the anti-Christ. Thus, even though the Jew Bill exists as an unhappy reminder of an ingrained English anti-Semitism, the chant also testifies to the success of Tudor propagandists who were able to sever the emotional connections between English consciousness and the Roman Church.[8] The visceral response of the mob to the bill did not result from any real or even perceived threat to the material existence of any but a handful of London merchants; rather, the mere thought of Jewish naturalization undermined the national self-image, the myth by which the people defined themselves as Englishmen. From this perspective, British Romanticism can be viewed as the intellectual process by which the insulating Tudor myth, which for centuries had defined England as a Protestant nation, was amended to accommodate the realities of a colonizing empire that would attempt, at least, to integrate racially, theologically, and culturally diverse peoples into a single "imagined political community."

Historically, from the sixteenth century on, British identity has been consolidated around the Anglican Church.[9] In order to complete the break with Rome, the Tudors, above all, had to reconfigure the way the British thought about themselves. In pre-Reformation England, the terms Christian and Catholic were synonymous, there being only one valid church in the West, headed by the pope. Therefore, when Henry VIII broke with Rome, he needed to do more than simply institutionalize the Anglican Church. He had to reorient the British thought process so that Catholicism and Christianity would automatically be differentiated in the people's minds. To do so, his chroniclers launched a massive propaganda campaign. Retaining the duality found in popularized versions of Christianity, they recast the traditional poles of good and evil. Heretofore, the *good* was associated with Christianity, which was equivalent to the Roman Church, and *evil* was the non-Christian, under the control of the demonic force that opposed what was presented as the true Christian religion. After the break with Rome, however, the *good* became more narrowly defined in terms of Protestantism, especially Anglicanism; and *evil* was associated with any non-Protestant faith, though especially Catholicism. As the religious turmoil of the mid-sixteenth century demonstrates, Henry's reformation was not exactly welcomed by all of his children, much less the populace. Therefore, it was necessary to generate a myth that would reinforce the differences between Anglicanism and Catholicism. In its most overt literary formulation, Book I of Edmund Spenser's *The Faerie Queene*, Gloriana—Elizabeth as head of the Anglican Church—sends Red Crosse, the true Christian Knight, to liberate Adam and Eve. He is opposed by Duessa/Fidessa, the false faith of Catholicism, who disguises herself as Una, the true church. While initially, the Red Crosse Knight is confused by the substitution of Fidessa for Una, he eventually recognizes the one truth and is thereby armed to confront the demonic dragon. Although Duessa lives, she is ultimately revealed as the hag she truly is.

With its blend of British folklore and Protestant theology, *The Faerie Queene* is part of the larger attempt to restructure the national identity from European Catholicism, in which England was subordinate to the central authority of the pope, to Anglicanism, in which the constitutionally established erastian relationship between throne and altar made the monarch both the secular and the religious head of the island nation, now cut off from the continent theologically, as well as geographically. Historically, as continuing religious upheavals leading up to the bloody revolution of 1642 and the bloodless revolution of 1688 demonstrate, the British could hardly be said to have universally embraced Anglicanism; yet, mythically, they continued to view themselves in terms of their national church, whose control by the monarch provided at least the illusion of stability. Thus, when Catholics, on one side, or Puritans, on the other, threatened the hegemony of the established church, religion trumped race, as the English turned to continental Protestants, rather than risk losing their Anglican identity to an ethnically British ruler.

By the Enlightenment, the myth began to lose its viability. In addition to religious dissent, the 1707 Act of Union with Scotland initiated two centuries of expansionism that undermined the basis of English self-identity. Never really a homogeneous island nation, the putative English had descended from racially distinct invading forces that had transformed the Celtic Britains into nominal Anglo-Saxons and then Anglo-Normans. With the incorporation of Scotland into the Empire, the British formally reintroduced the Celts into the commonweal, though—at least, the English consoled themselves—the Scottish national church was Protestant. However, the Irish, to be incorporated a century later in 1801, though cousins to the Scots, were Catholic, not Protestant. In addition, expansionism into Asia and the Americas introduced the dilemma of integrating non-Europeans, and even non-Christians, into the Empire, as well. More important, the Enlightenment raised questions about the viability of theocracies in the industrialized world. Because capitalism requires a literate work force, the church could no longer control the intellectual development of the populace. People who read thought more independently and were less amenable to the imposition of a single religious authority. Moreover, industrialism initiated the process that has evolved into today's globalization, as individual nations perforce established commercial alliances not only beyond the range of more narrow sectarianism, but frequently inconsistent with theological doctrine. The resulting conflict between their self-concept and the exigencies of material reality forced the British to reconfigure their national myth. The eighteenth-century Hanoverians, however, faced a greater challenge than had the Tudors, for they could not, as had Henry VIII's propagandists, simply replace one form of Christianity with another. Rather, in severing the connections to the older national myth, which for centuries had enabled the monarchs to use the established church to control the populace, they required some method by which to incorporate increasingly diverse populations into the British Empire, but one that would not destroy the "imagined political community" that would keep the Empire together for another century.

This transformation of the British self-identity is reflected in the evolution of Anglo-Jewish history between the passage and repeal of the Jewish Naturalization Bill in 1753 and emancipation in 1858. The emotional response of working-class Englishmen, who had neither economic stakes in the bill, nor personal relationships with the Jews, reflects the success of the Tudor myth. In fact, the bill constituted little legal or rational threat to the commonweal; however, as a step toward legitimization of the Jewish community in Great Britain, the "Jew Bill" presaged the destruction of the older self-identity as a Protestant nation unified around the constitutionally established Anglican Church. The Jews were hardly the first, much less the largest, threat to Anglican hegemony; still, they were never formally emancipated.[10] Rather, among the reforms instituted in the first half of the nineteenth century, the legal disabilities that had prevented Jewish integration were individually eliminated.

> "I have no pupil and not even any one to
> whom I can speak on Talmudic subjects"[11]

Thus laments David Tevele Schiff (d. 1792), rabbi of London's Great Synagogue from 1765 to 1792, who considered ignorance of traditional learning the most disturbing characteristic of English Jewry. Born in Frankfort, and serving variously in Vienna and Worms before going to England, Rabbi Schiff disparages the paucity of Jewish learning in a community that for another century would have to turn to the Continent to train its spiritual leaders; yet simultaneously, Rabbi Schiff anticipates the direction to be taken by the English *Haskalah*, the acculturating movement that would prepare the community for emancipation in 1858. By the time Lionel Rothschild assumed his seat in Parliament, the rabbinate was Anglicized. Nathan Marcus Adler (1803–1890), who was elected chief rabbi of the United Hebrew Congregations of the British Empire in 1844, was born in Hanover, then under the British crown.[12] As a modern Orthodox rabbi, Adler modeled the Anglo-Jewish community after the traditional Church of England, instituting an episcopal system among the synagogues, subverting the nascent Reform Movement, insisting on decorum in services that now had English-language sermons, and establishing the Jews' College in 1855, a seminary that did *not* provide ordination for the rabbinate. Adler's own son Hermann studied in Prague.[13]

Comparable to the dominant British community, English Jewry had historically developed in ways distinct from the Continent. In 1290, Edward I expelled the Jews from England. Although they would not be formally readmitted until the seventeenth century, almost immediately after the expulsion, a few Jews began returning. Soon thereafter, Iberian Sephardim, whether *conversos* (New Christians) or *marranos* (crypto-Jews), fleeing the Inquisition, came to England, at first under the guise of being Spanish Catholics, though as the country grew more firmly committed to Protestantism, eventually reverting to their Jewish origins.[14] By the end of the sixteenth century, there existed a small, though secure Jewish community in London, one that had developed its own "national" identity around its synagogue. Because the core of the community had been isolated from Jews on the Continent, its organization evolved in conjunction as much with the dominant community as with other Jews throughout the world.

In contrast to those Jews who faced variously anti-Semitic pogroms and edicts of expulsion, English Jews were relatively secure. By and large, it was felt that if they proved themselves loyal servants to the king, without calling too much attention to themselves, they could exist as a "nation" within a "nation." Consequently, rather than establishing the kinds of religious institutions that would consolidate their Jewish identities, they sought to assimilate. Therefore, when Eastern European Ashkenazim, fleeing from persecution on the Continent, began arriving in the seventeenth and eighteenth centuries, Anglo-Jewry provided the kinds of educational and financial assistance that would enable the newcomers to become acculturated, without jeopardizing the social standing of the upper-class Sephardim. While, in time, the Ashkenazim, chafing under the dominance of the Sephardim, broke away and established their own synagogues, they still sought a closer identification with the British than with other Jewish communities.

As a result, English Jews resembled more the British nation than their ethnic counterparts on the Continent. Because of its relative security, the Anglo-Jewish community gained fairly early a sense of its place within the dominant "nation." During this period, a fairly steady stream of new immigrants, mostly poor and uneducated Ashkenazim from Eastern Europe, provoked a combination of anti- and philo-Semitic conversionist activities from the British, in particular from the London Society for Promoting Christianity amongst the Jews, formally established in 1809.[15] As much to defend themselves from perceived threats against their community as to assist their less fortunate coreligionists, the upper-class Sephardim established Jewish charities and schools so that the newcomers might integrate more smoothly into the community. At the same time, native-born English Jews felt secure enough to participate in the dominant intellectual controversies of the time, including debates on Bible translations, Hebrew language studies, Deism, political radicalism, and Newtonian science.[16] David Levi, in particular, had no qualms about disputing with Joseph Priestley or Thomas Paine.[17]

Politically, the attitude of the British toward Jewish emancipation, in contrast to their continental counterparts, had less to do with Jewish beliefs and habits than with English identity.[18] Rather than granting a single governmental act, Parliament, between 1830 and 1871, incrementally eliminated individual disabilities that had been in place against the Jews. Before the 1830s, the existing restrictions had affected only a small portion of the population, so most Jews were content to live within these limitations. However, as the Anglo-Jewish middle class became consolidated, the disabilities proved embarrassing, especially for those who moved in more genteel circles. In the dominant community, opposition to Jewish emancipation, primarily among Tory High Churchmen and ultraconservative evangelicals, was countered by four different groups of Christians (often with conflicting motives): (1) the faction of Whigs that was ideologically committed to religious freedom; (2) progressive Tories; (3) evangelical Tories; and (4) Radicals and Nonconformists. After 1829, when the Irish Catholics were granted the right of citizenship, the British could no longer view themselves as an Anglo-Saxon Protestant nation. In addition, by the 1850s, when Rabbi Nathan Adler began reconfiguring his community so that it would resemble the dominant Anglican episcopacy, the Jews no longer protruded like an alien enclave within the British Commonwealth. Thus, by 1858, the two separate "nations" had merged. For its part, the dominant community, though still retaining a nominally established Church of England, granted religious freedom to its non-Protestant, non-Anglo-Saxon components. Similarly, the Jewish minority had effectively differentiated itself from other Jewish communities throughout the world, establishing its own Anglo-centric religious, cultural, and educational institutions through which a Jewish identity could be retained, but without jeopardizing a patriotic loyalty toward the Crown. Consequently, Rabbi Schiff's complaint about the paucity of Jewish learning transcended his own narrow focus. By importing their rabbis, English Jews were attempting to negotiate between their commitments to their heritage, on the one hand, and their nationality, on the other.

Neither a sequel nor a companion to *British Romanticism and the Jews: History, Culture, Literature*, a collection of original essays published by Palgrave/Macmillan in 2002, *The Jews and British Romanticism: Politics, Religion, Culture* is designed to explore some of the more dynamic ramifications of the intersection between the Jewish and British "nations" as they responded to their respective enlightenments during the Romantic Period and beyond, into the twentieth century, if not the twenty-first. Written by an international group of scholars, the fourteen chapters comprising this volume are truly interdisciplinary, including historical, philosophical, cultural, as well as literary analyses. Grouped into three major categories, with a coda at the end, the volume is designed to reveal some of the political, religious, and cultural implications of the Jews and British Romanticism.

British Culture and the Jews

The collection opens with Part I on British Culture and the Jews, containing four chapters that explore the relationship between the British and Jewish cultures during the Romantic Period. The first chapter, though dealing with the later part of the period, initiates the volume because its thesis has such broad implications. In "Mr. Punch at the Great Exhibition: Stereotypes of Yankee and Hebrew in 1851," Frank Felsenstein explores the issue of anti-Semitism in the public press, specifically by contrasting the attitudes toward Africans and Jews in those issues of the magazine *Punch* that coincided with the Great Exhibition of 1851. Through his analysis, Felsenstein exposes the contradiction between the British self-righteous condemnation of slavery, on the one hand, and the ingrained xenophobic anti-Semitism, which survived long after the Romantic Period, on the other. Complementing Felsenstein's view of the public press is Michael Ragussis's discussion of cross-dressing Jews in the theater. In "Passing for a Jew, On Stage and Off: Stage Jews and Cross-Dressing Gentiles in Georgian England," Ragussis argues that the popular stage trope of passing for a Jew articulated "a deepening anxiety over the increasingly fluid border between Jew and Gentile."

The third chapter in Part I, Marsha Keith Schuchard's "William Blake and the Jewish Swedenborgians" reveals one aspect of that fluidity: religious nonconformity among both Jews and Christians. In her attempt to rationalize the apparent contradictions inherent in William Blake's attitude toward the Jews, Schuchard delves into the history of the English Swedenborgians, to find in their midst the "enigmatic, controversial figure" of Dr. Mordechai

Gumpertz Levison (1741–1797), a Kabbalist and physician who traveled in occult circles. The part ends with a close analysis of Blake's method for incorporating biblical themes in his British prophecies. Focusing on one particular passage in *Jerusalem*, R. Paul Yoder, in "Blake and the Books of Numbers: Joshua the Giant Killer and the Tears of Balaam," reveals how Blake conflates popular culture with three particular episodes from the book of Numbers "to suggest that the legitimate line of prophecy need not depend on one's nationality."

Jewish Writers and British Culture

As the four chapters in Part II demonstrate, the Jews, too, felt anxiety over the borders between the two cultures, though their concern focused primarily on the central problem of how to negotiate between the conflicting pulls of their ethnicity and their nationality. Describing the least assimilated of this group, Michael Scrivener's "Following the Muse: Inspiration, Prophecy and Deference in the Poetry of Emma Lyon (1788–1870), Anglo-Jewish Poet" introduces an almost forgotten figure of Anglo-Jewish culture, the poet Emma Lyon, whose unfortunate experiences after the publication of her single book of poetry caused her to retreat back into the Jewish community, never to publish again. Though less timid than Lyon, Isaac D'Israeli also failed to establish his reputation in the dominant community. Rather, as Stuart Peterfreund demonstrates in "Identity, Diaspora, and the Secular Voice in the Works of Isaac D'Israeli," D'Israeli used the eighteenth-century attitude toward Orientalism as the vehicle through which to create for himself a cultural space as an assimilated Jew, but one who neither questions nor repudiates his origins. In this regard, according to Peterfreund, D'Israeli anticipates the position assumed by many Jewish professors of the twentieth century, a paradigmatic example being Erich Auerbach.

Taking the problem of acculturation to a more concrete level, Judith W. Page discusses "Anglo-Jewish Identity and the Politics of Cultivation in Hazlitt, Aguilar, and Disraeli." Centering on several "Jewish" country houses, Page traces the attitude toward land—the basis of Hazlitt's 1831 defense of Jewish emancipation—as it is manifested in works by Grace Aguilar and Benjamin Disraeli, both of whom "use narrative scenes of gardening and agriculture to negotiate the slippery terrain of British–Jewish identity in the early- to mid-nineteenth century." Finally, the last chapter of this part considers an Anglo-Jewish woman who made the opposite choice. In "Charlotte Dacre's Zofloya: The Gothic Demonization of the Jew," Diane Long Hoeveler discusses Charlotte Dacre—daughter of the notorious "Jew" King—who made a concerted effort to dissociate herself from both her heritage and her father, to the point of demonizing him in the titular character of her novel *Zofloya, or the Moor: A Romance of the Fifteenth Century.*

The Jews and British Romanticism
Outside of England

The next three chapters extend the perspective on the Jews and British
Romanticism beyond the more localized phenomenon that occurred on the
British Isles between the 1750s and 1850s. On the Continent existed a multiplicity of romanticisms with which both the British and the Jews were
familiar, so it would be simplistic to reduce the subject to a one-to-one
relationship. Rather, the fluid geographical, historical, and temporal boundaries of what we call Romanticism allowed and perhaps encouraged certain
conflicting aspects in the interaction between British Romanticism and
different phases of Jewish Revival. Beyond that, it is necessary to acknowledge that the dissemination of British culture was a byproduct of imperialism
and colonialism; and the admixing of British Romanticism with other
cultures, though possibly originating at a particular historical juncture, could
manifest itself in any number of ways, at any time from the nineteenth
century on. Similarly, the migrations of the Jews in the nineteenth and twentieth centuries brought them into contact—both directly and indirectly—
with different manifestations of British Romanticism, some authentically
British, others derivative through second or even third cultures. Reeva
Spector Simon's "Commerce, Concern and Christianity: Britain and Middle
Eastern Jewry in the Mid-Nineteenth Century," the first chapter of this part,
establishes the historical context for this broader perspective, delineating the
Middle Eastern policy in which "the British advocated citizenship, liberty
and freedom for the Jews who were under Muslim rule," while at the same
time supporting a domestic policy that "was largely determined by a reluctance to incorporate Jews into the body politic at home."

A component of British expansionism was an international interest in British
literature, though not everyone could read English. For that reason, in "Jewish
Translations of British Romantic Literature (1753–1818): A Preliminary
Bibliography," Sheila A. Spector generates a preliminary bibliography of
Hebrew and Yiddish translations of British romantic literature—ranging from
the mid-1850s to the present—to provide an overview of the kinds of materials that might have been available to those Jews who did not read English. As
this bibliography suggests, romantic texts and models could be adapted and
interiorized very belatedly by Hebrew writers, a point which is seminal to the
premise of Lilach Lachman's chapter "The Reader as Witness: 'City of the
Killings' and Bialik's Romantic Historiography." Relocating the discussion
from English to Hebrew literature, Lachman uses Hebrew poet Hayyim
Nahman Bialik as the examplar for exploring the role that British models
played in the construction of the Jews' internal sense of history, demonstrating
that the contact between British Romanticism and modern Hebrew poetry
extends beyond primary texts to secondary materials. Bialik's reception in the
twentieth century and the reading of his long poem reflect the extensive
deployment of British romantic models by contemporary Israeli scholars.

Coda: Coleridge and Judaica

A collection such as this sometimes gives the false impression that coverage is comprehensive, that there might be little more to say about a particular topic or writer than is discussed in a single chapter. Therefore, in contrast to the other parts, the concluding "coda" does not survey a broad range of topics; rather the last three chapters explore in more depth the plenitude of a single, though complex aspect of the Jews and British Romanticism: the relationship of Coleridge to Judaica. Opening this section, Stanley J. Spector's "Coleridge's Misreading of Spinoza" explores the apparent contradiction between Coleridge's repeated adulation of Spinoza the man, but rejection of his philosophy. From a close reading of what Coleridge says specifically about Spinoza's *Ethics*, Spector concludes that Coleridge could not possibly, as is generally believed, have actually read the text. In contrast, Frederick Burwick, in "Mendelssohn and Coleridge on Words, Thoughts, and Things," analyzes the marginalia found in Coleridge's copy of Moses Mendelssohn's treatise *Morgenstunden*, to conclude that though Coleridge did not agree with everything that he read, he was fully engaged with Mendelssohn's philosophy. Finally, to conclude this part and the collection as a whole, Lloyd Guy Davies demonstrates how the two cultures complement each other, in "Standing at Mont Blanc: Coleridge and *Midrash*" using the Jewish exegetical technique of *midrash* as a means of justifying—against accusations of inauthenticity—Coleridge's stance in the problematic "Hymn before Sun-rise, in the Vale of Chamouni."

This introduction would not be complete without my acknowledging the assistance I have received completing *The Jews and British Romanticism: Politics, Religion, Culture*. Most important are the contributors who, both with their own chapters and with their generous advice for the book as a whole, made this collection possible. In addition, I received enormous support from colleagues and from reviewers of *British Romanticism and the Jews: History, Culture, Literature*. The idea to compile a second collection came from readers who believed—a belief validated by the chapters in this volume—that we had but scratched the surface. Yet, as this collection demonstrates, while we have, I believe, expanded the parameters of the field, there is still much left to do. Also, it is conventional at this point to mention the forbearance, if not assistance, of one's family. I, however, have an enormous debt to acknowledge: my sister Reeva Spector Simon and my brother Stanley J. Spector have both brought their expertise to the project, each agreeing to write an entire chapter to help expand the book's focus beyond my own more limited abilities. Finally, I would like to thank the editorial and production staffs at Palgrave/Macmillan. I learned from the first volume the importance of a good publisher; for this reason, I furthered my working relationship with Palgrave/Macmillan. It is to all of these that the strengths of this volume are due; its shortcomings are my own.

Notes

1. There is no consensus about either the definition of Romanticism, or its dates, each being dependent upon the other. Because of the virtual coincidence with the seminal dates of Anglo-Jewish history—1753 and 1858—for the purpose of this volume, Romanticism will be defined in terms of the so-called romantic long century, a suggestion made by Susan J. Wolfson in her "50–50? Phone a Friend? Ask the Audience?: Speculating on a Romantic Century, 1750–1850," *European Romantic Review* 11, 1 (winter 2000): 1–11.

2. On European Jewish history, see David Vital, *A People Apart: The Jews in Europe 1789–1939*, Oxford History of Modern Europe, gen. ed. Lord Bullock and Sir William Deakin (Oxford: Oxford University Press, 1999). On nineteenth-century European protectorates of Jews, see Reeva Spector Simon's "Europe in the Middle East," in *The Jews of the Middle East and North Africa in Modern Times*, ed. Simon, Michael Menachem Laskier and Sara Reguer (New York: Columbia University Press, 2003), 19–28; and on the British protectorate in particular, see her contribution to this collection, "Commerce, Concern and Christianity: Britain and Middle-Eastern Jewry in the Mid-Nineteenth Century."

3. Historically, the word "nation" did not refer strictly to geographical delineation, but more significantly, to cultural and racial association. According to the *O.E.D.*, a "nation" is an "extensive aggregate of persons, so closely associated with each other by common descent, language, or history, as to form a distinct race or people, usually organized as a separate political state and occupying a definite territory." More recently, Benedict Anderson has defined "nation" as "an imagined political community—and imagined as both inherently limited and sovereign." As he explains, "Communities are to be distinguished . . . by the style in which they are imagined. . . . The nation is imagined as *limited* because even the largest of them, . . . has finite, if elastic, boundaries, beyond which lie other nations. . . . It is imagined as *sovereign* because the concept was born in an age in which Enlightenment and Revolution were destroying the legitimacy of the divinely-ordained, hierarchical dynastic realm. . . . Finally, it is imagined as a *community*, because, regardless of the actual inequality and exploitation that may prevail in each, the nation is always conceived as a deep, horizontal comradeship" (*Imagined Communities: Reflections on the Origin and Spread of Nationalism* [London and New York: Verso, 1991], 6–7).

4. The most recent studies of the *Haskalah* are Shmuel Feiner's *Haskalah and History: The Emergence of a Modern Jewish Historical Consciousness*, tr. Chaya Naor and Sondra Silverton (Oxford and Portland, OR: Littman Library of Jewish Civilization, 2002); and the anthology Feiner edited with David Sorkin, *New Perspectives on the Haskalah* (London and Portland, OR: Littman Library of Jewish Civilization, 2001).

5. The classic study of Reform Judaism is Michael A. Meyer, *Response to Modernity: A History of the Reform Movement in Judaism* (New York and Oxford: Oxford University Press, 1988).

6. On British history of the period, see Linda Colley, *Britons: Forging the Nation 1707–1837* (New Haven: Yale University Press, 1992). On Anglo-Jewish history, see the major studies by David S. Katz: *The Jews in the History of England,*

1485–1850 (Oxford: Clarendon Press, 1994); and *Philo-Semitism and the Readmission of the Jews to England, 1603–1655* (Oxford: Clarendon Press, 1982). On the late eighteenth and early nineteenth century in particular, see Todd Endelman's *The Jews of Georgian England, 1714–1830: Tradition and Change in a Liberal Society* (Philadelphia: The Jewish Publication Society of America, 1979; reprint, with a new preface, Ann Arbor: University of Michigan Press, 1999). Most recently, Endelman has published *The Jews of Britain, 1656 to 2000*, Jewish Communities in the Modern World, ed. David Sorkin (Berkeley: University of California Press, 2002). Finally, on the *Haskalah* in England, see David B. Ruderman, *Jewish Enlightenment in an English Key: Anglo-Jewry's Construction of Modern Jewish Thought* (Princeton: Princeton University Press, 2000).

7. On the Jewish Naturalization Bill, see Alan H. Singer, "Great Britain or Judea Nova? National Identity, Property, and the Jewish Naturalization Controversy of 1753," in *British Romanticism and the Jews: History, Culture, Literature*, ed. Sheila A. Spector (New York: Palgrave/Macmillan, 2002), 19–36.

8. This is Edwin Jones's thesis in *The English Nation: The Great Myth* (Phoenix Mill: Sutton, 1998).

9. This summary is from the first chapter of Jones's *The English Nation*, "Building the Official Version of the English Past," 31–60.

10. It is important to note that during the 1830s, that is, the period when Jewish disabilities were being reexamined, the established church was being threatened on the right, by the Oxford Tractarians who advocated a return to strict Catholicism, and on the left, by the disestablishmentarianists, who wished to sever completely the ties between church and state.

11. Charles Duschinsky, *The Rabbinate of the Great Synagogue, London, from 1756–1842* (London: Oxford University Press, 1921; reprint, with a new bibliographical note by Ruth P. Lehmann, Farnborough, Hants: Gregg, 1971), 94.

12. For a brief overview of Adler, see Endelman, *Jews of Britain*, 115–120. More extensive discussions of both Adler and his son Hermann can be found in Eugene C. Black, "The Anglicization of Orthodoxy: the Adlers, Father and Son," in *Profiles in Diversity: Jews in a Changing Europe, 1750–1870*, ed. Frances Malino and David Sorkin (Detroit: Wayne State University Press, 1998; reprint of *From East and West: Jews in a Changing Europe, 1750–1870* [London: Basil Blackwell, 1991]), 295–325.

13. On the Reform Movement in England, see Anne J. Kershen and Jonathan A. Romain, *Tradition and Change: A History of Reform Judaism in Britain, 1840–1995* (London: Vallentine Mitchell, 1995), especially the first two chapters, "Schism, 1840," 3–30, and "Founding Fathers, 1842–1870," 31–57.

14. The composition of the Sephardic community is extremely complex. Before the Spanish expulsion, some Jews chose to convert to Christianity, while others underwent forced conversion. Of the *conversos*, or New Christians, some remained crypto-Jews, or *marranos*, who pretended to accept Christianity but retained whatever vestiges of Judaism was possible under the circumstances. Once free of the Inquisition, some *conversos* reverted to Judaism, while others remained Christian. The standard study of Sephardic Jewry is Jane S. Gerber, *The Jews of Spain: A History of the Sephardic Experience* (New York: Free Press, 1992).

15. On conversionism, see Michael Ragussis, *Figures of Conversion: "The Jewish Question" and English National Identity*, Post-Contemporary Interventions, ed. Stanley Fish and Fredric Jameson (Durham: Duke University Press, 1995), especially chapter 1, "The Culture of Conversion," 1–56.
16. Ruderman discusses these topics in *Jewish Enlightenment in an English Key*.
17. On David Levi in particular, see Michael Scrivener, "British-Jewish Writing of the Romantic Era and the Problem of Modernity: The Example of David Levi," in *British Romanticism and the Jews: History, Culture, Literature*, ed. Sheila A. Spector (New York: Palgrave/Macmillan, 2002), 159–177.
18. On emancipation, see Endelman, *Jews of Britain*, 100–110.

PART I

BRITISH CULTURE AND THE JEWS

CHAPTER 1

Mr. Punch at the Great Exhibition: Stereotypes of Yankee and Hebrew in 1851[1]

Frank Felsenstein

In his panoptic study of the early years of *Punch*, Richard Altick comments on the periodical's traditional "mild xenophobia" in its depiction of foreigners and outsiders.[2] The intention of the present essay is to try to substantiate this by reference to the magazine's representation of two particular groups, the Jews (or "Hebrews") and the Americans (or "Yankees") in the year of the Great Exhibition. A principal reason for selecting these two groups is to probe the strange variance between *Punch*'s sharp yet self-righteous condemnation of America's failure to free its slaves, and its simultaneous maintenance of an almost incessantly negative stance toward the emancipation of Britain's Jews. Coincidentally, on the very day—May 1, 1851—when the Great Exhibition opened its doors to the public, Parliament was debating Jewish emancipation, causing the prime minister to miss the grand inauguration. The two volumes of *Punch* for 1851, issued exactly ten years after Mark Lemon with others had founded the journal, are volumes XX and XXI. In many respects, the attitudes represented in these two volumes characterize many of the intriguing contradictions and paradoxes concerning race and nationhood that are evident in the early years of the periodical as a whole and, by extension, in the bourgeois world of mid-nineteenth-century England.

Great Exhibition of 1851

"The Great Exhibition of the Works of Industry of All Nations" (to give it its full title), though prompted by the success of the French Industrial Exposition of 1844, was really the first truly international exposition and the model for many such later enterprises that were to be repeated in different locations (for example, New York, Paris, Montreal, Osaka, Brussels, Hanover, etc.) through the whole of the twentieth century. The venue of the Exhibition was Joseph Paxton's glass structure, built in Hyde Park, comprising 772,784 square feet (19 acres), with the addition of 217,100 square feet of galleries. It has been estimated that the edifice was four times the size of St. Peter's in Rome, and six times the size of St. Paul's in London. It attracted 17,000 exhibitors from all over the world. During the five months that it was open, from May 1 through October 11, 1851, it drew in approximately six million visitors. Despite the many naysayers who had opposed Prince Albert's plan, the Great Exhibition actually made a handsome profit; much of which was ploughed into building the complex of Kensington museums (the Science Museum; the Natural History Museum; the Imperial [later "Commonwealth"] Institute; and the Victoria & Albert Museum).

Punch and the Great Exhibition

From the beginning, *Punch* took an almost proprietary interest in the exhibition, especially so since the more popular name by which it became known, "The Crystal Palace," was first coined by the magazine in its issue of November 2, 1850.[3] In fact, John Tenniel's title page (figure 1.1) to *Punch*, volume XX, shows Mr. Punch as a kind of latter-day classical magister or writer ("The Modern Aesop") presiding over the Crystal Palace and its proceedings. The visitors to the Exhibition are represented as so many animals (notice the American eagle to the right holding a revolving pistol), and, as he informs us in the preface to the volume, *Punch* will be the venue for a series of modern fables about the mingling of "the self-respecting People of England . . . in amity and brotherhood with men of all climes in that Crystal Palace."

Adopting the idiom of the fable, the modern Aesop grandiosely proclaims that

> As in the Great Hive to which the World's Bees have contributed their labours, PUNCH has here concentrated the treasure of his own hive, in which, though there may be a little taste of the sting, there is no lack of the honey.

His Exhibition has the same object in view as that now collected in the Crystal Palace, to which he stood Sponsor, and gave the name

THE ADVANCEMENT AND HAPPINESS OF MANKIND,
With the Peace and Goodwill of all Nations. (iv)

In other words, Mr. Punch's promise is that the high ideals of the Exhibition concerning the bringing together from the four corners of the earth all of mankind will be reflected in the pages of the journal. Indeed, as we learn

Figure 1.1 Title page to *Punch, or the London Charivari* 20 (1851).

from a description of the exhibition at its opening ("Visions in the Crystal," XX, 188),

> Immediately on his first peep into the Crystal, Mr. Punch found himself fulfilling the request of JOHNSON—
>> Let Observation, with extensive view,
>> Survey mankind from China to Peru.

He beheld the whole of ADAM's race collected together for the first time since they were scattered on the plains of Shinar—shaking hands together, with JOHN BULL in their midst, instructing them in that only genuine mode of fraternizing. The resonance of the biblical allusion here is that not since the destruction of Babel have the nations of the world shared a common language; yet it is the grandiose duty of Great Britain to bring them together in amity.

In this and other prints depicting the Exhibition, the nations of the world are shown rubbing shoulders with one another at Hyde Park. In each of these representations, the world is made to play to the British tune. The idea of play or of the game is an important register by which we are made to associate the values of Great Britain with Empire and with power. In such situations, Mr. Punch is almost always the superior player, though usually magnanimous at the failure of those others who, by accident of birth or circumstance, are inevitably less privileged than he. However, we should recall that Mr. Punch himself is by origin—as he appears in puppetry—something of a gamester and a bully with a bludgeon, who thinks nothing of beating up or murdering those who oppose him. *Punch and Judy* is the dark side of the same game that here represents Mr. Punch as the benign face of Empire.

Despite or perhaps because of the implicit and often explicit assumption by Mr. Punch and his writers of an innate superiority, the humor of the journal leaves one in no doubt of the general expectation that the rest of the world will turn up and play according to the civilized rules devised by the British. If the relationship of the native Englishman to the foreigner is frequently expressed in terms of game playing, then playing at cricket—of all sports the most quintessentially English—can be seen as a radical way of defining one's national superiority. I don't know when the modern English phrase "that's just not cricket!" was first coined, but it has come to mean "that's not playing fair," "that's not being sportsmanlike," "that's not being very English." Significantly, American idiom has developed no equivalent in relation to the national sport of the United States—"that's not baseball!" remains meaningless, though, it might be conceded that the Jewish American phrase, "that's not quite kosher!" comes strangely close to being comparable. It's apposite in this context that *Punch* should represent its eponymous principal as a batsman at the crease (figure 1.2). As the epitome of Englishness, Mr. Punch appears here as anything other than a sporting hero, with his extended potbelly, puppet's hump, beak-like nose and protruding chin; yet, as an article, "Punch on Cricket" (XX, 249), also of 1851, claims,

> The game [of cricket] is essentially English; and though our countrymen carry it abroad wherever they go, it is difficult to inoculate or knock it into the foreigner. The Italians are too fat for Cricket, the French too thin, the Dutch too dumpty, the Belgians too bilious, the Flemish too flatulent, the East Indians too peppery, the Laplanders too bowlegged, the Swiss too sentimental, the Greeks too lazy, the Egyptians too long in the neck, and the Germans too short in the wind.

Figure 1.2 "Going Before the Wind," *Punch, or the London Charivari* 21 (1851): 114.

By such rules, perhaps there is ultimately no hope for the foreigner! Perhaps, too, this is a good moment to turn to *Punch*'s representation of Yankee and Hebrew.

Yankees

The Yankee has a prominent place in *Punch* of 1851, since the Crystal Palace had a large exhibition space reserved for the United States. As well as "Yankee," the most common epithets that *Punch* employs in allusion to white Americans are "Yankee Doodle" and "Jonathan"; for Afro-Americans, as we shall see, it is almost invariably "Sambo." According to *Brewer's Dictionary of Phrase and Fable*, the phrase "to consult Brother Jonathan," supposedly first used by George Washington, provided the origin of the term "Jonathan," as a collective name for the people of the United States.[4] In the pages of *Punch*, Jonathan is graphically represented as a lank, even slightly gaunt, figure, invariably wearing an oversized round hat and smoking a long cheroot. He is sometimes shown sporting a colt revolver and sometimes too a bowie knife. "Brother JONATHAN," remarks the wry Mr. Punch at the advent of the Great Exhibition, "was observed . . . converting his cow-hide into shoe leather, and unrivetting the fetters of a black man, to whom he afterwards offered a glass of cherry cobbler and a cigar. The same gentleman also appeared grinding his bowie-knife into a pruning-hook, and selling his revolving pistol to a marine-store keeper" (XX, 188). In general, Jonathan is depicted as something of a country boy, outlandish and lacking urban sophistication, but also a figure who is by nature without scruples, very sure of himself, and always jumping for opportunities that will proceed to his own unfair advantage.

The stereotype of the white American that emerges from the pages of *Punch* in 1851 may further be delineated in terms of the following perceptions, which for convenience I shall call the six stereotypical *S*'s: Sedition; Space or Scale; Steam Power; Sailing; Style; and most important for the present discussion, Slavery.

(i) Sedition. America is out to sow sedition by importing its republican and revolutionary notions into the sovereign state that three-quarters of a century before it had renounced. As one of several songs to the tune of "Yankee Doodle" announces,

> YANKEE DOODLE's come to town,
> To see the Exhibition,
> And strike a blow at England's Crown,
> By stirring up sedition . . .
> Chorus—YANKEE DOODLE, &c. . . .
> YANKEE DOODLE's come to town,
> In all his force and power,
> He means to burn the Abbey down,
> Bank, Parliament, and Tower.
> Oh! yes—and fire the Thames as well . . .
> Chorus—YANKEE DOODLE, &c. (XX, 161, verses 1 and 9)

Similar comic forebodings that an American presence at Crystal Palace will be a catalyst to republican sentiments in England prompt Mr. Punch to speculate that Kensington is on the point of becoming a commonwealth and "that the leading men of Liverpool are about to declare Liverpool, Lancashire, and Wales a republic; a pretty mess or puddle for the Liverpuddlians to get their feet into." However, he adds contemptuously, "This is the sort of stuff we expect to hear from America, but as we are not very likely to hear it from any other source, it does not much signify" (XX, 163). "The Revolution . . . anticipated by certain Yankees," he concludes later, "has been entirely confined to the wheels of the steam-engines and clock-work that are revolving in the Crystal Palace" (XX, 206).

(ii) Space or Scale. The space that the United States had reserved for itself at the Crystal Palace seems to have far exceeded the number of exhibits that initially reached London from America. This was to occasion several humorous stabs from *Punch*. The empty spaces in the American showcase typify for Mr. Punch a country that is large in scale but sparse in population, big on bravado but empty in substance. Among those "rare goods" still awaited from America, he itemizes "A Mattrass for the Falls of Niagara," "The Whip

with which America flogs all creation—especially the coloured portion of it," and (probably with the likes of Emerson and Longfellow in mind), "The tremendous Wooden Style that separates America from the English Fields of Literature" (XX, 218).

(iii) Steam Power. Although the Great Exhibition was intended primarily as a showcase of the technological prowess of Britain and her Empire, the American exhibit was perhaps the first occasion to demonstrate to the European public at large that the United States was in process of rapidly becoming a serious rival to British industrial strength. The version of the song "Yankee Doodle" already quoted (which *Punch* purportedly reprints from *The New York Weekly Herald*) also warns John Bull that America has "produce to display, that shall / Amaze your cotton-spinner." Great Britain should be alerted that "the sile [*sic*] of Freedom" across the Atlantic is cutting "out an Empire from the woods, / The greatest ever heerd [*sic*] on" that will make "Light work to fell the British Oak" (XX, 161). American innovation through steam power, as a later rendering in *Punch* of the same song maintains, will promote Yankee Doodle to beat the British "Downright in Agriculture, / With his machine for reaping wheat, / Chaw'd up as by a vulture" (XXI, 117). If prior to the event the British public was blithely unaware of the nascent economic power of the United States, the Great Exhibition brought that shocking news home as never before.

(iv) Sailing. In the very same year as the Great Exhibition, the advance of the United States was trumpeted in a different way when a Yankee crew entered the annual yachting contest at Cowes—with a sloop appropriately named "America"—and, to everybody's astonishment but their own, trounced all the British boats. Britain's sense of superiority, as we have seen so often registered in terms of sports and games, was severely shaken. As *Punch*'s "Last Appendix to 'Yankee Doodle'" makes evident,

> YANKEE DOODLE had a craft,
>   A rather tidy clipper,
> And he challenged, while they laughed,
>   The Britishers to whip her.
> Their whole yacht-squadron she outsped,
>   And that on their own water;
> Of all the lot she went a-head,
>   And they came nowhere arter.
> *Chorus*—YANKEE DOODLE, &c. (XXI, 117)

Amid comic qualms that the U.S. yacht would likely soon be followed by a U.S. bred Derby-winning horse, Mr. Punch warns his compatriots that "we really must look about us a little, if we do not wish to be utterly eclipsed by the stars and flogged by the stripes of America" ("America *versus* England," XXI, 128). Yet, recognizing the technical superiority of the yacht "America" over her British rivals, another column in *Punch* tries to find consolation in the fact that the losers behaved as only true Englishmen can: "We have taken our thrashing with perfect good-humour. No men were ever *whapped* who bore so little malice as the Cowes gentlemen" ("Why Did the 'America' Beat Us?" XXI, 118). The Americas Cup, which has yet to be won back by Great Britain, began as a result of this event.

(v) Style. Ante-Bellum America is not primarily known for its innovations in style or ladies' fashion, but was nevertheless responsible for what has been hailed as "the most important dress reform of the nineteenth century." This was the introduction of the "bloomer," a female costume made up of a "short skirt and loose trousers gathered closely round the ankles," named after a New Yorker, Mrs. Amelia Bloomer, editor of a monthly journal entitled *The Lily; a Ladies' Journal, Devoted to Temperance and Literature,* through the pages of which she had tried to introduce the fashion in 1849.[5] Her cause was taken up more successfully by a certain Elizabeth Smith Miller of Peterboro, New York, who succeeded in making a fad out of "bloomerism" just in time for it to be imported sensationally into England during the Great Exhibition. The effect of the new fashion was, if anything, more revolutionary than the putative plan to usher in American republicanism. The gendered opposition to bloomerism, which it was claimed would "unsex" the female kind by encouraging her to be the one to wear the trousers, prompted women to group together in what some historians have interpreted as an early manifestation of feminism and of what was eventually to become in both the United States and Britain the movement that demanded equal rights for women.

For *Punch*, of course, bloomerism provided a fertile source for male wit, and, in a different context, its manifestation deserves extended study. Here, I only describe one of the many prints in *Punch* intended to deride the new fashion. In John Leech's cartoon, "Bloomerism—An American Custom" (figure 1.3), we are presented with female renderings of "Jonathan," two American lady visitors dressed in bloomers and smoking cigarettes or cheroots, while being jeered at by an unruly crowd of British boys. The millinery shop that the women are strolling past, displays more conventional fashions in complete contrast to the flat and broad-brimmed frontier-style hats that they are sporting. The taunts of the boys are reflected more politely though no less incredulously in the eyes of their adult compatriots who glance disbelievingly in the direction of the two outlandish American visitors. Elsewhere, Jonathan is accused of stirring sedition, but, in their apparent trans-dressing, his womenfolk are actually far more successful than he in fomenting no less radical a change in the world of style and, by extension, in challenging established gender attitudes. Among those supposedly affected by bloomerism, surmises Mr. Punch at his most risible, even the uncivil Shadrach, that "stiff-necked Hebrew [who] makes it a part of his daily thanksgiving that he was not born a woman," will soon be found "wildly pulling his sordid beard that he came into the world the inheritor

Figure 1.3 John Leech, "Bloomerism—An American Custom," *Punch, or the London Charivari* 21 (1851): 141.

of that badge of weakness" (XXI, 189) which goes with being born a mere man.

(vi) Slavery. On the crucial question of slavery, Mr. Punch can constantly assert the superiority and independence of the British over the Americans (slavery having been abolished from Great Britain in 1807 and from its colonies in 1833). It is a reiterative theme in *Punch*, by no means confined to the year of the Great Exhibition. The American Civil War, in which slavery was a central issue, was to be fought in the following decade (1861–1865).

A centerpiece of the U.S. presentation at Crystal Palace was Hiram Powers' much admired marble statue, "The Greek Slave" (1843), a sculpture closely indebted for its inspiration to the Venus de' Medici in Florence, where the sculptor kept his studio (figure 1.4). "The Greek Slave" (copies of which are now among other places in the Corcoran Gallery in Washington, D.C., and at the Newark Museum, New Jersey) depicts a naked Christian maiden made captive by the Turks and exposed for sale at Constantinople (figure 1.5). Her physical bondage is denoted by the chains that bind her arms. When it was taken on a national tour across America during 1847–1848, the statue was extolled for its representation of sublime female virtue under duress, very few of its admirers openly making a connection between the aesthetic object and American slavery. When it was brought over to Crystal Palace, it created no less a sensation than it had in America,

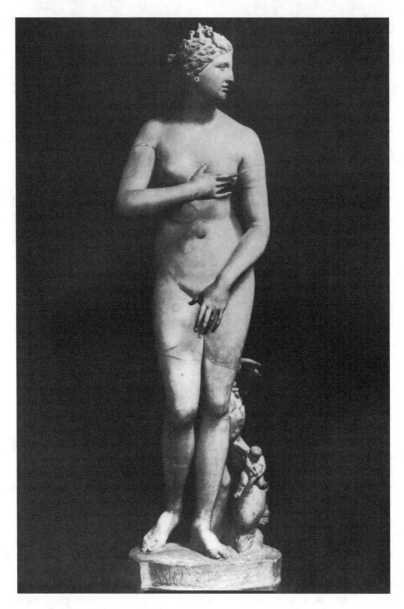

Figure 1.4 *Venus de' Medici*, Uffizi Gallery (Tribuna), Florence.

but for a British *cognoscente* like Mr. Punch it was an irresistible cue to invoke the horrifying specter of American slavery. *Punch* cynically derided it as "a Model Slave from the Model Republic" (XXI, 11).

John Tenniel's cartoon, "The Virginian Slave. Intended as a Companion to Power's 'Greek Slave'" (figure 1.6), graphically adumbrates *Punch*'s forceful condemnation of slavery elsewhere in the journal. Instead of the nude figure of a virginal white European, Tenniel's manacled black slave woman is clothed

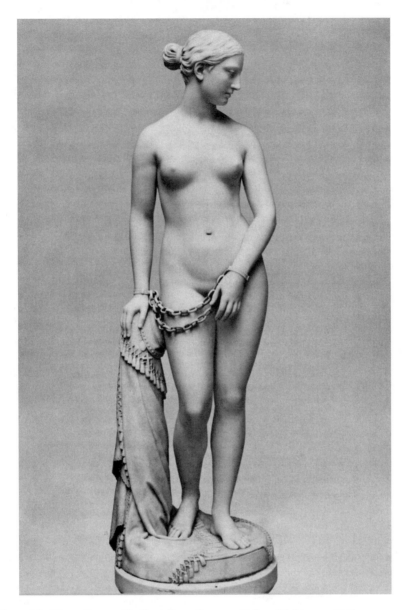

Figure 1.5 Hiram Powers, *The Greek Slave*, Corcoran Gallery, Washington, D.C.

in a loin-cloth (with the strong inference that she is concealing that she has been sexually abused by her owner), while the raised plinth upon which she stands is decorated in mock-celebration with ropes, chains, and bull-whips. The American ideal of unity in multiplicity (*e pluribus unum*) provides an ironic legend to the engraving. The same issue of *Punch* comments upon the empty space of the American showcase at Crystal Palace, and ironically

Figure 1.6   John Tenniel, "The Virginian Slave. Intended as a Companion to Power's 'Greek Slave,'" *Punch, or the London Charivari* 20 (1851): 236.

demands why there had not been chosen from "the treasures of America . . . some choice specimen of slaves? We have the Greek Captive in dead stone—why not the Virginian slave in living ebony?" (XX, 209). Beneath the text is a small illustration, entitled "Sample of American Manufacture" (figure 1.7), showing a whip-bearing Jonathan—with the implanted head of an American eagle—gesticulating and snarling orders at a group of shackled black slave children. "As we cannot have a black baby show," remarks Mr. Punch sarcastically, "let America hire a black or two to stand in manacles, an American manufacture, protected by the American Eagle."

Figure 1.7 "Sample of American Manufacture," *Punch, or the London Charivari* 20 (1851): 209.

On the same topic later in 1851, *Punch* introduces a dialect poem, purportedly written by an Afro-American slave named Sambo, and addressed to Hiram Powers' "Greek Slave." Though less exalted a poem than Elizabeth Barrett Browning's sonnet on the same theme, "Sambo to the 'Greek Slave'" is a persuasive indictment both of enslavement and of the mind set that would seem to revile white slavery yet remain coolly indifferent to the situation of blacks:

You a berry pretty image; ob dat dere am no doubt;
And HIRAM POWERS him clebber chap, de man dat cut you cut;
And all de people in de world to look at you dey go,
And say you am de finest ting dat 'Merica can show.
But though you am a lubly gal, I say you no correct;
You not at all de kind ob slave a nigger would expect;
You never did no workee wid such hands and feet as dose;
You different from SUSANNAH, dere,—you not like coal-black ROSE.

Dere's not a mark dat I see ob de cow-hide on your back;
No slave hab skin so smooth as yourn—dat is, if slavee black.
Gosh! if I war a slave again, all down in Tennessee,
In such a skin as that of yourn is where I'd like to be.

I 'spose de reason why your face look mellumcholly sad,
Is 'cause dey gone and torn you from your lubber and your dad.
How hard! say MASSA JONATHAN—oh, what a cruel shame!
Ob course you know him nebber serve a nigger gal de same.

But now no fear of floggee, nor from lubly wife to part,
And here I stands and speaks my mind about de work ob Art;
De nigger free de minute dat him touch de English shore,
Him gentleman ob colour now, and not a slave no more! (XXI, 105)

Entirely skeptical that such a model of perfection as that created by
Hiram Powers could ever truthfully have suffered as a slave ("not a mark I
see ob de cow-hide on your back"), the ventriloquized voice of Sambo is dis-
missive of the morals of "Massa Jonathan" and, by extension, questions the
whole ethos of American slavery. However, the counterpoint within the poem
to American slavery is the freedom that Sambo and friends will enjoy the
moment they set foot on British soil. Ultimately, what is celebrated is
the moral superiority of Britain over America, and the belief that, far from
being merely gestural, British liberty is tangible and real and to be shared by
all its denizens, whatever their national or ethnic origin. The piety of the
expression encompasses an endemic belief among Mr. Punch and many of his
compatriots that Britain (rather than America) is truly—and perhaps
uniquely—the land of liberty. It is ironic that, in the selfsame year as the Great
Exhibition, Parliament once again failed to extend that liberty in its fullness
to Britain's Jews.

Hebrews

On Thursday, May 1, 1851, an Oath of Abjuration (Jews) Bill, sponsored by
the British Prime Minister, Lord John Russell, received its second reading
in the House of Commons.[6] The purpose of the bill was to allow a Jew
elected to the House to be allowed to take his seat without having to swear
the full Oath of Abjuration that included (what for him were) the compromising words "upon the true faith of a Christian." The bill was passed by a
mere twenty-five votes, a far smaller margin than its proponents had hoped.
The likely reason for the slim majority was the foreseeable absence of a large
number of Liberal members of parliament whose presence was required at
the joyous inauguration of the Great Exhibition a short distance away in
Hyde Park. A few days later, the Bill was introduced into the House of Lords
where, with several bishops leading the opposition, it was predictably
defeated and thrown out.

Following the failure to achieve full citizenship for Britain's Jewish community in 1830 (the year after it had been granted to Roman Catholics),
attempts were made over practically the next three decades to bring about
such legislation. Finally, in 1858, on the fourteenth attempt and with some
residual opposition, both Houses of Parliament assented to the Jewish Relief
Act, and Jewish emancipation was achieved. Lord John Russell's unsuccess-
ful bill of 1851 was merely one such attempt on a very long and sometimes
painfully bumpy road.

During 1850 and 1851, two practicing Jews with strong political creden-
tials, Baron Lionel Rothschild and David Salomons, had each been elected

to Parliament but, because their faith disqualified them from the full Oath of Abjuration, were refused permission to take their seats. *Punch* represents them in "Distressing Case of Desertion," a cartoon by John Leech (figure 1.8), as two young babes abandoned in a Moses basket by a guilty-looking matron (Lord John Russell). The matron's right forearm is covered by her cloak but her hand appears to be amputated, perhaps ironically alluding to the biblical saying, "If I forget thee, O Jerusalem, let my right hand forget her cunning" (Psalms, 137:5). The pronounced features

Figure 1.8   John Leech, "Distressing Case of Desertion," *Punch, or the London Charivari* 21 (1851): 59.

and libertine posture of the two babes, the one sipping from a miniature flask, the other legs akimbo over the edge of the basket, hint at their assumed depravity. Their place of abandonment is at the door of the House of Lords, inside which the succession of bills to emancipate the Jews had consistently been voted down. A short mock advertisement, entitled "Child Dropping," which faces the illustration, announces that "tied to the knocker of the House of Lords [have been found] two promising male children, apparently of the Hebrew-Caucasian family." The announcement ominously adds: "This is to give notice, that the children so left will *not* be taken in; and the Police have orders to apprehend any persons making a similar attempt" (XXI, 58).

Punch's hostility to the Jews is occasionally tempered by a note of apparent support for the cause of emancipation, though even here there is evidence of studied ambivalence. When, earlier in 1851, Lord John Russell decided to reintroduce legislation on the question of the admission of Jews into Parliament, Mr. Punch appears to be speaking up in their favor. "We trust," he announces magisterially, "that bigotry and intolerance will no longer deprive the House of Commons of the services of a class of men so eminently calculated as the Hebrews to participate in its labours; for never let us forget that the whole business of Parliament may be defined to be a series of bill-transactions" (XX, 147). The Jews, it is jokily implied here, would fit well in the Commons since they are already among the most adept in dealing with bills, if only on the stock exchange. Their antiquity as a people, maintains Mr. Punch elsewhere, singularly qualifies them for acceptance even in the House of Lords. "Surely," he writes, "the long-descended Hebrew—whose name occurs in records long prior to the Roll of Battle Abbey, should be welcome to those who pique themselves on their pedigree." Yet, he adds sarcastically, there will surely be a difficulty in finding "an appropriate Solomonic or Levitical title" for an ennobled Jew, unless perhaps he chose to call himself "LORD DISCOUNT" (XX, 196). In straining for such humor, *Punch* reveals once again its incipient streak of anti-Semitism.

Where the journal tried, however unsuccessfully, to swallow or minimize its "mild xenophobia"[7] in the presence of so many foreign visitors to the Great Exhibition, that lesson remained unlearned in terms of its representation of the Jews. Because the Jews of 1851 (almost a full century before the foundation of the state of Israel) could not present themselves as a country or nation in an exhibition devoted to the "works of Industry of all Nations," there is almost no allusion to them in the context of the event itself. To be sure, among the china teapots, "cannons rare," and other items that are displayed as examples of British "industry" are "shuits of clothes by MOSES" (XX, 171). However, where the presence of America and Americans (and indeed of so many other nations) at Crystal Palace elicits reaction from the authors and illustrators of *Punch*, in the case of the Jews there is silence. That in itself would not be surprising, except that, outside the Exhibition, the Jews are a constant source of humorous and frequently anti-Semitic comment throughout the early years of *Punch*, and the volumes for 1851 are no exception. Among the common (and frequently denigratory or sneering) epithets used to describe the Jews in 1851 are "the Firm of Noses," "Messrs. Smouchey" [i.e., "of Moses"], "Israelites," the "Denizens of the Minories, . . . Holywell Street, or Houndsditch," and, of course, "Hebrews." The metaphor of clothes, which in the context of the Yankee allows Mr. Punch to go full vent in caustic commentary on the *avant-garde* vogue for bloomerism, turns distinctly unfashionable in his depiction of Jews as dealers in rags and old clothes.

In researching the first twenty-one volumes of *Punch*, I find little to support the view put forward by Ann and Roger Cowen in their book, *Victorian Jews through British Eyes*, that "when put to coming out with its views *Punch* was honest and forthright and not anti-semitic."[8] We only have to look at the evidence, both visual and textual, to question that conclusion, since what is constantly revealed is a frighteningly well-preserved palimpsest of the old medieval image of the Jew as a perceivable threat to the Christian *status quo*. Despite an apparent new dawn during the early years of the nineteenth century in the heyday of the romantic era, when enlightened writers like William Hazlitt and James Leigh Hunt had openly expressed their abhorrence of the old negative stereotype, traditional anti-Semitism remains depressingly alive and well in the pages of *Punch* in mid century.

However, in a climate of tremendous social change, when it might have seemed inevitable to many that eventually the Jews would follow the Catholics in achieving full emancipation, the tenor of anti-Semitism has changed, too. *Punch* may reflect the era's belief in religious and political liberty, but it does so in a manner that is frequently compromising toward the Jews. This can be seen, for instance, in a report about the Jews of the Austro-Hungarian Empire, who, in exchange for an assurance of the continuation of their present liberties, were persuaded to underwrite a fairly massive government debt (the Austrian Loan). *Punch* sees this as "very illustrative of the Hebrew mind," demonstrating "a fine philanthropy" as a means of enjoying "an enlarged sense of the blessings of religious liberty." The imputation here is that the Jews are accustomed to resort to bribery in order to maintain their liberty. "If the synagogue may stand," comments a thoroughly nasty Mr. Punch, "money will be supplied for the destruction of Christian cities: if the halter be kept from the Hebrew neck, the Hebrew will undraw the purse-strings of Europe" (XXI, 150). Apparently, for Mr. Punch, Jewish emancipation is not a good idea.

Everywhere, the Jews are represented as less than holy in their incessant wheeling and dealing. If the Yankee Jonathan is a figure considered untrustworthy but also rather lacking in calculation, the Hebrew is depicted as robotically devious and underhanded in his scheming actions and immorality of behavior. In a short "Domestic Melo-drama," entitled *Temptation*, the first of the two main figures is the Jew, Smouchey, described as "*a Dealer in worn-out Garments, whose cry of 'Old Clo'!' is a cloak for dishonesty.*" His victim is the London shop-boy, Sneakey, who is importuned and finally cornered by Smouchey into stealing indigo (an expensive dye) from his gentile master. When Sneakey is apprehended by a police officer, he confesses to his crime and admits to having been "over-persuaded by a rascal Jew," but, instead of Smouchey being arrested then and there, it is Sneakey who is dragged away protesting to prison. Smouchey's calculated duplicity is deemed responsible for the undoing of a gullible English boy, whose *ill-regulated mind* is easily subverted by the Jew. The playlet reenacts with utter lack of subtlety Fagin's undermining of Oliver Twist, Dickens's novel (1837–1839) looming ominously in the background. The moral of this "drama for every-day life" (as *Punch* calls it) is that the presence of Jews in England will only serve to debilitate the nation, while simultaneously providing undeserved material enrichment for these devious intruders. With his heavily Germanized accent, Smouchey links himself with the putative cartel of international Jewish bankers, who, like him, "often puy and shell vot's not our own. / The politishan bargains, trades, and shells / On shentiments that never vere his own" (XX, 28–29).

In terms of its overall treatment of the Jewish poor, *Punch* is no less derisory, reconstructing sometimes by brief allusion a host of social slurs that are used to explain its unwillingness to associate with such trash. "Christians," it insists, "will not fraternise with the denizens of the Minories" (a rundown quarter associated with the buying and selling by Jews of old clothes) (XXI, 51). Here and elsewhere, Jewish impoverishment is as much a source of criticism as Jewish affluence: "Holywell Street [another place of habitation associated with many of London's poorest Jews] [has] been a long-lived abomination; sinners there have grown grey in their nastiness. . . . In Holywell Street Infamy took up its freedom and was a protected citizen . . . " (XXI, 116).

If such smears are not always directed at Jews in general, they are frequently individualized through *Punch*'s constant barrage of attacks against Benjamin Disraeli (himself a convert from Judaism), who had long been a target of the journal's most disparaging salvoes. *Punch* never allowed Disraeli to forget his Jewishness, and satirical smears against the politician are most often openly anti-Semitic. *Punch*'s treatment of Disraeli deserves separate treatment, but in the present context, we should observe that his preoccupation with clothes and frequent representation as a dandy (e.g., figure 1.9, "Dressing for a Masquerade. Mr. D—sr—li as a Great Protectionist Leader") suggest a kinship, however distant, to the dealer in rags. At the same time, the modish apparel adopted by a wealthy convert or anglicized Jew is never sufficient to leave his ethnic origin unrevealed.

The marginal status of both Jews and converts from Judaism is a frequent topic for *Punch*. When just before Christmas some Jews from "the Firm of NOSES" in the Minories apparently advertised their wares with "showers of verses thrown into railway cabs and omnibuses," *Punch* advised its readers to beware of "The Poetical Thanksgiving of Jew Tailors, for the Love and Mercy associated with Christmas. On such a theme—and for such a money-making purpose—JUDAS ISCARIOT were worthy to be Laureate" (XX, 10). The accompanying cartoon (figure 1.10) shows two formally dressed Jews greeting each other with "I wish you a Merry Christmas," their seeming affluence contrasting with the poverty of the half-starved English

Figure 1.9 "Dressing for a Masquerade. Mr. D—sr—li as a Great Protectionist Leader," *Punch, or the London Charivari* 20 (1851): 87.

beggar girl outside their shop. It seems quite likely that the piece on "Firm of NOSES" is intended to allude to Jews who have undergone conversion to Christianity, not out of any deep religious awakening or conviction, but as a shortcut to achieving legal emancipation. Either as Jews or Christians, these figures are (as the placard proclaims) "Sham Abraham[s]."

I want to end by concentrating briefly on one such slur that occurred early in 1851 and is unmistakably the immediate source for *Temptation*, the little melodrama involving the defrauding of Sneakey by Smouchey. *Punch*

Figure 1.10   "Christmas in the Minories," *Punch, or the London Charivari* 20 (1851): 10.

devotes a fairly lengthy piece, "The Mystery of 'Clo'" (XX, 19), to describing the entrapment by a Jew, one Henry Hart, of a gentile lad of sixteen, James Thomas Newland, into stealing clothes from his employer and pawning them for profit. Newland is sympathetically represented as a "HUGH OF LINCOLN" figure, a latter-day victim not of ritual murder but of being "trepanned" into crime by the dastardly Jews. The piece was followed shortly after by John Leech's cartoon: "THE DEALER IN OLD CLOTHES TEACHING THE YOUNG IDEA HOW TO STEAL" (figure 1.11). A scurrilous-looking Jew is seen dropping a small coin into the palm of one of his neophytes, who, in turn, is handing a stolen item of jewelry to him. The inscription surrounding the traditional pawnbroker's sign states: "MONEY LENT UPON EVERY DESCRIPTION OF VALUABLE PROPERTY," making it all too clear that the wicked Jew is not merely a dealer in old clothes. The cartoon relates to the story of Hart, but has direct links back to Fagin's corruption of Oliver Twist. The implication is that the Jews, from their putative medieval ancestors found guilty of torturing to death little Hugh of Lincoln through to and beyond their nineteenth-century fictional representation in the evil Fagin, are everywhere the same.

Ironically, in the selfsame issue in which Leech's cartoon had appeared, *Punch* issued *An Apology to a Poor Hebrew* (XX, 27) for publishing what amounted to a malicious libel—the magazine later paid damages to Hart for having so misrepresented him—though this did not stop Hart himself from

Figure 1.11   John Leech, "The Dealer in Old Clothes Teaching the Young Idea How to Steal," *Punch, or the London Charivari* 20 (1851): 25.

being "convicted and sentenced to fourteen years' transportation" to Botany Bay.[9] Henry Hart's treatment by *Punch* is indicative of the marginal status accorded to the Jewish population in England in the era immediately before emancipation, demonstrating how easy it was to deem a Jew guilty merely because he was a Jew. Hart was certainly no angel but had he been anything less (or more?) than a Jew, his situation would probably have passed without opprobrious censure from *Punch*.

Punch was certainly aware that the Jews suffered from ill treatment in early Victorian England. In one instance, it has a respectable Jew, one

Alderman Moses, relating that "we [Hebrews] are unjustly treated, and yet . . . we don't complain . . . [;] we are persecuted, and yet . . . we don't threaten to rebel, or call foul names, or utter falsehoods, or incite to hatred and fury against those who do us wrong" (XXI, 123). Yet, Mr. Punch, that puppet Englishman, rarely shows himself capable of laying off in his frequent and foul treatment of this disadvantaged minority. It remains a sad irony that, in the international climate of 1851, neither Parliament nor the authors of *Punch* demonstrate much awareness of the inherent contradiction of at once celebrating the sturdy independence of the British, who, unlike the Americans would not tolerate slavery, while simultaneously denying fundamental rights of citizenship and representation to Britain's Jewish population. Even though Jewish Emancipation was finally adopted by Parliament in 1858, it would be many more years before Jews would be allowed to join in on an equal playing field in the game of cricket.

Notes

1. This chapter is based on an invited paper delivered at the "Jewish Identities and American Writing" conference, organized by the Rothermere Institute, University of Oxford, in October 2001. The choice of topic was prompted by the sesquicentennial of the Great Exhibition. It is intended as part of a larger work on representations of the Jews and of race and nationhood in Victorian popular culture.
2. *Punch: The Lively Youth of a British Institution 1841–1851* (Columbus: Ohio State University Press, 1997), 622.
3. Altick, *Punch*, 618.
4. *Brewer's Dictionary of Phrase and Fable*, revised and enl. fifth ed. (London: Cassell, 1959), 149, 512.
5. *Brewer's Dictionary of Phrase and Fable*, 119.
6. Abraham Gilam, *The Emancipation of the Jews in England 1830–1860* (New York and London: Garland Publishing, Inc., 1982), 102.
7. Altick, *Punch*, 622.
8. (London and Portland, Or.: Littman Library of Jewish Civilization, 1986; reprint, 1998), xxii.
9. Altick, *Punch*, 269–270.

Some Further Reading

Felsenstein, Frank. *Anti-Semitic Stereotypes: A Paradigm of Otherness in English Popular Culture, 1660–1830*. Baltimore: The Johns Hopkins University Press, 1995.
——. "Caricature." In *Encyclopedia of Antisemitism, Anti-Jewish Prejudice and Persecution*, ed. Richard Levy. New York: ABC-Clio, scheduled for publication, 2004–2005.
——. "Punch." In *Encyclopedia of Antisemitism, Anti-Jewish Prejudice and Persecution*, ed. Richard Levy. New York: ABC-Clio, scheduled for publication, 2004–2005.
Haskell, Francis and Nicholas Penny. *Taste and the Antique: The Lure of Classical Sculpture 1500–1900*. New Haven and London: Yale University Press, 1981.

Salbstein, M. C. N. *The Emancipation of the Jews in Britain: The Question of the Admission of the Jews to Parliament, 1828–1860.* East Brunswick, NJ: Fairleigh Dickinson University Press, 1982.

Spielmann, M. H. *The History of "Punch."* London: Cassell & Co., 1895. Reprint, Detroit: Gale Research Company, 1969.

Wohl, Anthony S. "'Ben JuJu': Representations of Disraeli's Jewishness in the Victorian Political Cartoon." In *Disraeli's Jewishness*, ed. Todd M. Endelman and Tony Kushner, 105–161. London: Valentine Mitchell, 2002.

Wunder, Richard P. *Hiram Powers: Vermont Sculptor.* Taftsville, VT: The Countryman Press in Cooperation with the Woodstock Historical Society, 1974.

CHAPTER 2

PASSING FOR A JEW, ON STAGE AND OFF: STAGE JEWS AND CROSS-DRESSING GENTILES IN GEORGIAN ENGLAND

Michael Ragussis

It is not surprising that the general public became fascinated with—even to the point of mimicry—a people that had been banished from England from 1290 until the 1650s, and that were suddenly seen in the eighteenth-century as a defining feature of the new commercial identity of England.[1] In this essay I examine the ways in which the figure of the Jew in Georgian England became a highly visible and significant theatrical construct, the product of professional actors on the stage and the public at large off the stage, from the time when the fiasco of the "Jew Bill" put the Jews on the national agenda in the 1750s through the opening decades of the nineteenth century. The explosion of new plays containing Jewish characters in this period allowed, and perhaps even encouraged, the public at large to participate in the performance of Jewish identity: the stage Jew often existed as a farcical exaggeration that was easily mimicked at masquerades and in street theater. I begin by recording the ways in which the general public embraced the act of passing for a Jew, frequently in more or less overt political demonstrations. Passing for a Jew was not mere comic sport; it became the means of expressing a deepening anxiety over the increasingly fluid border between Jew and gentile, and the location of Englishness in relation to Jewishness. I then turn to the way in which, through the trope of the cross-dressing gentile, the stage examined its own representations of Jewish identity as well as the theatricalization of Jewish identity in the culture at large.

Both the new visibility of the Jews in London and the growing preoccupation with mimicking them are apparent in the debut of a weekly journal, *The Connoisseur*, whose opening number January 31, 1754 describes a general tour of London that begins immediately with visiting the common haunts of the Jews, for the writer confesses "A . . . desire of penetrating into the most secret springs of action in these people."[2] This desire leads him to follow in the footsteps of a famous actor, Charles Macklin (though not identified by name): "When a comedian, celebrated for his excellence in the part of Shylock, first undertook that character, he made daily visits to the centre of business, the 'Change and the adjacent coffee-houses; that by a frequent intercourse and conversation with 'the unforeskinn'd race,' he might habituate himself to their air and deportment" (January 31, 1754). The tour of London begins by following an actor's search—not simply for Jews, but for a mode of representation: how to represent, to mimic, to copy this strange people who now populated the city becomes an important object of inquiry. So, Jewish representation entered a new phase in Georgian England, opening up the possibility that anyone could produce a Jewish portrait, merely through observation. For the first time in several centuries, Jews were evidently no longer merely figures of fantasy but were available for empirical observation. Visible and accessible, Jews were suddenly before everyone's eyes, at the coffee houses, at the Royal Exchange, in the theater pit and boxes—there, in other words—to be copied and mimicked.

Playing the Jew became a popular public phenomenon in an era that was already obsessed with performance, with the theatricality of everyday life. This was a time when the border between theater and everyday life was at its most liminal—the time, for instance, of amateur theatricals and masquerades, when theatrical amusement meant not merely attending the theater, but bringing the theater into one's own lived experience, the time when everyone was an actor as well as a spectator. Amateur theatricals became the craze,[3] and were even the subject of such professional theatricals as Isaac Jackman's *All the World's a Stage* (1777) and James Powell's *Private Theatricals* (1787). As one contemporary observer noted, "the phrenzy for spouting and acting . . . has not only shown itself in the parlours of private houses, but even descended into the kitchen and stables, the very footmen and grooms becoming Romeos and Alexanders."[4] In Jane Austen's *Mansfield Park* (1814), a novel that anatomizes this kind of theatricality, we recall Henry Crawford's declaration: "I could be fool enough at this moment to undertake any character that ever was written, from Shylock or Richard III down to the singing hero of a farce. . . . I feel as if I could be any thing or every thing."[5] Henry's claim to "be any thing or every thing" starts with perhaps the greatest performative stretch of all, playing the Jew. Nonetheless, it was a role that had become immensely popular. At the beginning of the eighteenth century, in what was intended as a conscious embrace of the new commercial identity of England but, in retrospect, looks like an unconscious symptom that would characterize the culture at large throughout the century, Addison declared in the opening number of *The Spectator*, "I have been taken for a Merchant upon the *Exchange* for above these ten Years, and sometimes pass for a *Jew* in the Assembly of Stock-Jobbers at *Jonathan*'s."[6] The Jewish disguise became especially popular at masquerades, a fact that Terry Castle's otherwise excellent *Masquerade and Civilization* overlooks. In Samuel Richardson's *Pamela* (1740), for instance, the heroine recalls a masquerade at which someone appeared as a Jewish Rabbi, and a fictitious epistle in *The Spectator* reports on a masquerade at which "a *Jew* eat me up half a Ham of Bacon" (no. 14 [March 16, 1711]). But it is not necessary to rely on fictitious accounts; there are also frequent journalistic accounts of real masquerades that record the appearances of "several female Jew Pedlars," or "a Jew Pedlar, talking German and broken English," or "the Hon. Mr. M-ntag-e in Shylock."[7] In its reports on public masquerades, *Westminster Magazine* records in June, 1777, "two Jew Shoe-blacks" and "an Israelite money-lender" (along with "a Highlander" and "a Welch Pauper," to complete what I have elsewhere called "multiethnic spectacle");[8] and, on another occasion, in June 1778, "Jews, Turks, Sailors, and Dominos." Castle reproduces an engraving from 1771 entitled "The Masquerade Dance" in which one man is dressed as a Jew (Castle simply identifies the group as "all-male").[9] And novels such as Tobias Smollett's *Expedition of Humphry Clinker* (1771) and William Godwin's *Caleb Williams* (1794) portray characters that hide their identities by assuming a Jewish disguise, while in Maria Edgeworth's *Harrington* (1817), "good Christian beggars . . . dressed up and daubed" as Jews—"the tone, accent, and action, suited to the parts to be played."[10]

The phenomenon of passing for a Jew flourished in the most liminal theatrical spaces. During the Old Price Riots at Covent Garden Theatre in 1809,[11] when rioters protested the new ticket prices, there is, for example, the record of a gentile cross-dressed as a Jew. This Jewish performance takes place off the stage but still in the theater. The episode suggests how complex and how powerful transgressing the border between stage actor and public spectator could become in Georgian England. The management had hired some Jews, most notably the pugilists Daniel Mendoza and "Dutch Sam," to contain the rioters, and soon the Jews themselves became one of the primary objects of opprobrium during the months that the riots dragged on. There was, for example, the audience's constant display of handbills, placards, mottos, epigrams, in addition to shouts from audience members: "Turn out the Jews"; "And lo! it came to pass, that John Bull was sorely vexed, and smote the Israelites"; "Oppose Shylock and the whole tribe of Israel"; "Shall Britons be subdued by the wandering tribe of Jerusalem"; "The Covent Garden Synagogue, Mendoza the Grand Rabbi"; "Genius of Britain support our cause / Free us from Kemble and Jewish laws"; and so on.[12] During the particular episode that I have in mind, the pit "joined in expressing a sort of mock indignation against a man, who appeared in the garb of a venerable Jewish rabbi." The "assumed" dress consisted of "a large black beard, and slouched hat." In this way the popular convention of the stage Jew became the property not of the actors on the stage, but of the audience in the pit: anyone could assume the role of the Jew, and audience members were obviating the need for the trained actor and for the playhouse in their dispute over rising theater prices; they could, in effect, stage their own performance of Jewish identity. The mock Jewish rabbi "suffered himself to be pushed about the pit, by his companions, without betraying the slightest symptoms of displeasure. While he was the object of attack, many exclaimed, 'a Jew! a Jew! turn him out.' The sham Israelite kept up the deception until he was quite exhausted."[13] A similar incident was recorded in *The London Evening-Post* (December 1–4, 1753), when a group of Jews in one of the balconies was met with the cry, "No Jews, out with them," but now the incident becomes a ritualized performance: the shouts are aimed not at real Jews but at a mock Jew, a cross-dressing gentile. By 1809, the audience had become acculturated to the performance of Jewish identity. In other words, this audience's performance of the pelted rabbi reproduced and ritualized what it had seen on the stage, week after week; it was copying offstage the scapegoating of the Jew that occurred on stage in a variety of plays, both old and new.

The public put on the performance of the venerable rabbi as a realization of its own power to expel the Jew from its midst. The social power of performance in the mini-farce of the rabbi, buffeted by shoves and jeers in every direction, the object of derision and ostracism ("a Jew! turn him out"), was realized in a ritualized form of expulsion. In this way the public reenacted what was perhaps the most dramatic event of Anglo-Jewish history—namely, the expulsion of the Jews from England in 1290. In fact, the guardianship of Englishness was connected in Georgian England with what were seen as patriotic performances of the expulsion of the Jews. On another evening during the Old Price riots, real Jews were ejected from the theater in what became a ritualized celebration of Anglo-centrism: "Repeated exclamations now came from the audience of 'Turn out the Jews;' and a ruffianly [*sic*] Hebrew, who was in the pit on the preceding night . . . now again grossly insulted the whole audience." A scuffle ensued, the Jew was turned out into the lobby and then knocked down, and he finally retreated with some other Jews. "A cry soon resounded from the pit, signifying that the Jews were turned out, and three loud huzzas were given immediately by the audience, followed by 'God save the King,' in universal chorus."[14] We have here a mini-opera that stages, offstage in the pit, the kinds of mottos that the rioters constructed to represent the Jews as a threat to Englishness.

Such incidents suggest how the public could empower itself to formulate English identity through the theatrical performance of the expulsion of the Jew. They recall an episode recorded in *The London Evening-Post* a half century earlier, at the time of the clamor over the Jewish Naturalization Bill: "On Saturday Night last amidst the Rejoicings for the celebrating his Majesty's Birth-Day in the Borough of Southwark, the populace dress'd up the effigy of a Jew, and burnt him in a large Bonfire" (November 13–15, 1753). The dressed-up Jewish effigy was a popular theatrical device used to represent the Jew as a kind of puppet figure in important ideological battles. There was, for example, the drunken Tory mob that paraded with a Jewish effigy in 1753.[15] Such representations made their way into plate 1 of Hogarth's *Election Series*, where the Tories parade with a Jewish effigy and a sign "No Jews."[16] Like the mock rabbi of the Old Price riots, the Jewish effigy functions as part of a ritualized public performance of expulsion, and suggests, through a kind of theatrical dressing up of a figure as a Jew, the ways in which the public used the lessons it learned nightly at the theater about staging Jewish identity.

While the performance of Jewish identity sometimes had a specific political agenda—as in the cases of the "Jew Bill" or the Old Price Riots—I wish to argue that the public's appropriation of the performance of the stage Jew was a response to what was seen more generally, with increasing anxiety, as the newly porous borders between (foreign) Jew and (English) gentile in the culture at large. This fluidity between identities was everywhere in evidence. For example, it was during the eighteenth century that the name *Jew* began to slip and slide, opening up the overlapping middle ground between Jew and gentile, Jew and Englishman. As early as May 27, 1727, in *The Craftsman*, we read: "Among the Christians with whom I reside there are a peculiar Sort called Stock-Jobbers. The Christians themselves nickname them Jews, as a mark of Reproach. . . . Those, who are the natural Jews, may be known by their Complexions and a sort of lingua Franca." So, there are "natural" Jews, and there are Jews by habit, behavior, or performance. During the clamor over the Naturalization Bill, those who campaigned against the bill substituted the word *Jew* for *Whig*, the Pelhams were called the Jewish brothers, and their supporters the Jewish candidates. In fact, the Jewish effigy paraded in Oxfordshire actually represented a Whig candidate— a vivid and politically charged example of the cross-dressing gentile (cross-dressed against his will).[17] Similarly, during the Old Price riots, Kemble was nicknamed "Mr. Jew Kemble" and caricatures depicted him with a very large nose.[18] And when a stockbroker in the audience criticized the Old Price rioters, they immediately called out, "Put him in the *Stocks*, he is a *Jew*."[19]

It was probably Charles Lamb who best summed up this culture's confusion and discomfort: "I do not relish the approximation of Jew and Christian, which has become so fashionable. . . . Jews christianizing— Christians judaizing—puzzle me. I like fish or flesh."[20] This new "approximation" was quite evident in the culture at large, including the newly familiar social relations between Jews and gentiles, not to mention the increased fervor to convert Jews to Christianity, as well as such sensational events as the conversion of a nobleman like Lord George Gordon to Judaism in the late 1780s, or the claim that the English were descended from the ancient Jews, made famous by Richard Brothers in the 1790s. There was in this culture, then, the paranoiac dissociation of English identity from Jewish identity, using exaggerated stage markers to locate Jewish difference, and epitomized by the ritualized performance of the expulsion of the Jews from England, at the same time that English gentiles began more and more to socialize with Jews, to marry Jews, and to name themselves Jews, usually pejoratively but not always (as in the cases of Gordon and Brothers), while Jews sometimes converted, sometimes took gentile names, and generally assimilated in large numbers.[21] In short, the theatrical performance of Jewish identity was often used to rigidify the border between gentile and Jew precisely as it began to become more and more porous.

At the same time, the performance of Jewish identity—in which Jew and Englishman seemed mixed, coterminous—could become a strikingly material realization of the culture's paranoiac fears about the new "approximation" between Jew and gentile. The performance of Jewish identity, after all, required the gentile to be hidden and absorbed in the figural body of the Jew. What are the ways in which Georgian theatrical culture used and explored the embodiment of Jewish difference in general and the exchange of Jewish and gentile bodies in particular? In this culture, we have numerous examples of the public's growing spectatorial appetite for the embodied figure of the Jew, and I now turn to an especially grotesque version of what I have called the new visibility and accessibility of Jewish identity in order to explore the ways in which the Jewish body became a focus of this culture's attention. I quote from the newspaper reports that followed the Chelsea murder case in 1771, when four Jews were executed on the charge of murder:

> The Curiosity and Impatience of the People to see the dead Bodies of the Jews exposed at Surgeons Hall on Tuesday late was so great, that it was with the utmost Difficulty that any Gentlemen of the Faculty could gain Admittance; the Mob was never so numerous and unruly upon a like Occasion. . . . The Professor of Anatomy and Mr. Bromfelld were obliged to climb in at a Window, to the no small Diversion of the Crowd, which at last became so great, that it was impossible to open the Gates to any one. . . .
>
> As Mr. Bayford was returning from the Hall after the Lecture, he was stopped by the Wife of the Jew Doctor, earnestly begging the Body of her Husband for Interment; which Request however could not be complied with, as the Skeleton of this Criminal is to be hung up in Surgeons Hall.[22]

What the opening number of *The Connoisseur* described as the goal of "penetrating into the most secret springs of action in these people" has become, twenty or so years later at Surgeons Hall, a mob inspection of the secret sites of the Jewish body; the hunt through the streets of London described in *The Connoisseur* has become a scavenger hunt. And while *The Connoisseur* concluded that "one might almost doubt, where money is out of the case, whether a Jew has 'eyes, hands, organs, dimensions, senses, affec-tions, passions,'"[23] at Surgeons Hall these parts are nakedly displayed— "exposed"—in death. The skeleton of the Jew hung up in Surgeons Hall mimics the Jewish effigy paraded through the streets or burned in celebra-tion. In such cases, the mob functions as spectatorial audience, whether on the real or the mock Jewish body. I wish to press the special theatricality of such a scene in which the Jewish body is displayed in a public arena: the events at Surgeons Hall suggest how the public at large, outside the domain of the conventional theater, could be constituted as spectators in what amounted to a kind of theater of the dead.

But the fascination with the Jewish body does not stop here, as the news-paper account makes clear:

> Two eminent Tooth-Drawers of this Town had a Scramble for the Teeth of the four Jews: One of the Gentlemen, however, had nearly extracted three whole

Sets before the second Operator arrived, who was therefore obliged to content himself with the Teeth of the fourth poor Wretch, (the Doctor) which he soon dislocated, and put into his Pocket, and they will probably ere long adorn the Mouths of some of the *Bon Ton*; a Jew's Eye is proverbially precious,—why not a Jew's Tooth?[24]

While for us an eerie anticipation of the Holocaust, for an eighteenth-century audience this account echoes the famous historical anecdote in which King John draws the teeth of a Jew to extort money from him; in this sense, the account is part of a cultural tradition that demonstrates English attitudes toward the Jews, except that the newspaper account is meant to satirize the apparently more polite and fashionable world of Georgian England, where the teeth of the executed Jews eventually adorn the beaux and belles of London. So, in a culture in which the actor and the masquerader attire themselves in the Jews' long whiskers and slouch hats, the city's fashionable set wears the Jews' teeth in an especially grotesque mirror of the performance of Jewish identity, a telling example of the fascination with the intersection of Jewish and gentile bodies. The newspaper account moves from the inspection of the dead Jewish body, to its invasion—the extraction and dislocation of the teeth—to end finally with its incorporation into the gentile body. This movement from inspection to invasion to incorporation suggests an allegory of the steps by which Jewish identity was, at this historical moment, popularly staged by this culture. It inadvertently warns about the ways in which the newly popular theatrical staging of Jewish identity functioned transgressively and suggests that the spectatorial obsession with the new Jewish visibility was, in fact, rapacious. Did the performance of Jewish identity require the absorption and incorporation of the Jewish body in the gentile body, and was the stage Jew being constructed on the corpse of Jewish identity, a uniformly static and grotesque figure that parasitically fed off a real and diverse population?

The picture we have here of the gentile invasion of the Jewish body functions as a corollary to—even as a defense against—the fear of the Jewish invasion of the gentile body, most notably expressed time and again during the uproar over the Jewish Naturalization Bill. In fact, I wish to claim that an important new figure, the circumcised gentile, emerged during the propaganda campaign against the "Jew Bill" and led directly to the popular phenomenon of the cross-dressing gentile. The anxiety over the naturalization of foreign-born Jews in 1753–1754 took its most potent form in the fear of a Judaized England, expressed in many forms in newspapers, pamphlets, and satirical engravings that imagined St. Paul's converted into a synagogue, Jews sitting in Parliament, but most notably, the mass circumcision of Englishmen.[25] The figure of the circumcised gentile was especially popular in the satirical prints of the time. In *A Scene of Scenes for the Year 1853* (a prediction of an entirely Judaized England one century after the 1753 "Jew Bill"), a figure is being circumcised, while several bishops and judges who had supported the "Jew Bill" witness the circumcision as they await their turn. In *A Stir in the City*, a satire on the General Election of 1754, a group of butchers is introduced to perform the rite for any voters who wish to become Jews, with the cry: "Are ye ready for circumcision?" In *The Jews shaving the Par*l*m**t*, set in a barber shop with a Jewish barber, a seated gentile cries out, "They will Circumcise us next." The satirical print *The Circumcised Gentiles, or a Journey to Jerusalem* shows a Jew, with the typical markers of beard and slouch hat and dialect, along with two gentile figures who have been converted and circumcised. It is no surprise, then, that a typical quip at this time nicknamed the "Jew Bill" "your Circumcition Bill [*sic*]."[26]

The opponents of the "Jew Bill" claimed that "the unconverted Jews can never incorporate with us,"[27] and I am arguing that the "Jew Bill's" proposal to incorporate the Jewish body into the English body politic led to two opposing but corollary images: the assimilated Jew (the Jew who has become an Englishman) and the Judaized Englishman (the Englishman who has become a Jew)—in the latter case, the English body incorporated into the Jewish body, represented in the demonstrably corporeal figures, first, of the circumcised gentile, and then, of the cross-dressed gentile. What all these figures have in common is the merging and meeting, or even worse, the indistinguishability, of (foreign) Jew and (English) gentile. Hence the renewal of medieval claims that visible markers existed to identify Jews, and the efforts of the theater to mark Jewish difference. According to a political weekly of 1753, *The Protester*, Jews are marked by nature: "their very Breed . . . is in general of the lowest, basest, and most contemptible Kind, distinguishable to the Eye by peculiar Marks, odious for that Distinction, and what, if once communicated to a Family, becomes indelible."[28] But, if these marks go unnoticed or are hidden, the Jew can be deliberately marked; an advertisement in *The London Evening-Post* explains how *An Historical Treatise concerning Jews and Judaism in England* demonstrates "that a Jew has no Right to appear in England without a yellow Badge fix'd on the upper Garment" (September 13, 1753). In many ways, the theatrical props of the beard and the hat and the dialect were the ways in which, through performance, the Jew was marked in Georgian England; they were the theatrical equivalents of the yellow badge. With "Jews christianizing—Christians judaizing," the stage was performing the important social function of untangling this confusion by marking the Jew clearly and unambiguously.

In this way the larger history of the Jews, not just the immediate social and political events of the time, informed the performance of Jewish identity in Georgian England. The accoutered stage Jew reminds us that the history of the Jews is in so many ways the history of the signifying body par excellence—in fact, arguably the most well-known and most dire history of the use of the inscribed body, from the bodily mark of circumcision to the well-known stereotypical bodily signs (from noses to odors) used to locate and expel the Jewish body from Christian societies throughout Europe from the Middle Ages through the twentieth century. This history includes the special identifying marks of both garment and body (the specially colored hat or badge, the concentration camp number) that various European cultures imposed on Jews as an unmistakable sign of Jewish identity. It is no accident, then, that when the Jew emerged as a central stage character in Georgian England, the question of such bodily markers was recalled and reinvented. The theater, the spectacle of the moving, speaking body, reinvested the Jews with its own set of markers—the long beard, the slouch hat, the garbled dialect.

In fact, such stage markers became the means of re-judaizing the Jew, reinventing even the real Jew as Jewish, as super-Jewish. The re-judaization of the Jew was necessary because "[i]n matters of dress, manners, speech, living habits, and cultural aspirations, they were ceasing to be identifiably Jewish."[29] So, street theater, the masquerade, and the stage assumed the function of re-judaizing the Jew, making the conventional markers show and stick. Satirical prints worked in the same way; in *The Grand Conference or the Jew Predominant* (1753), for example, Samson Gideon (a famous financier who was an extremely popular figure in Jewish caricature at the time) is represented as speaking with an accent more commonly associated with foreign-born Eastern European Jews, despite the fact that he was a London-born Sephardi.[30] This figure of the super-Judaized Jew, forced to play the role of the theatrical Jew, reaches its most remarkable articulation in Charles Dickens's *Our Mutual Friend* (1865), when the Jew Riah performs publicly the role of hard-hearted Jewish usurer, a Shylock, as the cover for the real usurer, the gentile Fledgby—a scenario that Dickens took from a Georgian play, Richard Cumberland's *The Fashionable Lover* (1772). So, precisely insofar as Jews were assimilating (and the government was pressing to naturalize more of them), there developed the need to mark them further, to reinvent the assimilating population as alien through representation. And I have been recording the ways in which the theater in particular, and the public in general, in the figure of the Jew on stage, at the masquerade, and in street theater, embraced and employed these markers.

While it was the work of the theater to invent and to disseminate these stage markers, it also became the work of the theater to expose their artificiality, to subvert the culture's wholesale theatricalization of Jewish identity. The surplus of Jewish representation and the supertheatricalization of Jewish identity led in fact to a crisis in representation. The sudden explosion of numerous new plays with Jewish characters, the public's broad embrace of Jewish performance in street theater and masquerades, and the exaggerated, satirical, and highly conventionalized nature of these theatrical representations eventually led to the specific theatrical trope I now wish to examine: the trope of the cross-dressing gentile. I mark here that historical moment when a surplus of Jewish performance produced another new theatrical phenomenon—namely, the pivotal scene when, on stage, a gentile character dons the costume and mimics the dialect of the Jew, thereby exposing the performative nature of Jewish identity in Georgian culture generally. So, in the theater at this time, audiences experienced a double—a doubling—phenomenon: plays that unselfconsciously and mimetically presented Jewish characters, and plays within which a gentile character, in a critical scene, would suddenly appear dressed up and speaking like the stage Jews the audience had seen presented mimetically perhaps only the night before. Even this experience was eventually staged in a single theatrical entertainment when in some plays there occurred the extraordinary meeting between the cross-dressed gentile and the "real" Jew whose part he was playing, in what was supposed to be an uproariously funny, and what became an ontologically searching, encounter between *fake* and *real* Jews. Such scenes in which the audience was exposed to the performance of Jewish identity—especially scenes where the *fake* Jew was believed over the *real* Jew by the other characters in the play—challenged the conventional mode of representing and recognizing Jewish identity on the stage.

The apparently seamless conventional performance of Jewish identity on the stage began to be punctured, then, when the action of a play was interrupted to disclose, almost as a kind of confession made on the part of the theater, the way in which Jewish identity was constructed for, and performed on, the stage. In other words, what was normally hidden backstage, as part of the actor's craft, was suddenly announced publicly on stage in an extraordinary piece of metatheater: we witness the gentile plan to equip himself with beard, with slouch hat, with dialect, and we see him appear moments later transformed into a Jew, and sometimes we see that persona stripped from him right on the stage, returning him to his gentile identity. In this way, what I am calling the surplus of representation overflowed into meta-representation, metatheater, when the audience was suddenly given a view not simply of the stage Jew, but also of the staging of the Jew, the act of (mis)representation itself.

If the conventional Georgian stage Jew was meant to represent the differences between Jew and gentile, the trope of the cross-dressing gentile also, at least initially, depended on and in some ways affirmed these differences; no such cross-dressing was possible if the differences between Jew and gentile were not apparent. The actual act of performing the Jew, the elaborate scheme of passing, meant that the Jew and the gentile were recognizably different. So, at one level, the trope of the cross-dressing gentile served the function of marking the Jew, of making him a comical exaggeration, of even controlling him like a puppet. Functioning as a largely unthreatening version of the figure of the circumcised gentile, the trope of the cross-dressing gentile was a theatrical experiment, forgoing the knife and the indelible mark of circumcision for the hat and the beard and the dialect, within the artificial and controllable arena of the theater: it was an experiment at playing becoming the Jew, even being lost and absorbed in the Jew. Moreover, the trope was a controlled experiment that could be reversed: all of the theatrical markers of Jewish identity could be laid aside, as they were when the cross-dressing gentile reemerged, as he always did, without his Jewish disguise. While from one vantage point the trope represented the absorption of the Englishman in the Jew (and his successful reemergence), the trope also functioned as an experiment that realized the communal or national desire to infiltrate the Jewish body, incorporate it, in order to imitate and control it, to make it do one's own bidding. Finally, however, the trope of the cross-dressing gentile did not simply stage this desire, but also explored and eventually exposed it, in what became the most signal hallmark of the trope—namely, its self-referentiality. From the beginning, all the plays that employed the trope of the cross-dressing gentile self-consciously explored theatricality in general and the construction of Jewish identity in particular.

The typical organizing feature of these plays is a comic marriage plot in which the *senex iratus*, a father or guardian, refuses access to his daughter or ward, and either the hero or his servant cross-dresses as a Jew in order to gain access to her. In *Love Laughs at Locksmiths* (1803),[31] for example, we have a plot in which the guardian keeps the heroine locked up, and the hero gains access to her through disguising himself as a Jew. In this play, the heroine is at once the captive ward of the guardian and the captive model of the artist, for the guardian is a painter who, "although he lets nobody behold the original, many . . . have seen the resemblance" (10). This play asks, like so many of these plays: Is it possible for the spectator to reach the original, behind the mask of the copy? The world the artist makes is of "sham men and women" (21), "busts and pictures . . . representing figures as large as life" (26)—in other words, the world of optical illusion, the world that these plays consistently show the cross-dressing gentile occupying. The comedy here depends on showing that the artist who insists on monopolizing the original for himself, and showing only the resemblance to others, is fooled (at least initially) by the figure of the cross-dressing gentile, when the hero cross-dresses as a Jew to fool the old guardian. Once the guardian discovers the disguise, he mimics a Jew by copying the hero who mimics a Jew: this multiplication of false Jews becomes part of the trope, exposing the potentially infinite play of representation and reproduction in the cultural construction of Jewish identity. So, in an allegory of the representation of Jewish identity, the artist who in his work copies the original (in the case of his ward), now copies the copy (in the case of the Jew).

In *The Wandering Jew: or, Love's Masquerade* (1797),[32] there is a similar self-consciousness about various forms of representation, and the play's humor and meaning work through a number of optical illusions and sight gags that draw attention to the power of art. In the main plot, we have a painter, whose dummy model several times incites confusion between the real and the copy, when, for example, the hero puts on the clothes of the mannequin and then is mistaken for a "walking model" (18). And in another scene, two characters place their heads in the holes that have been cut out of life-size portraits, making to the astonishment of everyone "living portraits" (54). This obsession with the real inhabiting, hidden in, obscured by, or animating the artificial becomes a consistent context for exploring theatrical impersonation in general and the figure of the cross-dressing gentile in particular. The hero impersonates not only the Wandering Jew but also an Italian count, Count Gran Contrasto del Camera Obscura, with the name here a play on the entire theme of illusion, representation, and artistic reproduction. In his impersonation of the Italian count, he must admit that he can speak no Italian, but neither can the woman he attempts to fool, so that he can speak "in Hebrew, Greek, Latin, Welch, or Irish" (24), and successfully fool her nonetheless. The ignorance of the spectator, then, is a central requirement in the successful performance of the *other*, and the parochial "English spectator" (25) is time and again singled out as the butt of the humor in these plays. In another scene, a character remarks about having been to the theater to see the actor Jack Bannister in a play (27), and of course, the audience knows that it is Bannister who is playing the Jew and the Italian in this play. The actor (Bannister), who plays the hero playing a Jew and an Italian, is told: "you'd make an incomparable actor! Do, go on stage" (23).

These plays thrive on this kind of inside joke between the actor and the audience, where all the fictions of theatricality are shared between the actor and the knowing audience member (as opposed to the gullible spectator located on stage). In other words, the meta-theatrical dimension of these plays keeps displacing the work of seeing and knowing onto the stage itself, where the play's characters enact the role of the audience by being consistently gulled. In this way, the cross-dressing actor and the sophisticated audience member collude, refusing the spell of theatrical illusion. It is in this way that these plays work to minimize character and story—what might be called the center of mimesis—in order to maximize the infinite play of dialects, makeup, and costumes, the equipment of performance itself. It is no accident, then, that the hero is often a former actor; in fact, these plays suggest the actor as hero—only the dissembling actor can outsmart the old guardian.

We can see this emphasis on the hero as actor, as role-player, in *The Invisible Girl* (1806).[33] In this play, only one character (played again by Jack Bannister), aptly named Allclack, does all the speaking. In the course of the play, he impersonates a Jew, a lord, and his own mother. In its reduction of speaking roles to one and in its entire focus on the many roles one actor can play, this play makes it especially clear that the plot of these plays exists merely to serve the series of performances given by the actor. We have here the hero as actor in the comic marriage plot and the actor as hero in the theater of impersonation. The series of cross-dressing performances swallows the plot, just as the hero-actor swallows the other characters (he is "all-clack"). The plot exists to stage a series of cross-dressings, and so becomes neither more nor less than the site of a special kind of theatrical spectacle, a kind of double watching and double listening. A double act of recognition structures such performance-plays. On the stage mis-recognition occurs when the gulled spectator mistakes Jack Bannister for Allclack for a Jew. But in the audience, a form of recognition occurs when the enlightened spectator recognizes that Allclack is impersonating the Jew, and even that Bannister is impersonating Allclack. In this spectacle of cross-dressing, performativity is put on display. One actor can play all the roles because theater is about performance, not mimesis. Instead of hiding its secrets, its constitutive conventions, theater exposes them in these plays, and makes sure that the audience recognizes them.

While in *The Invisible Girl* a real Jews exists, but only as a mere ghostly presence who at one point in the play silently beholds his speaking double in the actor's performance, in *Rochester; or, King Charles the Second's Merry Days* (1819),[34] the telling absence of a real Jew is marked by the multiplication of fake Jews. In *Rochester*, both Rochester and Buckingham put on "a Jew's dress and beard" to enter the old guardian's house to court the heroine. When both are so dressed (unbeknownst to each other), Rochester hears Buckingham's cry, "Ould clothes" (38), and is fooled into believing that Buckingham is a real Jew. While this is the phrase he himself cried a moment earlier, he nonetheless is fooled, failing to understand how anyone—in this case, Buckingham—can, like himself, work the script of Jewish identity, which is both unalterable and universally known. So even the cross-dressing gentile, although aware of his own theatrical construction of Jewish identity, is gulled into believing the fiction of the cross-dressing gentile. The power of such theatrical constructions, or our willingness to believe in them, seems universal. When Buckingham, cross-dressed as an old-clothes man, sees the cross-dressed Rochester, he similarly exclaims: "here's a real Jew here; I hope he won't detect me" (38). But Buckingham has nothing to fear: Rochester is not "a real Jew," and the theater, in Miles Peter Andrews's *Dissipation* (1781), had already shown that even a "real" Jew cannot detect a cross-dressing gentile, when a Frenchman absconds with a Jew's daughter by putting on the costume of a rabbi and speaking the dialect, thereby fooling the Jewish father. The power of the stereotype knows no bounds: it fools gentile and Jew alike, and it even fools those who work the fictitious construction themselves.

It is only when both cross-dressing gentiles raise the price they are willing to pay for some old clothes (in an effort to gain admittance to the house that holds the heroine) that each begins to realize the other cannot be a Jew—that is, each begins to fail to live up to the stereotype of the greedy Jew: "I suspect this fellow never can be a genuine Jew" (39). When one of the cross-dressed Jews accuses the other of being an imposter, the gullibility of the gentile about what constitutes Jewish identity is made clear when the old guardian responds: "how can he have such a beard, and not be a Jew?" (40). To prove that the other is an imposter, Rochester says (in a comical rendition of Othello's famous speech): "I'll shave him directly. I took the uncircumcised dog by the throat and smote him thus—dere—(*pulls off Buckingham's beard*)" (40). The beard is shown as a false marker compared to the true marker, circumcision. The scene ends farcically with each fake Jew pulling off the other's beard. In other words, each cross-dressing gentile undresses the other—that is, undoes the construction of Jewish identity for all to behold. It is an important moment in the self-reflexivity of the trope of the cross-dressing gentile: we are shown the way in which the trope undoes itself, exposes itself. At the same time, there is no "genuine Jew" in the play; he has been displaced by the multiplication of false Jews. The "genuine Jew" becomes, if not a fiction, at least an absence. Jewish identity exists only in an apparently endless line of simulacra. The real Jew—whatever that is—is banished from the stage in favor of multiple doubles. The spectator is left to choose between two copies, and once their impersonations are discovered, no "real" Jew takes their place. In the absence of the stereotype, nothing appears.

What happens when a so-called genuine Jew enters a play to encounter directly, and interrogate, the cross-dressing gentile? While this is only imagined in *Rochester*, when both cross-dressing gentiles fear being discovered by a real Jew, such a scene does in fact occur in *Transformation; or, Love and Law* (1810).[35] Here, the attorney Makesafe uses his servants as sentinels to guard his house against the young hero's entrance. He imprisons his ward while he guards both her and her fortune against her will. The cross-dressing hero is an actor aptly named Cameleon, pinpointing this increasing association in the trope of the cross-dressing gentile: in Thomas Dibdin's *Family Quarrels* (1805), the servant Proteus is a former actor; in Dibdin's *Humphrey Clinker* (1818), the hero Wilson is also a former actor; even Mr. Hardy in Hannah Cowley's *Belle's Stratagem* (1780) goes not to a Jew, but to an actor, in order to learn how to impersonate a Jew. The protean actor, chameleon-like, is the man who knows the tricks of performance that can create the figure of the Jew.

Transformation makes explicit the case for the power of the actor and the gullibility of the spectator when Cameleon recalls his days as a strolling player, working with the Strutt family. Mr. Strutt, who is eulogized as "a fine actor," is comically characterized as being "four feet high" and having "squinted, waddled and snuffled" in real life; "yet in Macheath he was thought to excell." Mrs. Strutt is another example of the enigma of the mesmerizing power of acting: "twice as high" as her husband, she "hobbled" in real life but excelled in dancing roles and in playing Columbine (10–11). Are such characterizations a eulogy to the mysterious, self-transformative powers of the actor, or a comic satire on the public and its willingness to be fooled by impersonation and masquerade?

The hero in *Transformation* plays three roles—a woman, a Jew, and a Yorkshireman—where the trope of cross-dressing emphasizes the comical otherness of the roles played. Makesafe gives his two servants the description of the only three people whom they can let enter the house—"so exact a description, that it will be impossible for you to mistake them" (5). When Cameleon decides to impersonate these three figures in order to gain access to the imprisoned heroine, he models his impersonations on these written descriptions. Never having seen the actual people, the actor copies not from life, but from a written description—in other words, from a representation— so that his performance is at a double remove. The play here suggests the way in which the performance of Jewish identity on the stage, or even the representation of Jewish identity in general—in novels, engravings, pamphlets—may in fact be a copy of a copy. While the written descriptions that the servants record incite in them a desire for authenticity, for the original—"Their portraits are so very interesting, that I long to be acquainted with the originals" (7)—the servants meet the copies of the originals, namely the actor Cameleon impersonating the originals. The written descriptions recreate and expose the myth of the distinguishing feature, the real marker, that stamps identity and so makes it recognizable. Malachi, the Jewish moneylender, is described as having "a red beard, and a red head, a broad brimmed hat . . . , and a long dark coat, almost down to his heels" (7). Intended to assist the servants in recognizing the Jew with whom Makesafe has business, these features actually assist the actor Cameleon in his job of mimicry—they become the recognizable marks by which he can gull the servants. Performance is exposed here as occurring through the citation of a text, the dominant culture's text of Jewish identity. The spectator recognizes Jewish identity through the representations that have been dictated: "write what I dictate" (5), Makesafe tells his servants, as he describes the Jew.

The farce examines the power of representation, both in written descriptions and performed behaviors, through a series of (mis)recognition scenes. By staging encounters between the cross-dressing hero and the people he is impersonating, the farce shows how the servants are unable to tell the copy from the original; in each case the servants mistakenly choose the cross-dressed Cameleon, the actor, as the real person. In the case of the Jew, this farce marks an important development in the trope, because here the cross-dressing gentile encounters the Jew he is impersonating, thereby deepening the issue of theatricality: even when compared with the *real* Jew, the cross-dressing gentile is believed, taken for real. Such a scene calls into question the entire notion of the *genuine Jew* as it figures in all modes of representation because the "genuine Jew" (19) in the play is himself only a performed mask, played by an actor. When one of the servants sees the two Jews, he exclaims: "All the people walk about today in company with their own ghosts" (19). Representation is exposed as a deadly form of reproduction, in which the original and the ghostly double are inextricably entwined, enmeshed with each other. The original, the authentic, no longer exists. When the two Jews see each other, both exclaim; when named, they bow simultaneously. The name *Jew* names only a fiction.

In this light, Jewish identity seems displaced from itself: the servant addresses Malachi, "Are you yourself—or is that you?" The servant then takes out his written description of the Jew, and examines the two Jews minutely: "Are you he—or is he you? For one of you certainly must be the other, that's clear" (19). Jewish identity is entirely destabilized; it seems to exist outside itself. In a comical song in which Malachi attempts to authenticate his identity, he sings, "I am de true Malachi, vat ish call'd the original Jew, / Vat shells every thing as sheep as can be" (20), just as Cameleon the actor copies him. The "original Jew" seems to exist only in his double, in the stereotype of the cunning peddler, the man who gulls us in the first place by telling us that he "shells every thing as sheep as can be." The original Jew, then, is already a copy, as is the man who plays the original Jew here, just another actor. The so-called original Jew, of course, is the stereotypical Jewish peddler who has been conventionalized in play after play, in graphic print after print. Even the so-called genuine Jew is amazed at the copy of himself that he sees, leading him to make an anti-Semitic comment to his convincing double: "You must be de tevil!—or you would not be so like me" (21). The Jew sees himself outside himself, and, as it were, momentarily authenticates the negative stereotype of Jewish identity; the stereotype is so profound, so thoroughly diffused in the culture, that even the Jew (mis)recognizes himself by it.

This scene exposes not only how performable the *other* is, according to a communally scripted description of otherness, but also how spectators are socially constructed in their belief in certain conventional visual and aural identity markers—what we call stereotypes. So, in such a scene, the spectator himself is shown as a social construction manipulated by ideologies of difference and otherness. The servant tries to solve the dilemma through his belief in spectatorship, in the great English tradition of empiricism: "You, sir, come here, and let me look at you—and you, sir, if you please" (19). This scene repeats the kind of inspection of Jewish identity that occurred frequently on the stage, when a Jew's exaggerated dress was marked and mocked by another character on stage, but now the spectator is puzzled because two Jews are under inspection, with the serious suspicion that one is real and the other fake. Previously, Jewish identity was always recognizable precisely insofar as it was distinguishable from English (or some such "normative") identity (and vice versa); but here, Jewish identity must be distinguished from its copy, so to speak.

Finally, the (English) spectator's own identity is challenged, insofar as the recognition of the *other* is the ground of one's own identity, when the servant exclaims: "Next time I come into the room, I shall expect to see my double here ready to fight it out with me—whether I am myself or somebody else" (25). A new question now emerges: who is the man who (mis)recognizes the Jew? Does the subject/spectator himself become someone else, alienated from himself, doubled, when he sees double, when he no longer can adequately recognize the Jew as other? Finally, one must wonder about the status of the audience proper in such a scene: while the audience typically shares the joke of the cross-dressing gentile, in the scene that I am now examining, the audience could be genuinely fooled in its attempt to distinguish between the cross-dressed hero and Malachi, depending on the performance choices the actors make in playing the scene. In such a case, even the apparent sophistication of the theater audience is overthrown, when the gulled spectator on the stage mimics the gulled spectator in the audience. The recognition of Jewish identity has become a puzzle that even the spectator in the audience cannot solve. In this way, the destabilization of Jewish identity functions to destabilize the normative English spectatorial position.

Structured through a variety of metatheatrical strategies aimed at the audience (such as shared jokes between actors and audience members, or the figure of the gulled spectator on the stage), these plays began to function intertextually as the basis of a specific cultural community, so much so that they became part of a theatrical project collectively shared by playwrights, actors, and audience. This is illustrated particularly well in Hannah Cowley's *The Belle's Stratagem* (1780) when Mr. Hardy, in order to cross-dress as a Jew at a masquerade, copies not from nature but from the stage, by going "to my favourite little Quick [in order to] borrow his Jew Isaac's dress. . . . [H]e shall teach me—Ay, that's it—I'll be cunning little Isaac."[36] Here, in *The Belle's Stratagem*, Cowley depends on her audience's recognition of a direct citation of Richard Brinsley Sheridan's *The Duenna* (1775), in which the well-known actor John Quick (1748–1831) was celebrated for his performance of the Jew Isaac Mendoza. Cowley points to the artificiality of the Jew in Sheridan's play by having Mr. Hardy borrow from the actor the Jewish costume and learn from him how to perform the Jewish role. The pure theatricality of the stage Jew becomes apparent: the construction of Jewish identity is mobile, able to be imported to a number of settings and performed by a number of (even unprofessional) actors. This kind of intertextual citation acknowledges the audience's knowledge of Sheridan's celebrated play, and even of the particular players on the London stage, for in certain productions of *The Belle's Stratagem* it was Quick himself who played Mr. Hardy citing Quick, another one of those metatheatrical jokes shared between actor and audience that underscored the artificiality of constructions of Jewish identity. In such ways the audience became a constituent player in the theater's demystification of the stage Jew. In a similar intertextual strategy, John Tobin's *The Faro Table; or, the Guardians* (1816), a patent rewriting of Sheridan's *School for Scandal* (1777), forces on Sheridan's Sir Oliver, now named Mr. Barton, what Sir Oliver has avoided—namely, cross-dressing as a Jew. But such a revision was inevitable, because certainly by the time of Tobin's play no one in the audience could have taken Sir Oliver's protest seriously: "how the Plague shall I be able to pass for a Jew?"[37] The question had been answered too often, on stage and off. So, the trope of the cross-dressing gentile became the necessary supplement that haunted the stage Jew and the theatricalization of Jewish identity generally. In the cases of both Cowley and Tobin, for example, the trope functioned as a citation to an earlier play and a corrective demystifier. In this way, audiences were involved in reviewing the staples of the theatrical repertory, as they were being rewritten through the addition of the trope of the cross-dressing gentile.

In such ways, these plays began to imagine and even to constitute an English theatrical community engaged in working out the question of Jewish identity from play to play and from performance to performance. As a fluid theatrical sign, Jewish identity began to move with ease between and among a variety of plays, and the act of cross-dressing articulated and signaled such cross-movement. The trope of the cross-dressing gentile demonstrated that anyone could borrow the script of Jewish identity, anyone could occupy the position of the Jew; Jewish identity was an infinitely performable script, to be cited and renewed and revised and circulated time and again. The plays, the performers, and even the audiences of the London stage seemed to be participating collaboratively in the (re)formulation and demystification of the Jew as a collective construction. When we recall that, in addition to the sheer number of new plays with Jewish characters in the last quarter of the eighteenth century, four of the most popular plays of this period were *The Duenna, The School for Scandal, The Belle's Stratagem*, and *The Merchant of Venice*,[38] we realize that the theater and its public in some profound sense were given over to this question of Jewish identity. With its corollary features of the masquerade, the optical illusion, the gulled spectator, the figure of the double, and the (mis)recognition scene, the trope of the cross-dressing gentile became the broadest and most probing inquiry into the nature of the representation of Jewish identity that had ever been produced in England. In play after play, the trope investigated and subverted the representation of Jewish identity as a coherent and fixed theatrical construct—even as a kind of social institution—shared by the culture at large.

Notes

1. Following the lead of Joseph Addison in *The Spectator*, Voltaire locates Jewish merchants at the heart of the new commercial England, the Royal Exchange (*Letters Concerning the English Nation*, ed. Nicholas Cronk [Oxford and New York: Oxford University Press, 1994], 30), and in the words of another foreign visitor to England, "commerce is considered England's strength; and care has been taken not to drive away anyone who contributes to build it up. Jews are therefore protected" (quoted in J. Rumney, "Anglo-Jewry as Seen Through Foreign Eyes, 1730–1830," *Transactions of the Jewish Historical Society of England* 13[1932–1935]: 329).
2. In James Ferguson, ed., *The British Essayists* (London: Barnard and Farley, 1819), 30:1–2.
3. Allardyce Nicoll, *A History of English Drama 1660–1900*, 6 vols. (Cambridge: Cambridge University Press, 1952), 3:19; James J. Lynch, *Box, Pit, and Gallery: Stage and Society in Johnson's London* (Berkeley and Los Angeles: University of California Press, 1953), 226.
4. A reviewer for the *London Chronicle*, quoted by Lynch, *Box, Pit, and Gallary*, 226.
5. Ed. James Kinsley (Oxford and New York: Oxford University Press, 1998), 111.
6. See Joseph Addison and Richard Steele, *The Spectator*, no. 1 (Mar. 1, 1711), in *The Spectator*, ed. Donald F. Bond, 5 vols. (Oxford: Clarendon, 1965), 1:4.
7. Aileen Ribeiro, *The Dress Worn at Masquerades in England, 1730–1790, and Its Relation to Fancy Dress in Portraiture* (New York and London: Garland, 1984), 70 and 77–78.
8. See Michael Ragussis, "Jews and Other 'Outlandish Englishmen': Ethnic Performance and the Invention of British Identity under the Georges," *Critical Inquiry* 26(Summer 2000): 773–797.
9. Terry Castle, *Masquerade and Civilization: The Carnivalesque in Eighteenth-Century English Culture and Fiction* (Stanford, CA: Stanford University Press, 1986), 50.
10. Maria Edgeworth, *Harrington*, vol. 9 of *Tales and Novels* (New York: AMS Press, 1967).
11. For an excellent general discussion of the Old Price Riots, see Marc Baer, *Theatre and Disorder in Late Georgian London* (Oxford: Clarendon, 1992).

12. See *The Covent Garden Journal*, ed. John Joseph Stockdale, 2 vols. (London: J. J. Stockdale, 1810), 1:184, 1:182, 1:183, 1:190, 1:189, 1:196. John Philip Kemble (1757–1823), famous actor and playwright, was the manager and part owner of Covent Garden at the time of the riots.

13. *The Covent Garden Journal*, 1:232.

14. *The Covent Garden Journal*, 1:187.

15. *Jackson's Oxford Journal*, December 28, 1753.

16. See *Hogarth's Graphic Works*, compiled and with a commentary by Ronald Paulson, 2 vols. (New Haven and London: Yale University Press, 1965), 1:229.

17. Thomas W. Perry, *Public Opinion, Propaganda, and Politics in Eighteenth-Century England: A Study of the Jew Bill of 1753* (Cambridge: Harvard University Press, 1962), 74–75.

18. *The Covent Garden Journal*, 2:522. See Baer, *Theatre and Disorder*, 216.

19. *The Covent Garden Journal*, 1:213.

20. See "Imperfect Sympathies" (*Elia*, 1823), in *The Works of Charles and Mary Lamb*, ed. E. V. Lucas, 5 vols. (New York: AMS Press, 1968), 3:62.

21. On these new developments in Anglo-Jewish culture, see the excellent study by Todd M. Endelman, *The Jews of Georgian England, 1714–1830* (Philadelphia: The Jewish Publication Society of America, 1979; reprint Ann Arbor: University of Michigan Press, 1999); on Gordon, Brothers, and the culture of conversion, see Michael Ragussis, *Figures of Conversion: "The Jewish Question" and English National Identity* (Durham and London: Duke University Press, 1995).

22. *Public Advertiser*, December 14, 1771.

23. "No. 1. Thursday, January 31, 1754," in Ferguson, *The British Essayists*, 30:1–2.

24. *Public Advertiser*, December 14, 1771.

25. For detailed discussions of the Jew Bill, see Alan H. Singer, "Great Britain or Judea Nova? National Identity, Property, and the Jewish Naturalization Controversy of 1753," in *British Romanticism and the Jews: History, Culture, Literature*, ed. Sheila A. Spector (New York: Palgrave/Macmillan, 2002), 19–36, and Frank Felsenstein, *Anti-Semitic Stereotypes: A Paradigm of Otherness in English Popular Culture, 1660–1830* (Baltimore and London: The Johns Hopkins University Press, 1995), 187–214.

26. For a more comprehensive study (and reproduction) of these satirical prints, see Israel Solomons, "Satirical and Political Prints on the Jews' Naturalization Bill, 1753," *Transactions of the Jewish Historical Society of England* 6 (1912): 205–233. Also see the excellent analysis of some of these prints, and the anxiety over circumcision, in Felsenstein, *Anti-Semitic Stereotypes* 139–146 and 192–200.

27. William Cobbett, ed., *Parliamentary History of England*, 36 vols. (London: T. C. Hansard, 1806–1820), 14:1380.

28. *The Protester, on Behalf of the People*, "by Issachar Barebone, one of the People," 10:58.

29. Endelman, *Jews of Georgian England*, 11.

30. Felsenstein, *Anti-Semitic Stereotypes*, 207–209.

31. Page numbers in parentheses refer to George Colman, the Younger, *Love Laughs at Locksmiths: A Musical Farce*, in *Lacy's Acting Edition of Plays* (London: Thomas Hailes Lacy, n.d.), vol. 94.

32. Page numbers in parentheses refer to Andrew Franklin, *The Wandering Jew: or, Love's Masquerade* (London: George Cawthorn, 1797).

33. Page numbers in parentheses refer to Theodore Edward Hook, *The Invisible Girl* (London: C. and R. Baldwin, 1806).

34. Page numbers in parentheses refer to William Thomas Moncrief, *Rochester: or, King Charles the Second's Merry Days* (London: John Lowndes, 1819).

35. Page numbers in parentheses refer to [John Allingham], *Transformation; or, Love and Law* (Baltimore: J. Robinson, 1814).

36. Hannah Cowley, *The Belle's Stratagem* (London: Longman, Hurst, Rees, and Orme, n.d.), 44.

37. *The Dramatic Works of Richard Brinsley Sheridan*, ed. Cecil Price (Oxford: Clarendon Press, 1973), 1.389.

38. See Charles Beecher Hogan, *The London Stage, 1776–1800: A Critical Introduction* (Carbondale and Edwardsville: Southern Illinois University Press, 1968), clxxi–clxxii.

CHAPTER 3

WILLIAM BLAKE AND THE JEWISH
SWEDENBORGIANS

Marsha Keith Schuchard

> *I am sure This Jesus will not do*
> *Either for Englishman or Jew.*[1]

In 1820, the sixty-three-year-old William Blake drew a symbolic self-portrait, in which he sketched a *menorah* on his forehead. Raymond Lister observes that "This symbol, derived from the Jewish seven-branched candlestick modelled on the Tree of Life, expresses spiritual enlightenment, being in effect a third 'spiritual' eye."[2] Though Blake was attracted to the visionary theosophy of the Jewish Kabbalah, he—like other Christian "philo-Semites"—viewed it from a conversionist perspective.[3] In his illuminated prophecy *Jerusalem*, he issued an "Address to the Jews," in which he proclaimed: "You have a tradition, that Man anciently contain'd in his mighty limbs all things in Heaven & Earth," but "now the Starry Heavens are fled from the mighty limbs of Albion" (E 171). While drawing on kabbalistic traditions of Adam Kadmon, the macrocosmic Grand Man, for his portrayal of Albion, Blake veered between praise and mockery of the Jews. At one time, he affirmed that "The Hebrew Nation did not write it / Avarice & Chastity did shite it"; at another, he scoffed that Jesus turned the devils into swine, "That he might tempt the Jews to Dine / Since which a Pig has got a look / That for a Jew may be mistook" (E 516, 877). In 1818, Blake scorned equally the Jewish and Christian upholders of repressive Mosaic laws:

> The Vision of Christ that thou dost see
> Is my Visions greatest Enemy:
> Thine has a great hook nose like thine,
> Mine has a snub nose like to mine. (E 524)

But two years later, he portrayed himself as a Judaized Christian with a *menorah* on his forehead. In this chapter, I suggest that Blake's complex and ambivalent attitude toward the Jews was rooted in his early Moravian–Swedenborgian religious background and developed through his access to a Jewish–Christian subculture within Illuminist Freemasonry.

Questions about the religious background of Blake's family have long perplexed scholars, but my recent discovery of documents in the Moravian archives at Muswell Hill, London, has provided new answers—as well as raising new questions. These eighteenth-century church diaries reveal that Catherine Armitage, William Blake's mother, Thomas Armitage, her first husband, and John Blake, almost certainly William's paternal uncle, attended Moravian services at the Fetter Lane chapel in the 1740s and that the Armitages were accepted into the highly selective Congregation of the Lamb in November 1750.[4] John Blake's acceptance apparently took place in the late 1740s. After Thomas Armitage's death in September 1751, Catherine remarried their close neighbor and fellow hosier James Blake (John's brother?) in October 1752 and subsequently withdrew from the private "Congregation of the Lamb."[5] However, according to the nineteenth-century Blake facsimilist William Muir, the Blakes continued to attend the public services at Fetter Lane, at least during the early years of their marriage.[6] He and other critics suggested the influence of Moravian hymns and theology on the lyrics and symbolism of works produced by Catherine's third child, William, born in 1757, but they did not explore further the biographical links.[7]

What is relevant to William Blake's complex attitude to the Jews is the fact that the Armitage–Blake involvement with the Moravian Brethren (the *Unitas Fratrum*) occurred during the turbulent "Sifting Time," when their leader, Count Nicolaus Ludwig von Zinzendorf (1700–1760), implemented a radically antinomian program of sexual and visionary experimentation, which included the *Judenmission*, a secretive outreach program to kabbalistic Jews.[8] In 1749, when John Blake petitioned for membership in the Congregation of the Lamb, he addressed his letter to Reverend Peter Boehler, who had returned from service in the American colonies, where he often preached in synagogues: "he could expound the Psalms in Hebrew, much to the delight of the Sons of Abraham."[9] When Boehler was persecuted by the colonial authorities, only the Jews continued to support him. Returning to London in 1746, Boehler superintended for the next six years "the whole English work," which included the local *Judenmission*. In 1750, Zinzendorf and Boehler ordered a Jewish Moravian couple, David and Esther Kirchof, to buy a house in the Jewish quarter in London and to establish a "*judenchristliche Gemeinschaft unter Juden*" (a Jewish–Christian community under or among Jews).[10] This represented a change in strategy from the earlier Jewish–Christian congregations "*unter Christen*" and represented Zinzendorf's intensified effort at rapprochment with Jews. While the "*geheimbunde*" (secret congregation) discussed the kabbalistic "*geheimlehre*" (secret teaching), participants should be discrete, so as not to arouse opposition from orthodox rabbis.[11] As members of the inner Congregation of the Lamb, the Armitages and Blakes would have been fully informed about these affairs.

Complicating this unusual religious context was the participation of Emanuel Swedenborg (1688–1772) in Moravian affairs in Amsterdam and London in the 1740s.[12] Since his university days at Uppsala, Swedenborg had been exposed to the Christian Kabbalism of Rabbi Johann Kemper, a former Sabbatian Jew, who converted to Christianity, moved to Sweden, and developed a daring Zoharic interpretation of the New Testament.[13] For Kemper, the conversion to Islam by Sabbatai Zevi, the "false messiah," in 1666, bore striking parallels to Jesus's self-abasement and salvific crucifixion.[14] The post-conversion disciples of Sabbatai Zevi developed an antinomian theology of "holy sinning," in which one descends into the evil of false religion in order to transmute it into true Zoharic Judaism. For many, this included permission to publicly convert to the dominant religion of their region, whether Islam, Christianity, or orthodox Judaism, while privately maintaining their belief in the messianic role of Sabbatai Zevi and the kabbalistic leaders of his posthumous movement. As Elliot Wolfson observes, "Rabbi" Kemper drew on the antinomian hermeneutics of Sabbatianism to become a genuine Judaeo-Christian, one who managed to "keep a foot in both camps."[15] For seven years, while Swedenborg lived with Eric Benzelius, his brother-in-law and intellectual mentor, Benzelius was working closely with Kemper on researches into kabbalistic theosophy and its Christian application. After Kemper's death in 1716, Benzelius and his son-in-law Anders Norrelius (Swedenborg's nephew-by-marriage) struggled for decades to publish Kemper's theses, which they believed would reinvigorate Christianity by bringing it back to its Jewish mystical roots.

By the time Swedenborg sought Moravian membership in London in the 1740s, he was already familiar with the kind of Judaized Christianity advocated by Zinzendorf and the *Judenmission*. In 1744, while living with a Moravian near Fetter Lane, he was visited by two unnamed Jews, who witnessed his ecstatic trance, and he tried to preach his messianic message in the local synagogue.[16] In 1748–1749 in London, he referred again to contacts with Jews and Moravians and, though he began to criticize Zinzendorf's antinomian theosophy, he continued to use the Moravian publisher John Lewis. By his next visit in 1758, he had completely broken with the Brethren and wrote bitter "spirit-world" accounts of their deceptive practices and magico-erotic rituals. However, the Moravian's kabbalistic concept of "mystical marriage" would continue to influence his own notions of "conjugial love" and his oddly sexualized interpretations of the Hebrew scriptures.[17] Thus, it is provocative that William Muir and his colleague, the biographer Thomas Wright (who were accurate about the Moravianism of Blake's mother) claimed that the Blake family moved on from Moravianism to Swedenborgianism during William's youth (1:2). Such a shift, which was replicated by many other theosophical questers, sheds light on William's always heterodox, often conflicting opinions about the Jews. It also provides a

context for the surprising emergence of Swedenborgian Jews in the 1770s
and 1780s.

Though Zinzendorf and Swedenborg were Christian conversionists, their
fascination with kabbalistic sexual and visionary theosophy made them
stretch their Christian theology almost to the breaking point, in order to
assimilate Jewish mystical traditions into its framework. The Moravians'
establishment of secret Jewish–Christian associations for Christianized study
of Kabbalah provides a clandestine context for Swedenborg's strange diary
descriptions of the antinomian, magical, and erotic rituals of certain
Moravians and Jews.[18] The Hebrew- and Yiddish-speaking Moravian missionaries lived in the Jewish quarters of London, Amsterdam, and other
cities, and they participated fully in Jewish religious and social affairs. To
avoid Jewish objection to claims for the divinity of Jesus, "Rabbi" Samuel
Lieberkuh—the main missionary—stressed the full "humanation" of Jesus,
the God-Man, a concept influenced by the kabbalists' cosmic Adam
Kadmon, and developed later by Swedenborg into the Grand Man or Divine
Human.[19] Lieberkuhn so Judaized himself that his Hebrew friends called
him "the converted Israelite," and even Zinzendorf worried that he was
becoming "a secret Socinian."[20] In the 1740s and 1750s, while Swedenborg,
the Armitages, and Blakes attended Moravian services, Zinzendorf urged the
Brethren to infuse Hebrew and kabbalistic terminology into their hymns, as
well as to celebrate *Yom Kippur*, to keep the Jewish Sabbath as a day of rest,
and to perform sacramentalized conjugal intercourse ("the holy joining") on
the Saturday Sabbath.[21] Lieberkuhn and Zinzendorf attempted to keep
kosher, refusing to eat foods forbidden to the Jews.[22]

Both Zinzendorf and Swedenborg were students of the Hermetic sciences
and developed in London contacts with a clandestine network of
"Rosicrucian" alchemists, who shared kabbalistic interests and "irregular"
Masonic affiliations.[23] Wolfson notes that Rabbi Kemper's acceptance by
Christian Hebraists in Sweden occurred within an emerging Rosicrucian–
Masonic milieu:

> The messianic task of Kemper was to cultivate a religious philosophy that
> would simultaneously foster a Jewish Christianity for the Jews and a Christian
> Judaism for Christians. With respect to this project Kemper clearly was
> indebted to the bold hermeneutic of the Sabbatian form of Kabbalah, which
> pushed the halakhic tradition to its limit by narrowing the gap separating the
> sacred and profane . . . but it fit in as well with the larger cultural patterns of
> his historical moment and geographical setting attested in the post-
> Reformation fraternities of neo-Rosicrucians and Freemasons, which loosened
> considerably the boundaries between Judaism and Christianity, in large meas-
> ure due to the interest of these occult fraternities in Jewish esotericism.
> (142, 146)

During their residences in London, Zinzendorf and Swedenborg both
participated in this "historical moment" of Rosicrucian–Masonic "loosening
of the boundaries."[24] Moreover, it is possible that Blake's precocious,

adolescent interest (before 1776) in Paracelsus and Boehme was rooted in his parents' earlier exposure to Hermetic philosophy through the Moravians, Swedenborgians, and "Ancient" Freemasons.[25] For all three groups, alchemical studies were relevant to their overtures to Jews, for, as Elisheva Carlebach observes, "Medieval religious usage borrowed the term *conversion* from the al/chemical sciences, in which one substance was changed into something utterly different by a mysterious process."[26]

I discuss in *Why Mrs. Blake Cried* the Moravians' contacts with crypto-Sabbatian Jews, such as Jonathan Eibschütz in Hamburg and Jacob Frank in Poland, and Swedenborg's probable association with their sympathizer, Dr. Samuel Jacob Falk, the controversial kabbalist known as "the *Baal Shem* of London." Frank's sensational conversion to Catholicism in 1759, followed by thousands of his supporters received wide press coverage in London. The young artist Richard Cosway, who would become Blake's teacher and lifelong friend, contributed to the Frankist debate when he provided the frontispiece portrait for a tract by Edward Goldney, who responded to the Polish conversions by seeking contact with London Jews and urging them to become Protestants rather than Papists.[27] Cosway, who was interested in Moravianism and Swedenborgianism, was so sympathetic to Jews that Giacomo Casanova assumed that he was actually Jewish.[28] During this period, rumors also circulated about the alleged conversions of Eibeschütz and Falk. Though they publicly identified themselves as Jews, the Sabbatian paradox provided them—as it did Rabbi Kemper—with a religious vision that was both deracinating and liberating. As Carlebach observes,

> Lines between Judaism and Christianity became more tangled as post-Sabbatian outgrowths continued to proliferate. Collective subversive conversions, such as that of the Frankists, and the many cases of Sabbatians who remained Jews but syncretized Christian elements into their belief systems assured the continued existence, and even broadening, of areas of social and intellectual congruence between Jews and Christians.
>   . . . The invention of multiple identities by famous failed messiahs such as Reubeni, Zevi, and Frank expanded the possibilities for self-renewal and re-invention which form the core experiences of conversion. (87)

Within these "tangled lines" of Jewish–Christian interchange, Falk and Swedenborg expressed similarly mixed views. In 1768, Falk recorded a provocative note about Abraham and Simon, the sons of his patron, the wealthy Dutch banker Tobias Boas. According to Solomon Schechter, when Falk spoke of the sons, he said that he did not like them to have a religion in which their ancestors did not believe, but he added, "I myself have a choice."[29] Schechter suspected that Falk referred to his Sabbatian accommodation to Christianity. The anti-Sabbatian polemicist Jacob Emden accused Falk of gaining adherents to establish in London "a Sabbatian club," while others claimed that he seduced wealthy Christians to his "brotherhood." Swedenborg was aware that his close friend and political ally, the Swedish ambassador Joachim Frederik Preis, was often assisted by Tobias Boas in secretive Swedish–Jewish negotiations at The Hague and in London, which sometimes had Sabbatian overtones.[30] Thus, it is curious that after spending the summer of 1769 as a close neighbor of Dr. Falk in Wellclose Square, Swedenborg's attitude toward the Jews changed from recently expressed hostility to a new sympathy, at least for certain Jews who seemed to share his "Kemperian" interpretation of the Hebrew "Word":

> When they [the Jews] are told that interiorly there is within the Word a spiritual sense, which largely treats of Christ or the Messiah, they reply that it is not so. Some of them, however, say that interiorly in the Word, that is, in the depths, there is nothing but gold; and they make other statements of the same nature.[31]

One year later, Swedenborg contacted another mysterious figure, who seemed to live with "a foot in both worlds." In summer 1770, while traveling from Stockholm to Amsterdam, he stopped over in Hamburg, where he stayed with Johannes Müller (*Élie Artiste*), the mysterious Rosicrucian kabbalist, who had contacted Eibeschütz in 1761 and apparently maintained links with his crypto-Sabbatian disciples.[32] Müller subsequently wrote a circular letter about his relations with Swedenborg, in which he accepted his visions as genuine but criticized aspects of his theosophy. Swedenborg's defender, Friedrich Christoph Œtinger, annotated the letter with the following comment: Elias (Müller) possessed "the true sense and understanding of the Talmud and the Rabbis. Toward gathering all the people in one Belief and one God."[33] Like Elias, Œtinger participated in a shadowy Rosicrucian network, and he had long been aware of the Moravian *Judenmission*. He had earlier instructed Zinzendorf in Hebrew and Kabbalah, and he believed that Swedenborg was a Christian Kabbalist.[34] Two years after Swedenborg's visit in Hamburg, Müller wrote a *Lettre à l'Ober Rabbiner der Judenschaft in Frankfurt am Main* (August 14, 1772), addressed to Pinchas Halevi Horowitz, a heterodox kabbalist and disciple of Dov Baer, late leader of the Hassidic movment in Poland.[35] When Müller later moved to Riga, he participated in the *Gold-und Rosenkreutzer* network, one of whose members claimed that from Swedenborg "come all the new Rosicrucian writings."[36]

Though these shadowy, clandestine links between Christian Rosicrucians and Sabbatian/Hassidic Jews still puzzle scholars, it is suggestive that when Swedenborg arrived in Amsterdam, his friend J. C. Cuno described his meeting "Jews and Portuguese with whom he joined in, without distinction" (the latter were probably Marranos).[37] Swedenborg then added to the last sections of *True Christian Religion* (1770) a description of the heavenly bridegroom wearing "a tunic and an ephod, like Aaron" and a scene of "Jews in the Spiritual World," in which "converted Jews are set over them, who warn them not to speak disrespectfully of Christ."[38] He noted that some of the Jews, "when in the world, had thought from reason on various subjects, and lived accordingly. These consist mostly of Portuguese Jews." The spirit of Moses appears to them and affirms that "the Messiah is Christ"; then,

"Those who pay heed to the warning are sent to synagogues of converted Jews, where they receive instruction." In the 1780s, William Blake would read these passages, which may have influenced his own Judaeo-Christian notions.[39] Meanwhile, when Swedenborg moved on to London in September 1771, he was visited by a French artist, Phillipe Jacques de Loutherbourg, who shared his Hermetic and kabbalistic interests; in the months before Swedenborg's death in March 1772, Loutherbourg painted his portrait from life. According to Stephen Lloyd, Loutherbourg also painted the great, mystical portrait of Dr. Falk that captures so brilliantly the mixture of shadow and luminosity of his personality.[40]

As Yehudah Liebes demonstrates, there was an actual "synagogue of converted Jews" in Amsterdam, who lived outwardly as Jews until the death of their leader, Rabbi Eibeschütz, in 1764, when they completed their conversion to Christianity.[41] Relevant to the Blake family is the fact that survivors of this "crypto Judaeo-Christian Sect of Sabbatean Origin" established (or reestablished) links with the Moravians in London from 1772 until 1780. The manager of the renewed association was the Moravian minister Benjamin La Trobe, whose family developed ties with the artistic circle of Cosway and Blake.[42] Moreover, La Trobe chose as his agent to the sect his veteran missionary, Christian Dober, who was the nephew of Leonard Dober, a leader of the *Judenmission* in Amsterdam and London during the earlier period of Swedenborg–Armitage–Blake participation in the Brethren's affairs.[43] Given the overlap between former Moravians and current Swedenborgians in the 1770s, this clandestine Sabbatian–Christian rapprochement provides an illuminating context for the first "Jewish Swedenborgian" to be discussed in this paper.

The enigmatic, controversial figure of Dr. Mordechai Gumpertz Levison (1741–1797) continues to puzzle historians, who attempt to trace his unusual intellectual and spiritual development. Heinz Moshe Graupe portrays him as a "much neglected" man, "whose work is an example of 'unknown intellectual history,'" while David Ruderman describes him as "perhaps the most colorful Jewish intellectual of his times."[44] As we shall see, Blake may have met Levison in 1779, and the Jewish savant's influence would definitely influence Blake's experiences among the Swedenborgians in the 1780s. More importantly, Levison's complex personality sheds light on Blake's self-image as a Judaized Christian and on his heterodox notion of the Jewish Jesus.

Levison was born and educated in Berlin under Rabbi David Frankel, former teacher of Moses Mendelssohn, who encouraged his student's wide reading in the natural as well as supernatural sciences. But Levison's family was originally from Hamburg, where his grandfather served on the rabbinical tribune of the Three Communities (Hamburg, Altona, and Wandsbeck). It was probably through his family connections that Levison met Jonathan Eibeschütz, who served as Chief Rabbi of the Three Communities, which were under Danish control. Eibeschütz joined Frankel in giving the fourteen-year-old Levison "a rabbinical authorisation."[45] Graupe suggests that Levison's "extensive use of Kabbalistic literature" in his later writings was possibly "a sign of Eibeschütz's continuing influence" (10). Though little is known about Levison during the "mystery years" (1760s), he moved to London circa 1770 in order to study medicine. He was accepted as a student by the Scottish physicians John and William Hunter, who maintained many heterodox interests in religion and science.[46] Blake would later (1779–1781) study anatomy under the Hunters, who taught students at the Royal Academy of Arts. William Hunter owned Swedenborg's *Regnum Animale* (1744), as well as a rich collection of Jewish medical writings and kabbalistic–Hermetic works, which he recommended to his students.[47]

It was possibly the Hunters who introduced Levison to their collaborator Peter Woulfe, a Fellow of the Royal Society and brilliant chemist *cum* alchemist, who had met Swedenborg in 1769 and became an early Masonic supporter of his theories.[48] Woulfe also collaborated with Benjamin La Trobe during the period when the Moravian minister maintained links with the "crypto Judaean-Christian sect of Sabbatean origin" in Amsterdam.[49] Levison was also befriended by Dr. William Smith, who had studied Kabbalah under Dr. Falk and who was Swedenborg's "intimate friend" and physician, and by Dr. Husband Messiter, who had associated with the Moravians at the time of the *Judenmission* and who was currently Swedenborg's confidante and physician.[50] Woulfe, Smith, and Messiter were keen students of Jewish theosophy and Hermetic alchemy, subjects of equal interest to the erudite Jewish medical student. Did they, in turn, introduce Levison to Swedenborg? After Swedenborg visited Müller in Hamburg, who probably informed him about his own overtures to Hassidic Jews, and after mixing with "Jews and Portuguese" in Amsterdam, he arrived in London in September 1771.

In the meantime, in 1771, Levison published in London his first major Hebrew work, *Ma'amar ha-Torah ve-ha-Hokhmah* ("A Dissertation on the Law and Science"). According to Ruderman, Levison's spiritual–scientific argument was heavily influenced by the Swedish scientist Carl Linnaeus, whose views on the sexuality of plants seemed consistent with those of the kabbalists.[51]

Another (and stronger?) influence possibly came from Linnaeus's cousin and colleague, Swedenborg, who extended the sexuality of plants into the sexuality of angels and spirits in heaven. As Ruderman summarizes Levison's argument in his Hebrew treatises,

This "great chain of being" suggests a natural pattern even in the world beyond man, a world of intelligences, spirits, and angels. If the anatomist can uncover a remarkable web of interactive relations between muscles, organs, and brain, revealing "a vitality that dwells in their midst, you can imagine a spiritual pattern from all these powers that travel from the brain to every part of the body and back . . . and thus there is no doubt an analogy in this spiritual realm, in the uppermost heights . . . and thus you will understand the words of the kabbalists on the primordial man [Adam Kadmon] and similar notions . . . Therefore, through an examination of the natural order, the existence of angels and the succession of levels can be proven."[52]

This argument bears striking resemblances to Swedenborg's notions of the Grand Man, who contains within himself all natural and supernatural beings and whose dynamic relationships can be deciphered by the "science of correspondences."

After studying Kabbalah with Falk, Dr. Smith became intrigued by the Hebrew linguistic theories of John Hutchinson, and it is curious that he and another Hutchinsonian, the Edinburgh-educated physician Dr. Andrew Wilson, encouraged Levison's ambitious publications in Hebrew and English. Both men maintained close associations with the Scottish medical schools, at a time when Dr. Messiter was sending Swedenborg's works to various professors in Scotland.[53] Swedenborg himself wrote of his friendships with various Scots in London, including an "Edinboro gent."[54] In 1775, it would be Smith and Wilson who sponsored Levison's medical accreditation from Marischal College, Aberdeen.[55] A long-time, mutual friend of Smith and Swedenborg, the German-born physician and alchemist John Frederick Hampe, joined Dr. Messiter in attending Swedenborg on his deathbed in March 1772.[56] Like Levison and his later Swedish–Masonic collaborators, these men believed that Swedenborg's scientific and mystical theories held a key to alchemy.

Though it is unknown whether Dr. Wilson was interested in Swedenborgianism, he shared Smith's interest in Jewish medical and mystical lore. Described as "a man of some mental power," Wilson was an ardent and erudite defender of the uncorrupted purity of biblical Hebrew, and he recommended its study to all serious students of science and religion.[57] In *The Creation the Groundwork of Revelation, and Revelation the Attempt to Demonstrate that the Hebrew Language is Founded Upon Natural Ideas, and that the Hebrew Writings Transfer Them to Spiritual Objects* (Edinburgh, 1750), he expressed many themes that would be of interest not only to Levison but to his Swedenborgian colleagues. The proper study of the natural sciences should reinforce one's spiritual beliefs, for "Adam and all his progeny were to be instructed in spiritual things, by the knowledge of natural things, and were to compare one with the other" (12, 20). Moreover, from Hebrew studies and "from revelation, we may also learn to decypher all the hieroglyphics, fables, mysteries, etc. of the antients." Levison, who argued that it was the author of the *Zohar*, not Linnaeus, who first noticed "the sexuality of plants," would have been pleased by Wilson's argument that the Jews discovered the circulation of the blood long before Harvey and the principles of Fire, Light, and Air long before Lavoisier and Fourcroy.[58]

After receiving his Scottish medical accreditation in 1775, Levison became a physician at the General Medical Asylum, founded by the Duke of Portland as "an institution for out-patients, providing free medical treatment and medication to the poor."[59] He also collaborated with Dr. Messiter in establishing the "Amico Medical Society," while Messiter encouraged his alchemical experiments. Besides the Swedenborgian alchemist Peter Woulfe, Levison probably met Messiter's intimate friend, Dr. Benedict Chastanier, who also studied alchemy, Kabbalah, and Swedenborgianism, and who was Levison's close neighbor when both lived on Tottenham Court Road. Hans Joachim Schoeps believed that Levison became a Freemason in London, but neither he nor Graupe could verify his membership.[60] However, both Messiter and Chastanier were Masons and affiliated with Franco-Scottish (*Écossais*) rites that were considered "irregular" by orthodox English Masons. Chastanier's next-door neighbor was the French engraver Lambert de Lintot, who directed an Illuminist Rite of Seven Degrees (also called "Heredom of Kilwinning"), which merged kabbalistic with Swedenborgian themes. Among its members were Dr. Falk and the eclectic Swedenborgian, General Charles Rainsford. The Rite of Seven Degrees survived into the 1780s, and it is pos-sible that Blake took the name of his illuminated prophet, Los, from Lintot's ritual use of that word.[61] In 1769, Chastanier founded in London the Rite of *Illuminés Théosophes*, and in 1776 he and his initiates organized the London Universal Society for the Promotion of the New Jerusalem Church, which had the public purpose of the "Preservation of Baron Swedenborg's Posthumous Works." The *Illuminés* established links with the Swedish Masons (also called *Illuminés*) who would later welcome Levison to Stockholm.

For Levison, who had been charged with antinomian behavior and expelled from the Duke's Place Synagogue, these heterodox Christians must have seemed more open-minded and welcoming than his orthodox coreligionists. Within this context, his self-identification as a Jew and a Swedenborgian becomes more plausible. Though these Jewish–Swedenborgian associations may seem distant from what we know of Blake's interests in the 1770s, it is possible that his and Levison's paths crossed at the end of the decade, when Blake subscribed to the Reverend Jacob Duché's *Discourses on Various Subjects* (1779), a rather bland collection of his American sermons.[62] Besides various Swedenborgians, there were two Jewish subscribers—Dr. Phillip de la Cour, who often brought Christian visitors to meet Dr. Falk, and Naphtali Hart Mier, who defended Levison when he was attacked in the Duke's Place Synagogue.[63] In the second edition (1780), the names of subscribers omitted from the first edition were added, including a "Mrs. Levison," who was possibly the wife of Dr. Levision. Though it has long been assumed that he was unmarried, his enemies in London accused him of "adultery," thus suggesting a first wife before his known marriage in Hamburg in 1786.[64]

As an Anglican minister in Philadelphia, Duché's restless spiritual quest had taken him through Rosicrucianism, Behmenism, Moravianism, and cur-rently Swedenborgianism.[65] Though he served as chaplain to the First Continental Congress, his loyalist fears about the colonists' revolution led to his emigration to London in 1777, where he initially settled in Hampstead and held discussion meetings on mystical and occultist topics. Besides theos-ophy, Duché was greatly interested in medicine, and he could have met

Levison during the physician's "close engagement" with the Hampstead suburb, when, according to Graupe, he was in charge of treating a local diptheria epidemic in 1777–1778 (8). Another link was possibly provided by Peter Woulfe, a mutual friend of Levison and Duché, or—more intriguingly— by Blake's close friend, the Swedenborgian printer and engraver, William Sharp. When Levison published *An Account of the Epidemical Sore Throat* (1778), based on his Hampstead experiences, one of the sponsoring printers was "W. Sharp." At the end of the volume, W. Sharp advertised himself as "the sole bookseller for Levison's 'lately published' works, *An Essay on the Blood* and *The Spirit and Union of the Natural, Moral, and Divine Law.*"[66] One year later, Sharp paid for the printing of Duché's *Discourses*, and his engraved frontispiece (after Benjamin West's design) "caused much remark at the time."[67] As Morton D. Paley notes, the frontispiece shows male and female angels, and "thus correlates with a Swedenborgian doctrine—the existence of sex in heaven."[68]

Duché's gatherings were perhaps the object of the long walks to Hampstead that Blake remembered taking in his youth.[69] At a time when Blake was reading Paracelsus and Boehme, as well as Duché, he could have learned of Levison's similar interests. However, given the sparcity of information on Blake in 1779–1780, it is impossible to know whether they met. From this point on, any influence from Levison on Blake's Judaeo-Christian notions would come at second hand, through Levison's collaboration with a visiting Swedish alchemist, Augustus Nordenskjöld, whose Swedenborgian theories of "eternal virile potency" and "concubinage" would create much controversy in the Swedenborg society that Blake and his wife Catherine attended in 1789. According to Jan Häll, it was Dr. Messiter who introduced Levison to Nordenskjöld, when the latter arrived in London in late 1779, bringing with him unpublished manuscripts by Swedenborg for publication by Chastanier's Universal Society.[70] Augustus and his brother Carl Frederick were the sons of Finnish Moravian parents and nephews of a Rosicrucian alchemist, and they became early Masonic adherents of Swedenborg. Their radical sexual theories drew upon Zinzendorf's and Swedenborg's kabbalistic concept of the mystical nature of conjugal sex, which they assimilated into their alchemical, economic, and political projects.

As a skilled chemist and metallurgist, Augustus was so impressed with Levison's theoretical knowledge that he moved into the Jew's new residence in Soho Square, where they collaborated in alchemical studies. In the square, they were close neighbors (or possible housemates?) of another Kabbalist and Hermeticist, General Rainsford, who maintained an alchemical lab in which they could have practiced.[71] Rainsford also shared his esoteric studies with Blake's artistic colleagues Cosway, Loutherbourg, Sharp, and Thomas Spence Duché, son of Jacob; Blake's close friend George Cumberland would later make fun of Rainsford's and their "illuminist" enthusiasms.[72] Nordenskjöld probably learned that Rainsford was an old friend of the Moravian minister James Hutton, who had known Swedenborg in the 1740s, and that he considered Swedenborg, whom he called "that Great

Man," to be a fellow Kabbalist.[73] Thus, during Levison's residence in Soho Square, he was at the center of Swedenborgian enterprises that combined practical science with Hermetic and kabbalistic research.

That Rainsford definitely knew Nordenskjöld and probably met Levison raises a new question about the Jewish physician's religious position, for Rainsford was then working with Dr. Falk on a secretive Masonic project, in which the Rosicrucian "Order of Asiatic Brethren" would recruit Christians and Jews to study Kabbalah together, without pressure to convert to either religion.[74] A later Christian member of the Order recorded that it drew upon the teachings of Eibeschütz, Frank, and Falk.[75] Other Illuminist Masons believed that Falk had links with Frank.[76] Though no evidence of a link between Falk and Levison has emerged, the latter could have learned more about the *Baal Shem* from his friend Dr. John Coakley Lettsom, physician to Falk's main patrons, Abraham and Benjamin Goldsmid.[77] After Falk's unexpected death in April 1782, Rainsford lamented that their plan was interrupted, but it is curious that Levison, after his move from London to Hamburg in 1782, would collaborate with Dr. Johann Christian Anton Theden, a high-ranking member of the *Gold-und Rosenkreuzer*, whose history was obscurely linked with the Asiatic Brethren.[78] Samuel Beswick claimed that Theden was "an intelligent Swedenborgian," who had met Swedenborg at a lodge in Berlin and then furnished information about his Masonic career to Friedrich Nicolai.[79]

In the meantime, in Soho Square, Levison helped Nordenskjöld produce an English translation of his treatise, *A Plain System of Alchymy*, which featured an epigraph from "Philalethes" expressing the Swede's radical economic and millenarian religious program:

> I do hope and expect, that within a few years, money will be like dross; and that prop of the Antichristian beast will be dashed in pieces. The people are mad, the nations rave, an unprofitable weight is set in the place of God. These things will accompany our so long expected and so suddenly approaching redemption, when the New Jerusalem—Believe me, ye young men, believe me ye fathers, because the time is at the door. I do not write these things out of a vain conception, but I see them in the Spirit.[80]

The pamphlet was dedicated to the distinguished Swedish chemist Torbern Bergman, and it drew on Nordenskjöld's genuine expertise as a practical chemist and metallurgist. Like Levison, he cited respected natural scientists (such as Boyle, Macquer, Lavoisier, and Lewis), as well as alchemists (Hermes Trismegistis, Isaac Hollandus, Kunkel, and Henkel). But, he argued, the real key to alchemy was revealed by Swedenborg in his book *Sapientia Angelica de Divino amore et de Divina Sapientia* (1763) (12n).

Levison was especially interested in the medical applications of Nordensköld's experiments, and the two alchemists subsequently changed their plans. Stopping the printing at page 16, they decided to travel to Sweden to present King Gustaf III, a Swedenborgian Mason, with their proposal for a royal alchemical laboratory and philanthropic hospital (the latter to be based on Levison's and Messiter's "Amico Medical Society").[81] In January 1780, Levison left for Stockholm, where he was welcomed by the Illuminist Masons at the Swedish court, several of whom had been personal friends of Swedenborg. According to Carl Frederick Nordenskjöld, because Levison "gave himself out as a Swedenborgian, we wished to show him all possible hospitality."[82] In March, the physician was presented to the king, who agreed to his plan and provided him with 1,000 Pound Sterling.[83] Levison made a short trip to London, and then he and Augustus Nordenskjöld (who returned *incognito*) established their secret laboratory at Drottningholm Palace in Stockholm. Levison also proposed the foundation of a charitable hospital, with a research component, and he published a work in Swedish that expressed not only his medical but also his alchemical notions.

In a chapter on "The Passions," Levison discussed the melancholy caused by false and bigoted religious notions, and he argued that "barmhårtighet" (mercy, compassion, pity) is the essence of true religion.[84] The final emblem portrayed God (or a Prophet) with a Christian cross next to two tablets of the Mosaic law and the New Testament, surrounded by rays shining through clouds. The image certainly suggests a Judaeo-Christian syncretism. In May, when Gustaf III gave Levison the title of Professor, it was considered one of the first appointments of a Jew in modern history. However, hostile courtiers subverted the funding for the alchemical lab, and Levison suddenly left Sweden, under mysterious circumstances. It is possible that his Jewish iden-tification negated his Swedenborgian affiliation—especially among the more conservative Masons. Despite efforts by some liberals to change the Masonic rules, only Christians were allowed to join Swedish Masonic lodges, which—ironically—utilized rituals heavily infused with Kabbalism. Nevertheless, after moving to Hamburg in 1782, Levison resumed a cordial correspondence with the tolerant Gustaf III, and he was appointed physician to the Swedish consulate, with some kind of diplomatic status. In 1784, he published a work in which he affirmed that "the coming of the Messiah to him is the coming of everlasting peace, and the belief of all in one creator; it is the time of the cessation of religious hatred."[85] As Pelli observes, he thus "seemed to accept the relativity of all religions." In 1784, when Carl Frederick Nordenskjöld visited the London Swedenborgians, he probably informed them about the activities of this unusual Swedenborgian Jew.

In the meantime, another alleged Jewish–Christian, the Masonic adven-turer "Count" Cagliostro, began to play a role in Swedenborgian affairs in England. Cagliostro had earlier, in 1772 and 1776, resided in London, where he collaborated with Dr. Falk in developing the rite of Egyptian Freemasonry.[86] In 1780, when Cagliostro travelled to Russia, the Swedenborgian Masons believed that he would reveal to them the secrets of the London *Baal Shem*. After an angry Catherine the Great expelled Cagliostro, he was invited to Sweden by Levison's alchemical patron, King Gustaf III. At that time, Augustus Nordenskjöld discussed Cagliostro's alchemical techniques in a letter to Levison.[87] However, Cagliostro turned down the Swedish invitation and instead settled in Strasbourg in late 1780, where he was welcomed by the mystical Masons. His ambiguous religious pronouncements puzzled his Masonic patron, Frederick Rodolphe Saltzmann, who recorded:

> He [Cagliostro] says much good about Swedenborg and complains that he had been persecuted. In vain the Swedes want at present to almost resuscitate his ashes, but they will discover nothing. The greatest man in Europe is the celebrated Falke in London. There are in that capital some 5 or 6 masons who have the [secret] knowledge, but they lack the key. He [Cagliostro] tells me that when operating it is necessary to have circles, words—four circles—and hieroglyphs. He seems to me to incline to Judaism; however, that is only a hypothesis that I cannot give as truth.[88]

In June 1786, in the wake of the sensational Diamond Necklace Trial in Paris, an acquitted Cagliostro fled to London, where he sought recruits among the local Swedenborgians. On November 2, he published an advertisement in the *Morning Herald* in which he called upon "all true Masons" to join the Swedenborgians in "building the New Temple or New Jerusalem" and identified himself as "a Mason and a Member of the New Church." That Blake was aware of Cagliostro's efforts among the Swedenborgians is suggested by his allusion in *The Marriage of Heaven and Hell* to the bizarre affair of the promiscuous baboons.[89]

While Cagliostro was still in London, the Swedenborgians were visited by another controversial kabbalistic *guru*, Count Thaddeus Grabianka, a wealthy Polish nobleman, who had received a magical book from the heir of "an old Cabalon." After he joined the Swedenborgian *Illuminés* at Berlin and Avignon, the adepts utilized a kabbalistic oracle, based on Grabianka's text and developed by "Élie Artiste," the Rosicrucian patron of Swedenborg.[90] Though Grabianka was outwardly a Catholic, his heterodox views reflected the mixed religious atmosphere of his (and Falk's) home territory in Podolia, where Sabbatian and Sufic mysticism mingled with esoteric Christianity.[91] For over eleven months, Grabianka met weekly with forty or more Swedenborgians at the residence of Jacob Duché, who now lived at the Lambeth Asylum for Female Orphans, and it seems likely that Blake attended some of these meetings. Perhaps influenced by the grandiose ambitions of Jacob Frank, whose Zionist proclamations were widely known in Podolia, Grabianka dreamed of becoming the "King of the New Israel," and he planned an actual military expedition to reclaim Jerusalem. Drawing on his kabbalistic studies, he developed an antinomian, erotic theosophy that went far beyond Swedenborg's "conjugial love." He merged the Jewish *Shekhinah* into the Catholic Mary, and the Avignon initiates worshiped the female potency within the Godhead in hallucinatory and orgiastic rituals.

Though it is unknown if Grabianka himself was part Jewish (as were so many Polish aristocrats), it is provocative that one of his agents in London in 1788 was "a converted Jew, whose name was Samuel," who has since disappeared from official New Church records.[92] Samuel attended

Swedenborgian services at the Great Eastcheap Chapel, where Blake and his wife Catherine also participated. At one such service, Samuel met John Wright, a millenarian carpenter from Leeds, who had been directed to the chapel by a Swedenborgian neighbor on Tottenham Court Road. According to Wright, at first Samuel contended very warmly for this New Jerusalem Church, but a disappointed Wright replied that he "saw nothing but old forms of worship established by man's will, and not according to the will of God." Wright argued that the Holy Spirit informed him that "when the new Jerusalem Church was established, it would be established by the Spirit and Power of Elias," and the ministers would perform "signs and wonders, and miraculous works." Samuel then conversed about "his own people returning to their own land," which Wright assured him would soon come to pass.

Apparently spotting a recruit for Grabianka's "hidden servants of the New Israel," Samuel then took Wright to meet William Bryan, a Swedenborgian printer and close friend of William Sharp. Bryan had earlier met Grabianka and other Continental *Illuminés* during their visits to London. He was also friendly with Peter Woulfe, who had already visited Avignon and now acted as a liaison to the Swedenborgians in London, and with General Rainsford, who collected manuscripts on the kabbalistic and mesmeric techniques used by the Avignon *Illuminés*.[93] Bryan had recently heard from Jacob Duché that his son, the talented young artist Thomas Spence Duché, had benefitted from Grabianka's magical–medical treatment during his visit to Avignon and that he was currently collaborating with Rainsford on similar experiments in Hermetic therapy.[94] Thus, Bryan and Wright determined to travel to the southern French city, a journey prepared behind the scenes by Samuel and his fellow *Illuminés*. Though nothing more is known of Samuel, he was possibly a Masonic colleague of Dr. Levison, for a "M. Levyson" and "Samuel Samuel" were earlier listed as visitors to the "Reconciliation" lodge.[95] There may have been other Jewish Swedenborgians, for in 1792 Robert Hindmarsh received support from Jacob Barnet, "a converted Jew," in his Swedenborgian argument against Joseph Priestley.[96] Rainsford and another Swedenborgian, Henry Servanté, referred to their friendship and experiments in animal magnetism with Dr. Isaac Benamore, who had earlier collaborated with Cagliostro and the Swedenborgian magnetizers Cosway, Loutherbourg, and Dr. de Mainaduc.[97]

In John Wright's later account of the Zionistic prophecies of the Avignon oracle, there emerged—once again—a peculiar syncretism of Jewish and Christian beliefs. With Grabianka as "King of the New Israel," Palestine will become the center of the new faith, which will welcome "les juives illuminés" to a universalist Christian religion.[98] After their return to London in late 1789, Wright and Bryan maintained low profiles, while informing a few select friends about their revolutionary political visions.[99] In the meantime, the Swedenborg Society at Great East Cheap was riven by schisms, as the Nordenskjöld brothers, Chastanier, J. A. Tulk, and other liberals struggled against the increasing sexual prudery and political conservatism of many of the English congregants. In spring 1789, while William and Catherine Blake participated in the Great Eastcheap Conference, the proposals by Augustus Nordenskjöld to allow a regulated form of concubinism (as advocated by Swedenborg in *Conjugial Love*) and to maintain a secret interior order for alchemical projects precipitated the expulsion of the liberals and the eventual domination by the conservatives. Though many English *Illuminés* (such as Cosway, Loutherbourg, Sharp, Rainsford, and Tulk) continued to study Swedenborg (along with Paracelsus, Agrippa, and Boehme), they—like the Blakes—no longer participated in the increasingly conservative East Cheap congregation. In a defiant passage in *The Marriage of Heaven and Hell,* Blake seemed to echo the antinomian Kabbalism of Frank and Grabianka. As Randall Helms explains, when Blake portrayed a naked Isaiah and a dung-eating Ezekiel, he knew that these were acts "directly contravening the Law of Moses."[100] For Blake, "It is of great moment . . . that the voice of prophetic inspiration can contravene the Mosaic Law."

When Prime Minister Pitt's "white terror" was implemented from 1792 on, the New Church sectarians determined to distance themselves from the revolutionary Illuminism of Avignon and Stockholm. However, some of the "faithful hidden servants" of Grabianka did emerge in the tumultous movement launched by Richard Brothers, an early initiate of Avignon. In 1794, Brothers proclaimed himself "Prince of the Hebrews," who would reveal the Jewish origins of Englishmen, who would then join their Hebraic brothers in a return to Jerusalem where they would rebuild the Temple.[101] Wright and Bryan became enthusiastic partisans and now published sensational accounts of their visionary experiences in Avignon.[102] Brothers' bizarre campaign was supported by many millenarian radicals, and he initially appealed to Blake, Sharp, Cosway, Loutherbourg, Rainsford, and other Swedenborgians. Cosway so Judaized himself that he grew a long patriarchal beard and insisted that his four-year-old daughter be instructed in Hebrew.[103] Loutherbourg so immersed himself in Hebrew and kabbalistic studies that his artistic admirers feared he would withdraw from the Royal Academy.[104] In *The Four Zoas* (1796–1804) and other works, Blake expressed antinomian sexual and spiritual themes that were strikingly similar to those of Cagliostro and Grabianka, and it is provocative that Grabianka allegedly revisited London in 1796 and 1800, before moving on to a controversial Illuminist career in Russia.

In 1803, after three years of William Hayley's suffocating patronage at Felpham, Blake returned to London, where he renewed his study of Hebrew and joined Cosway's circle in their magical and magnetic experiments.[105] In 1805, Cosway sketched a mystical self-portrait, in which he "positioned himself between the two Masonic columns, while pointing to the Star of David, which is revealed in a manuscript he holds."[106] In 1806, he drew "an extraordinary and complex self-portrait as Esau," which "reveals his profound involvement with Christian mysticism":

> The whole image is a manifesto of his highly syncretic religious beliefs. These are signified by references to esoteric Freemasonry and the Cabbala, in the

form of the two columns of the Temple of Jerusalem, on the bases of which are represented the Two Tablets of the Old Testament Law (on the left) and the two interlocking triangles (on the right), the latter a reference to the artist's fascination with the occult tradition . . . His identification with Esau is explained by the fact that the elder twin of Jacob—and son of Isaac—was considered to be the precursor of the Gnostic and Masonic traditions of hidden knowledge. Cosway . . . presents himself as trampling on the earthly powers, indicated by the globe, coins, manuscripts, and the mask which is infested by a snake.[107]

Cosway's mystical self-portraits, like Blake's *menorah* self-portrait, were possibly rooted in their association with a Jewish–Christian Rosicrucian society in London. According to nineteenth-century oral traditions reported by William Butler Yeats, who was editing Blake's works, Blake joined "mystics and students of magic" in "an important secret society" under "three brothers named Falk":

> There is reason to believe that he acquired at this time some knowledge of the Kabala and that he was not unacquainted with certain doctrines of the Rosicrucians. It is possible that he received initiation into an order of Christian Kabalists then established in London, and known as "The Hermetic Students of the G.D." [Golden Dawn]. Of course this conjecture is not susceptible of proof. He would have said nothing about such initiation even if he had received it. The "students" in question do not name themselves, or each other, and the subject of their study is nothing less than universal magic . . . his contemporary, the miniature painter Cosway, kept a house for the study and practice of magic, and left behind him at his death, a considerable bundle of magical formulae . . . It must have been at this time that he [Blake] acquired what he knew of Hebrew. Several of the names in the very earliest of his mythic books are direct adaptations of that tongue. He also used Hebrew characters on some of his designs, which show that he had learned the unfamiliar way of writing them, known to some occult students as the "Celestial Alphabet."[108]

Though Yeats and his Rosicrucian colleagues issued conflicting and confused identifications of the brothers Falk, they all sensed some connection with the late *Baal-Shem*.[109] Yeats's fellow initiate Dr. Wynn Wescott later claimed that "Dr. Falk could not have been fully affiliated to any Rosicrucian College because he was a strict Jew, and the members of all true Rosicrucian Colleges have always been Christians," but then he contradicted himself, admitting that "many Christians have adopted the modification of the old Jewish Kabalah, so perhaps some Jews have been allied with Christian Rosicrucians."[110] As the research of Jacob Katz, Gershom G. Scholem, and Christopher McIntosh has shown, some Jewish Masons did indeed become Rosicrucians in the Order of Asiatic Brethren.[111] Sheila Spector reinforces Yeats's claims about Blake's study of the mystical use of Hebrew letters and of kabbalistic theosophy, noting further that his illuminated prophecy *Jerusalem* (1804–1820) might have been influenced by the *Kabbala*

Denudata.[112] Kathleen Raine and others have speculated that Blake must have had a real Jew as instructor, but the matter remains a mystery.[113]

When Blake issued his peculiar conversionist challenge "To the Jews," it was as though he looked through, not with, the "third 'spiritual' eye" on his forehead:

> Jerusalem the Emanation of the Giant Albion! Can it be? . . . Ye are united O ye Inhabitants of Earth in One Religion. The Religion of Jesus: the most Ancient, the Eternal: & the Everlasting Gospel . . . Amen! Huzza! Selah! . . .
>
> You have a tradition, that Man anciently containd in his mighty limbs all things in Heaven & Earth. . . .
>
> If Humility is Christianity; you O Jews are the true Christians; If your tradition that Man contained in his Limbs, all animals, is True & they were separated from by him by cruel Sacrifices: and when compulsory cruel Sacrifices had brought Humanity into a Feminine Tabernacle, in the loins of Abraham & David: the Lamb of God, the Saviour became apparent on Earth as the Prophets foretold? The Return of Israel is a Return to Mental Sacrifice & War. Take up the Cross O Israel & follow Jesus. (E 171–174)

From Blake's own pronouncements in *The Everlasting Gospel* (ca. 1818), it is clear that the Jesus to be followed was an antinomian lawbreaker, a sexualized savior, and a fully human embodiment of the divinity. As Blake's God tells Jesus, "Thou art a Man God is no more / Thy own humanity learn to adore" (E 520). When Crabb Robinson "put the popular question to him—Concerning the imputed Divinity of Jesus Christ," Blake answered, "He is the only God—but then he added—And so am I and so are you."[114] Though he wryly remarked that "This Jesus will not do / Either for Englishman or Jew," he may have known that for some Jewish Swedenborgians, the Kabbalists' Grand Man and Swedenborg's Divine Human subsumed all religious divisions.

Notes

This paper draws on the extensive contextual material provided in my previous publications and in a forthcoming book, *Why Mrs. Blake Cried: William Blake and the Sexual Basis of Spiritual Vision* (London: Random House). To avoid lengthy duplication of that documentation, I refer to those works for background but provide new citations for additional information.

1. William Blake, "The Everlasting Gospel" (ca. 1818), *The Complete Poetry and Prose of William Blake*, ed. David V. Erdman, revised ed. (1965; New York: Doubleday/Anchor Press, 1988), 524. Subsequent references to the Erdman edition will be cited parenthetically, and abbreviated E.
2. Raymond Lister, *George Richmond: A Critical Biography* (London: Robin-Gorton, 1981), 132.
3. For the best study of Blake's kabbalistic interests, see Sheila A. Spector, *"Wonders Divine": The Development of Blake's Kabbalistic Myth* (Lewisburg: Bucknell University Press, 2001), and *"Glorious incomprehensible": The Development of Blake's Kabbalistic Language* (Lewisburg: Bucknell University Press, 2001).

4. London, Moravian Church Library: MS. C/36/158–159; Congregation Diary, V (1751), 61, 80; Petitions for Membership—"John Blake." The records include earlier Blakes and Wrights (Catherine's maiden name) who were possibly relatives. These documents are reproduced in Keri Davies and Marsha Keith Schuchard, "Recovering the Lost Moravian History of Blake's Family," *Blake: An Illustrated Quarterly* 38, 1 (summer 2004): 36–43. They are reproduced and fully explicated in my book, *Why Mrs. Blake Cried: William Blake and the Sexual Basis of Spiritual Vision* (London: Random House, forthcoming). I am grateful to Paul Hewitt, former librarian at the Moravian Church Library, for permission to use these documents.

5. In 1743, John Blake lived in the same house with James Blake, William's father, and they were probably brothers; see Gerald E. Bentley, Jr., *Stranger from Paradise: A Biography of William Blake* (New Haven: Yale University Press, 2001), 3. Catherine Blake's withdrawal was possibly required by her marriage to James Blake, who was not a member of the Congregation of the Lamb, thus making her ineligible for participation in the highly selective group. Moreover, the demands of the Congregation were extremely time-consuming for a wife who would soon bear five children and work in the family shop. She and her new husband would be allowed to attend the public services at Fetter Lane.

6. Muir communicated the Moravian information to Thomas Wright, who published it in *The Life of William Blake* (1929); reprint (New York: Burt Franklin, 1969), 1:2, and to Margaret Lowery, who repeated it in *Windows of the Morning: A Critical Study of William Blake's Poetical Sketches, 1783* (New Haven: Yale University Press, 1940), 14–15, 210 n57.

7. Nancy Bogen, "The Problem of William Blake's Early Religion," *The Personalist* 49 (1968): 509, 517; and Jack Lindsay, *William Blake: His Life and Work* (London: Constable, 1978), 3–4, 275–276.

8. For the "Sifting Period," see Craig Atwood, "Blood, Sex, and Death: Life and Liturgy in Zinzendorf's Bethlehem" (Ph.D. diss., Princeton University, 1995); and Colin Podmore, *The Moravian Church in England, 1728–1760* (Oxford: Clarendon, 1998). For the Moravian *Judenmission*, see Christiane Dithmar, *Zinzendorfs nonkonformistische Haltung zum Judentum* (Heidelberg: Universitäts Verlag C. Winter, 2000).

9. J. P. Lockwood, *Memorials of the Life of Peter Boehler, Bishop of the Church of the Moravian Brethren*, intro. Thomas Jackson (London: Wesleyan Conference Office, 1868), 116, 126.

10. Lockwood, *Memorials*, 186–189, 243.

11. Gustaf Dalman and Diakoms Schulze, *Zinzendorf und Lieberkuhn: Studien in der Geschichte der Judenmission* (Leipzig: Hinrich, 1903), 43, 68, 84, 88.

12. See the Introduction to Lars Berquist, *Swedenborg's Dream Diary*, trans. Anders Hallengren (West Chester, PA: Swedenborg Foundation, 2001), 3–75.

13. George Dole, "Philosemitism in the Seventeenth Century," *Studia Swedenborgiana* 7 (1990): 5–6; also, my article, "Leibniz, Benzelius, and Swedenborg: The Kabbalistic Roots of Swedish Illuminism," in *Leibniz, Mysticism, and Religion,* ed. Allison Coudert, Richard Popkin, and Gordon Weiner (Dordrecht: Kluwer Academic, 1998), 84–106.

14. Hans Joachim Schoeps, *Barocke Juden, Christen, Judenchristen* (Bern und München: Francke, 1965), 60–67.

15. Elliot Wolfson, "Messianism in the Christian Kabbalism of Johann Kemper," in *Millenarianism and Messianism in Early Modern European Culture*, vol. 1,

Jewish Messianism in the Early Modern World, ed. Matt Goldish and Richard Popkin (Kluwer: Dordrecht Academic, 2001), 140.

16. Benedict Chastanier, *Tableau Analytique et Raisonée de la Doctrine Céleste* (London, 1786), 21–21; Berquist, *Swedenborg's Dream Diary,* 55.

17. See my on-line article, "Why Mrs. Blake Cried: Swedenborg, Blake, and the Sexual Basis of Spiritual Vision," *Esoterica: The Journal for Esoteric Studies* 2 (1999): 1–58 <http://www. esoteric. msu>.

18. Pierre Deghaye, *La Doctrine Ésotérique de Zinzendorf (1700–1760)* (Paris: Klincksieck, 1969), 161–169; Bergquist, *Swedenborg's Dream Diary,* 180–181, 211–213, 247, 284, 298, 317; Emanuel Swedenborg, *The Spiritual Diary,* trans. James Buss (London: Swedenborg Society, 1977), #3449–3453, 3717, 3765–3773, 4331, 4496, 4525, 4791–4815, 5988–5995. His odd descriptions of orgiastic Quakers evidently referred to those who participated in Moravian rituals.

19. Craig Atwood, "Sleeping in the Arms of Jesus: Sanctifying Sexuality in the Eighteenth-Century Moravian Church," *Journal of the History of Sexuality* 8 (1997): 34–44. I discuss at length the Jesus–Adam Kadmon parallels in *Why Mrs. Blake Cried.*

20. J. E. Hutton, *A History of the Moravian Missions* (London: Moravian Publication Office, 1922), 149, 154.

21. Dithmar, *Zinzendorfs nonkonformistische Hattung,* 134, 145–146; Atwood, "Sleeping," 44. For the Jewish and kabbalistic requirement concerning sex on the Sabbath, see David Biale, *Eros and the Jews* (New York: Basic Books, 1992), 54, 101–118.

22. Hutton, Moravian Missions, 150; Peter Voght, "Zinzendorf's Theology of the Sabbath," in *The Distinctiveness of Moravian Culture: Essays and Documents in Moravian History in Honor of Vernon H. Nelson on his Seventieth Birthday,* ed. Craig Atwood and Peter Voght (Nazareth, PA: Moravian Historical Society, 2003), 206, 213, 223–224.

23. Berquist, *Dream Diary,* 336; for his references to writings on Kabbalah, Rosicrucianism, and Hermeticism, see Emanuel Swedenborg, *A Philosopher's Notebook,* ed. Alfred Acton (Philadelphia: Swedenborg Scientific Association, 1931), 30, 158, 160, 178, 232, 250, 258–259, 314, 508. For the Moravians' Rosicrucian interests, see Julius Sachse, *The German Sectarians of Pennsylvania, 1742–1800* (1899–1900; rpt. New York: AMS, 1971), 1:39, 290, 427–430, 466.

24. See my articles, "Yeats and the Unknown Superiors: Swedenborg, Falk, and Cagliostro," in *Secret Texts: The Literature of Secret Societies,* ed. Hugh Ormsby-Lennon and Marie Roberts (New York: AMS, 1988), 114–168; and "Jacobite and Visionary: The Masonic Journey of Emanuel Swedenborg," *Ars Quatuor Coronatorum,* 115 (2002): 33–72.

25. See E 707. London, Grand Lodge: Atholl Register, Lodge #38—lists James Blake, possibly Blake's father, as a member from 1757 to 1761. His lodge brothers were mainly liberal shopkeepers and artisans.

26. *Divided Souls: Converts from Judaism in Germany, 1500–1750* (New Haven: Yale University Press, 2001), 1.

27. See G. [Goldney], "Friendly Address to the Jews," *Gentleman's Magazine,* 29 (1759): 269–270; Edward Goldney, *Epistles to Deists and Jews* (London: printed for the author, 1759), 2: iii, viii, 1–12.

28. *A Catalogue of the . . . Library of Richard Cosway* (London: Mr. Stanley, 1821), 4–5; John Nichols, *Literary Anecdotes of the Eighteenth Century* (1812–1815; rpt. New York: AMS, 1961), 3: 435–437; Alfred Rubens, "Early Anglo-Jewish Artists," *Transactions of the Jewish Historical Society of England* 14 (1935–1939): 10.

29. "The 'Baalshem'—Dr. Falk," *Jewish Chronicle* (March 9, 1888): 15–16.

30. Hugo Valentin, *Judarnas Historia i Sverige* (Stockholm: Albert Bonniers, 1924), 112–135; Carl Sprinchorn, "Sjuttonhundratalets Svenska Kolonisationsplaner," *Svensk Historisk Tidskrift* 43 (1923): 132–135; Charles Duschinsky, "Jacob Kimchi and Shalom Buzaglo," *Transactions of the Jewish Historical Society of England* 7 (1915): 282–289; Cecil Roth, "The Amazing Clan of Buzaglo," *Transactions of the Jewish Historical Society of England* 23 (1971): 11–22.

31. Emanuel Swedenborg, *The True Christian Religion Containing the Universal Theology of the New Church*, trans. W. C. Dick (1770; London: Swedenborg Society, 1950), 845.

32. For Swedenborg's visit, see Brumore's letter to Thomé, published in the *Journal Encyclopédique* (December 1, 1785): 295; for Müller and Eibeschütz, see Reinhard Breymayer, "'Élie Artiste': Johann Daniel Müller de Wissenbach/Nassau (1716 jusqu'a après 1785), un aventurier entre le piétisme radicale et l'Illuminisme," in *Actes du Colloque International Lumières et Illuminisme*, ed. Mario Matucci (Université de Pisa: Instituto di Lingua e Letterature Françese, 1985), 75 n46.

33. Reinhard Breymayer, "Von Swedenborg zu Elias Artista: Der 'Prophet' Johann Daniel Müller aus Wissenbach/Nassau (1716 nach 1785), Gegner Moses Mendelssohn und Lessings, kritischer Freund Emanuel Swedenborg," in *Emanuel Swedenborg, 1688–1772. Naturforscher und Kundiger der Überwelt* (Stuttgart: Württenbergischen Landesbibliothek, 1988), 91.

34. Deghaye, *La Doctrine*, 164–167; Friedrich Christoph Œtinger, *Swedenborgs und andere Irrdische und Himmlische Philosophie* (Frankfurt und Leipzig, 1765).

35. Reinhard Breymayer, "Ein unbekannter Gegner Gotthold Ephraim Lessings: Der ehemalige Frankfurter Konzertdirektor Johann Daniel Müller aus Wissenbach/Nassau (1716 bis nach 1785)," in *Pietismus-Herrnhuterum-Erweckungsbewegung: Festschrift für Erich Beyreuther,* ed. Dietrich Meyer (Köln: Rheinland-Verlag GmbH, 1982), 135 n65; Yehoshua Horowitz, "Horowitz, Phinehas (Pinhas) Ben Zevi Hirsch Ha-Levi," *Encyclopaedia Judaica* (Jerusalem: Keter, 1972), 8: 999–1001; and Esther (Zweig) Liebes, "Dov Baer (The Maggid) of Mezhirech," *Encyclopaedia Judaica* (Jerusalem: Keter, 1972), 6: 180–184.

36. After referring to Swedenborg in his diary, J. H. Schröder wrote, "Daher kommen alle die neuen Rosen-Kreutzer-Schriften" (see Henry F. Fullenwider, "Friedrich Christoph Œtinger, Theophil Friedrich Œtinger, und die Spätrosenkreuzer," *Blätter für Wurttembergische Geschichte* 7 [1975]: 53).

37. Quoted in Cyriel Odhner Sigstedt, *The Swedenborg Epic* (London: Swedenborg Society, 1981), 416.

38. Swedenborg, *True Christian Religion*, #841–842.

39. E 41; David V. Erdman, *Blake: Prophet Against Empire*, revised ed. (Princeton: Princeton University Press, 1969), 144–145, 177.

40. Dr. Lloyd, Assistant Director of the Scottish National Portrait Gallery, examined the portrait, with the permission of its owner, Mrs. Cecil Roth. He doubted the previous attribution to John Singleton Copley and concluded that it was more likely by Loutherbourg (personal communication from Dr. Lloyd).

41. "A Crypto Judaeo-Christian Sect of Sabbatean Origin," *Tarbiz* 57 (1988): 110, 349–384 (in Hebrew with English abstract).

42. Gustaf Dalman, "Documente eines Christlichen Geheimbundes unter den Juden im achtzehnen Jahrhundert," *Saat auf Hoffnung. Zeitschrift die Mission der Kirche an Israel* 28 (1890): 18–59. I give details on the La Trobe family's contacts with the Cosway-Blake circle in *Why Mrs. Blake Cried*.

43. Dalman and Schulze, *Zinzendorf und Lieberkuhn*, 68.

44. Heinz Moshe Graupe, "Mordechai Shnaber-Levison: The Life, Works, and Thought of a Haslakah Outsider," *Leo Baeck Institute Yearbook* 41 (1996): 15; David Ruderman, *Jewish Thought and Scientific Discovery in Early Modern Europe* (New Haven: Yale University Press, 1995), 345.

45. Graupe, *Haslakah Outsider*, 7.

46. W. F. Bynum and Roy Porter, *William Hunter and the Eighteenth-Century Medical World* (Cambridge: Cambridge University Press, 1985).

47. Mungo Ferguson, *The Printed Books in the Library of the Hunterian Museum in the University of Glasgow* (Glasgow: Jackson, Wylie, 1930), 347. A bequest of his books was made by William Hunter (d. 1783) "to provide teaching material in science and the humanities." Thus, it is relevant to Levison's medical–alchemical career that Hunter included works by Swedenborg, Hermes Trismegistus, Paracelsus, Agrippa, Postel, Dee, Fludd, Digby, etc.

48. Levison refers to his collaboration with Peter Woulfe in *An Essay on the Blood* (London: T. Davies, 1776), 95n. See also "Peter Woulfe," *DNB*; James Partington, *A History of Chemistry* (London: Macmillan, 1962), 3:99, 245, 290, 300, 547; Benedict Chastanier, *A Word of Advice to a Benighted World* (London, 1795), 20–23.

49. Peter Woulfe, "Experiments on Some Mineral Substances, Communicated by the Desire of William Hunter, FRS," *Philosophical Transactions of the Royal Society* 69 (1779): 22.

50. Bergquist, *Swedenborg's Dream Diary*, 55–57; Cecil Roth, "The King and the Cabalist," *Essays and Portraits in Anglo-Jewish History* (Philadelphia: Jewish Publication Society of America, 1962), 139–164.

51. Ruderman, *Jewish Thought*, 359. However, the alleged influence of Linnaeus's *Nemesis Divina* on Levison is inaccurate, for selections of the manuscript were not published until 1848, and it was not published in its entirely until 1968 (in English 2001).

52. Ruderman, *Jewish Thought*, 362. Translated from Levison's *Shelosh-Esre Yesodai ha-Torah*, 94a-b. This was published at Altona in 1792 but probably written during Levison's London years.

53. Rudolph Tafel, *Documents Concerning the Life and Character of Emanuel Swedenborg* (London: Swedenborg Society, 1875), 2: 522–527.

54. Swedenborg mentioned Dr. Alexander Bruce, Stamp Brooksbanks, and "P. C., Esquire, an Edenboro gent"; see Sigrid Sigstedt, "Chronological List of Swedenborg Documents" (1943), typescript in Swedenborg Society London, 2:#2876, 2154, 2265–2266.

55. Kenneth Collins, "Jewish Medical Students and Graduates in Scotland," *Transactions of the Jewish Historical Society of England* 29 (1982–1986): 79.

56. Sigstedt, *Swedenborg Epic*, 431, 434; John Henry Hampe, F. R. S., *An Experimental System of Metallurgy* (London: J. Nourse, 1777), biographical advertisement. Nourse also published Swedenborg's early scientific works.
57. "Andrew Wilson, M.D.," *DNB*.
58. Ruderman, *Jewish Thought*, 361; Andrew Wilson, *Horae Davidicae*, 87n, 180. The Emory University copy lacks the title-page, but the catalogue lists it as published in Edinburgh in 1748. However, references to Antoine-François, comte de Fourcroy (1755–1809), and Antoine Laurent Lavoisier (1743–1794) suggest a later edition.
59. Graupe, *Haslakah Outsider*, 8.
60. Graupe, *Haslakah Outsider*, 12, n37.
61. William Wonnacott, "The Rite of Seven Degrees in London," *Ars Quatuor Coronatorum* 39 (1926): 63–98; George Draffen, "Some Further Notes on the Rite of Seven Degrees in London," *Ars Quatuor Coronatorum* 68 (1956): 94–110; London, Grand Lodge: MS. BE 166—Livre des délibérations de la loge de l'Union, #70 (ca. 1772–1790). For Blake and Los, see my article, "The Secret Masonic History of Blake's Swedenborg Society," *Blake: An Illustrated Quarterly* 26 (1992): 40–51.
62. Revealing his eclectic religious outlook, Duché recommended as aids to Christian worship the sacred writings of the heathens, including "thrice-great Hermes," Socrates, Epictetus, Zoroaster, and Confucius (285). The third edition of Duché's *Discourses* (1790) included additional "Discourses Preached at the Asylum" in Lambeth, which deal more enthusiastically with the "inward man" and other Swedenborgian themes.
63. Roth, "King and the Kabbalist," 146; Graupe, *Haslakah Outsider*, 8 n27.
64. Moshe Pelli, *Mordechai Gumpel Schnaber: The First Religious Reformer of the Hebrew Haslakah in Germany* (Beer-Sheva: University of Negev, 1972), 9.
65. Clarke Garrett, "The Spiritual Odyssey of Jacob Duché," *Proceedings of the American Philosophical Society* 119 (1975): 143–155; also by Garrett, "Swedenborg and the Mystical Enlightenment in Late Eighteenth-Century England," *Journal of the History of Ideas* 45 (1984): 67–81.
66. Gumperz Levison, M. D., *An Account of the Epidemical Sore Throat* (London: printed for B. White, Fleet Street; J. Bew, No. 28, Paternoster Row; and W. Sharp, in the Strand, opposite Somerset House, 1778). For William Sharp as bookseller, see Ian Maxted, *The London Book Trades, 1775–1800* (London: Dawson, 1977), 202.
67. Anon., "The Reverend Jacob Duché," *The Monthly Observer* 1 (1857): 81.
68. *The Apocalyptic Sublime* (New Haven: Yale University Press, 1986), 48.
69. For the walks, see Bentley, *Stranger From Paradise*, 28.
70. *I Swedenborgs Labyrint: Studier i de Gustavianska Swedenborgarnes liv och tänkande* (Stockholm: Atlantis, 1995), 88.
71. The Rainsford Papers in the British Library and at Alnwick Castle are the major source for the Illuminist underground in England and its ties with similar developments in Europe. See Gordon P. Hills, "Notes on the Rainsford Papers in the British Museum," *Ars Quatuor Coronatorum* 26 (1913): 93–130.
72. Gerald E. Bentley, Jr, "Mainaduc, Madness, and Mesmerism: George Cumberland and the Blake Connection," *Notes and Queries* 236 (September 1991): 294–296.
73. Bergquist, *Swedenborg's Dream Diary*, 267–269; British Library: Rainsford Papers, MS. 23,669. f.290; Hills, 110; Alnwick Castle: Rainsford Papers,

MS. 600. ff. 181, 250, 294, 430. I am grateful to Colin Smithson, archivist to the Duke of Northumberland, for permission to examine the Rainsford Papers in the family's possession.

74. Gordon P. Hills, "Notes on Some Contemporary References to Dr. Falk, the Baal Shem of London, in the Rainsford Manuscripts at the British Museum," *Transactions of the Jewish Historical Society of England* (1918), 125. Rainsford and his Swedenborgian-Masonic colleagues Lambert de Lintot and Ebenezer Sibly owned various works about the Asiatic Brethren, who gained recruits among the Swedenborgian *Illuminés* in Copenhagen (Prince Carl of Hesse-Cassel) and Stockholm (Carl Boheman). Asiatic emissaries also visited London. For the Order's acceptance of Jews and the fusion of Jewish–Christian symbolism, see Jacob Katz, *Jews and Freemasons in Europe, 1723–1939* (Cambridge: Harvard University Press, 1970), 26–53; and Christopher McIntosh, *The Rose Cross and the Age of Reason* (Leiden: Brill, 1992), 161–177.

75. For Franz Joseph Molitor's MS. history of the Order, see Gershom G. Scholem, *Du Frankisme au Jacobinisme* (Paris: Le Seul Gallimard, 1981), 39. For some reason, this important study by Scholem is rarely consulted by historians.

76. For Polish Masons' linking of Falk and Frank, see Jacob Schatzky, *The History of the Jews of Warsaw* (in Yiddish) (New York: Yiddish Scientific Institute, 1947–1953), 1:89. For French Masons' similar linking, see *La Monde Maçonnique,* 15 (1873–1874): 164, for a letter read in 1787 to the assembled *Philaléthes* about "un juif devenu chrétien, nommé Franc, qui, d'aprés son extérieur, selon le récit de l'écrivain, parait avoir des rapports avec le fameux Falc, mort à Londres." The French Masons considered Rainsford to be a major source of information on Falk and Swedenborg. For their further inquiries, see J. E. S. Tuckett, "Savalette de Langes, Les Philaletes, and the Convent of Wilhelmsbad, 1782," *Ars Quatuor Coronatorum* 30 (1917): 131–171.

77. Levison refers to "my ingenious friend Dr. Lettsom" in *An Account of the Epidemical Sore Throat,* 54. For the Goldsmids, see James Johnston Abraham, *Lettsom: His Life, Times, Friends, and Descendants* (London: William Heinemann, 1933), 444–445. Also, see Mark L. Schoenfield, "Abraham Goldsmid: Money Magician in the Popular Press," in *British Romanticism and the Jews: History, Culture, Literature,* ed. Sheila A. Spector (New York: Palgrave/Macmillan, 2002), 37–60.

78. On Theden, see Ferdinand Runkel, *Geschichte der Freimaurer in Deutschland* (Berlin: Reimar Hobbing, 1932), 2: 114–119; Karl Frick, *Die Erleuchteten* (Graz: AkademischeDruck-u. Verlagsanstadt, 1973), 360–361.

79. Samuel Beswick, *The Swedenborg Rite and the Great Masonic Leaders of the Eighteenth Century* (New York: Masonic Publishing Company, 1870), 46–49. Unfortunately, Beswick does not provide documentation for his Masonic claims, which are a perplexing mix of verifiable fact and credulous fantasy.

80. [Augustus Nordenskjöld], *A Plain System of Alchymy,* inscribed by the author, London, Soho Square, December 1, 1779. Copy in Royal Library, Stockholm.

81. Hans Joachim Schoeps, "Läkaren och Alkemisten Gumpertz Levison: Ett Bidrag till den Gustavianska Tidens Kulturhistoria," *Lychnos* (1943): 23, 40–41.

82. Bryn Athyn, Academy of New Church: Academy Collection of Swedenborg Documents, #1664.31, p. 13–14 (C. F. Nordenskjöld to C. B. Wadström, London, January 31, 1784). I am grateful to David Glenn for permission to use these documents.

83. Oscar Patric Sturzen-Becker, "Gustaf de Tredjes Guldmakere," *Månadsskrift* (Oct.–Dec. 1864): 730.

84. George Levison, *Utkast til Physica Anmärkningar öfver Lefnadstattet I Stockholm . . . af en Engelsk Läkare* (Stockholm, 1780), 96–100.

85. Pelli, *Mordechai Gumpel Schnaber*, 11, 14.

86. For the context and detailed documentation, see my articles, "Yeats and the Unknown Superiors," 145–148, and "Dr. Samuel Jacob Falk," 203–226.

87. Sturzen-Becker, "Gustaf," 732.

88. London, Wellcome Institute of History of Medicine: Lalande MS. 1048 (letter from C. G. Salzmann to P. J. Willermoz, December 31, 1781); translation from the original French is mine.

89. E 42; see my article, "William Blake and the Promiscuous Baboons: A Cagliostroan Séance Gone Awry," *British Journal for Eighteenth-Century Studies* 18 (1995): 185–200.

90. M. L. Danilewicz, "'The King of the New Israel': Thaddeus Grabianka (1740–1807)," *Oxford Slavonic Papers*, n.s. 1 (1968): 49–75; Alice Joly, "La 'Sainte Parole' d'Avignon," *Les Cahiers de la Tour Saint-Jacques* 2–4 (1960): 98–116.

91. Clarke Garrett, *Respectable Folly: Millenarians and the French Revolution in France and England* (Baltimore: The Johns Hopkins University Press, 1975), 102.

92. John Wright, *A Revealed Knowledge of Some Things that Will Speedily Be Fulfilled in the World, Communicated to a Number of Christians, Brought Together at Avignon, by the Power of the Spirit of God, from all Nations* (London, 1794), 4–5.

93. British Library: Rainsford Papers, MS. 23,675, ff. 26, 33.

94. Rainsford Papers, 26,669, ff. 129–130.

95. John Shaftesley, "Jews in English Regular Freemasonry, 1717–1860," *Transactions of the Jewish Historical Society of England* 25 (1977): 182, 187.

96. Robert Hindmarsh, ed., *The New Jerusalem Journal* 2 (September 1792): 50.

97. Rainsford Papers, Add. MSS. 23,670.f.71; "Epistolary Correspondence of the Earlier Members of the Church," *Monthly Observer and New Church Record* 3 (1859): 281. Dr. Benamore's magnetic therapy was praised by the poet William Cowper.

98. Wright, *Revealed Knowledge*, 18–19, 27–28.

99. Garrett, *Respectable Folly*, 111–113, 175–178.

100. E 38; Randall Helms, "Why Ezekiel Ate Dung," *English Language Notes* 15 (June 1978): 280–281.

101. Morton D. Paley, "William Blake, the Prince of the Hebrews, and the Woman Clothed with the Sun," in *William Blake: Essays in Honour of Sir Geffrey Keynes*, ed. Paley and Michael Phillips (Oxford: Clarendon, 1973), 260–293; G. R. Balleine, *Past Finding Out: The Tragic Story of Joanna Southcott and Her Successors* (New York: Macmillan, 1956), 28.

102. Wright, *Revealed Knowledge* (1794); William Bryan, *A Testimony of the Spirit of Truth Concerning Richard Brothers* (London, 1795).

103. According to Gerald Barnett, the Hebrew instruction was "because of the strong Hebraic influence of Emanuel Swedenborg"; see his *Richard and Maria Cosway* (Tiverton: West Country Books, 1995), 140.

104. Paley, *Apocalyptic Sublime*, 64–65.

105. E 505; for the magnetic–magical context, see my article, "Blake's Healing Trio: Magnetism, Medicine, and Mania," *Blake: An Illustrated Quarterly* 23 (1989): 20–31.

106. Stephen Lloyd, *Richard and Maria Cosway: Regency Artists of Taste and Fashion* (Edinburgh: Scottish National Portrait Gallery, 1995), 127, plate #160.

107. Lloyd, *Richard and Maria Cosway*, 127, plate #161.

108. Edwin Ellis and William Butler Yeats, eds., *The Works of William Blake* (London: Quaritch, 1893), 1:24–25; W. B. Yeats, ed., *The Poems of William Blake* (London: Lawrence & Bullen, 1893), xv–xvii.

109. For the various conjectures, see Schuchard, "Yeats and the Unknown Superiors," 114–117, 151, 153.

110. Wynn Westcott, "The Rosicrucians Past and Present," in *The Magical Mason: Forgotten Hermetic Writings of W. W. Westcott*, ed. Robert Gilbert (Wellingborough: Aquarian Press, 1983), 43.

111. Katz, *Jews and Freemasons*, 38–69; Scholem, *Du Frankisme*, 28–39; McIntosh, *Rose Cross*, 161–177.

112. Spector, *"Wonders Divine,"* 31–35, 140–168; also, "Blake's Graphic Use of Hebrew," *Blake: An Illustrated Quarterly* 37 (2003): 75–79.

113. Kathleen Raine, *The Human Face of God: William Blake and the Book of Job* (New York: Thames and Hudson, 1982), 7, n.303.

114. Bentley, *Blake Records* (Oxford: Clarendon Press, 1969), 539–540.

CHAPTER 4

BLAKE AND THE BOOK OF NUMBERS: JOSHUA THE GIANT KILLER AND THE TEARS OF BALAAM

R. Paul Yoder

William Blake's last major poem, *Jerusalem the Emanation of the Giant Albion*, is a challenging and often obscure work in which one is rarely sure of the validity of statements and claims made by the various characters. Often characters make flatly contradictory statements, as when both Jesus and Satan claim divine authority in the poem. Indeed, the entire action of the poem depends on Albion's decision as to which "God" to follow: Jesus (associated with freedom, forgiveness, and peace) or Satan (associated with Natural Philosophy, judgment, punishment, and war). Repeatedly in the poem, Satan insists, "I am God," and the question is: how does Albion know that he is not? The question is important because, as Blake saw it, people and states often claim for themselves divine authority to justify their actions, when in fact their actions are led by more human drives like greed or pride or ambition. They use the pretense of divine authority to control others. Through all its difficulty, these are the issues that drive *Jerusalem*. Blake seems to have recognized that similar issues are played out in the biblical account of the Israelite conquest of Canaan, primarily that narrated in the book of Numbers and completed in the book of Joshua. Indeed he invokes three crucial episodes from Numbers as the biblical context for his poem— the report of the spies about giants in Canaan, Balaam's attempt to curse the Israelites, and the battle of Peor—and he uses that context to suggest an alternative to war as a means of conquest, and to suggest that the legitimate line of prophecy need not depend on one's nationality.

A Change in Reference: "To me who believe the
Bible & profess myself a Christian"[1]

William Blake is known as one of England's most biblically oriented poets. His often unorthodox Christian beliefs are readily evident in his writing, from the relatively early *The Marriage of Heaven and Hell* (1793), *America A Prophecy* (1793), and *The Songs of Innocence and of Experience* (1794), to the later works *Milton* (1815) and *Jerusalem* (1820). Moreover, Blake was interested not only in the Christian New Testament, but also in the Old Testament, roughly equivalent to the Jewish *Tanakh*; his *The [First] Book of Urizen* (1794) is a parody of Genesis; and in *The Marriage of Heaven and Hell*, Blake famously claims to have dined with Isaiah and Ezekiel and quizzed them on their prophetic style.[2] Despite the prominence of Isaiah and Ezekiel in *The Marriage of Heaven and Hell*, most of Blake's biblical references in his earlier works are rather less explicit. Even Jesus is referred to only obliquely in the early works, except for *The Marriage of Heaven and Hell*. Rather than name names, Blake invokes patterns—the shepherd or lamb in *Songs of Innocence*, or the seven days of creation in *The Book of Urizen*. A less famous, but equally characteristic instance involves Fuzon, whose actions at the end of *The Book of Urizen* recall Moses and Exodus:

> So Fuzon call'd all together
> The remaining children of Urizen:
> And they left the pendulous earth:
> They called it Egypt, & left it. (28:19–22, E 83)

In *The Book of Ahania* (1795), Fuzon transmutes into a Christ-figure as

> The corse of his [Urizen's] first begotten
> On the accursed Tree of MYSTERY
> On the topmost stem of this Tree
> Urizen nail'd Fuzon's corse. (4:5–8, E 87)

In those earlier works, Blake invokes plot patterns (leaving Egypt) and linguistic tropes ("first begotten") from the Bible in order to create his own myth of creation and fall that also critiques the biblical patterns of creation and fall.

After about 1798, and especially beginning in the 1800s, Blake's approach to biblical reference changes. This change occurs during a period in which Blake had stopped producing new illuminated books: the period 1793–1795 saw the printing of at least eight new illuminated books, but no new books are printed after that until about 1815, with the first complete copy of *Milton*. This is not to say that Blake was not writing, however. In fact, he was working on *The Four Zoas* for much of this time, a massive poem that would be the culmination of Blake's mythological efforts of the 1790s, but which he never brought to press.[3] Instead, when Blake returned to etching illuminated books, he embarked on a very different sort of work with a very different set of biblical references. Instead of invoking general patterns from the Bible, Blake is much more explicit in his reference. He becomes focused on the Israelite military campaign into the promised land as described in the book of Numbers. In Blake's work, there is no explicit reference to Canaan, for example, before 1798, but after that, there are forty-one references to Canaan, thirty-one appearing in *Jerusalem* alone. There are perhaps two references to Moses by name before 1798, and twenty-three after that date. The Daughters of Zelophehad, whose inheritance problems comprise a short scene in Numbers, provide the names for Tirzah and four of her sisters in *Jerusalem*. Blake seems especially concerned with the battle of Peor and the events leading up to it, again none of which is mentioned explicitly in Blake's work before 1798.

The change I am suggesting in Blake's referencing the Bible is first evident in his annotations to Bishop Richard Watson's *An Apology for the Bible*, written in response to Thomas Paine's commentary on the Bible in *The Age of Reason*.[4] It is also in these annotations that Blake makes some of his most caustic statements about Jews. For example, Blake states that he is "one who believe [*sic*] the Bible & profess [*sic*] myself a Christian," but he refers to the "Jewish Scriptures" as "only an Example of the wickedness & deceit of the Jews & were written as an Example of the possibility of Human Beastliness in all its branches" (E 614). Blake makes such charges because he reads the Bible, not as a literal example of how people should act, but as "Examples given to us of the perverseness of some & its consequent evil & the honesty of others & its consequent good" (E 618). For Blake, "The Bible or <Peculiar> Word of God, Exclusive of Conscience or the Word of God Universal, is that Abomination which like the Jewish ceremonies is for ever removed & henceforth every man may converse with God & be a King & Priest in his own house" (E 615). Blake identifies the individual conscience with the "Word of God Universal," and advocates that conscience should govern a radical individualism in interpreting the sacred text or "the Peculiar Word of God." Within such a framework, Blake contends in these annotations that "The laws of the Jews were (both ceremonial & real) the basest & most oppressive of human codes. & being like all codes given under pretence of divine command were what Christ pronounced them The Abomination that maketh desolate. i. e. State Religion" (E 618).

Here we get to the crux of the issue—the "pretence of divine command" used to establish "State Religion," or as Blake had described in *The Marriage of Heaven and Hell*:

. . . [A] system was formed, which some took advantage of & enslav'd the vulgar by attempting to realize or abstract the mental dieties from their objects: thus began Priesthood.

Choosing forms of worship from poetic tales.

And at length they pronounced that the Gods had orderd such things. (plate 11, E 38)

Blake recognized the power behind the claim of divine command, and as he saw it, the example of how ancient Hebrews had used the claim of divine command to establish a state religion provided a model for critiquing his own Christian contemporaries: "That the Jews assumed a right <Exclusively> to the benefits of God. will be a lasting witness against them. & the same will it be against Christians" (E 615). Further, Blake was especially concerned with how such a state religion was used against non-adherents, and here is where Joshua enters the picture. Again from Blake's annotations to Watson's *Apology for the Bible*:

> God never makes one man murder another nor one nation . . . the destruction of the Canaanites by Joshua was the Unnatural design of wicked men To Extirpate a nation by means of another nation is as wicked as to destroy an individual by means of another individual which God considers (in the Bible) as Murder & commands that it shall not be done. (E 614–615)

In Blake's rather Augustinian reading of the Bible, the moral laws are fairly clear and are used to judge the actions of individuals. God says not to murder, so large-scale murder could not have been ordered by God; it must have been the work of wicked people.

Blake's critique of the campaign into Canaan is not that different from the way modern Jews read the Torah and the rest of the TaNaKH.[5] David, for example, was a great king, but he also had human failings that we regularly recognize and lament. No one takes David's treatment of Uriah as an example of how one should act. And certainly, the account of Joshua's campaign into Canaan, as recounted in the book of Joshua, is enough to give anyone pause. City after city—Makkedah, Libnah, Lachish, Eglon, Hebron, Hazor—we are told, is destroyed and the Israelites "put it and all the people in it to the sword, letting none escape" (Josh. 10:30). In Hazor, we are told, "Not a soul survived" (Josh. 11:11). In the Negeb, the Shephelah, and the slopes, Joshua "let none escape, but proscribed everything that breathed—as the Lord, the God of Israel, had commanded" (Josh. 10:40). For Blake the slaughter of so many people, apparently including women and children, is bad enough, but the real power move is the claim that the Lord had commanded it. For Blake, such a divine command was simply impossible; it is not God who would order such a thing. So if God did not command it, who did? The obvious answer is Joshua.

As I have noted, the sort of explicit reference to Joshua or Canaan that Blake makes in his annotations to Watson's *Apology for the Bible* are relatively rare in his earlier work. There are one or two references to Canaan and Moses in *The Four Zoas*, but it is not until *Milton* and especially *Jerusalem* that such explicit references reach a sort of critical mass, drawing in correspondences among biblical history, English folklore, contemporary English culture and Blake's own life. In the discussion that follows I focus on one particular passage from *Jerusalem* that brings together three important events from the book of Numbers: the sending of the spies in advance of the army, the attempt of Balak to hire Balaam to curse the Israelites, and the battle of Peor, in which Balaam was implicated. Blake's densely packed allusions to these events together focus on the question of how best to conduct the conquest of the promised land, and collaterally the question of who best to succeed Moses. Moreover, Blake's allusions to Numbers connect the biblical story with both English folklore and Blake's own biography in a way that allows him to assume for himself and for England the mantle of biblical prophecy.

Joshua the Giant Killer: Bread for Us

For reasons nobody has satisfactorily explained, the Preface to chapter 2 of *Jerusalem* is addressed "To the Jews."[6] Without attempting to explain that address, I shall note only that Blake's references to the events of Numbers reach a sort of crescendo in chapter 2, and nowhere is this more evident than in Los's speech to the friends of Albion in the middle of the chapter. As Albion flees into the wilderness of "Eternal Death," his friends stand, paralyzed with horror and fear. Los then makes a speech intended to rouse them to action. Throughout the poem, the rebellious Sons of Albion are, like their father, presented as giants, and in his speech to the friends of Albion, Los uses the rhetorical figure of prosopopeia—quoting or speaking in the voice of someone else—to depict the threats of these giants against Albion and his friends. The giants, as quoted by Los, say,

> We smell the blood of the English! we delight in their blood on our Altars!
> The living & the dead shall be ground in our rumbling Mills
> For bread of the Sons of Albion: of the Giants Hand and Scofield.
>
> (38[43]: 46–50, E 185)

If their threat sounds familiar that is because Blake is adapting one of England's most famous folktales—Jack and the Beanstalk—for their speech. *Funk & Wagnalls Standard Dictionary of Folklore Mythology and Legend* identifies the Jack and the Beanstalk story as "an English folktale, popular especially in the British Isles and the United States as a nursery story," and says that "the story belongs to the famous Jack [the Giant Killer] tale cycle" known in most English colonies and across Europe; *Funk & Wagnalls* also gives the lines Blake echoes here, which many of us recall from childhood:

> Fee-fi-fo-fum
> I smell the blood of an Englishman
> Be he live or be he dead
> I'll grind his bones to make my bread.[7]

Blake repeats, "smell the blood of the English," "the living and the dead," and the grinding of the victim to make bread. By putting these words into the mouths of the giant sons of Albion, Blake connects his own myth of Albion's fall with the folktale of Jack and the Beanstalk, aligning Los and the friends of Albion with the folk hero Jack, and the Giant Sons of Albion with the giant who terrorized Jack and his neighbors.

There are also more personal allusions in this brief passage, for Los's rendering of the giants' threats ends by identifying the Giant Sons of Albion as "the Giants Hand & Scofield" (38[43]:50, E 185).[8] In this identification, the drama of the poem and the folktale spill out into Blake's own life and England's artistic culture around 1800. "Hand" is named after the editorial mark—a pointing hand—used by the Hunt brothers, who championed writers like Keats, but who had offended Blake and hurt him professionally in their reviews of his work in the *Examiner*. "Scofield" refers to Private John Scofield who in 1803 initiated the charges of sedition against Blake, which punctuated his stay in Felpham under the patronage of William Hayley. Blake stood trial and was acquitted, but he never forgot the incident, and Scofield is only one of those involved in the trial who lend their names to the villainous Sons of Albion. Thus, Los and the friends of Albion are now associated with Jack the Giant Killer, and with Blake himself, and these figures are leagued against giants who include villains from both English folklore and England's early nineteenth-century artistic, military, and legal establishments.[9]

So, where does Numbers come into all this? In the midst of his plea to the friends of Albion to fight the giants and not to fear them, Los presents a catalog of the effects of Albion's fall. Among these effects, Los includes the facts that

> Oshea and Caleb fight: they contend in the valleys of Peor
> In the terrible Family Contentions of those who love each other:
> The Armies of Balaam weep—no women come to the field
> . . .
> But Death! Eternal Death! remains in the Valleys of Peor. (38[43]:37–39, 45, E 185)

The references to "Oshea and Caleb," Balaam and the valleys of Peor all relate the action of the poem to the middle chapters of the Book of Numbers, roughly chapters 13–25, plus chapter 31, as the Hebrews move deeper into Midian and Moab, and prepare for the campaign into Canaan.[10] The reference pairing Oshea and Caleb is particularly telling: Oshea's (Hosea's) name is changed to Joshua in Numbers 13:16, when he is chosen, along with eleven others, including Caleb, to go as spies into Canaan. When the spies return, they bring reports of giants—the Anakites (members of the Nephilim)—inhabiting the land, and only Joshua and Caleb stand to urge the Hebrews to trust in God and continue with the divine plan for moving into the promised land. Los's speech to the friends of Albion concerning the prospect of taking on the giant sons of Albion is thus a recognizable analogue to the urging of Joshua and Caleb to the reluctant Hebrews concerning the prospect of battling the giant Anakites. Like the friends of Albion, the Israelites were paralyzed with doubt about what action to take; like Los, Caleb had stood up and urged action: "Let us by all means go up, and we shall gain possession of it [the land], for we shall surely overcome it" (Num. 13:30). Even after the Israelites threaten to stone Caleb and Joshua, the two men continue in this plea, urging, "the Lord is with us. Have no fear of them" (Num. 14:9).

It is easy to see how this episode would have attracted Blake's attention, for it is a crucial moment in the history of the Exodus. Because the Israelites "despised" the land that God had promised them, God decrees that of the adults among them, only Joshua and Caleb will enter the promised land; as for the rest, their "carcasses shall drop in this wilderness, while [their] children shall roam in the wilderness for forty years" (Num. 14:32–33). The reluctance of the Hebrews is a defining moment on the path to the promised land, as is the reluctance of Albion's friends in responding to his plight. Thus, Blake aligns the friends of Albion with the doubting Hebrews, and Los—whose speech opens, "Why stand we here trembling around / Calling on God for help; and not ourselves in whom God dwells" (38[43]:12–13, E 184)—with Joshua and Caleb, who urge the reluctant Israelites, "The Lord is with us. Have no fear of them." In Blake's larger allusive web, Joshua and Caleb are associated not only with Los, but also with Jack the Giant Killer and Blake himself, while the giant Anakites are associated with the giants of English folklore and culture who threaten them; indeed, a few plates later, Anak is explicitly mentioned as one of the "Giants of Albion" (49:56, E 199). Just as Blake elsewhere in *Jerusalem* combines biblical and English geography by overlaying the map of the Tribes of Israel atop the map of England, here Blake combines Jewish history as recorded in Numbers with the English tales of Jack the Giant Killer, and his own personal history of artistic, military, and legal persecution.

These overlapping tales of heroic encounters with giants conflate biblical and British traditions into a single larger history. In this history, there is apparently a core story of an encounter with giants, and the different versions of the story suggest the sort of culturally specific adaptation that Blake had described much earlier in *All Religions are One*: "The Religions of all Nations are derived from each Nations different reception of the Poetic Genius. . . . As all men are alike (tho' infinitely various) So all Religions & as all similars have one source" (E 1–2). Nevertheless, the different derivations of the poetic genius are important, for Los's rendering of the giants' threats echoes not only the giant from the English folktale, but also, ironically, Caleb and Joshua themselves who say to the Israelites, "Only rebel not ye against the Lord, neither fear ye the people of the land; for they are bread for us" (Num. 14:9). That is the King James translation, but the passage is apparently troubling enough that in the edition of the Torah edited by W. Gunther Plaut, the passage is translated as "they will be our prey," even though Plaut acknowledges in a footnote that *lakhmanu* should be translated literally as "'our food' or 'our bread.'"[11] Citing seventeenth-century commentator Ephraim Lenczic, J. H. Hertz notes that Joshua and Caleb's reference to bread may be intended to recall the manna which God gave to the Hebrews in the desert and which melted when the sun grew hot

(Exodus 16:21), so that the passage suggests that the enemy would disappear like manna.[12] In either case, the biblical commentator clearly registers some discomfort with a literal interpretation of Joshua and Caleb's words. My point is that in the English folklore version of the story, the version from which Blake adapts the speech of the Sons of Albion, it is the giant who threatens to make bread of the English; in the biblical version of the story, which Blake invokes as the context of the scene and the model for Los's speech, it is the Hebrews who threaten to make bread of the giants, an attitude that to Blake must have foreshadowed Joshua's handling of the campaign into Canaan.

By invoking the two giant stories so closely together, Blake creates what Robert Gleckner has called a "significant allusion," that is, an allusion that invokes an entire context so that the invoked context and the moment in Blake's poem comment on each other. In this case, the interaction of Bible, folklore and poem calls attention to the fact that Joshua and Caleb refer to the giants as bread or food. Further, Joshua and Caleb use this cannibalistic rhetoric in exactly the opposite way from how such rhetoric was usually deployed in Blake's day. Peter Kitson has noted that the accusation of cannibalism "was used as the process by which imperial Europe distinguished itself from the subjects of it [sic] colonial expansion while concomitantly demonstrating a moral justification for that expansion."[13] Los does not represent "imperial Europe," but that strategy of demonizing the Other with the charge of cannibalism clearly parallels Los's argument when he quotes the threats of the giant Sons of Albion to make bread of the English in order to rouse the friends of Albion to action. In Numbers 14:9, however, the situation is different: Joshua and Caleb do not charge the Anakites with cannibalism; rather, they invoke the rhetoric of cannibalism for themselves as an index of their own power. Almost certainly Joshua and Caleb do not intend their rhetoric literally, and generations of biblical interpretation have argued for a figurative reading of the passage, but as we have seen, those figurative readings themselves testify to the discomfort the rhetoric creates in readers, if not in the immediate audience of Joshua and Caleb. It is this discomfort that Blake foregrounds in Los's speech when he draws together the figures of "Oshea and Caleb" and the giant at the top of Jack's beanstalk. In the instance we have been considering, Blake seems to want to appropriate for Los the inspiration and trust in divine guidance claimed by Joshua and Caleb in the face of a terrifying opponent. When he brings in the Jack and the Beanstalk reference, he then opposes that inspiration and trust to the cannibalistic threats of the giants. But the allusion to Jack also has the effect of criticizing the cannibalistic rhetoric of Joshua and Caleb. Given such rhetoric, it should be no surprise that one of the implications of Albion's fall is that Oshea and Caleb fight for eternal death in the valleys of Peor.

The Tears of Balaam

Blake does see an alternative to the slaughter of the indigenous populations, and to see that we must return to the densely allusive passage cited earlier, now more fully quoted:

> Oshea and Caleb fight: they contend in the valleys of Peor
> In the terrible Family Contentions of those who love each other:
> The Armies of Balaam weep—no women come to the field
> Dead corses lay before them & not as in Wars of old.
> For the Soldier who fights for Truth, calls his enemy his brother:
> They fight & contend for life, & not for eternal death!
> But here the Soldier strikes, & a dead corse falls at his feet
> Nor Daughter nor Sister nor Mother come forth to embosom the Slain!
> But Death! Eternal Death! remains in the Valleys of Peor.
>   (38 [43]:37–45, E 185)

The lines on war here are certainly in keeping with Blake's critique of Joshua expressed in the annotations to Watson. That Oshea (Joshua) and Caleb fight in the "valleys of Peor" suggests that the action has moved forward from the report of the spies and Joshua's claim that the Anakites will be "bread for us." Blake opposes this fighting in the "valleys of Peor" to the "Wars of old" in which the "Soldier who fights for truth, calls his enemy his brother," where "They fight & contend for life, & not for eternal death." These wars of old, fought for truth, are the mental fight that Blake thinks of as paradisal; it is intellectual combat leading to fuller life, not corporeal warfare leading to the "dead corse." It is not clear what Blake means by the "terrible Family Contentions"; these contentions could be the squabbling among the Israelites, but they more likely perhaps refer to the impact of the battle of Peor on the intimate relationships between some Israelites and the Midianites, relationships developed on the advice of Balaam to the Midianites. The battle of Peor is the climax of Numbers, the last major battle before Moses dies and the Israelites cross the Jordan; and Balaam is blamed by Moses for the need to slaughter all the males and the nonvirgin females among the prisoners captured in the battle. This slaughter of women and children may account for Blake's vision in which none come to "embosom the Slain." Moreover, by blaming Balaam for the need to kill the prisoners, Moses may also have finally put an end to a rivalry that begins earlier in Numbers, and earlier still in Midrash.

In Numbers, Balaam plays a key role both in recognizing God's promise to the Israelites, and in advising (however disastrously) the Midianites on how to deal with the Israelites' arrival in their territory. The main story of Balaam is the longest sustained episode in Numbers and comprises the center of the book. Balaam is a not a Hebrew, but he is a prophet of some repute, living in Aram; he is hired by Balak, the king of Moab, to curse the invading Israelites, but each of the three times he tries to curse them, God turns his curses into blessings. The story is, however, more complicated than that. Take, for example, Balaam's relationship with the Hebrew God. When approached by Balak's emissaries, Balaam asks God for guidance. God tells him not to go and Balaam obeys. When the emissaries return to ask a second time, Balaam again asks God for guidance, and this time God tells him to go with them. Balaam goes with them, even though he warns them that "Though Balak were to give me his house full of silver and gold, I could not do anything, big or little, contrary to the command of the Lord my God" (Num. 22:18); he tells Balak himself, "I can utter only the word that God puts into my mouth" (Num. 22:38). Even though Balaam is hired to curse the Israelites and is not a Hebrew himself, it is clearly the God of the Hebrews who guides his behavior and speech; repeatedly in the Torah's account of the Balaam story God is referred as either "YHVH (Adonai)" or "Elohim." Historically, there is some debate about Balaam's sincerity in serving God, but all accounts agree that Balaam's third oracle is a masterfully rendered vision, inspired by YHVH. In the eighteenth-century English tradition, Bishop Robert Lowth, in his *Lectures on the Sacred Poetry of the Hebrews* (a text Blake knew), says of Balaam's third oracle, "I do not know that the whole scope of the Hebrew poetry contains any thing more exquisite or perfect. [It] abounds in gay and splendid imagery copied immediately from the tablet of nature; and is chiefly conspicuous for the glowing elegance of the style, and the form and diversity of the figures"; and he calls it the prime example among the shorter biblical prophecies of the "order, disposition, and symmetry of a perfect poem of the prophetic kind."[14] In Jewish tradition, this "perfect poem," which begins, "*Ma tovu ohalekha Yaakov*" ("How fair are your tents, O Jacob"), has become a staple in the liturgy.

Despite the praise for and acceptance of his prophecy, Balaam is remembered as a villain, and *midrash* even extends his villainy well before his first appearance in the Torah. The folktales recorded in *Mimekor Yisrael: Classical Jewish Folktales* place Balaam in Pharaoh's court in Egypt at the beginning of Moses's life, advising Pharaoh to "Command that every son who is born among the Children of Israel should be slain," including the infant Moses.[15] When Moses survives and is brought into Pharaoh's household, it is Balaam who devises a plan for testing the presence of divine wisdom in the young child by offering him a choice between a precious stone and a hot coal; when Moses reaches for the precious stone, an angel pushes his hand away so that he grabs the coal and burns his lips and tongue, "and thereby became slow of speech."[16] When Moses returns to Egypt, and he and Aaron stand before Pharaoh asking for the freedom of the Israelites, Balaam is the chief magician who challenges Aaron when his staff transforms into a serpent.[17] Tracing this tradition of a villainous Balaam, Geza Vermes notes that the references to Balaam in Numbers combine three layers—the J-E tradition, the D tradition, and the P tradition—and that the J-E and D layers offer no support for such an anti-Balaam interpretation. Instead, he argues that the late addition of the P layer, referring to Balaam's complicity with the Midianites in Peor, "completely altered the figure of its principle character."[18] Read in this way, in the shadow cast backward from Peor, Vermes argues, Balaam is never given a fair hearing in his interaction with Balak; all of his actions are seen to be driven by "cupidity, pride and hatred."[19] Among the ancient commentators discussed by Vermes, only

Pseudo-Philo rejects the "pejorative interpretation" of the "priestly redactors" of the Torah.[20]

What these priestly redactors add specifically is Balaam's involvement in what Moses calls "the matter of Peor" (Num. 31:16). Balaam issues his prophecies for Balak from Mount Peor, but there was also apparently a shrine to Baal at Peor, identified as Baalpeor in Numbers 25:3. According to Moses in Numbers 31:16, the women of Midian had "at the bidding of Balaam induced the Israelites to commit trespass [in Num. 25:1 that 'trespass' is 'whoring'] against the Lord in the matter of Peor, so that the Lord's community was struck by the plague." The plague among the Israelites is usually understood to have been a venereal disease, some sort of sexual plague resulting from the 'whoring' of the Midianite women with the Israelite men, and for this reason, after the bloody defeat of the Midianites, Moses also orders the soldiers to "slay every male among the children, and slay also every woman who has known a man carnally" (Num. 31:17). The charge leveled against Balaam by Moses accounts for the negative reading of Balaam's story—he conspired with idolaters to seduce the Israelites, and he also allowed himself to be hired by Balak (even if he consulted God and was led by God).

In English literature before Blake, references to Balaam reflect the Balaam traditions both pro and con. Despite the praise of Robert Lowth and others for his prophecies, by the end of the eighteenth century, Balaam's name had become almost synonymous with greed, a tradition traceable to the statement in 2 Peter that Balaam "loved the wages of unrighteousness" (2:15). This is the tradition invoked by Alexander Pope at the end of the *Epistle to Bathurst* in the portrait of Sir Balaam, whom the Devil "tempts by making rich, not making poor."[21] Before Pope, Milton had invoked a more complex view of the Balaam tradition, this one focusing less on the element of greed and more on the opposition between Balaam's blessing the Israelites and the charges leveled against him by Moses at Peor: in *Paradise Regained*, Satan asks permission to return to Jesus the next day, remarking that God "vouchsaf'd his voice / To *Balaam* Reprobate, a Prophet yet / Inspir'd" (1:490–492).[22] The Son's response to Satan is a paraphrase of Balaam's own words: "do as thou find'st / Permission from above; thou canst not more" (1:495–496).

Blake invokes this same passage from the Balaam story to describe his own work in a letter to Dr. Trusler of August 16, 1799. Blake is apologizing for not following suggestions from Dr. Trusler for a design illustrating "Malevolence," but he says that he is like Milton, to whom the Muse dictated *Paradise Lost* and "also in the predicament of that prophet who says I cannot go beyond the command of the Lord to speak good or bad" (E 701), quoting Balaam's remark to Balak almost exactly. Blake may be getting paid by Trusler, as Balaam had been paid by Balak, but his art is governed by a higher power. It is not news that Blake saw himself as a latter-day prophet, but what is important here for Blake as a non-Jewish Englishman is that Balaam demonstrates that a prophet of Adonai does not have to be Jewish.

If Blake identified with Balaam, he also seems to have sympathized with his politics. Blake refers to Balaam twice by name, both times in *Jerusalem*: the first time is in the passage on which I have been focusing; the second time is at the end of chapter 2 in a kind of summary of the chapter. In the first instance, Los says that "The Armies of Balaam weep" (38[43]:39, E 185), apparently referring to the Midianite forces defeated at Peor and the captives slaughtered after the battle; in the second instance, Erin says that "Og & Sihon in the tears of Balaam / The Son of Beor, have given their power to Joshua & Caleb" (49:58–59, E 199). The victories of the Israelites transferred the power of Og and Sihon to Joshua and Caleb, leaving Balaam and his army in tears. In *A Blake Dictionary*, S. Foster Damon says that this image of the weeping Balaam is "not mentioned elsewhere,"[23] but Damon could not have known when he wrote the dictionary about a rather amazing discovery made in 1967 at an archaeological dig at Deir 'Alla. This discovery was a fragment of wall plaster on which was written an account of the prophet Balaam weeping after a night vision he has been given of the drought and desolation that the "council of the gods" (the *shaddayin*) has decided to inflict on the land.[24] In the Deir 'Alla fragment, Balaam apparently weeps because of the grim vision he is given of the future; Blake may have imagined Balaam weeping for similar reasons, for even in Balaam's triumphant third vision, he sees that the Israelites "shall devour enemy nations, Crush their bones, And smash their arrows" (Num. 24: 8). The claim in the vision that Israel shall "devour enemy nations" recalls Joshua and Caleb's claim that the giants shall be "bread" for the Israelites. Perhaps Balaam became an adviser to the Midianites in an effort to help them avoid the harshness of this fate, even if the final triumph of the Israelites was inevitable.[25]

Even without knowledge of the Deir 'Alla fragment, Damon contends that Blake interpreted the Balaam story along the lines I have suggested. Where Numbers says that Balaam counseled the Midianites to lead the Israelites into whoredom and trespass, Damon says that he counseled the Midianite women to "fraternize" with the "lads of Israel," and he suggests that Blake saw this tactic as an attempt to prevent the coming war, and "an essential step towards the Brotherhood of Man."[26] In other words, Blake seems to have understood Balaam to have advocated a "make love, not war" approach to the defense of Midian. Blake may or may not have accepted the story about a sexual plague, but certainly Moses's response to the open sexuality advocated by Balaam—the killing of all males and all sexually active females—would have seemed to Blake as yet another manifestation of a Urizenic suppression of sexual freedom and pleasure. This suppression of sexual freedom was necessary to support the war effort because the relationships that would develop out of the fraternization between the lads of Israel and the Midianite women would surely make it more difficult for the Israelites to accept the position of Joshua and Caleb, who saw the inhabitants of Canaan as "our bread."

Gunther Plaut notes that the slaying of the prisoners at Peor "contains historical and moral problems of a high order." After noting that the facts as related in Numbers cannot be correct historically, Plaut adds that this historical inconsistency only "exacerbates the moral question." He phrases the moral question about Peor in much the same way that Blake had questioned the issue of Joshua's conduct of the Canaan campaign: "How can the idea of slaughtering so many prisoners be reconciled with the humanitarian ideals and the deep sense of compassion that are the very heart of the Torah?" Plaut notes a *midrash* that also makes the same interpretive move as Blake: the *midrash* "attempts to relieve God of responsibility and comments that Moses' anger brought him to sin, implying that it was not God but Moses who issued the fatal command."[27] Blake does not comment much on Moses's involvement at Peor; the closest he gets is in the closing plates of Chapter 2 of *Jerusalem*, where he has Erin say that Jehovah is "Building the Body of Moses in the Valley of Peor: the Body / Of Divine Analogy" (49:57–58, E 199). For Blake the body contains the shrunken forms of mortal perception fallen from the expanding and contracting senses of the divine, but the body is also a merciful gift for it prevents the human from falling into complete chaos. The "Body of Moses" appears to suggest both positive and negative qualities: it is associated with the slaughter of captives at Peor, but it is also a state, created by God in order that the "Eternal Human" may be distinguished from "those States or Worlds in which the Spirit travels" (49:72–74, E 199). Indeed, in his *A Vision of the Last Judgment*, Blake writes that "it ought to be understood that the Persons Moses & Abraham are not here meant but the States Signified by those Names the Individuals being representatives or Visions of those States as they were reveald to Mortal Man in the Series of Divine Revelations. as they were written in the Bible" (E 556). That is, in Blake's reading of the Bible, Abraham and Moses, for example, signify roles that an individual might play, "states" through which an individual may pass like a traveler. Elsewhere in his work, Blake tends to praise Moses; he regularly includes Moses in lists that also include Solomon, Paul, David, and Ezekiel, positive role models for Blake. But at Peor something else happens; by ordering the death of the captives, Moses sets an example for Joshua's bloody campaign west of the Jordan. Moses becomes a state into which Joshua may enter.

I began this paper by noting that at the core of Blake's *Jerusalem* is the question of how to distinguish valid claims of divine authority from invalid claims. For Blake, this question was crucial not only for himself but also for his country: he saw himself firmly in the biblical prophetic tradition, but also saw that he was at odds with the prevailing cultural, political, and religious conditions. Blake also saw that in Numbers, the same question was implied in the interplay of Joshua, Balaam, and Moses in the events surrounding the battle of Peor. Blake believed that core values had been lost in Joshua's rhetoric of cannibalism and in Moses's order to slay women and children, even while the two leaders claimed divine authority. In the lost values of the Israelite leaders, Blake saw an example of the lost values of his own leaders in England. The arts were in the hands of commentators and editors like the Hunt brothers who repeatedly attacked Blake's work; the military was in the hands of soldiers like Scofield who harassed civilians and lied about their actions; the law was in the hands of the courts that tried Blake on the lies of the soldier; the Church of England created a "State Religion," "The Abomination that maketh desolate." As Blake has Los say in his speech to the friends of Albion, "A pretence of Art, to destroy Art: a pretence of Liberty / To destroy Liberty. a pretence of Religion to destroy Religion" (38[43]:35–36, E 185). Clearly the mantle of leadership must fall to another, to someone outside the main line, to a prophet of true vision, regardless of whether he is a Jew or not. Someone like Balaam. Or someone like Blake.

Notes

1. William Blake, Annotations to R. Watson, *An Apology for the Bible* (London, 1797), in *The Complete Poetry and Prose of William Blake*, ed. David V. Erdman, newly revised ed. (New York: Doubleday/Anchor Press, 1988), 614. Future references to the Erdman edition, abbreviated E, are indicated parenthetically in the text, and include plate and line numbers, as well as page numbers.

2. Leslie Tannenbaum's *Biblical Tradition in Blake's Early Prophecies: The Great Code of Art* (Princeton: Princeton University Press, 1982) remains the most complete commentary on Blake's biblical references in his earlier work.

3. Blake's work on *The Four Zoas, Milton,* and *Jerusalem* overlapped a good bit in the early 1800s, and some passages from *The Four Zoas* resurface in both *Milton* and *Jerusalem*. For a fuller discussion of this process see Morton Paley, *The Continuing City: William Blake's "Jerusalem"* (Oxford: Clarendon Press, 1983): 3, 35–42, and Joseph Viscomi, *Blake and the Idea of the Book* (Princeton: Princeton University Press, 1993): 317–320.

4. For a fuller discussion of the background for Blake's annotations to Watson's *Apology for the Bible*, see Florence Sandler, "'Defending the Bible': Blake, Paine, and the Bishop," in *Blake and His Bibles*, ed. David V. Erdman with an introduction by Mark Trevor Smith (West Cornwall, CT: Locust Hill Press, 1990), 41–70.

5. TaNaKH is an acronym for the Hebrew Bible, comprising *Torah* (the five books of Moses), *Nevi'im* (Prophets), and *Ketuvim* (other writings). Unless otherwise specified, references to books in the *Tanakh* are to *JPS Hebrew–English Tanakh*, second ed. (Philadelphia: Jewish Publication Society, 2000 [1999 on title page]). Book, chapter, and verse will be cited parenthetically in the text.

6. See, e.g., James Ferguson, "Prefaces to *Jerusalem*," in *Interpreting Blake: Essays*, selected and ed. Michael Phillips (London, New York and Melbourne: Cambridge University Press, 1978), 164–195, or more recently, Fred Dortorte, *The Dialectic of Vision: Contrary Readings of William Blake's "Jerusalem"* (Barrytown, NY: Station Hill Arts, 1998).

7. Ed. Maria Leach (New York: Funk & Wagnalls, 1972).

8. The most recent biography of Blake is Gerald E. Bentley, Jr.'s *Stranger from Paradise: A Biography of William Blake* (New Haven: Yale University Press, 2001).

9. John Adlard, in *The Sports of Cruelty: Fairies, Folk-songs, Charms & Other Country Matters in the Work of William Blake* (London: C. & A. Woolf,

1972), discusses giants in Blake's work, but makes no mention of Jack the Giant Killer.

10. As we shall see, there is some confusion about the distinction between Midianites and Moabites. Numbers 25:1–8 speaks specifically of the "whoring" of the Moabite women, but these women are clearly associated with the "Midianite woman" who, with her Israelite lover, is killed by Phinehas. In Numbers 31:16, Moses speaks specifically about the Midianite women and children, even though he seems to have the sexual transgression of the Moabite women in mind. The confusion may be explained by the fact that the Midianites were a populous tribe, many of whom lived in Moab, a smaller region along the southeastern Dead Sea. Where the biblical text is explicit in referring to one nation or the other, I have kept that reference, but the exegetical tradition has generally made little of the distinction.

11. This reference to the book of Numbers in the King James Version and a later reference to the Epistles are to *The Holy Bible* (Nashville: Thomas Nelson Publishers, 1972). References to Plaut are to *The Torah: A Modern Commentary*, ed. W. Gunther Plaut (New York: Union of Hebrew Congregations, 1981).

12. *The Pentateuch and Haftorahs*, ed. J. H. Hertz, second ed. (London, Soncino Press, 1971), 627.

13. "Romantic Displacements: Representing Cannibalism," in *Placing and Displacing Romanticism*, ed. Kitson (Aldershot: Ashgate, 2001), 204.

14. Trans. G. Gregory (Boston: Joseph T. Buckingham, 1815), 286–287.

15. Collected by Micha Joseph bin Gorion, ed. Emanuel bin Gorion, trans. I. M. Lask, intro. Dan Ben-Amos, 3 vols. (Bloomington and London: Indiana University Press, 1976), 1:77.

16. *Mimekor Yisrael*, 1:78.

17. *Mimekor Yisrael*, 1:86–87.

18. *Scripture and Tradition in Judaism*, Haggidic Studies, second rev. ed. (Leiden: Brill, 1973), 175–176. The J, E, D, and P designations derive from the "Documenatary Hypothesis" of how the Torah was written. This hypothesis, in one form or another the most commonly accepted theory today, argues that the Torah was written at different times and by different authors before being put into its canonical form by a redactor. "J" is so called because the author refers to God as "YHVH" or "Jehovah" in English; "E," roughly contemporary with J, is so called because the author refers to God as "Elohim." The "D" author contributed Deuteronomy. "P" stands for the "priestly" author(s); P is generally accepted to have been written at several times over perhaps 500 years, but also includes the latest additions to the Torah, including Numbers chapters 25–36. For a discussion of the Documentary Hypothesis, see W. Gunther Plaut's "General Introduction to the Torah," in his edition of the Torah, xxi–xxiv, or Edward L. Greenstein, "Sources of the Pentateuch," in *Harper's Bible Dictionary*, gen. ed. Paul J. Achtemeier (San Francisco: Harper & Row, 1985), 983–986.

19. Vermes, *Scripture and Tradition*, 174.

20. Vermes points out that Pseudo-Philo's *Biblical Antiquities (Liber Antiquitatum Biblicarum)* was published by G. Kisch in 1949 for the first time since the sixteenth century. Pseudo-Philo's work is generally dated from the first century C.E.

21. In *The Twickenham Edition of the Works of Alexander Pope*, vol. III, pt. ii, *Epistles to Several Persons (Moral Essays)*, ed. F. W. Bateson (London: Methuen;

New Haven: Yale University Press, 1951), 348. Bateson suggests that Pope had Thomas Pitt in mind in his depiction of Sir Balaam, assuming a correspondence between Pope's reference to a "Diamond" (361–364) and Pitt's immense profit from the resale of the Pitt Diamond.

22. In *The Riverside Milton*, ed. Roy Flannagan (Boston, New York: Houghton Mifflin, 1998).

23. *A Blake Dictionary: The Ideas and Symbols of William Blake*, revised ed. with a new foreword and annotated bibliography by Morris Eaves (Hanover and London: University Press of New England for Brown University Press, 1988), 36.

24. This discovery is documented in Jacob Milgrom's commentary in *The JPS Torah Commentary, Numbers: The Traditional Hebrew Text with the New JPS Translation* (Philadelphia and New York: Jewish Publication Society, 1990), 473–476.

25. The anti-Balaam tradition, of course, has it that after finding that he could not curse the Israelites, Balaam "persuaded the Midianites to seduce the Israelites at Baal-peor" (see Milgrom's commentary, 259).

26. Damon, *A Blake Dictionary*, 36.

27. Plaut, *The Torah*, 1230.

PART II

JEWISH WRITERS AND BRITISH CULTURE

CHAPTER 5

FOLLOWING THE MUSE: INSPIRATION, PROPHECY, AND DEFERENCE IN THE POETRY OF EMMA LYON (1788–1870), ANGLO-JEWISH POET

Michael Scrivener

There is no disputing that Emma Lyon's poetry has been neglected.[1] Her first and only volume of poetry was published in 1812 when she was twenty-three years old, as she enjoyed a brief moment of public attention. Her *Miscellaneous Poems*[2] was reviewed favorably but condescendingly in the *Monthly* and *Critical*, and Isaac Nathan (1792–1864), a former pupil at her father's boarding school, composed music for one of her songs, "The Soldier's Farewell," which was sung by the famous Jewish tenor, John Braham (1774–1856). (Nathan and Braham were involved with Lord Byron's *Hebrew Melodies* of 1815[3]). Also, in April of 1812, a poem of hers was sung at the annual meeting of a prominent charity, the Society of Friends of Foreigners in Distress. Lyon's literary career was beginning with some modest success, but her public career seems to have ended after she got married to Abraham Henry (1789–1840) in 1816 and gave birth to ten children between 1817 and 1830.[4] Some of her poetry after her marriage was recited at the Jews' Hospital and the Jews' Free School, and we know that she continued to write poetry but "*en amatrice*," as an amateur.[5] Her manuscript poems still might show up eventually, but as for now, they are not known to have survived.

Lyon's book was presented to the public as a charity case, not an unusual mode of publication for women in the eighteenth and nineteenth centuries. Lyon's apologetic preface declares that "necessity," not "choice," compelled her to publish her poetry as a way to raise money for her large family that was financially distressed because of the blindness of her father,

Solomon Lyon (1754–1820). The book was published by subscription, with most of the subscribers from Oxford, Cambridge, and Eton where Lyon had taught Hebrew. At ten shillings six pence a copy with over 350 subscribers, the book would have raised a considerable sum of money—over £151—for Emma Lyon and her fourteen siblings. One narrative to account for her short literary career is simply that because her father recovered his sight after his cataract operation in 1815 and because she married, the "necessity" that compelled her to publish no longer held sway. Moreover, she had children of her own to care for and from 1840, when her husband died, sole responsibility as parent. The repressive norm of female modesty that discouraged women's literary ambition would be powerful enough to account for Lyon's literary silence after 1812, but a prominent theme in Lyon's poetry is her poetic ambition, her relationship to the Muse and sources of cultural authority. Uncomfortably aware of the norms under which she wrote, she did not simply internalize those norms. Also, women with large families did indeed publish—Charlotte Smith (1749–1806), an obvious influence on Lyon's poetry, also had ten children—and women found numerous ways to work around the modesty norm, notably writers like Grace Aguilar (1816–1847) who defended Judaism within the parameters of the separate-spheres ideology.[6] As a first book by a twenty-three-year-old, *Miscellaneous Poems* is such a promising and ambitious effort that it is truly disconcerting that she published no more. Even as an only book, Lyon's work is interesting for a number of reasons: one of the first Anglo-Jewish women to publish poetry— the daughters Sophia and Charlotte of Jonathan "Jew" King seem to have been the first[7]—Lyon produced writing that raises issues of gender, religion, and cultural identity by means of exploring the implications of poetic inspiration. In my conclusion I speculate on why Lyon—both a promising Romantic and a silenced Victorian—did not publish any more of her poetry during her long lifetime.

Observers of women's eighteenth- and nineteenth-century poetry will remark on several things: women were not supposed to write poetry, but large numbers of women wrote anyway—and even larger numbers of women wrote in other genres as well, especially the romance and the novel. Prior to the full articulation of the "Angel in the House" norm that Virginia Woolf deconstructed in her "Professions for Women" (1942), separate-spheres ideology was powerful enough to force from almost every woman writer some gesture of visible obedience to its authority. The most interesting women writers also ironize this gesture and thereby call into question the entire ideology. Sandra Gilbert and Susan Gubar developed the concept of a "poetics of duplicity" to describe women's writing and that concept pertains to certain aspects of Lyon's poetry.[8] Gilbert and Gubar write of "submerged meanings"—"meanings hidden within or behind the more accessible, 'public' content of [women's] works, so that their literature could be read and appreciated even when its vital concern with female dispossession and disease was ignored" (72). These "palimpsestic" texts "simultaneously" conform to and subvert "patriarchal literary standards" (82). I set aside here the question of whether it is only women's writing that operates under a poetics of duplicity and suggest that part of Lyon's work seems to be palimpsestic in the way described by Gilbert and Gubar. Lyon appears to obey the rules of female modesty, but contrary meanings frequently undermine the modest persona. She writes of both her "blushing Muse" (*Miscellaneous Poems* 3) afraid of public notice and an insistently ambitious desire for fame and authority that is realized most boldly in her assuming the role of an inspired prophet. She sometimes employs allegory or other forms of literary indirection to undermine modesty, and she also simply contradicts the modesty norm as though she were not doing anything transgressive. Her strategy is reminiscent of the method of concealment in Poe's story, "The Purloined Letter," where the best hiding place is in open view. I maintain that she can so boldly violate the norms she elsewhere upholds because of the process of framing: her poetry is carefully framed as culturally deferential, so that the actual poetry has much latitude of expression. Deferential framing is so omnipresent in women's writing that we notice usually only when it is absent, as in Mary Wollstonecraft, not when it is routinely present, as in Charlotte Smith's preface to the sixth edition of *Elegiac Sonnets* (1792), where she self-deprecatingly devalues her literary accomplishments by pointing to the sphere that really counts for women: "The post of honour is a private station."[9]

As a woman and a Jew, Lyon wrote at two removes from the cultural norm. As an observant Jew, she wrote poetry that does not seem to have offended her largely Christian readership; only about 7 percent of her subscribers appear to be Jewish. At a time when there were intensive efforts in London to convert Jews to Christianity, when an emerging model for the woman writer was the pious Christian,[10] Lyon deployed a sentimental idiom of personifications to explore the issues of poetic identity in one part of the book, and in another she used poetic versions of nine psalms to affirm Jewish values not obviously incompatible with Christian values. When her final poem expresses an urgent messianic hope, the palimpsestic text both refers to a Jehovah with whom Christian readers of the King James Bible would have been familiar, and echoes for Jewish readers liturgical invocations of the Messiah. One strategy, then, is a rhetorical Judeo-Christian approach, avoiding those points of irreconcilable difference between Christianity and Judaism.

Before the reader gets to the poetry as such, the reader's perception gets shaped by a strenuous framing process. The structure of the poetry's public meaning was fashioned by the subscription mode of publication, the dedication to Princess Charlotte, and the apologetic preface. Lyon performs a "respectful deference" (ix–x) to the cultural authorities in order for her work to be published in the subscription format. Deference is inscribed in the title page: "Miscellaneous Poems, / by / Miss Emma Lyon, / Daughter of the Rev. S. Lyon, / Hebrew Teacher." The title page highlights her status as daughter who omits any mention of herself being a teacher of Hebrew. The adjective "miscellaneous" suggests a lack of structure and pattern in the volume of poems, but in fact, the book has been shaped into a discernible form hardly as careless as the word miscellaneous would suggest. As one proceeds from the title page, there are further layers of deferential gesturing. The whole second page is a dedication to Princess Charlotte, who is the occasion for the volume's very first poem, occupying pages three and four. Lyon has placed the royal most favored by the Whigs and liberals in the position of patroness. Lyon then assumes a self-deprecating tone appropriate for the obligatory apologetic preface: her writing is "simple," her imagination "uncultivated," and "necessity" not "choice" brings her unworthy productions before the public. Then follows the list of subscribers, "respectable" to say the least: six royals, innumerable Oxford, Cambridge, and Eton worthies, concluding with a list of names from the Society of Friends of Foreigners in Distress, a well-known charity supported by the political elite. If the academic, religious, political, and social leaders have attached their names and money to a publication, then one can only assume that the poetry is ideologically inoffensive.

Thus is the way the reviews treat Lyon's volume, as the two reviews accept the book's appeal for charity, and exempt her poetry from the ordinary aesthetic strictures. In the *Critical Review*, the actual poetry of the "authoress" is not taken seriously, as only one ode ["Stanzas to the Moon"] is mentioned, and almost all the attention in the brief review is to the preface and the dedication to Princess Charlotte.[11] Neither review mentions Emma Lyon's religion or preoccupation with poetic identity, nor does either review comment on the ambitious nine metrical psalm paraphrases. The *Monthly Review* refers to Lyon's "pretty little poems."[12] The reviewers are correctly reading according to the public script dictated by the deferential framing. However, there is a subtext of discontent, ambition, and protest that undermines the overall appearance of cultural harmony and that appears in almost all the poems, not just the psalms.

The 152 pages of *Miscellaneous Poems* consist of fifty-seven separate poems of several different kinds: most are short odes using personifications and a sentimental idiom; there are three sonnets, six ballads or songs, one blank-verse meditation, and nine "Paraphrases upon Psalms." Lyon relies on rhymed quatrains, usually pentameter or tetrameter, for thirty of her fifty-seven poems, and more than a third of the poems are in couplets. One prominent theme in the poetry is her relationship to her muse and to poetry in general. Poetry gives extraordinary pleasure, but her gender, her social situation, and especially her lack of a classical education seem to disqualify her from becoming a complete poet. Nevertheless, she speaks of her vocation as a poet, even a prophetic calling. When she tells us that "necessity" alone compels her to publish her poetry, we also know that she expresses herself with such enthusiasm about the pleasures of poetry even from "earliest infancy" (Preface, vii).

Many of the poems explicitly explore "inspiration" as it affects and is affected by cultural authority. The poetry is ambivalent about "fame" and its attendant processes, like competition, envy, and masculine power, but the nine psalms and final poems that conclude the volume resolve the ambivalence by incorporating the earlier figures of inspiration into a model of prophecy and by transforming poetic ambition into eagerness to spread the wisdom of God.

The book's first poem positions Lyon in relation to the dominant masculine culture in "Address to the University of Oxford." Her "weak" feminine Muse hesitantly and tremblingly appears among "contemplation's studious sons" (l. 2). While ostensibly describing her situation as a timid, unlearned young woman, these lines also record a note of protest:

> Had it been mine in learning's path to tread,
> The Muse, perchance, had smil'd as fancy led:
> But fortune's cloud gloom'd o'er my earliest hour,
> And cares domestic drove me from her bow'r;
> Or I had haply trac'd each mystic page,
> And reap'd, like you, the fruits of ev'ry age.
>
> (ll. 13–18)

It is hardly just gender that kept her from learning at Oxford; Jews, of course, could not enroll at either Cambridge or Oxford where her father could teach Hebrew, but not with the full privileges of a professing Christian. She also declares throughout the book a muse that is hobbled by a lack of learning, a lack about which she is not quiet, so that while she appears to be modest, making no excessive claims for her writing, she is also calling attention to an injustice.

The second piece, "Lines to D. F*****, Esq. Barrister," is another poem of positioning, in this case in relation to a gentile friend, Daniel French, the husband of one of her good friends, to whom she also writes a poem. Providing encouraging advice and a sympathetic reading of her work, Daniel French was one of Emma Lyon's Hebrew students, and he intervened on her behalf shortly after the publication of the book when she was assaulted by a William Simmons, who lived in the same London building as Emma Lyon.[13] (I discuss this incident in the conclusion.) A "patron," a sympathetic mediator between herself and the public before which her "blushing Muse still shrinks" (l. 10), French validates the poet's sincerity, honesty, and modesty—her "moral" status, in short. It is almost as if he is cosigning a loan she is taking out, in this case, a purchase on the reading public's attention. As a gentile barrister, he can play the role of authorizing presence to permit Lyon's imagination to explore her relationship with her muse, who is called here "Goddess" and addressed in the second person. The classical idiom of the Muses and their shrine describes her relationship to her own poetry in many of the other forty-seven poems that precede the nine psalm paraphrases; in these poems there is a proliferation of female deities and female-gendered personifications that provide the basis for Lyon's poetics.

The tribute to French is an important poem because the patterns it establishes recur throughout the book. The poem has a five-part structure, beginning with a prologue (ll. 1–14) that pays tribute to French's generosity and encouragement while echoing the preface in renouncing poetic ambition: "No thought of fame, or yet ambitious pride / Bade me all fearful to the world confide" (ll. 7–8). Before these forbidden masculine values of competition, her Muse blushes and shrinks, but the speaker's first encounter with the Muse (ll. 15–36) seems to come from the world of Romance. After "heaven's sweet zephyrs play'd around my head" and first breathing in for the first time "[t]hy sweets, fair fancy," she vows and prays to the Muse, her goddess, who then speaks to her:

> Sure some rude thorn
> Impels to seek me in life's early morn;
> They seldom wander near my mystic cell,
> Whom pleasure has not bid a long farewell.
> But if thou com'st a lonely hour to cheer,
> Remember! 'tis not happiness dwells here:
> The pow'r I boast is but to soothe the mind,
> When cares perplex, and fortune low'rs unkind.
>   (ll. 25–32)

The Muse sternly directs the poet to stay within the bounds (and bonds) of female modesty, but the Muse also speaks of the power and creativity of imagination, as well as a "mystic" (l. 58) power to which only the few, the elect, and the spiritual elite ever have access. Although only those who are unhappy seek the Muse for solace, the pleasures of poetry seem more than just compensatory and therapeutic. The Muse's words are described thus: "so gently flow'd / Each accent sweet, that still my bosom glow'd; / Still long'd to trace the varying shades of rhyme, / And catch the glimm'rings of a thought sublime" (ll. 33–36). Like someone who has just fallen in love, she realizes that her body, her feelings, and her intellect long for the presence of her Muse.

Precisely at this moment of her greatest pleasure—acquainting herself with her desire and identity as a poet—and her greatest embarrassment when she is aware of her poetic inadequacies in relation to the source of her inspiration, she returns to the figure of French for reassurance and guidance (ll. 37–54). As a gentile man supposedly educated in the most prestigious kinds of secular poetry, he is Lyon's projection of cultural authority, whether he was really knowledgeable or not. By thanking French so profusely, she distracts herself and us from the more powerful and decisive encounter with her Muse who reappears in the next section side by side with French (ll. 55–72). French's presence both authorizes the Muse, "the fair Queen" (l. 62), and her "Sisters" (l. 58), and acts like a restraint on the Muse. Lyon steels herself against harsh criticism with the following logic: if French approves of the poetry, then so will the critics (ll. 65–66). Reassured and strengthened, she turns again to her Muse, referring to the necessity of *reining* her "erring fancy" with "wisdom" because of all that she lacks: an education in Milton, Homer, and Virgil (ll. 67–71). For effect, she seems to be exaggerating her ignorance and unfamiliarity with Milton and classical culture. Through several allusions it is evident she has read Milton, at least *Paradise Lost*, and it would have been quite unremarkable for her to have had access to Homer and Virgil through the numerous translations. Her son remarks that his mother Emma Lyon was "well educated" and received at Cambridge University "exceptional educational opportunities"—"an astounding thing in her days."[14] Nevertheless, here and elsewhere the poem's speaker abases herself before the icon of a masculine, gentile, classical culture whose authority she seems to accept, but whose figures of the Muses and model of inspiration she makes her own. "Milton" seems to signify a forbidding cultural authority throughout the volume, but this same "Milton" also authorizes poetic inspiration and the figures of the muses. The effect the poem is seeking is a continuation of the deferential framing process: by accepting her inferiority, even by exaggerating her lack of knowledge, she pacifies the censorious authority that otherwise would question the poetry's ideological soundness. The very Muse that will ultimately rule over an alternative poetic world developed throughout the volume of poetry receives a symbolic imprimatur in the first two poems through Lyon's strategic representation of French, Oxford, and classical culture.

The allegory that concludes the poem (ll. 73–88) depicts "Nature's" Muse in whose garden she is a lowly, orphaned "weed" (l. 74) afflicted by a "tempest" (l. 76); she finds shelter and comfort with "thee, poor Muse" (l. 80) who oversees the trembling, unchecked, unguided strivings of the novice poet who looks toward the "rich wand'rings" (l. 87) of the Muse's genius. A classical education seems too remote to acquire but to develop from a "weed" to something more attractive in the garden of her Muse does not seem impossible. Allegorically her "poor" Muse is the same one that inspires the "wisdom" and "genius" of "classic" culture which she only "in vain" tries to imitate, but the Muse provides her with "a sheltering home" (ll. 80, 86–88). There are two effects that the concluding section produces, a secure sense of belonging to and being accepted by the feminine Muse, and an extreme, if not theatrical sense of inferiority to the "bright effusions of a tow'ring mind" (l. 82) identified with the masculine classical culture. The book as a whole depicts a conflict between these two centers of value, the poet's own validating and supportive feminine Muse, and a disapproving masculine culture. The conflict is also between a culture of sensibility and a neoclassical culture.

A cluster of eight other poems develops the figures, images, symbols, and logic of the inspirational model Lyon is adopting ("Ode to Genius," "An Ode on Solitude," "An Ode to Sleep," "Lines to the Muse," "An Ode on Death," "An Ode on Sympathy," "An Ode on the Fear of Criticism," and "Lines to Melancholy"). Inspired poetry, which is distinct from classically educated poetry, is aligned with the values of sensibility, like solitude, melancholy, suffering, authentic feeling, and existential truth. Using "An Ode to Genius," I illustrate the way a single poem works through aspects of poetic inspiration. First, I quote the poem in full:

All glorious power! Of keen celestial eye,
   Genius! tumultuous ruler of the breast,

By nature wing'd with wond'rous speed to fly,
    Yet seldom visiting an earthly guest!

Descend for once with all thy glowing fire,
    And make my soul thy transitory shrine:
Or oh! Forgive me if I deck my lyre
    With gems or ornaments that are not thine!

Come, guide my fancy when it seeks the Muse
    That still to thee directs her daring flight!
Through my chill veins one gentle beam infuse
    Of splendor, visible to mortal sight!

Lead to the bow'rs where haunt thy heavenly train,
    And I will distant watch their mystic tread;
From their rich harvest glean the scatter'd grain,
    To weave a band fantastic for my head.

By me unenvied, flattering crowds may throng,
    Where Poets trace the never-varying round;
If thou, bright genius! animate my song,
    My name shall live, with endless glory crown'd.

"An Ode to Genius" suggests a compensation for the lack of a classical education: "genius" descends to inspire the poet with unexpected, indeterminate creativity whose sources are once again the Muse and her "mystic" and "fantastic" powers. The last two lines of this five-stanza poem affirm competition for fame in a way the tribute to French seemed to make impossible: "If thou, bright genius! animate my song, / My name shall live, with endless glory crown'd" (ll. 19–20). Nowhere in the poem can one find expressions of female modesty and the apologetic "necessity" that compels the reluctant poet to make her verse public. Inspiration, introduced in the French poem, provides Lyon with a poetic model that is both classical (deriving from Plato's *Ion* and other classical sources), and anticlassical in its sensibility-based values. The most authentic kind of poetry, according to Lyon, is poetry that is unwilled, spontaneous, "descending" from somewhere outside the self and momentarily dwelling within the soul. One can hear anticipations of Keats's preference for poetry coming as naturally as the leaves on a tree—or not at all—or Shelley's descriptions of inspiration in his *Defence of Poetry*. The moment of inspiration is intense but momentary— "transitory" (l. 6). The fourth stanza suggests Ruth gleaning the barley, as Lyon imagines herself in the Muse's bowers, looking on from a distance, and coming later to pick up the remnants of the most glorious moments of inspiration (when composition begins, as Shelley said, inspiration is already waning). Despite the modesty of the gesture, she also imagines making for herself a "band fantastic" for her head. The final stanza contrasts Lyon with the poets whose creativity is diminished by uniformity but who nevertheless enjoy the attention of the "flattering crowds"; if Lyon's prayers for inspiration are granted, she will not envy the popular poets. One must also take note of the poem's stanzaic form, its appropriating Gray's "Church-Yard" elegy for the obscure, the mute inglorious Miltons, the socially and culturally marginal without a voice.

Other poems develop different aspects of the sensibility repertoire of themes. The compensation for alienated solitude is a sense of power from "wisdom" and "the purest joy" from "melancholy" ("Ode on Solitude"). Melancholy is also a "goddess" and "[s]orceress" with the powers of "magic" ("Lines to Melancholy," ll. 1, 9). The enchanted ground of poetry is not exclusively feminine, for Lyon also writes of solitude's "sequester'd grove, / Where sons of contemplation rove!" ("Ode on Solitude," ll. 5–6). The moon is the symbol of creativity that shines upon the insomniacs who are estranged from the sun-drenched world where the wicked prosper and the innocent suffer ("An Ode to Sleep" and "An Ode on the Fear of Criticism"). The poet experiences common ties with the criminal, another victim of "fate" and "fortune" ("Lines to the Muse"). Assisted by the Moon and the Muse, the poet's feminine mentors and protectors, she combats the masculine cultural powers and produces a "wild" song:

> Me hope inspires, with whisp'ring breath,
>   To tempt the air sublime,
> To triumph o'er the shades of death
>   And injuries of time.
>
> But lo! The Critics' grizly band!
>   That dash the fairest crown,
> Already lift the wasteful hand
>   To hurl me trembling down.
>
> Yet still in fields where fame is sought,
>   For fame shall Emma sigh,
> And shudder at the dismal thought,
>   To close th' inglorious eye.
>
> Still wildly singing all night long,
>   While Cynthia wond'ring views,
> With rude simplicity of song
>   Call down th' inspiring Muse.
>   ("An Ode on the Fear of Criticism")

Although the published reviews of her book were not harshly critical, even if they were condescending, the imagined critics are severe, forbidding, and violent, as they "dash" the crown from the head, and "hurl" her down. The imaginary conflict with masculine critics perhaps reflects the treatment of Anna Barbauld's ambitious poem, *Eighteen Hundred and Eleven*; the harsh criticism ended the poetic career of one of the most prominent women poets at the time.[15] The "fame" that Lyon and women are not supposed to want inspires the poem's speaker to attempt the arduous "sublime" represented effectively in the poem's last stanza where her alienation, solitude, insomnia, and persistence are turned into a striking image of almost Maenad-like abandon and fierceness. Although called here by its classical name, Cynthia, Lyon also may have had in mind the significance of the Moon in Judaism, as the Jewish calendar is lunar, not solar, and special women's observances sometimes commemorated the new moon (*Rosh Hodesh*). The last six lines of "Lines to Melancholy," however, strike another note—of depression and abjection—that is also a part of this cluster of poems.

> But not to me, with kind relief,
> Thy [Melancholy's] soft approach e'er tempers grief;
> Thou doom'st me all the sighs to know,
> That lay thy destin'd victim low;
> And these worn eyes with tears to steep,
> Till time brings on eternal sleep!

Echoing perhaps Charlotte Smith, the great poet of abjection and gloom, Lyon imagines her poet figure being felled not by the masculine cultural powers but by the feminine power of melancholy, one of the goddesses. Fresh creativity emerges from the pain and isolation of the suffering woman poet, but that same condition for creativity is also fatal to the well-being of the poet as a human being. The poet thrives on the misery of the person, a terrible paradox developed with frightening rigor much later by Sylvia Plath in her final poems.[16]

There is a similar dialectic of hope and despair in the four poems on the seasons. It is not until the final poem on winter that Lyon is able to balance the awareness of time, mortality, and the ephemeral nature of existence—the *tempus fugit* theme that is prominent in works like *Kohelet* (Ecclesiastes) in the Hebrew Bible—with a sense of inner power and poetic strength, a confidence in the effectiveness of the "visionary light" (l. 28) from the Muse to dispel the dreariness of cyclical temporality. Poetry, the imagination, the creative mind can overcome nature, but nature too overcomes poetry: "Sweet Hope, thy fair anchor my motto shall be, / My soul shall repose, tho' deluded, in thee" ("Sonnet on Hope," ll. 13–14).

One image Lyon provides for the wages of hope is the love-lorn woman who is desperate or even mad. In "Stanzas to the Moon" a lonely, unhappy "Ellen" wanders alone in the moonlight, praying to the moon for mental relief. Those who have what they want are peacefully asleep, while those who yearn for what they cannot have disturb the night with their entreaties. The effectively anapestic song, "The Maniac," is another representation of the love-lorn woman, this time "Anna," who becomes another instance of Lyon's transcendence. Still a third poem, "Willow," represents another woman character—Agnes—who has lost her lover and is distraught and sleepless. Although conventional, these moony women with disyllabic names (like Emma) symbolize a desire that cannot be satisfied in the sunny world where the powerful rule over the weak and suffering.

The companion piece to the opening poem on Oxford is the "Lines Addressed to the University of Cambridge," her second poetic encounter with the established culture. As in the first, there are moments of humiliation and weakness, as she calls herself "unletter'd" with "my rural verse" (l. 9), but there is also here a stronger sense of inspiration and its power, as she affirms her "wild" song with its "ethereal fire" as she attempts to "catch Divinity's inspiring breeze" (ll. 23–25, 37). Indeed, here is a rare instance when the lack of a classical education becomes a virtue: "No learning checks me as I wildly sing" (l. 23). The tribute to Cambridge's Bacon, Newton, and Milton acquires some ironic edge as the poem enacts a performative contradiction: she makes a poetic homage to the great minds of the past, but she is not supposed to have the authority to make such a tribute. There is also an intriguing contrast between the blind Milton and his daughters, and the blind Solomon Lyon and his poetic daughter, as Solomon's blindness is the condition, which enables the daughter to become a public poet, whereas Milton's daughters were merely used to record the father's verse. The "Sonnet to my Father" expresses strong affection for the man who most likely taught Lyon Hebrew well enough to be able to teach it herself; indeed, her teaching Hebrew like her father indicates a degree of identification with the father one sees with some other women writers like Maria Edgeworth.[17] There is also the tradition of the rabbi's exceptional daughter whose intellectual brilliance was recognized, if begrudgingly. The most famous example of the type was Beruriah, wife of R. Meir, daughter of R. Hanina ben Teradion. Of Beruriah it was said that she could "master three hundred *Halakhot* [religious laws or practices] a day."[18] Rather than be overwhelmed by the priority of Milton—or the authority of her father—she finds a way to use an aspect of his poetry—and her father's learning—for her own purposes.

From Milton she makes use of his model of inspiration, which she then thoroughly feminizes. Lyon adds to her feminine pantheon in "An Ode to Sorrow" by installing in it Minerva, goddess of wisdom, and Cecilia, saint of music. Perhaps the latter was influenced by Pope's "Ode for Musick, on St. Cecilia's Day," a poem that includes other elements which recur in Lyon's book, including melancholy, the muses, sleep, envy, and inspiration. Even the form of the short, Horatian ode that Lyon uses frequently (twenty-three times) could have been modeled after Pope's five-stanza, twenty-line "Ode to Solitude."[19]

A minor but not insignificant theme in Lyon's book is political, especially protesting against war. In "Beggar-Boy," before the happy ending resolves the action, a press-gang, still quite active in 1812, has separated a father from his family. The existence of the unpopular war is also registered in a poem like the "Soldier's Farewel," while "Wild Roses" is an effective song about begging, an activity of which there was no shortage in the famine year of 1812, the year also of Luddite riots. Her most Shelleyan poem, "An Ode on Hope," of course precedes Shelley's mature work by a number of years, so there is no question of influence—unless Shelley was influenced by her, a real possibility.[20] In this poem there is an apocalyptic hope—"Celestial bliss may yet be nigh"—(l. 8) attached to volcanic imagery that works just as Shelley's symbolism of revolution does: pent up, repressed energies are bursting from confinement with violent heat and explosive light, as the emergence of the new entails destruction as well as birth. The "ensanguin'd field" (l. 82) of the last stanza alludes to the war, a symptom of the historical disturbance that seems to portend mighty changes. The Shelleyan current in her work is safely ensconced in the middle parts of the book, the radicalism of which is disguised somewhat by the same kind of abstractions that Shelley also used.

However artful and interesting are the poems of sensibility that describe her emergent and conflicted poetic identity, the nine psalm paraphrases are surprising for their confident voice, as though the poet had finally discovered the kind of poetry she could write without self-division. Also, hardly any of the other poems even allude to God or religious themes, so the turn to explicitly biblical material is surprising; the dominant theme of the other poems is inspiration with rarely even hints at a religious motif. The psalms are not necessarily "pretty little poems," as the *Monthly Review* called her poetry, but could be read as ambitiously competitive and culturally central, especially if her psalm paraphrases suggested an engagement with theology rather than merely pious sentiment.[21] Lyon's prestigious precedents include the metrical paraphrases by Isaac Watts, Thomas Sternhold, and John Hopkins; moreover, as liturgy in the Christian churches the psalms were hardly peripheral. Lyon achieves continuity with the rest of the poetry in her book, however, by turning inspiration away from a sentimental idiom and toward a biblical, prophetic discourse, and she does so in a provocatively bold manner, presenting herself as a prophetic voice inspired by God. Her turn from a sentimental to a biblical idiom mediated by the figure of inspiration suggests the validity of Jon Mee's contention that the discourse of "enthusiasm" was broad enough to encompass different styles and ideological commitments.[22]

Beginning in the sixteenth century and influentially justified in Sir Philip Sidney's *Apologie for Poetrie* (1595), translated, metrical psalms were seen not just as devotional texts but also as poetry.[23] Thomas Wyatt's "highly introspective and complex translations" of the Penitential Psalms, which were well outside the parameters of devotional literature,[24] were published in 1550,[25] preceding the ambitious metrical versions of the psalms by Sidney himself and his sister.[26] By the late sixteenth century, according to Rivkah Zim, psalm paraphrases were a secure literary kind that required no special pleading.[27] The writing of psalm paraphrases was viewed as a type of imitation that was not "an inferior, non-creative activity."[28] The poet–translator was "not obliged to preserve the author's meaning in the author's words" but the expectation was that the paraphrase would be "respectful" of the "original author's meaning." Readers were so familiar with the psalms that a paraphrase's proximity or distance from the original was an aesthetic variable, so that the paraphrase generated a kind of palimpsest effect, with the poet's own version imposed on the already existing version—which for Emma Lyon's audience would have been the King James translation.[29] Two other versions of the psalms were so well known as to constitute yet another layer of context, the Sternhold–Hopkins metrical psalms (1562)—the most popular volume of verse published in the early modern period[30]—and especially Isaac Watts's version, of which there were numerous editions in the eighteenth and nineteenth centuries.[31]

Lyon's choice of nine psalms reflects her preoccupation with inspiration and social justice, as she makes two emphases: validating the poet as God's prophet inspired by God's wisdom, and vindicating God's justice in a world where the wicked seem to prosper while the righteous seem only to suffer. Her paraphrases also accentuate language, orality and consciousness, bringing into prominence a linguistic stress and an inwardness present in the original but heightened by Lyon. Three of the psalms she chooses are didactic, coming out of the "wisdom" tradition (19, 49, 73); two are prophetic exhortations (50, 58); others are a liturgy (15), a royal psalm (72), a Zion hymn (76), and a psalm of individual confidence (91). She notably ignores all the Penitential Psalms, general hymns, and laments (more than half of all the psalms are within these three subgenres).[32] To illustrate the overall quality of the psalm paraphrases, I discuss two.

The psalm first presented is Psalm 19, which is striking for its last stanza that is only tangentially related to the original. She turns the Authorized Version's verse 14, the last verse, "Let the words of my mouth, and the meditation of my heart, be acceptable in thy sight, O Lord, my strength, and my redeemer," into the following:

> O Thou, who erst on David's holiest lyre,
> Didst dart thy sacred vehemence of fire,
>   Come, teach me to reveal thy ways,
>   And scatter round a dazzling blaze;
> Unfolding bright, inspir'd with silent awe,
> The' unclouded prospect of thy heavenly law!
> (ll. 55–60)

The actual Hebrew of verse 14 is *"y'hu l'ratzon imrei fi v'higion libi lifanecha Adonai tsuri v'goali,"* a very familiar sentence spoken in the prayers after the *Amidah*;[33] it is something with which Lyon would have been entirely familiar. Lyon transforms a cluster of words that deals with the proper state of mind for praying into a statement about prophetic inspiration. The grammar shifts from a petitionary "may" to an invocatory "come" and "scatter." The stanza here is not unlike the last stanza of Shelley's "Ode to the West Wind," where the imperative verbs call for prophetic power. From God to David to Emma Lyon, the divine authority passes, as the stanza invokes God's power in a way that is at once modest—she is after all *praying* for inspiration—and bold—she is claiming the mantle of a prophet. She is deferring to traditional authority but transgressing the gender code, vowing obedience to God's law but claiming for herself a role, one that was not permitted at the time by religious institutions, in transmitting the law.

Although Psalm 19 is one of David's psalms in everyone's canon, the final stanza explicitly distinguishes between a first-person speaker and David. The only way to read Lyon's paraphrase, then, is to read the first-person in the eighth stanza as referring to Lyon, not David, or better, Lyon impersonating David, appropriating his role, his status, prestige, and authority:

> O give me, Lord! Thy glorious tracks to see,
> To find my solace and delight in thee;
>   To feel that holy fear within,
>   That makes it agony to sin;
> Thy laws are amiable and sweet indeed,
> As virgin honey from the flowery mead!
>   (ll. 42–48)

In one sense, what could be more pious and socially inoffensive than psalm paraphrases, one of the genres deemed feminine enough for women writers? In another sense, what could be more daring for a twenty-three-year-old Jewish woman in the early nineteenth century than assuming the Davidic role? As the first paraphrase, as the only psalm appearing out of order, its importance has to be ascribed to the role of prophet Lyon is here assuming.

Other psalm paraphrases also develop the theme of prophetic election. In Psalm 15, the fourth stanza focuses on the idea of prophetic poetry: "Who dares to give free utterance to truth, / Beneath the frowns of a tyrannic foe" (ll. 15–16). First, the idea of speaking truth to power is nowhere to be found in the original Psalm 15, and second, speaking truth to power reinforces the theme of prophetic vocation that she introduced in Psalm 19. The person worthy of God's favor, then, is a fearless prophet who also—in the last stanza—protests against and sheds tears over the "undeserv'd" sufferings of the "good." The idea of undeserved suffering, which is also lacking in the original Psalm 15, is another important theme in Lyon's psalms. Lyon turns Psalm 49 into a poem about inspiration and vindicating the morally worthy who are not socially powerful. Psalm 50, originally about divorcing ritual sacrifice from truly moral behavior, Lyon makes into a prophetic address to the "priests" about the false and true "music" for God. The next paraphrase, of Psalm 58, another prophetic exhortation, continues to distinguish between corrupt and innocent speech by contrasting "words of innocence" with "guile," "falsehood," flattery, seduction, "slander," and "deceit." Lyon's paraphrase of Psalm 72 mixes contemporary and historically remote references, plays with the equivalence of poet and king (both David and Solomon were poets), and supplies a subtext of political exhortation advocating justice for the poor, "the sons of toil" (l. 16) and "the orphan" (l. 34).

I want to examine closely Lyon's version of Psalm 49 for the way it brings together inspiration and prophetic statement that vindicates the morally righteous who are not socially powerful. The original is a wisdom psalm about the "transitory nature of wealth and pleasure" and the paradise with God that awaits the just man,[34] but Lyon makes her psalm relate to prophetic truth, as it lays claim to the allegiance of the "nations" (l. 1), the obedience of "royalty" (l. 3), and as it takes possession of the prophet herself:

> Heaven's holy Spirit breathes upon my lyre,
>   And cheers the fainting courage of my soul;
> The truths I sing no mortal tongues inspire,
>   From heaven's high fount the sacred numbers roll.
> (ll. 5–8)

The second line makes the reader think inevitably of the poet's self-doubt that has been developed throughout the volume. Whereas Psalm 19 invoked holy inspiration, in this paraphrase she can announce confidently that the "Spirit breathes upon my lyre." In the original Psalm 49 there is nothing whatsoever about inspiration, so that the innovation is wholly Lyon's. She also turns the psalm's message of the transience of wealth and pleasure into a mode of political protest as her paraphrase notes with satisfaction that the most powerful members of society cannot avoid death, the sublime equalizer. Lyon imagines the humiliation of the rich and powerful in their existential moment of facing their ultimate destiny: they either repress awareness or face a death they cannot comprehend.

> Slaves to the pride and emptiness of life,
>   Alone reflection is your deadly foe;
> But when she comes, with momentary strife,
>   Ye veil the gulph that ever yawns below.
> (ll. 41–44)

It is noteworthy that "reflection" is a she, joining Lyon's vast feminine pantheon of exalted virtues and powers. As the activity associated with reason and intellect, not feelings and sentiment, reflection is marked as feminine, counter to the gendered norms of the cultural code. The socially powerful, labeled here "the sons of crime" (l. 52), cannot avoid death or God's judgment, as even their immoral "fame" (l. 46) will not endure—anticipating Shelley's "Ozymandias" sonnet. Echoing traditional Jewish doctrine, the paraphrase affirms the immortality of the righteous. The Authorized Version's psalm lacks the edge of class conflict that is prominent in Lyon as well as in many of the metrical psalms in Isaac Watts's collection. The King James translation warns the rich man and gives him advice; Lyon's version gloats over his ruin and celebrates the triumph of the powerless. All three of the paraphrases of Psalm 49 in Watts's collection emphasize strongly the wickedness of the rich and the dire fate that awaits them; typical is the following quatrain in the conventional fourteener with alternating rhymes: "Why doth he [the man of riches] treat the poor with scorn, / Made of the self-same clay, / And boast as though his flesh was born / Of better dust than they?"[35] It appears that the poverty of the Lyon family, the widespread social suffering in 1812, and the specific disabilities and prejudices with which Jews were afflicted assisted Lyon's identification with other poor people and permitted her to draw upon the egalitarian themes in the Watts psalms.

If Lyon's paraphrases share the edge of class resentment in the Isaac Watts Psalter, they differ from Watts fundamentally in their Jewishness. The Watts psalms invoke, despite the anachronism, the name of Jesus Christ in numerous metrical paraphrases. The psalms were a secure part of the Christian liturgy and devotional service, both Catholic and Protestant. Her choice of psalms, the omissions and *midrashic* inventions in her paraphrases, and the subtle shadings have a this-worldly, ethical focus on social justice. She uses the psalms to establish her status as an inspired poet with prophetic authority, thus linking the earlier poems with the psalms.

The two poems that conclude her book, "Stanzas Sung with great applause at the Anniversary Meeting of the Society of Friends of Foreigners in Distress, Held at the New London Tavern, April 27, 1812," and "Conclusion," use nationalism and messianic hope to punctuate her complex treatment of poetic inspiration. She exploits her connection with the Society to emphasize her acceptance as a poet and as a moral agent by the most powerful members of society. Established in 1807, the Society of Friends of Foreigners in Distress granted "pecuniary relief and other assistance to FOREIGNERS of any nation in this country, who, from misfortune, may fall into distress" and who do not qualify for parish assistance. Of the over 4,000 people the Society had helped between 1807 and 1816, only a small number—forty—received "pensions" to stay in Britain, while the others were assisted in returning to their country of origin.[36] Two of the three trustees of the Society in 1816 were subscribers to Lyon's poetry, Sir William Paxton, and William Vaughan. The only other prominent Society figure who was a subscriber is D. H. Rucker—four of the Ruckers subscribed to Lyon's poetry. The Society was not designed to assist only or principally Jews, but Nathan Rothschild was one of the directors, and one of the fourteen "cases" represented in the 1816 report seems to be Jewish, although no one is identified by religion, only country (*Report* 13–21). A large proportion of those receiving assistance in 1816 were from the German-speaking parts of Europe, precisely where most of the Ashkenazi Jews—like Solomon Lyon from Bohemia who in his blindness could not, as a foreigner, seek parish assistance—came from who settled in Britain at that time. The Society provided a vehicle for helping foreign Jews in distress but in an ecumenical way that was not politically controversial. Indeed, the Society had the support of the royal family as well as the Russian and Prussian leaders.

She also uses her own identity as a needy outsider requiring assistance as a point of departure to establish Britain as a multicultural haven for exiles and victims of tyranny. The third stanza, which was censored at the Meeting, is restored in her book:

> When flying from a tyrant's sway
>   In quest of freedom's glorious ray,
> The famish'd exiles wander here,
>   Safe shelter'd from the murd'ring spear;
> They bless the hospitable Isle,
>   And through the clouds of sorrow smile,
> Reposing in the hallow'd rest
>   Of *Friends to Foreigners distrest!*

Probably because both the Russian and Prussian governments supported the Society and would not have appreciated these allusions to murderous tyranny, especially from a Jewish woman, the authorities in charge suppressed the stanza. Lyon's intention, however, is quite apparent: by flattering the generosity of the British, she hopes to generate a myth of national identity quite unlike what was actually normative in 1812. In fact, most of the recipients of aid from the Society were sent back to their country of origin; only the exceptional cases were permitted to receive aid and remain in Britain. Lyon's song does not go as far as Emma Lazarus's "The New Colossus," for the fourth stanza refers approvingly to the distressed foreigner returning to his native home, but the principle of assisting everyone who has a need, regardless of religion or national origin, in conjunction with the rhetoric of foreign tyrannies from which people are justifiably fleeing, prepares the way for the myth of a multicultural haven—something a later Anglo-Jewish writer, Grace Aguilar, will develop further.

The final poem in her volume affirms and underlines Lyon's role as an inspired prophet, as she invokes the source of poetic inspiration: "Descend, O Muse, with more than wonted fire, / Ere deadly silence steals upon my lyre" (ll. 1–2). The self-fashioned image of modest young woman fearful of public exposure is displaced with expressions of "soaring pride" in her spreading the name of Jehovah "far and wide" (l. 7). She echoes the sentiment of the *Aleinu* prayer[37] and assumes the messianic tones of the prophet Isaiah in her hope that all the nations will hearken to the divine message of social justice:

> A language that all nations hear
> Alike with one harmonious ear:
> No clime so dark, no ignorance so blind,
> But reads the splendor of th' Almighty mind.
>   (ll. 17–20)

The appeal here is as universal as the previous poem was nationalistic. Lyon has skillfully placed her Jewish themes in contexts designed to win favor with British, Christian readers. The pedagogy of her poetry implies a progressive revelation from multicultural nationalism to a higher universal emancipation. The final stanza affirms that God works an ethical effect through history by means of the exemplary "good man" whose "upright heart" and "pure unsullied hand" enjoy the protection of a militant God, who "fights" for the morally virtuous.

The anxiety about public poetry and transgressing her gender role is resolved by her writing nationalist and religious poetry that displaces the guilt of representation and competitive struggle onto political and moral conflict. The inadequacies of her education become less debilitating when the poetic subject is biblical and political. On the Hebrew Bible and the experiences of the outsider she is much more expert than the gentlemen from Oxbridge. Her ability to shift the terms of cultural debate in a way favorable to her suggests a sure grasp of the possibilities available to her within the kind of book she was permitted to write. These poems seem anything but "miscellaneous"; rather, the volume is a well-crafted whole with a very particular design. There is a progression from the earlier poems with their sentimental idiom, feminine pantheon of goddesses, nearly ecstatic celebrations of the inspired pleasures of poetry, and gloomy excursions into the melancholic world of madness and sleepless nights, to the self-assured psalms and final poems. There are numerous points of continuity between the secular–sentimental and religious–prophetic poems, including the themes of social justice and political protest, not just the inspirational model for creating poetry. With such strong command over her poetry, with such confidence, it is difficult to understand why she ceased publication after 1812. Perhaps the reason was not the modesty norm and the separate-spheres ideology but an episode of violence with which she would always associate her ambition and moment of fame. Perhaps she came to associate her moment of poetic glory with humiliation.

I return to the incident alluded to earlier when she was assaulted by William Simmons. According to the London *Times*, there were conflicting versions of what had happened in Emma Lyon's apartment building on the weekend of June 13–14, 1812. The version that was accepted by the jury is as follows: on Saturday Simmons engaged in "violent conduct" against Emma Lyon, so that when Daniel French and his wife visited her on Sunday, she was "confined to her room, by the very severe indisposition occasioned, as she informed Mrs. French, by the violent conduct of Mr. Simmons towards her." Mrs. French urged her husband to speak with William Simmons who lived in Emma Lyon's building. When Simmons heard the name of Emma Lyon, he called French "a damned Jew" and accused French of trying to murder him. A fight ensued between French, Simmons, and a friend of Simmons who was a "peace officer." French, who was beaten up, was dragged to a watch-house and kept in jail until ten o'clock at night when he was finally released by a magistrate. The version of events presented by Simmons and his friend Squires was that Daniel French attacked Simmons without any provocation; they made no mention apparently of the assault of Emma Lyon.

What can we make of this story? Let me offer a narrative that mixes fact and speculation: Emma Lyon is living alone in an apartment shortly after the publication of her poetry book and the public meeting where her poem—minus one crucial stanza—was read before royalty and dignitaries. She is teaching Hebrew and has just experienced the satisfaction of having assisted her large family. Her younger sisters take care of her father and the youngest siblings, so that her living alone is framed as one less mouth to feed. On Saturday, most likely she would have spent the Sabbath with her family and would have gone back to her apartment after sundown. Presumably, it was while she was returning on Saturday night that a possibly drunk Simmons confronted her. Was his violent conduct only verbal? If it were just verbal, would she have taken to her bed and confided first to Mrs. French? She was assaulted—at least verbally, perhaps physically—by a drunken, anti-Semitic

Simmons. After confiding to Mrs. French, Emma Lyon then witnesses her friend Daniel French beaten up, arrested, and tried for assaulting her attacker. Although French is acquitted and Simmons and his accomplice are convicted and sentenced to six months in the House of Correction, she now associates her literary ambition with violent anti-Semitism and public notoriety, if not shame, possibly rape. She had to testify in court on behalf of Daniel French, and we know she was accompanied by two of her brothers.

This incident might have decisively persuaded her to avoid further publication. The mainstream Jewish community of which she was a part did not prohibit women from publishing secular books, as the examples of the Moss sisters (Celia and Marion) and Grace Aguilar testify.[38] If, however, she associated efforts to promote her poetic fame with violence and public notoriety, she might have chosen to keep the rest of her poetry private. One cannot, however, underestimate the power of the separate-spheres ideology, with which Lyon struggled mightily in her single volume of poetry, to coerce women writers into silence and self-repression. Even a writer like Lyon—living on her own, teaching Hebrew at a time when even the issue of women's learning Hebrew was controversial within the Jewish community (and one can imagine how someone hostile to Jews and women might construe Emma Lyon giving Hebrew lessons to men), earning money for her family, and appropriating a prophetic role in her poetry—even she might not have been strong enough to overcome the cultural norm.

Notes

1. Versions of this chapter were given before several audiences whose comments and criticisms have improved the essay: at Wayne State University (Detroit, 2002), at the North American Society for the Study of Romanticism (NASSR) conference (London, Ontario, 2002), and at Temple University (Philadelphia, 2003).
2. (Oxford: J. Bartlett, 1812). The text is now available on-line through the University of California at Davis "British Women Romantic Poets" project <http://www.lib.ucdavis.edu/BWRP/Works/#L>.
3. Isaac Nathan, *A Selection of Hebrew Melodies, Ancient and Modern, and [text by] Lord Byron,* eds. Frederick Burwick and Paul Douglass (Tuscaloosa: University of Alabama Press, 1988).
4. A surprisingly large amount of information about Emma Lyon, her father Solomon, and the Lyon family has been published by one of the descendants of the family, Naomi Cream, in two publications, "Isaac Leo Lyon: The First Free Jewish Migrant to Australia?" *Journal of Australian Jewish Historical Society* 12:1 (1993): 3–16, and "Revd Solomon Lyon of Cambridge, 1755–1820," *Jewish Historical Studies* 36 (1999–2001): 31–69.
5. *The Jews Free School Governors Committee Minutes 1818–1831* of March 23, 1824 reports that at the anniversary dinner of February 11, one of the events was that "Amelia Adolphus . . . repeated an English Ode written by Mrs. Henry" (159). I thank Naomi Cream for this information. A letter (June 12, 1874) from her youngest son, Michael Henry (1830–1875), to historian James Picciotto (1830–1897), states that "[a]fter her marriage to my father, she

ceased to write except *en amatrice*; she wrote poems which were recited at public Institutions, such as Jews' Hospital, Jews' Free School & Society of friends for foreigners in distress. I have a printed poem of hers recited at the Free School 50 years ago." The letter (MS 116/59) is quoted by permission of the University of Southampton Library, Archives and Manuscripts.

6. On Aguilar, see Elizabeth Fay, "Grace Aguilar: Rewriting Scott Rewriting History," in *British Romanticism and the Jews: History, Culture, Literature*, ed. Sheila A. Spector (New York: Palgrave/Macmillan, 2002), 215–234. In this volume, see Judith W. Page's "Anglo-Jewish Identity and the Politics of Cultivation in Hazlitt, Aguilar, and Disraeli."

7. For the fascinating King sisters and their father, see Duncan Wu, *Romantic Women Poets* (Oxford: Blackwell, 1997), 358–363, and Todd M. Endelman, "The Chequered Career of 'Jew' King: A Study in Anglo-Jewish Social History," in Frances Malino and David Sorkin, ed., *From East and West. Jews in a Changing Europe, 1750–1870* (Oxford: Basil Blackwell, 1990), 151–181. On Charlotte Dacre's novel *Zofloya*, see Diane Long Hoeveler's contribution to this volume, "Charlotte Dacre's Zofloya: The Gothic Demonization of the Jew."

8. Susan Gubar and Sandra Gilbert, *The Madwoman in the Attic: The Woman Writer and the Nineteenth-Century Literary Imagination* (New Haven: Yale University Press, 1979), 82.

9. *Elegaic Sonnets, and Other Poems* (London: Jones and Company, 1827), ix.

10. For the importance of converting Jews, see Michael Ragussis, *Figures of Conversion: "The Jewish Question" and English National Identity* (Durham and London: Duke University Press, 1995); for the religious identity of the woman writer, see Cynthia Scheinberg, *Women's Poetry and Religion in Victorian England: Jewish Identity and Christian Culture* (Cambridge: Cambridge University Press, 2002).

11. 2 n.s. (Aug., 1812): 216.

12. 70 (Feb., 1813): 214.

13. 70 (Feb., 1813): 214.

14. Letter of Michael Henry to James Picciotto (June 12, 1874), University of Southampton Library, MS 116/59.

15. For the poem and the description of the negative reviews, see Duncan Wu, ed., *Romantic Women Poets: An Anthology*, 8–18.

16. Irving Massey discusses the tension between survival and art in "Yiddish Poetry of the Holocaust," in *Find You the Virtue: Ethics, Image, and Desire in Literature* (Fairfax: George Mason University Press, 1987), 79–112.

17. Professor Steven Newman, English Department, Temple University, pointed out to me the parallel between Lyon and Milton; for father-identified women writers, see Elizabeth Kowaleski-Wallace, *Their Fathers' Daughters: Hannah More, Maria Edgeworth, and Patriarchal Complicity* (New York: Oxford University Press, 1991).

18. Hayyim Nahman Bialik and Yehoshua Hana Ravnitsky, eds., *The Book of Legends = Sefer Ha-Aggadah: Legends from the Talmud and Midrash*, trans. William G. Braude (New York: Schocken Books, 1992), 446.

19. For Pope's influence on women writers, see Donna Landry, *The Muses of Resistance: Laboring-Class Women's Poetry in Britain, 1739–1796* (Cambridge: Cambridge University Press, 1990), 12, 43–55.

20. Shelley was in Oxford in 1810–1811; in 1812 he was in Ireland and Wales promoting political reform. As a recent Oxonian, he surely would have heard about Lyon, his blindness, and his daughter's volume of poetry; whether he read a copy is another matter.

21. Duncan Wu, distilling the literary criticism of Francis Jeffrey and other male Romantic-era critics who enforced the gendered aesthetic rules women were supposed to follow, correctly identifies "paraphrases of the Scriptures" as one of the genres allotted to women because such did not challenge "conventional notions of femininity," but any writing that gestured toward theology, an exclusively male province, was strictly forbidden to women (*Romantic Women Poets*, xxi).

22. Jon Mee, *Dangerous Enthusiasm: William Blake and the Culture of Radicalism in the 1790s* (Oxford: Clarendon Press; New York: Oxford University Press, 1992).

23. Sir Philip Sidney, *An Apology for Poetry*, in Hazard Adams, ed., *Critical Theory Since Plato*, revised ed. (New York, et al.: Harcourt Brace Jovanovich, 1992), illustrates one category of imitation (of the "horrible" made "delightful" by mimesis) with "that heavenly Psalm of Mercy" (151). Sidney also refers to "Holy Scripture" as having "whole parts in it poetical" (153). In her recent *Common Prayer: The Language of Public Devotion in Early Modern England*, Ramie Targoff points to the centrality of Sidney's *Apologie* ([Chicago and London: University of Chicago Press, 2001], 73).

24. Targoff, *Common Prayer*, 78.

25. Kenneth Muir and Patricia Thomson, eds., *Collected Poems of Sir Thomas Wyatt* (Liverpool: Liverpool University Press, 1969), xviii.

26. J. C. A. Rathmell, ed., *The Psalms of Sir Philip Sidney and The Countess of Pembroke* (New York: New York University Press, 1963). The Sidney Psalms circulated as manuscript poems among an influential elite readership but were not published until 1823 in a small edition (xxvii).

27. *English Metrical Psalms. Poetry as Praise and Prayer 1535–1601* (Cambridge: Cambridge University Press, 1987), 40.

28. Zim, *English Metrical Psalms*, 3.

29. Zim, *English Metrical Psalms*, 12–15.

30. John N. King, "Religious Writing," in *The Cambridge Companion to English Literature 1500–1600*, ed. Arthur F. Kinney (Cambridge: Cambridge University Press, 2000), writes of the Sternhold-Hopkins version: "*The Whole Book of Psalms* . . . was the most popular collection of English Renaissance verse" (126).

31. Between 1801 and 1815, there were eighty-two separate editions of English Psalters, four of which were the metrical version authored by Isaac Watts (1674–1748). There were no editions of Sternhold and Hopkins that were advertised as such, but it is likely that their translations were within some of the eighty-two editions published then (*Nineteenth-Century Short Title Catalogue*, series 1, 1801–1815, vol. 6 [Newcastle upon Tyne et al.: Avero, 1984]).

32. I am using the categories developed by S. E. Gillingham, *The Poems and Psalms of the Hebrew Bible* (Oxford: Oxford University Press, 1994), 231.

33. The *Amidah*, also known as *Shemonneh-Esreh* ("Eighteen," referring to the eighteen benedictions which it originally comprised), is the core element of the daily prayers.

34. Mitchell Dahood, S. J., ed., *The Anchor Bible. Psalms I. 1–50* (Garden City: Doubleday, 1966), 296.
35. Isaac Watts, *The Psalms, Hymns and Spiritual Songs of the Rev. Isaac Watts, D. D.* (Boston: Samuel T. Armstrong, Crocker, and Brewster, 1823), 124.
36. *Report and State of the Society of Friends of Foreigners in Distress* (London: W. Marchant, 1816), 23.
37. *Aleinu le-shabbe'ah* ("It is out duty to praise [the Lord of all things]"), prayer about the kingdom of God, originally part of the New Year's service, though now recited at the conclusion of statutory services.
38. Michael Galchinsky, *The Origins of the Modern Jewish Woman Writer: Romance and Reform in Victorian England* (Detroit: Wayne State University Press, 1996).

CHAPTER 6

IDENTITY, DIASPORA, AND THE SECULAR VOICE IN THE WORKS OF ISAAC D'ISRAELI

Stuart Peterfreund

D'Israeli, Language, and the Problematic of the Jewish Literary Identity in the Late Eighteenth and Early Nineteenth Centuries

Those who in our time discuss the Jewish literary voice and/or literary identity[1] proceed in the main without a clear sense of what it was like to be an educated, self-aware, and primarily secular European Jew seeking to establish or locate a literary identity in the late eighteenth and early nineteenth centuries. Without an autonomous homeland for more than sixteen centuries and counting, European Jewry's own foundational narratives tell over and over a tale of exile and belatedness. The chronicle of lost homelands includes the losses of Eden, the pre-Noachian earth, the monolingual Plains of Shinar, and the united kingdom of Israel, not to mention a wandering exile of forty years in the desert, after escaping enslavement that followed upon what had been a place of honor in ancient Egypt. Then there were the expulsions in Europe—from England in 1290, from France in 1394, and from Spain in 1492—to conjure with, as well as the constant persecution of the Jews by the Inquisition, especially in Mediterranean Europe.

Speaking of the situation of contemporary American Jewish poetry, but in a manner that seems equally applicable to the literary situation of the Jewish writer in D'Israeli's time, Harold Bloom accounts in part for that situation by observing, "Partly it's the immense difficulty that's involved in the whole issue of Jewish cultural transmission, and, I think, the kind of fossilization of Jewish culture which is involved in trying to maintain a second century formulation eighteen centuries later."[2] As D'Israeli himself observes acerbically in the title of the first chapter of *The Genius of Judaism* (1833), "With the Israelite Every Thing Is Ancient, and Nothing Is Obsolete."[3]

The expulsion from Spain and the Inquisition had a direct effect on the history of Isaac D'Israeli's family. His grandfather's settlement in Cento, Ferrara, and then his father Benjamin's emigration to London in 1748, were a part of the post-1492 movement—and legacy—of the exiled Spanish Jews (Sephardim). And Benjamin's business partner, whose sister-in-law became his first wife, was part of a family that fled the Inquisition in Portugal in 1730 and came to London.[4]

To be Jewish, as Sander Gilman observes, was to be "the obvious Other for the European, whether the citizen of the Roman Empire or of the Federal Republic of Germany," because "the rhetoric of European culture is Christianized, even in its most secular form" (18). The degree to which that rhetoric is Christianized descends down to the level of onomastics, the art of name giving: "Other than aristocrats and wealthy people Jews did not get surnames in Eastern Europe until the Napoleonic years of the early 19th century. Most of the Jews were ordered to get surnames for tax purposes."[5] Prior to this time, names primarily designated place of origin—*Berlin* or, in the case of the subject of this paper *Israel*[6]—or they were translations of the traditional patronymic, such as *Isaacson* for *Ben Yitzhak* or *Jacobson* for *Ben Yaakov*. One exception in this regard was the Holy Roman Empire, where Emperor Joseph II made Jews take last names in the late eighteenth century.

But Joseph II saw naming not only as the means of establishing the tax rolls. He saw naming as a revenue-generating opportunity in its own right, as well as a means of controlling the movement and dealings of Jews within the Empire by distinguishing between the tolerated Jews and those who had to live far from Vienna.[7] Those Jews who could afford to do so were constrained "to pay for their choice of names; the poor had assigned names."[8]

In the main, these last names resembled the run of Christian European names. As such, the names appeared to draw the Jews into the rhetorical orbit of Christian Europe. Many of the names described the male who bore it, for example, *Hoch* (*Tall*), *Kurtz* (*Short*), *Schwartz* (*Black*), *Weiss* (*White*); his occupation, for example, *Holtzman* (*Woodsman*), *Schneider* (*Tailor*); his city of origin or residence, for example, *Franfurter, Breslauer*. As a rule, such names seemed completely secular, save for names that identified the male bearer as *Cohen* (*Rabbi*), *Kaplan* (*Chaplain*), or *Levi* (*Temple Singer*).

But there were also the names that were purchased under a pricing plan that keyed the amount tendered to the value of the object denominated, for example, *Diamond, Stein* (*Glass*), *Rosen* (*Roses*). The mainly pleasant and complimentary associations with such names should not be allowed to conceal the opprobrium which they just barely contain, especially the names denominating jewelry and nearly allied precious objects. By the last quarter of the nineteenth century in Vienna, as Gilman notes, the word *Schmuck* (*jewelry*) had been conflated, through the mediation of the Yiddish-influenced Viennese urban dialect, with *Schmock*, "a standard slang term for the circumcised male penis" (87)—this in an age in which circumcision was almost universally a mark of religious difference. Such names, which were originally selected by those in charge and sold to the Jews, denominated the *Schmuck* that proclaimed the bearer of the name a *Schmock*—a synecdoche for a Jew, in other words. And then there were also the low-budget names assigned to the poor, such as *Plotz* (*To Die*), *Klutz* (*Clumsy*), and *Billig* (*Cheap*).

The othering that occurred took a number of variant forms. The Jewish body and mind were pathologized. Jewish sexuality and mental stability, and mental capability were impugned. Jewish designs on the Christian world were scrutinized and policed—on occasion violently.[9] But perhaps above all, Christian Europeans ridiculed the vernacular speech patterns of Jews.

Christian Germans spoke with contempt of "*Mauscheln*, the language ascribed to the Eastern Jew who attempted to speak German."[10] The very connotations of the term, derived from the Yiddish term meaning "to talk like a Jewish merchant," tell all. Common contemporary colloquial synonyms include "to secretly negotiate," "to transact business," and "to fiddle." The nominal form refers to one who cheats at cards. The language intended by this pejorative term is the singsong, affectively over the top, idiomatically fractured language of outsiders.[11]

The English had no specific term of opprobrium. But the language of the Jews—as satirized, for example, in such humor magazines as *Punch* and *The Butterfly*—was stereotyped by its singsong cadences and affective excesses, as well as by subject–verb agreement errors connoting at once foreignness and lower-class origins, its failure to recognize the phonetic distinction between *w* and *v* (*vy* for *why*), and its lisping failure to recognize the phonetic distinction between *s* and *th* (*thith* for *this*).[12] This last characteristic is of particular interest, since both Hebrew and Yiddish, although lacking the phoneme *w* (and thereby resorting to *v* as the closest approximation), do recognize the allophonic dyad *s-sh* but not the phoneme *th*. Perhaps the lisp is meant to signal the effeminacy or infantile nature of the speaker. But another way of accounting for this last feature of Jewish English of that time is to remember that most of the Jews in Western Europe—Isaac D'Israeli, for example—were Sephardic, not Ashkenazic. Accordingly, their language base was Castilian Spanish (and Ladino) rather than Old High German (and Yiddish). Castilian Spanish systematically substitutes *th* for what is *s* in other Spanish dialects. Whatever its provenance may have been,[13] the lisp called attention both to the uncouthness and the foreignness of the speaker.

Although not subjected to the vicious stereotyping found in the humor magazines—and, to a lesser extent in Charles Dickens' *Oliver Twist* (1838), and William Makepeace Thackeray's *Codlingsby* (1847), a satiric response to his son Benjamin Disraeli's *Coningsby* (1844)—Isaac D'Israeli's linguistic difference as a marker of his otherness was both apparent and noted on occasion. As James Ogden notes, because of the circumstance of "growing up in an Italian–Jewish home and receiving much of his early education abroad, it came as natural to him to write French as to write English." Accordingly, "gallicisms were always a feature of his style, especially early in his career: 'since I know myself,' for example." And "as late as 1823, a reviewer suggested that he wrote English as an acquired language" (14).

Cultural acceptance, if not passing outright, would come, more or less, with time, although the English republic of letters remained "suspicious of 'lively foreigners'" to the end of D'Israeli's life.[14] Washington Irving, writing in "The Art of Book-Making," collected in *The Sketch Book of Geoffrey Crayon, Gent* (1819; 1834) reports on an 1817 encounter with "one dapper little gentleman in bright-coloured clothes, with a chirping, gossiping expression of countenance, who had all the appearance of an author on good terms with his bookseller."[15] In 1832, in grateful recognition of D'Israeli's *Commentaries on the Life and Reign of Charles the First* (1828–1831), Oxford University, which at the time required those who wished to take a degree or hold a university post to subscribe to the Thirty-Nine Articles of the Anglican Church,[16] conferred on D'Israeli an honorary Doctorate of Civil Law.[17] And yet, despite the linguistic issues and the larger cultural concerns to which the linguistic issues adverted, and despite his own awareness, as expressed in the Anti-Jacobin novel *Vaurien* (1797), that "literary Jews must always be rare . . . their most malignant and powerful enemies will be found among their domestic associates,"[18] D'Israeli aspired to recognition— and, ultimately, to a career—in English letters. But the way to take toward that career was far less certain than D'Israeli's motivation to make his way.

Finding the Secular Voice; or, Just Write and Speak Like You are an Orientalist Who has Always Lived Here

D'Israeli's earliest published efforts present him in search of a durable secular voice that proclaims by its topic and manner that the writer at work crafting that voice is a capable and valued citizen of the English republic of letters. The very earliest published writings, the essays "Letter from Nonsense with Some Account of Himself and Family," and "Farther Account of the Family of Nonsense" (1784), both of which appeared in the short-lived and largely unread *Wit's Magazine*, show him affecting a tongue-in-cheek, often satiric urbanity that applies something like a Johnsonian morality to what is at its core a Shandean world.[19] The titular character's name and the narrative stance anticipate the names and the stance of *Vaurien* (Fr., *worthless*) and *Flim-flams* (1805).[20] The second essay, with its "attack on Roman Catholicism" offers D'Israeli a chance to capitalize on the English anti-Catholic sentiment that had fueled the Gordon Riots just four years earlier, while settling an old score with the Inquisition.[21] D'Israeli also undertakes to enter the culture of English letters by engaging in and going to the heart of one of the republic's ongoing debates—in this case the debate between the party of expressiveness and the party of decorum. In large part because the latter party looks to be more properly English than the former, which partakes of the emotional shrillness often ascribed to Jews, D'Israeli criticizes "the 'bombast' of Lee, Thomson, Shakespeare, and Dryden, which suggests that the author might have been sitting at the feet of Dr. Johnson."[22]

A letter of this time to the magazine's editor, the dramatist Thomas Holcroft, reveals a writer attempting to convey an impression of easy familiarity with English letters, even as he conveys an impression of obsequious deference to his correspondent. D'Israeli writes in part, "You say 'I am partial' I own it but does it not do me honour to be partial to Mr. Holcroft? I will not give too much way to the effusions of my mind. The spirit of the courser is known by his being withheld—Says Dan Pope."[23]

The reference to "the spirit of the courser" alludes to one of the better known couplets in Alexander Pope's *Essay on Criticism* (1711): "The winged courser, like a gen'rous horse, / Shows most true mettle when you check his course" (ll. 86–87).[24] In urging an esthetics of discipline and restraint, the speaker likens Pegasus, the winged horse symbolizing poetry, to a well-turned-out saddle horse, which shows its power and spirit to advantage when those are held in check because the horse is being ridden under tight rein. Just as a rider who keeps a mount under control shows both that mount and her/his craft to advantage, a poet who keeps his/her poem under tight esthetic control shows the worthiness of the subject and her/his skill to advantage. Such an esthetics would certainly be consistent with D'Israeli's contention that a lack of tight esthetic control results in bombastic Shakespearean characters such as Hamlet, Lear, and Macbeth, all three of these products of an out-of-control poetic imagination.

Perhaps more interesting than the first allusion is the second, contained in the reference to Pope as "Dan Pope." The title, derived from the Latin *dominus* (*lord, master*)—the same root that gives rise to the (Castilian) Spanish title *Don*—means *sir*, or *master*. To judge from Spenser's reference, in *The Faerie Queene* (1596), to "Dan Chaucer, well of English undefiled, / On Fame's eternal beadroll worthie to be fyled" (IV.ii.32),[25] *Dan* is an honorific that may be used by a poet-aspirant to identify a precursor-poet that s/he admires and/or aspires to emulate in some important way. And to be sure, D'Israeli does emulate Pope, "his favourite poet," in his choice of a "favourite verse-form, heroic couplets."[26] But what is explicit in Spenser's use of the term and implicit in D'Israeli's is the acknowledgment of operating within the same national literary tradition as the precursor-poet. Spenser's English poetry flows from its unsullied Chaucerian wellsprings, just as D'Israeli would have his English poetry flow from its Popean source.

In 1789, after spending much of that year and the preceding one studying and traveling in continental Europe, D'Israeli returned to England and once again inserted himself into a poetic controversy in the republic of letters with the publication of "On the Abuse of Satire," a poem defending the Poet Laureate, Thomas Warton, and execrating the satirical attacks mounted against him by "Peter Pindar" (John Wolcot). The poem, published anonymously, "was a minor sensation."[27] And the shifting dynamics of its reception are instructive. "On the Abuse" was originally thought to have been written by William Hayley, a patron of Blake's and a minor poet of the time, whom Wolcot had identified as a future object of his satire. In a gesture compounded of a gentleman's self-abnegation and an ephebe's self-promotion, D'Israeli took responsibility (and credit) for the poem in his first volume, *A Defence of Poetry [and] Specimens of a New Version of Telemachus* (1790), taking Wolcot to task for his inability to distinguish between D'Israeli's "rough and artless labour" and Hayley's "terseness and elegance."[28]

The fact that *The Gentleman's Magazine* made a point of quoting this acknowledgement might at first glance seem innocent enough, were it not for the fact that this same periodical in the very same review ventures the innuendo that suggests that D'Israeli's assessment of his talent as a poet is being taken at face value. Commenting on *Specimens of a New Version of Telemachus*, the reviewer observes, "'The beauteous grotto on the *acclivious* green Displays a wide *circuitry* of scene,' is not in Fénelon and should not be in D'Israeli: for it suits none but Christie the auctioneer."[29] The author of these lines is being belittled as a buyer and a seller, a member of the mercantile classes—the worthy descendant of the merchant of Cento, if not the merchant of Venice.[30] The sense of the descent from the divine to the demotic and from the mythic to the mercantile is reinforced by the response of *The Monthly Review* to *Narrative Poems* (1803): "Mr. D'Israeli's muse might truly say *Non sum qualis eram* [I am not what I once was], though she probably will not feel inclined to make the confession."[31]

At some point D'Israeli must have realized that he was not going to become a citizen of the republic of letters as an English poet among poets. But if he was not to gain that citizenship as an English poet, then how would he? He had to find some collective discourse that embraced his voice. One option in the near term was to involve himself in the discourse of Orientalism, as he does in *Mejnoun and Leila*.[32] The Orientalism operating in this text looks quite a bit different from Edward Said's version, in which the West controls the East "by making statements about it, authorizing views of it, describing it, by teaching it, settling it, ruling over it: in short, Orientalism as a Western style for dominating, restructuring and having authority over the Orient."[33]

Orientalism as it was practiced in the eighteenth and nineteenth centuries pursued likeness and interconnectedness rather than unlikeness and otherness. Caroline Franklin is right to note that "Said's Foucauldian model is too monolithic."[34] Naji B. Oueijian would seem to concur. He offers a useful corrective to Said's position by noting that the gradient of Islamic–Christian religious difference assumed by Said to underwrite Orientalism gave rise to what Oueijian calls "False Orientalism." Orientalism per se "is not limited to the study of Islam . . . Biblical scholarship is an integral and consequential part of Orientalism. Students of Christian theology (like Bede, and later Schelling, Hegel and several others) were certainly Oriental scholars because they were obliged to study the Biblical history of the East."[35] Indeed, Franklin observes that Byron in his Orientalist nationalism privileged claims for Greek and Hebrew emancipation over the prerogatives of "the traditional Western Other of Islamic Empire, for the Turks controlled both Greece and

Palestine." The Turks in their turn became the enemy for Byron, but an enemy of the East, not of the West: ". . . both Byronic nationalist ideals were, therefore, in opposition to British foreign policy which since 1791 had been to prop up the declining Ottoman Empire in order to keep open the route to India, and prevent the ambitions of Napoleonic France, Russia and Austria of extending their influence to the Mediterranean" (228).

In the cultural space of Orientalism, Jewish otherness, by being studied from a putatively Western perspective and associated with the rest of the East through the medium of a discourse that stresses common sources and origins over differences, and aspires to discover syncretism rather than otherness, is subject to a blurring effect that elides distinctions between Jews and the rest of the Oriental world—and, ultimately, between the Oriental world and the West.[36] The blurring that occurs between the Orient and the West is evident even at the beginning of the poem, in the "Advertisement" that prefaces *Mejnoun and Leila*, the first and longest of the texts collected as *Romances* (1799; 1803).

In the "Advertisement," D'Israeli observes, "the story of MEJNOUN and LEILA is as popular in the East, as the loves of ABELARD and ELOISA, or those of PETRARCH and LAURA in the West" (A2). The comparison helps to define *Mejnoun and Leila* as a tragic tale about star-crossed lovers, but in this instance, rather than the Oriental tale being *like* the two European tales, the two latter are *like* the much older Persian original, which is antecedent to them both in its historical setting and its date of composition. D'Israeli notes that the romance tells the story of "the son of an Arabian Chief, in the first age of the Mohammedan Empire" (A1)—the late seventh or eighth century, prior to the establishment of the Holy Roman Empire and the gradual waning of the Dark Ages. The story of Abelard and Eloisa, who, like Mejnoun and Leila, were interred together, is set in the twelfth century, and that of Petrarch and Laura, in the fourteenth century.

While D'Israeli defers on the matter to Sir William Jones, who "observes that there are no less than eleven or twelve poems on the story of Leila and Mejnoun" (A1), authorship of the poem is most commonly attributed to Sadi (ca. 1210–1290). Although the actual events comprising the story of Abelard and Eloisa predate Sadi—both lovers were dead by 1163—the epistolary narrative of their love story first appeared in a Latin version in 1616, was translated into French in 1697, and did not appear in English until John Hughes' translation of 1713. Alexander Pope's *Eloisa to Abelard*, which makes use of Hughes' translation, was first published in 1717. Petrarch's poetic tribute to Laura dates from a first encounter in 1327. Pride of place here is the Orient's.

Indeed, in glossing the epithet "hyacinthine locks," which is appropriated by Milton in *Paradise Lost* (IV.301–303), D'Israeli makes explicit what he elsewhere merely implies—that Western poetry is in some important respects descended from and derivative of ancient Oriental poetry: "*Hyacinthine locks* is frequent among the Arabic poets, and which Sir William Jones delightfully renders, 'The fragrant HYACINTHS of AZZA's hair, / That wanton with the laughing summer air.' From the Orientalists it passed to the Greeks, and our Milton adopts it: '*Hyacinthine locks* / Round from his parted forehead [that is, forelock] manly hung / Clustering, but not beneath his shoulders broad'" (133n).

It is significant that *Mejnoun and Leila* is in large measure about a star-crossed poet immortalized by his love-longings and the poetry that those love-longings gave rise to. "Fragments of his poetry are still repeated with rapture, and the best works of the Persians abound in an allusion to his sufferings" (A1–2), as D'Israeli states. Here, again, the Orient is accorded pride of place in the origination of poetic practices subsequently common in the West. In Venice, for example, the gondoliers to this day sing bits of Petrarch and Tasso, another disappointed poet-lover, as they ply the canals. And the story of Abelard and Eloisa, after being rendered by a poet of Pope's reputation,[37] was not only alluded to, but retold, albeit arguably not in the best works of the English. Parodies included Richard Cambridge's *An Elegy Written in an Empty Assembly Room* (1756), and *Eloisa en Dishabille, Being a New Version of That Lady's Celebrated Epistle to Abelard* (1801), attributed to John Matthews. Sequels include Thomas Ward's *Abelard to Eloisa: A Poetic Epistle, Newly Attempted* (1782) and Edward Jermingham's *Abelard to Eloisa: A Poem* (1792).

No less than Western preeminence in virtually every poetic genre is at issue. Of the Persian poets, D'Israeli concludes, "there is no poetical character of which they are not in possession; in the epic grandeur of Firdausi and Nizami; the philosophic poetry of Sadi; the anacreontic vein of Hafez; and the elegiac tenderness of Jami" (A4). Then, too, there are moments in the romance when *Mejnoun and Leila* is made to anticipate no less a poet than Shakespeare himself. For example, after the Emir, Leila's father, rejects Kais' suit, he behaves in a manner that would seem to anticipate Hamlet's erratic behavior following his father's suspicious death, even as Kais's intensely expressive physiognomy reveals characteristically oriental traits that are discussed below:

> He could no longer support the eye of the world. In his tortured sensations his language was inhuman. He called his mother the wife of his father, but no relative of her child; and he surlily dismissed his friends, one by one, for capricious, but inveterate dislikes. Sometimes his anger was loquacious, his taunt bitter, his repartee caustic, while at times he was obstinately mute; but his silence concealed not the disorder of his intellect, for then the vacillations of his countenance, and the glistening and rapid movements of his eye, expressed his phrenzy. (39)

And that moment at the end of the romance in which "the tribe of Mejnoun unite with the tribe of Leila" and "they raise a tomb to the memory of the lovers, and there depositing the bodies, the plant round many a gloomy cypress tree" (125) anticipates the conclusion of *Romeo and Juliet*.

The ancientness of the culture, as well as the access to knowledge that such wisdom grants, is perhaps most succinctly expressed in the discussion of the Effendi Lebid, at whose *madrasseh* in Isfahan Leila and Kais, who have each been sent to study there, first meet. Recounting the Effendi's accomplishments, the narrator says in part, "he preferred to interrogate Nature in a sublime solitude. In the plains of Shinaar he had accurately measured a degree of the great circle of the earth; on the shores of the Bosphorus he had taught the inhabitants the art of an invaluable fishery, and the voice of the population broke along these solitary skies" (2–3). The plains of Shinar, where the Tower of Babel once rose skyward, was a place where the Adamic knowledge of the natural world that arose with the naming of the animals (Gen. 2:18) descended to the furthest degree of chaos in ancient times, owing to the confounding of tongues (Gen. 11:1–9). The Effendi's determination of a degree of longitude at that site represents a taking back of some of that knowledge.

So, too, teaching those living on the Bosphorus, the strait that separates Turkey (and Asia) from Europe, to fish speaks both to the Effendi's ubiquity and to his command of worldly knowledge—in this instance knowledge of "the great whales, and every living creature that moveth" (Gen. 1:21) in the waters of the earth. Before commercial marine traffic and overfishing depleted its stocks, the Bosphorus was a major fish migration route between the Black Sea and the Sea of Marmara, and one of the migrant species to be found there was the sturgeon, prized for its roe, consumed as the luxury foodstuff caviar, the "invaluable fishery" to which the narrator alludes.

The knowledge that the Effendi Lebid possesses, then, is more deeply rooted in the syncretic history of the world than is the astronomical, chemical, and mathematical knowledge of the Islamic Middle Ages. Such knowledge at once underwrites the cultural interactions of the region and points to their common origin.

The deployment of the sweeping generalizations and parallel instances throughout *Mejnoun and Leila* is earnest of D'Israeli's bid to be considered an Orientalist among Orientalists, a goal that he hopes to attain by a prodigious display of erudition accompanying the poem in its apparatus. And indeed, the copiousness of the Orientalist scholarship accompanying the poem in the form of footnotes is noteworthy. Among the texts D'Israeli cites several times are John Bell's *Travels from St. Petersburgh in Russia to Various Parts of Asia* (1788), James Dallaway's *Constantinople* (1797), Sir William Jones's *Grammar of the Persian Language* (third ed., 1783), Carsten Niebuhr's *A Collection of Late Voyages* (1797), Major William Ouseley's *Persian Miscellanies* (1795), and two works by John Richardson— *A Dictionary of Persian, Arabic, and English* (1777–1780), and *A Grammar of the Arabic Language* (1776).

D'Israeli comes up with arcana such as the following note, triggered by the statement that Kais "pounded rubies to cover her [i.e., Leila's] rich confection" (50): "Mr. Dallaway in his 'Constantinople,' notices the *conserve of rubies*, so called as well from the richness of the other ingredients, as that *pounded rubies* are a part of its composition; so capricious are their preparations in the confectionary art" (127–128). Having recounted that

Kais, disguised as a Mevleheh Dervish, steals, Romeo-like, into Leila's family compound to see her, the narrator notes that Leila serves the disguised Kais a meal, which he washes down with "a bardak of fair and gelid water." D'Israeli, citing Niebuhr as his authority, quotes: "They put their water into *bardaks,* or unglazed pots made of porous earth" (21 and n). Recounting the travels together of Kais's father, Ahmed, and his tutor, Effendi Lebid, the narrator notes the effect of the climate on the two, "Both old men were fainting in the hot blasts, and they administered to them garlic and dried grapes to revive them." Citing Page's *Travels* (i.e., Pierre Marie François de Pagés, *Travels around the World in the Years 1767, 1768, 1769, 1770, 1771* [1791]—a translation of *Voyage autour du Monde* [1782]), D'Israeli explains, "the Arabs, when they travel, carry with them garlic and dried grapes, for the purpose of reviving such persons as may fall down fainting from the effects of the hot blast" (50 and n).

On one level, the scholarship is a self-representation of D'Israeli performing the work of literature and culture more generally in an effort to establish a place for himself, despite being a "'lively foreigner,'" in "the aristocracy of [British] literature."[38] But on another level, the scholarship underwrites a complex exilic motif. *Kais* just happens to be an anagram for *Isaac.* Kais, the given name of the *mejnoun*—an Arabic word that means, alternatively, "madman" or "a man inspired,"—is an exile. He woos Leila in part with his love lyrics, which help to win her over. Kais flees into the wilderness when Leila's father refuses to permit Leila to marry him. In the wilderness, he is effectively silenced, much as D'Israeli himself is silenced, and Kais's poems, which go for the most part unread in his own lifetime, become the only tangible evidence of the lovers' erstwhile relationship. In *The Genius of Judaism,* D'Israeli offers the following reflection on his own plight: "I might have been a prophet, who am now only an historian" (178).

Kais is prepared for his exile by reason of his wandering nature; he is descended from self-made Bedouin nobility: "Among the BEDOWEENS, or Pastoral Arabs," his father, "Ahmed Kais, was a distinguished Schieck [that is, sheikh]."[39] The characters in the romance operate in a cultural space in which lineage ("race") counts, although not in precisely the same way that it does in British cultural space. Leila's father manifests something roughly akin to hereditary nobility. He is an Emir who wears a green turban, marking him as one who "claims his descent from Fatima the wife of Mahomet" (4, 127n; see also 13). By his own representations, Kais stands at the beginning of a noble line. Facing the Emir and suing for the hand of his daughter, Kais argues,

Descendant of Fatima! Is humility held to be a vice in thy race? Comes not the noblest race from the humblest origin? The lovely fountain of juvenicia, while it wanders among flowers and sunshine, hides its head amidst rushes and darkness. The great Prophet, like myself, was of an obscure birth; and arrogance never marked the camel driver. Noble Emir! thy father was a son of peace, my father is a son of war; Honour wreathed thy cradle, Opulence pillowed the bed of my infancy; thou wert born illustrious, I to become illustrious; the glory of thy race devolved to thee, the glory of mine proceeds from me. (28)

And breeding will out, regardless of socioeconomic status. Bloodlines matter in *Mejnoun and Leila*, where the quality of the gaze, animation of the facial features, and, to a lesser extent, the luxuriance of the hair reflect spiritedness and the pedigree that gives rise to them. The example of Kais noted above, in which "the vacillations of his countenance, and the glistening and rapid movements of his eye, expressed his phrenzy" (39), is but one of several throughout the romance. For example, when Kais, disguised as a Dervish, gains access to Leila's tent, she remarks his altered appearance—the absence of "the beautiful light of thine eye, the tender bloom of thy check [*sic*]" (21–22)—commenting on Kais's normal appearance (glowing eye, blooming complexion) and the effect wrought by the lovers' involuntary separation.

When Kais again gains access to Leila's tent—this time disguised as a perfumer and confectioner—Leila notes that "the eyes of Kais are brilliant with love" (25). Shortly thereafter, when the Emir discovers the two lovers together, he has a fit of rage worthy of his bloodlines: "The green-turbaned despot at first could only indicate his passion by ferocious gestures, and with eyes red with rage, and lips quivering without articulation" (26).

As with Kais, so with Leila: D'Israeli's "Advertisement" states that the real-life Leila in fact "had no transcendent in any eyes but those of her lover. She had a swarthy complexion, and was of low stature" (A2). But she is represented otherwise in the romance. Rescued from the despotic sway of her father by Nousel, whose troops best the Emir's troops in an Oriental equivalent of a knightly tournament, Leila, awaiting the time of her marriage to Kais, unwittingly inflames Nousel's passions. Her "novel graces" include "the harmony of her features[,] the bloom of her complexion. . . . [t]he tenderness of her tones; and . . . the melody of her tongue," which Nousel forgot about when he gazed upon the "brilliancy" of her eyes (96). Later on, when Leila, her hopes for a life together with Kais dashed by a reversal of fortune, goes through the motions of an arranged marriage with Ebnselan, she is beautiful even in her sorrow. As the narrator describes her, Leila's "flowing hair, waving on her shoulders, was dressed with embroidered ribbons, and the long tassels of silk, wrought with gold and silver, reached to her feet" (104).

To understand some of the complex cultural negotiations that underwrite *Mejnoun and Leila*, it is helpful to consult Benjamin Disraeli's novel *Coningsby*, which may be read as an explanation and amplification, in an important retrospective sense, of the position staked out by his father in *Mejnoun and Leila* and elsewhere.[40] Indeed, in the novel, the Jew Sidonia, who is in an important sense Disraeli's double—he is of Sidon as Disraeli is of Israel[41]—also looks a bit like Disraeli's father's double, given his near remove from the Iberian Peninsula and the Inquisition.

Sidonia announces his ethnic identity to the protagonist Coningsby by stating, "I am of that faith that the Apostles professed before they followed their Master" (121). Such a characterization reverses Christianity's attempt to distance itself linguistically and culturally from Judaism[42] by noting, not only that Judaism historically precedes Christianity, but also that the two exhibit only one degree of separation.

In Sidonia's account, not only do the Jews exist at one degree of separation from the early Christians, but they exist in a close proximity to the Arabs as well. After his companion takes note of the pristine cleanliness of the table service, Coningsby, who has invited Sidonia to dine with him at the rural English inn where both have taken shelter from a sudden squall, speculates, "An inheritance from our Saxon fathers? . . . I apprehend the northern nations have a greater sense of cleanliness, of propriety, of what we call comfort?" Sidonia demurs: "By no means . . . the East is the land of the Bath. Moses and Mahomet made cleanliness religion" (116). In fact, Sidonia characterizes the Jews who settled in Spain—the line from which he as Disraeli's double is descended—as "Mosaic Arabs" that "had sojourned in Africa," most likely "the descendants of some of the earlier dispersions" (209).

And yet, despite repeated instances of diasporic exile and movement among the other peoples of the world, according to the narrator of *Coningsby*, the "Arabian tribes," who are Caucasians, and therefore "rank in the first and superior class, together, among others, with the Saxon and the Greek" (219), have remained racially pure. As the narrator observes, "Sidonia and his brethren could claim a distinction which the Saxon and the Greek, and the rest of the Caucasian nations, have forfeited. The Hebrew is an unmixed race. Doubtless, among the tribes who inhabit the bosom of the Desert, progenitors alike of the Mosaic and the Mohammedan Arabs, blood may be found as pure as that of the Scheik Abraham. But the Mosaic Arabs are the most ancient, if not the only, unmixed blood that dwells in cities" (219–220).

Not surprisingly, purity of lineage matters to Sidonia. His mount is what first attracts the attention of Coningsby. Showing the Arabian mare to Coningsby, Sidonia explains that her beauty and mettle are in large measure owing to her pedigree. His explanation also has the effect of inserting that pedigree into the tribal history of Arabia, as well as the history of the Ottoman Empire, a regional governor (Pacha) of which gave the horse to Sidonia as a gift. And in his valuation of the mare, Sidonia displays his erudition—he knows who the fourth-century BCE Greek sculptor Lysippus is and that he was known for rendering heroic subjects, albeit in bronze rather than gold—and he works to undercut the stereotype of Jews as being obsessed with possessing gold and jewels:

> She is not only of pure race . . . but of the highest and rarest breed in Arabia Her name is "the Daughter of the Star." She is a foal of that famous mare that belonged to the Prince of the Wahabees; and to possess which, I believe, was one of the principal causes of the war between that tribe and the Egyptians. The Pacha of Egypt gave her to me, and I would not change her for her statue in pure gold, even carved by Lysippus. (120)

Just as the pure Arabian lineage makes for "the remarkable beauty of the animal" (114), the pure Arabian lineage of the Jews in the novel makes for appearances that are at least striking and, in the case of women, extraordinarily beautiful. Sidonia himself is at once sensual and cerebral—"perhaps ten years older than Coningsby, [he] was still, according to Hippocrates, in the period of lusty youth. He was above the middle height, and of a distinguished air and figure; pale, with an impressive brow, and dark eyes of great intelligence" (114).

And the niece of Sir Joseph Wallinger—she is subsequently identified as Edith Millbank, the sister of one of Coningsby's schoolmates at Eton (316)—although nominally Spanish, displays the looks characteristic of the Oriental physiognomy shared in common by Arabian Jews and Moslems: "The finely-arched brow was a little elevated, the soft dark eyes were fully opened, the nostril of the delicate nose slightly dilated, the small, yet rich, full lips just parted; and over the clear, transparent visage, there played a vivid glance of gratified intelligence" (304).[43]

Underneath Sidonia's "impressive brow," itself perhaps reminiscent of Adam's hyacinthine lock-wreathed brow in *Paradise Lost*, there is a powerful intelligence at work. Despite being debarred by his religion from attending the Christian universities of Europe, "Sidonia was fortunate in the tutor whom his father had procured for him, and who devoted to his charge all the resources of his trained intellect and vast and various erudition." Not surprisingly, that tutor, Rebello, "a Jesuit before the revolution; since then an exiled liberal leader; now a member of the Cortes . . . was always a Jew."

Like recognized like. Rebello "found in his pupil that precocity of intellectual development which is characteristic of the Arabian organization. The young Sidonia penetrated the highest mysteries of mathematics with a facility almost instinctive; while a memory . . . seemed to magnify his acquisitions of ancient learning by the promptness with which they could be reproduced and applied." Like Isaac D'Israeli, Sidonia "had an unusual command over modern languages" (214),[44] much of it acquired in travels throughout Europe.

But he is a polymath as well as a linguist:

> Sidonia had exhausted all the resources of human knowledge; he was the master of the learning of every nation, of all tongues dead or living, of every literature, Western and Oriental. He had pursued the speculations of science to their last term, and had himself illustrated them by observation and experiment. He had lived in all orders of society, had viewed every combination of Nature and of Art, and had observed man under every phasis of civilization. He had even studied him in the wilderness. The influence of creeds and laws, manners, customs, traditions, in all their diversities, had been subjected to his personal scrutiny. (216)

Indeed, Sidonia's stock of lore is nothing short of Adamic, especially when the subject of conversation is women, the first of whom came from Adam's side. Sidonia is a guest favored by Lord Eskdale, according to the narrator, because Sidonia

> would tell you Talmudical stories about our mother Eve and the Queen of Sheba, which would have astonished you. There was not a free lady of Greece,

Leontium and Phryne, Lais, Danae, and Lamia, the Egyptian girl Thonis, respecting whom he could not tell you as many diverting tales as if they were ladies of Loretto; not a nook of Athenaeus, not an obscure scholiast, not a passage in a Greek orator, that could throw light on these personages, which was not at his command. (318)

But Sidonia lacks a social context, much as Isaac D'Israeli, in his search for his place in the republic of letters, lacked a social context: "His religion walled him out from the pursuits of a citizen; his riches deprived him of the stimulating anxieties of a man. He perceived himself as a lone being, alike without cares and without duties." And perhaps because of that lack of context, Sidonia has another burden to contend with: "In his organization there was a peculiarity, perhaps a great deficiency. He was a man without affections. It would be harsh to say he had no heart, for he was susceptible to deep emotions, but not for individuals" (217).[45]

With *Romances*—and above all, with *Mejnoun and Leila*, the major text in that collection—D'Israeli found an Orientalist context and achieved a modest success. The English press published a second edition in 1801, just two years after the publication of the first, at a price of four shillings, as compared to eight shillings for the first edition. An American edition followed shortly, in 1803. In 1808, John Braham's *Kais, or, Love in the Deserts*, an opera based on *Mejnoun and Leila*, was performed at Drury Lane and was well enough received to warrant publication by John Murray, the son of D'Israeli's first publisher of that name and a figure instrumental in helping D'Israeli to become a successful author.[46]

Ultimately, however, what *Romances* seems to have done for D'Israeli is to insert him into a cultural context and to establish his cultural authority in a manner indispensable to his major cultural work as a compiler, annotator, and curator of English literature and literary history. This work began prior to the publication of *Romances* with the appearance of the first edition of *Curiosities of Literature* (1791). But it accelerated markedly after 1799. *Curiosities* went to two volumes in 1797–1798, and to three thereafter. Four separate editions preceded the publication of *Romances*; nine followed during D'Israeli's lifetime. The two-volume *Calamities of Authors* followed in 1812, and the three-volume *Calamities of Authors* two years later.[47] And this list is far from exhaustive.

Der Ewige Jude

In arguing for the importance of the Jewish contribution to the progress of Western intellectual history, Sidonia focuses in part on how that contribution has manifested in Germany, home of D'Israeli's intellectual hero, Moses Mendelssohn.[48] Sidonia notes that "a second and greater Reformation . . . of which so little is known in England, is entirely developing under the auspices of the Jews, who almost monopolize the professorial chairs of Germany." Not surprisingly, the three professors mentioned—"Neander, the founder of Spiritual Christianity . . . who is Regius Professor of Divinity at the University of Berlin," "Benary, equally famous and in the same University," and "Wehl, the Arabic Professor at Heidelberg," who is "the author of the life of Mahomet" (250)—are scholars who work Oriental–Western cultural interconnections.[49]

While Sidonia may overstate the ubiquity of Jewish professors in German universities, he does point to what became an ever-burgeoning presence until the events of 1933 and the *Shoah* thereafter. What is interesting to note is that in some cases, despite an increasing influence of secularization and cultural dislocation, the Jewish scholars of the 1920s and after, up until their prewar and post-*Shoah* immigration to the United States and England, intervened in Western culture in ways that would have been recognized and understood by D'Israeli.

At this juncture, owing to the constraints of length, I focus on only one of the scholars who may be seen as fitting the definition of a Jewish professor— Erich Auerbach, "a completely assimilated Jew,"[50] but not a Jew given to questioning or repudiating his origins. Not that such a repudiation would have prevented his dismissal from the University of Marburg in 1933, the revocation of his veteran's pension in 1935, or the stripping of his German citizenship in 1938: Auerbach's life was profoundly and irrevocably affected by the rise of Naziism, and *Mimesis*, written while Auerbach remained for the duration of the war in Istanbul,[51] would not been the same book, absent his experience, as a Jew, written in response to the events of his time.[52] But I suspect that the argument to be made for Auerbach could be made, with appropriate nuancing, for another such as Walter Benjamin, and perhaps for Leo Spitzer as well.

The focus of Auerbach's meditation on his historical and cultural situation is chapter 1, "The Scar of Odysseus," although, as Jan N. Bremmer notes, other parts of the discussion—"the depictions of Barbarian rulers in Gregory of Tours and of a revolt of the lower classes in Ammianus Marcellinus," as well as "the last chapters where the pessimistic views of modern novelists are criticized because they would weaken our resolve in standing up to negative ideologies" (5)—also bear the imprint of the issues at hand.

In the first chapter of *Mimesis*, Auerbach compares two scenes. The former is "the well-prepared and touching scene in book 19 [of *The Odyssey*] when Odysseus has at last come home, the scene in which the old housekeeper Euryclea, who had been his nurse, recognizes him by a scar on the thigh" (3). The latter is "the account of the sacrifice of Isaac [Gen. 22:1–12], a homogeneous narrative produced by the so-called Elohist" (7–8).

A good deal is at stake in the comparison. In his retrospective concluding remarks, Auerbach notes that the two styles of realism under discussion,

> in their opposition represent basic types: on the one hand, fully externalized description, uniform illumination, uninterrupted connection, free expression, all events in the foreground, displaying unmistakable meanings, few elements of historical development and of psychological perspective; on the other hand,

certain parts brought into high relief, others left obscure, abruptness, suggestive influence of the unexpressed, "background" quality, multiplicity of meanings and the need for interpretation, universal–historical claims, development of
the concept of historically becoming, and preoccupation with the problematic.

And as the two basic modes of narrative realism, "the two styles have exercised their determining influence upon the representation of reality in
European literature" (23).

By grouping Old Testament narrative under the rubric of "European
literature," Auerbach makes a subversive move not unlike Disraeli, speaking
through Sidonia, when the latter notes that his religion is "that faith that
the Apostles professed before they followed their Master" (121). That is,
Auerbach works to preempt and defeat Christian Europe's persistent
tendency to dissever its cultural endowment from any connection with its
Oriental origins.

In Auerbach's case, as in the cases of those before him, the move arises
out of psychological necessity, as he finds himself involved, willy-nilly, in
identity criticism. While his focus is on Auerbach's response to Homeric realism, Egbert J. Bakker, who notes that *Mimesis*, as Auerbach understands the
term, represents "not only the reality of the epic tale, but also its telling,"
fails to see that the concept applies with equal validity to the Elohist text to
which the Homeric text is compared.[53] No less than the "the very performance of Homeric poetry becomes an act of representation," under the terms
of which the "'divine poet' (*Odyssey* 8.43) reenacts the prestigious past, but
is in turn reenacted himself," the very performance of Elohist poetry
becomes such an act of representation.

Auerbach observes that the appeal of Elohist narrative and Old Testament
narrative more generally arises from this dynamic of identification through
representation, a dynamic that both recapitulates and makes meaningful the
diasporic context of that narrative. Auerbach offers the following observations concerning Old Testament protagonists:

> There is not one of them who does not, like Adam, undergo the deepest
> humiliation—and hardly one who is not deemed worthy of God's personal
> intervention and personal inspiration. . . . The poor beggar Odysseus is only
> masquerading, but Adam is really cast down, Jacob really a refugee, Joseph
> really in the pit and then a slave to be bought and sold. But their greatness,
> arising out of their humiliation, is almost superhuman and an image of God's
> greatness. (18)

Such narratives are not the stuff of legend, and that is precisely the reason why
they are indispensable in times such as the historical present (1942–1945) in
which Auerbach writes—not creating, as Seth Lerer would have it, "a legend
of the writer in exile, remembering the texts and contexts of a past" (309),
but rather a *history* of the writer in exile. Legends make for easy moralizing.
"In the legends of martyrs, for example," he observes, "a stiff-necked and
fanatical persecutor stands over against an equally stiff-necked and fanatical

victim; and a situation so complicated—that is to say, so real and historical—as that in which the 'persecutor' Pliny finds himself in the celebrated letter to Trajan on the subject of the Christians, is unfit for legend" (19).

The passage just quoted leads into the core of Auerbach's argument for the superiority of history to legend. History bears moral witness, and in reading Old Testament narrative—or in writing about it in the context of the historical present—the reader or writer who puts his/her interpretive practices on the line in turn bears moral witness. Moral dilemmas and questions as to why events fall out as they do are virtually absent from the clean, well-lighted time and space of Homeric narrative. Those dilemmas and questions bedevil Elohist narrative, but they do so in a manner calculated to make those who re-present those narratives reenact the dilemmas and questions, to the end of articulating responses, if not answers outright. It may well have been the case in Auerbach's time that "the history which we ourselves are witnessing," including "the behavior of individual men and groups of men at the time of the rise of National Socialism in Germany," is a case-in-point of "how difficult it is to represent historical themes in general, and how unfit they are for legend [!]" As Martin Elsky notes, "Auerbach's criticism is itself an example of how the interpretation, as well as the production, of texts is an expression of cultural identity in particular places at particular times."[54] Auerbach himself is insistent that, when compared to Homer,

> Abraham, Jacob, or even Moses produces a more concrete, direct, and historical impression than the figures of the Homeric world—not because they are better described in terms of sense (the contrary is the case) but because the confused, contradictory multiplicity of events, the psychological and factual cross-purposes, which true history reveals, have not disappeared in the representation but remain clearly perceptible. (19–20)

Auerbach's own elusive, indirect, and discontinuous expository style—Lerer correctly notes that its irrepressibility "interrupts the reading of Odysseus's scar" (309)—is but one indicator of how one bears witness through mimesis as a critical practice, no less than through mimesis as realistic narrative. Sadly enough, it is a critical practice resting on an article of faith that the *Shoah* all but shattered—a faith that the Jews are blessed with a trait or instinct that has given them an ability to improvise, and in so doing to survive. The faith is evident in Sidonia's contemptuous observation regarding anti-Semitism in England: "Do you think that the quiet humdrum persecution of a decorous representative of an English university can crush those who have successively baffled the Pharaohs, Nebuchadnezzar, Rome, and the Feudal ages?" (250). This same faith may be glimpsed in Auerbach's observation that "the origins of prophecy seem to lie in the irrepressible politico-religious spontaneity of the people. We receive the impression that the movements emerging from the depths of the people of Israel–Judah must have been of a wholly different nature from those even of the later ancient democracies—of a different nature and far more elemental" (21–22).

Ultimately, Auerbach knew better. His final, prayerlike words in *Mimesis* are the following: "I hope that my study will reach its readers—both my friends of former years, if they are still alive, as well as all the others for whom it was intended. And may it contribute to bringing together again those whose love for our western history has serenely persevered" (557). *Shoah* is now as real as Old Testament narrative: next year in Jerusalem, perhaps, or perhaps Princeton, New Jersey, but never again in the Europe that allowed the Third Reich to rise and flourish, even as it ignored the plight of Auerbach's (and my) people.

Notes

1. Sander Gilman, *The Jew's Body* (New York: Routledge, 1991), 10–11.
2. Ellen Spirer, "Candidates for Survival: A Talk with Harold Bloom" < http://www.bostonreview.net/BR11.1/bloom.html > (March 13, 2004): 5.
3. (London: Edward Moxon, 1833), 1.
4. James Ogden, *Isaac D'Israeli* (Oxford: Clarendon, 1969), 5.
5. "How the Jews Got Their Names" < www.geocities.com/buddychai/Religion/Names.html > (March 13, 2004): 1; hereafter referred to as "Names."
6. Benjamin Israeli, Isaac's father, changed the family name to D'Israeli when he emigrated to England (Ogden, *Isaac D'Israeli*, 5). Jews in Spain had last names prior to their expulsion in 1492; Jews in England and France, from the sixteenth century onward.
7. As Murray Frost points out, the Edict of Toleration did not apply fully to the Jews, who did not attain full rights and citizenship in Austria until 1860–1861 ("The Edict of Tolerance and the Jews," *Deep Background: Delving Deeper into Jewish History on Stamps* < http://www.goletapublishing.com/jstamps/0102deep.htm > [March 16, 2004]: 1–2).
8. "Names," 1.
9. Gilman, *The Jew's Body*, passim.
10. Gilman, *The Jew's Body*, 21.
11. Gilman, *The Jew's Body*, 16.
12. Gilman, *The Jew's Body*, 14–15, 65. Also, on anti-Semitic satire in *Punch*, see "Mr. Punch at the Great Exhibition: Stereotypes of Yankee and Hebrew in 1851," Frank Felsenstein's contribution to this volume.
13. There may also be some connection between the stereotypical lisp and the story of the shibboleth (Judg.12). Having surrounded the Ephraimites, the Gileadites, who know that the Ephraimites made no distinction between *s* and *sh* and could not pronounce the latter—for example, in the word *shibboleth*, which means *ear of corn*—would not let the unidentified pass through their lines unless they could say the word. *Sibboleth* merited summary execution. The lisp, then, might serve to foreground the uses of sibilance.
14. Ogden, *Isaac*, 207.
15. Quoted in Ogden, *Isaac D'Israeli*, 114–115.
16. In large part to allow his own four children (Benjamin, James [Jacobus], Ralph [Raphael], and Sarah) to gain access freely to culturally or religiously restricted institutions such as Oxbridge, D'Israeli had the four baptized during the summer of 1817 (Ogden, *Isaac D'Israeli*, 201).

17. Ogden, *Isaac D'Israeli*, 160.
18. *Vaurien: or, Sketches of the Times, Exhibiting Views of the Philosophies, Religions, Politics, Literature, and Manners of the Age*, 2 vols. (London: T. Cadell, 1797), 2:250n.
19. "Father Account of the Family of Nonsense," *The Wit's Magazine: or, Library of Momus: Being a Compleat Repository of Mirth, Humour, and Entertainment* 1(1784): 177–179; "Letter from Nonsense with Some Account of Himself and Family," *The Wit's Maggzine* 1 (1784): 145–147.
20. *Flim-flams!: or, The Life and Errors of my Uncle, and the Amours of my Aunt!* 3 vols. (London: Printed for John Murray, 1805).
21. Ogden, *Isaac D'Israeli*, 11. See also *The Wit's Magazine* 1 (1784): 177–179, and Wilfrid S. Samuel, "D'Israeli: First Published Writing," *Notes and Queries* (April 30, 1949).
22. Ogden, *Isaac D'Israeli*, 11. See also *The Wit's Magazine* 1 (1784): 177–179.
23. Quoted in Ogden, *Isaac D'Israeli*, 11.
24. Alexander Pope, *Alexander Pope*, ed. Pat Rogers (New York: Oxford University Press, 1993), 21.
25. Edmund Spenser, *The Faerie Queene*, ed. Thomas P. Roche, Jr., assisted by C. Patrick O'Donnell, Jr. (New Haven: Yale University Press, 1978), 587.
26. Ogden, *Isaac D'Israeli*, 49.
27. Ogden, *Isaac D'Israeli*, 18. "On the Abuse of Satire," *Gentleman's Magazine* XIV:ii (1789): 748–749.
28. *Defence of Poetry*, in *A Defence of Poetry [and] Specimens of a New Version of Telemachus* (London: Stockdale, 1790), 22n.
29. Quoted in Ogden, *Isaac D'Israeli*, 50.
30. Isaac's father, Benjamin D'Israeli, was in fact a merchant—an importer of Italian goods, to be specific (Ogden, *Isaac D'Israeli*, 6).
31. *The Monthly Review*, second ser., XLIV, 333; as quoted in Ogden, *Isaac D'Israeli*, 51–52.
32. *Mejnoun and Leila*, in *Romances by I. D'Israeli. To Which Is Now Added a Modern Romance* (1799; Philadelphia: Samuel F. Bradford, 1803). Future references to *Mejnoun and Leila* are indicated parenthetically in the text.
33. *Orientalism* (1978; New York: Vintage, 1979), 2–3.
34. "'Some Examples of the Finest Orientalism': Byronic Philhellenism and Proto-Zionism at the Time of the Congress of Vienna," in *Romanticism and Colonialism: Writing and Empire, 1780–1830,* ed. Tim Fulford and Peter J. Kitson (Cambridge: Cambridge University Press, 1999), 222.
35. "Orientalism: The Romantics' Added Dimension; or, Edward Said Refuted," *EESE (Erfurt Electronic Studies in English)* < http://webdoc.gwdg.de/edoc/ia/eese/artic20/naji/3_2000.html > (January 10, 2003): 2.
36. Conversely, Gilman notes the way that Christianity worked from the time of the Gospels, its originating narratives, to establish a sharp distinction between the historical Jesus, who was an Aramaic-speaking Jew, and the Jesus of the Gospels, who ultimately is made to speak to gentiles in their own vernacular. In their rendering of Jesus's last speech on the cross, the four Gospels describe a movement away from Aramaic, "the 'hidden' language of the Jews[, which] is the magical language of difference," and toward that vernacular. What begins as *"Eli, Eli, Lama Sabachthani"* ("My God, My God, why hast thou forsaken me") in Matthew (27:46), and is rendered virtually identically in Mark (15:34), becomes "Father, into thy hands I commend my spirit" in

Luke (23:46), and then "it is finished" in John (19:30). To Gilman, "His language needs no translation; it is transparent, familiar not foreign" (13–15).

37. As Ogden notes, "D'Israeli's literary tastes . . . are those of the average cultivated Englishman of the period. . . . Among modern poets, Dryden Pope, and Gray are considered pre-eminent . . ." (*Isaac D'Israeli*, 38).

38. Ogden, *Isaac D'Israeli*, 207.

39. In terms of their nomadic life, the Bedouins recall the Israelites who, after being freed from bondage in Egypt, wandered for forty years in the desert before entering Canaan.

40. *Coningsby; or, the New Generation* (London: Longmans, 1900). Future references to *Coningsby* are indicated parenthetically in the text.

41. Sidon, today a city in Lebanon, was a Phoenician seaport mentioned throughout the post-Mosaic portion of the Old Testament (e.g., 1 Kings 11:5, Ezek. 28:20–21). In *Coningsby*, Madame Colonna tellingly refers to Sidonia as "Monsieur de Sidonia" (208), as does Lady Wallinger (348), thereby making the onomastic doubling of *Disraeli* and *Sidonia* identical down to the use of the quasi-noble *de*.

42. Gilman, *The Jew's Body*, 13–16.

43. It is perhaps a reminiscence of this passage that underwrites Thackeray's satirizing of Jewish physiognomy in *Codlingsby*. Walking through London's Jewish quarter just before the Friday night sunset and the start of the Sabbath, Codlingsby takes in the sights, among them the following:

> Ringlets glossy, and curly, and jetty—eyes as black as night—midsummer night—when it lightens; haughty noses bending like the beaks of eagles—eager quivering nostrils—lips curved like the bow of Love—every man or maiden, every babe or matron in that English Jewry bore in his countenance one or more characteristics of his peerless Arab race. (16)

Edith maintains the purity of Hebrew lineage that is emphasized by Sidonia. Disraeli makes a point of noting the she is not the daughter of Sir Joseph Wallinger and his lady, "but his niece; the child of his wife's sister" (305). Both sisters, along with the rest of their nominally Catalan family, fled "during a political convulsion to England" (321)—to Liverpool, to be specific. The family name, *Millbank*, is a curiosity in its own right, for it seems to be an adopted family name, albeit one adopted by the traditions of Jewish onomastics: a family name denoting a city of origin or residence. Although her travels take her to the most stylish places in many of the great capitals of Europe, Edith's "thoughts were often in her Saxon valley, amid the green hills and busy factories of Millbank." The name suggests the traditional connection of the Jews with manufacturing (Mill) and banking. The latter is in fact the family business of Sidonia and his relations.

To be a Spaniard of gentle birth in *Coningsby* is to be a Jew in all probability, since the religious pressure of the Inquisition in post-1492 Spain left two alternatives to fleeing: conversion or death at the stake. Sidonia's family, for example, was, on the surface, particularly close to the Church: "Besides several prelates, they counted among their number an archbishop of Toledo; and a Sidonia, in a season of great danger and difficulty, had exercised for many years the paramount office of Grand Inquisitor." Nor was Sidonia's family an exception: "[t]his illustrious family during all this period, in common with two-thirds of the Arragonese nobility, adhered to the ancient faith and ceremonies of their fathers; a belief in the unity of the God of Sinai, and the rights and observations of the laws of Moses" (209).

44. As a schoolboy D'Israeli "made very little progress with Greek or Latin, but began to acquire a considerable knowledge of modern languages." He acquired his languages while he "stayed with his father's agent at Amsterdam" (Ogden, *Isaac D'Israeli*, 9), albeit not at the homes of relatives, as Sidonia does (215). Benjamin Disraeli, on the other hand, was compelled to learn Greek and Latin at Higham Hall as a public-school boy.

45. Sidonia occupies an interesting middle ground between the Byronic hero and Emily Brontë's Heathcliff, on the one hand and the damaged male protagonist of the modern novel—F. Scott Fitzgerald's Jay Gatz, Ernest Hemingway's Jake Barnes, John Barth's Jack Horner, and of course Philip Roth's Alexander Portnoy.

46. Ogden, *Isaac D'Israeli*, 56, 74.

47. Ogden, *Isaac D'Israeli*, 210–213.

48. Stuart Peterfreund, "Not for 'Antiquaries,' but for 'Philosophers': Isaac D'Israeli's Talmudic Critique and His Talmudical Way with Literature," in *British Romanticism and the Jews: History, Culture, Literature*, ed. Sheila A. Spector (New York: Palgrave/Macmillan, 2002), 187–188.

49. Ferdinand Benary (fl. 1830) wrote on Hebrew levirate marriage (the marriage of a widow by her deceased husband's brother) in the context of laws and tradition pertaining to this custom, as well as on Sanskrit poetry.

50. Luiz Costa-Lima, "Auerbach and Literary History," *Literary History and the Challenge of Philology: The Legacy of Erich Auerbach*, ed. Seth Lerer (Stanford: Stanford University Press, 1996), 54.

51. *Mimesis: The Representation of Reality in Western Literature*, trans. Willard R. Trask (Princeton: Princeton University Press, 1953). Future references to *Mimesis* are indicated parenthetically in the text. It is interesting to note that it was the modern Turkey of Kemal Attaturk, the post–world war successor-state to the Ottoman Empire, which offered Auerbach a position teaching Western European literature at the University of Istanbul. Despite his own militant secularism and an unflattering history of dealing with Greek and Armenian elements of its bourgeoisie by deportation or genocide, Attaturk did continue the Ottoman history of friendly relations with the Jews that often led to their employment in positions of trust and/or responsibility (see Jan N. Bremmer, "Erich Auerbach and His Mimesis," *Poetics Today* 20, 1 [spring 1999]: 5; and Karen Armstrong, *The Battle Cry for God* [New York: Ballantine, 2000], 191).

52. Bremmer, "Enic Auerbach," 3, 5.

53. "Mimesis as Performance: Rereading Auerbach's First Chapter," *Poetics Today* 20, 1 (spring 1999): 17.

54. "Church History and the Cultural Geography of Erich Auerbach: Europe and Its Eastern other," in *Opening the Borders: Inclusivity in Early Modern Studies, Essays in Honor of James V. Mirollo*, ed. Peter C. Herman (Newark: University of Delaware Press, 1999), 325.

CHAPTER 7

ANGLO-JEWISH IDENTITY AND THE
POLITICS OF CULTIVATION IN HAZLITT,
AGUILAR, AND DISRAELI*

Judith W. Page

In 1830, William Cobbett challenged his readers to "produce a Jew who
ever dug, who went to the plough, or who ever made his own coat or his
own shoes, or who did anything at all, except get all the money he could
from the pockets of the people."[1] Cobbett repeats the old canard that Jews,
as international vagabonds, have no connection to the land and thus cannot
be legitimate Britons. Cobbett resented Jews for allegedly refusing to do real
work, and he also feared that if unfettered, Jews would buy up and degrade
the land meant for others to work. In response to the sort of worldview
promoted by Cobbett (if not in direct response to him), writers more
friendly to Jews and Judaism made land and cultivation central to their sense
of Jewish identity in nineteenth-century Britain.[2] These writers returned to
the biblical notion of the Jews as cultivators of fields and vineyards, and
presented Jews as adaptors of ancient traditions to contemporary Britain.
Beginning with William Hazlitt's passionate defense of Jewish emancipation
in 1831 and looking at several prints of "Jewish" country houses, I chart the
centrality of "the land" and ownership to the position of Jews in Britain.
Such writers as Grace Aguilar and Benjamin Disraeli use narrative scenes of
gardening and agriculture to negotiate the slippery terrain of British–Jewish
identity in the early- to mid-nineteenth century. Paradoxically, though, the
connection to the land in Aguilar leads to an affirmation of Anglo-Jewish
identity, while Disraeli's contrast between the landscapes of England and
Palestine makes accommodation more difficult. As a practicing Jew and child
of immigrants, Aguilar adheres to "the liberal dream of inclusion" and has
great hopes for making Britain a national home for Jews.[3] In contrast,
Disraeli, the most famous convert from Judaism to Christianity in

nineteenth-century England and an emerging proto-Zionist, develops an outlandish theory of Semitic racial superiority and imagines his superior Semites most at home in Palestine.

I

In "Emancipation of the Jews," William Hazlitt develops an agricultural metaphor at the center of his argument for civil emancipation. His passionate language both rehearses the traditional charges and transforms the literal notions of work and cultivation into a metaphor for understanding the plight of the Jews in history. Speaking for all Britons, Hazlitt argues that

> We [also] object to their trades and modes of life; that is, we shut people up in close confinement and complain that they do not live in the open air. The Jews barter and sell commodities, instead of raising and manufacturing them. But this is the necessary traditional consequence of their former persecution and pillage by all nations. They could not set up a trade when they were hunted every moment from place to place, and while they could count nothing their own but what they could carry with them. They could not devote themselves to the pursuit of agriculture, when they were not allowed to possess a foot of land. You tear a people up by the roots and trample on them like noxious weeds, and then make an outcry that they do not take root in the soil like wholesome plants. You drive them like a pest from city to city, from kingdom to kingdom, and then call them vagabonds and aliens.[4]

The literal condition of the Jews in history vis-à-vis the land becomes a metaphor of perpetual uprooting and stunted growth. Like Shakespeare's history plays, in which the health of the body politic is compared to the state of a garden, Hazlitt implies that the garden of Britain needs proper tending if the country is to thrive and progress. Furthermore, his shift from the third person "they" in reference to the Jews to the second person "you" implicates his readers in the process of Jewish oppression.

Hazlitt also argues against the notion that Jews can form no attachments to British soil because they hope to be restored to their promised land. While not denying the biblical promise or its eventual fulfillment, Hazlitt argues that this event "may be delayed eighteen hundred more [years]" and should thus not be an impediment to Jewish emancipation (322). Furthermore, Hazlitt posits that if Jews were connected to the land through work and ownership, Jews as a group would have a stake in British loyalty:

> Suppose a Jew to have amassed a large fortune in the last war, and to have laid by money in the funds, and built himself a handsome house in the neighborhood of the metropolis; would he be more likely by his vote in the House of Commons to promote a revolution, so as to cause a general bankruptcy; or to encourage the mob to pull down his house, or root up his favourite walks, because after all, at the end of several centuries, he and the rest of his nation indulge in the prospect of returning to their own country. (322)

Where Cobbett saw the potential destruction of traditional relationships to the land, Hazlitt argues that Jewish ownership of property will lead to greater stability. Once again, he uses the language of uprooting, but this time it is quite personal: the Jewish homeowner (implicitly) is attached to his "favourite walks," and has made England his home.

A similar argument ensues in the critical response to Disraeli's fiction. In reviewing the Young England trilogy (*Coningsby, Sybil,* and *Tancred*) in *The Times,* the reviewer argues that if the conversion societies will let the Jews alone, "they will Christianize themselves in less than a generation. Whilst Mr. Disraeli eloquently discourses of [*sic*] a speedy return to Jerusalem, Sidonia [Disraeli's Rothschild-like character] buys a noble estate in Bucks, and Sidonia's first cousin is high-sheriff of the county. . . ."[5] An official Jewish response comes from Jacob Franklin in *The Voice of Jacob* on April 23, 1847:

> If Sidonia buys a noble estate in Bucks, he not only does not act against the precepts of Judaism, but he literally follows the counsel of the prophet, who thus advised Israel, saying, "This captivity is long: build ye houses and dwell in them; and plant gardens and eat the fruit of them" (Jerem. xxix, 28); and if Sidonia's first cousin is high-sheriff of a country, he only follows the noble example set to him by Daniel, Hannaniah, Meshael, and Azariah; and surely England is worth Babylon, Queen Victoria, Nebuchadnezzar, and a Heathen empire a Christian. The truth is, the Jews never secluded themselves from the Christians—it was the Christians who excluded the Jews.[6]

Jacob Franklin, then, emphasizes not only that Jews can survive living amidst Christians, but that for Jews of the Diaspora, it is a *mitzvah* (an obligation under the Law) to cultivate the earth—to put down roots—wherever they find themselves. His argument is rooted in the Bible, but he does not necessarily refute the argument that such land-owning practices in the Diaspora may lead to "Christianizing."

Although Hazlitt does not acknowledge that Jews had been connecting to the English land for over a hundred years, more recently Malcolm Brown has documented the developing tradition of Anglo-Jewish country houses, both in the environs of London and more far afield, in Leicestershire and Sidmouth. The purchase or design of country houses was often accompanied by a parallel interest in gardening, including the cultivation of seeds and cuttings from as far away as America (27). Todd M. Endelman examines this movement of well-to-do Jews to country houses (often in addition to the London townhouse), distinguishing in general between the Sephardim, who began the practice in the eighteenth century, and the Ashkenazim, who continued it in the early decades of the nineteenth. According to Endelman, Sephardim were more likely to break ties with the Jewish community than the Ashkenazim. For Sephardim, "the purchase of a country property represented more than conformity to the social ideals of the landowning class. It also indicated a willingness to live, either permanently or temporarily, outside Jewish social circles and without access to synagogues and other religious institutions that are essential to Jewish observance."[7]

Paradoxically, Hazlitt's argument for emancipation could lead to assimilation so radical that Jews actually gave up their Judaism, a position expressed in the satirical *Punch*. Endelman argues that wealthy Ashkenazim left Judaism for "Material self-interest, social ambition, [and] religious indifference" (47). When it came to establishing and promoting homes in the country, this seems to be a prime motivation. Like other owners of country estates, Jews participated in the culture of promoting their homes and by extension their social status by subscribing to collections of prints of countryseats—and essentially paying for the inclusion of their own country house in the volume. In the 1800 edition of *Seats of the Nobility and Gentry in Great Britain and Wales in a Collection of Select Views*, this notice occurs:

> The Proprietor of this Work respectfully informs the Nobility and Gentry who honor him with their patronage, that owing to the great Advance on Paper, Printing, &c, and indeed on every Article of Life, he is under the Necessity of suppressing one Plate in this and future Numbers: he hopes this Arrangement will meet with their Approbation in Preference to advancing the Price, as it will enable him to bring forward the second Volume with more Expedition, which will complete the Work.[8]

Another such collection, *Picturesque Views of the Principal Seats of the Nobility and Gentry, By the most Eminent British Artists, with A Description of each Seat*, includes plates of the homes and verbal descriptions of at least three Jews or recent converts, M. Ximenes, Sir Sampson Gideon, and M. I. Levy.[9] Most of the prints in the volume conventionally place the house clearly in the background, usually centered, with human and animal figures in the foreground and a frame of trees, shrubs, and other signs of cultivation. The corresponding verbal description puffs the house and its owners, making it as attractive as possible to other members of the upper classes and to tourists alike. The "Jewish seats" represented in the collection are not identified as such, and except for the telltale name, there would be no way of identifying Jews or Jewishness. Like the other prints and descriptions, they are calculated to "place" the owners in the land and on the social scale. As Richard Wilson and Alan Mackley argue in *Creating Paradise*, "The value of a house was not viewed primarily in economic terms. It might, in adverse circumstances, be rented out, but generally owners wrote it off as an item of exceptional consumption, possessing, however, considerable social and political benefits."[10]

Consider, first, the print of the Ximenes estate in Berkshire, Bear Place (figure 7.1). The multistoried and -winged house sits in the background. In the foreground are both a laborer herding three animals and a lady guiding her dog through the park. The illustration shows the congruence of the elite (presumably owners of the estate) with the worker, or rather it shows that this is a working estate, but one with pleasant walks. There is a harmony in the little world of Bear Place. In addition to a verbal description of the house as "a handsome modern edifice" and "striking," the blurb states that

Figure 7.1   Gough maps 177 "Bear Place."

"The grounds are laid out with considerable taste, and the prospects are both numerous and pleasing." The writer goes on to say that there are several homes with the name Bear, "which they are said to have retained ever since the time of William the Conqueror; when a family of that name, or one of a similar sound, is supposed to have been put in possession of this part of the country for some distance round." Thus the description balances the modernity of the house with Norman tradition going back to William the Conqueror, presumably with no irony intended toward the current Jewish occupants, who surely would not have been welcome back then.[11]

The print of Sir Sampson Gideon's Belvidere House in Kent is equally conventional (figure 7.2). Once again, the house is centered in the background. In front of it sheep graze and in the immediate foreground a man rests from hunting, with one faithful dog by his side and the other leaping playfully. The man and seated dog rest under the canopy of a large tree, perhaps an oak, which would be a fitting symbol of their national devotion to England. The verbal description boasts about the spectacular view of the Thames (not visible in the print) and the constant traffic of ships "employed in the immense trade of London," perhaps a reference to the commercial world that the elder Samson [*sic*] Gideon was a part of. The current owner, Sir Sampson, who had been baptized as a child,[12] "has a fine collection of pictures by the very first masters, and other works of virtù, well worth the attention of the curious." Presumably when he is not hunting, Sir Sampson busies himself with his art collection, another mark of his social status and taste.

Figure 7.2   Gough maps 177 "Belvidere House."

Figure 7.3   Gough maps 177 "Prospect Place."

The third print is that of Prospect Place in Surrey, the seat of M. I. Levy (figure 7.3). Similar to the others, this print features the mansion in the background with two figures in the foreground: a lady with a parasol and her playful dog. But to the left, a coach is entering the road up to the house, perhaps signifying the proximity of the house to London and the larger world: "This Villa is most delightfully situated, on a rising ground, in the lane leading from Wimbledon to Kingston, at the distance of about ten miles from the metropolis." The description boasts of the "rich view of the country," and also focuses on the arts of cultivation: "The hot-houses, and forcing walls, are large and spacious; and they are remarkable for producing the earliest, largest, and finest fruits, in the country." Having excellent fruit trees is a mark of status. When the financier Abraham Goldsmid threw an elaborate housewarming at Morden Lodge (on a Friday night, yet, August 22, 1806), Dr. Hughson's guide book reported the gardens in this way: "The gardens are capacious, and well-stocked with every vegetable, flower, and fruit, foreign and native, that can be procured. The pineries, graperies, orangeries, & c are well worth the attention of the botanist and curious; in short, the gardens, hot and green-houses, & c do much credit to Mr Nicols, the present head gardener."[13] Of course, this kind of lavish display would only have confirmed a critic such as Cobbett in his claim that Jews will never be connected to the land; rather, they are dealers and "procurers."[14] Niall Ferguson, however, describes Amschel Rothschild's garden in his (and the first Jewish) home outside of the Jugenstrasse in Frankfort in very different terms. According to Ferguson, Rothschild bought the house in 1811 and then the garden next door in increments over the next several years in order to escape the oppression of the ghetto, but also with the fear that he, as a Jew, would lose the right to live there. Rothschild sometimes slept in the garden, described as his family's "paradise," and encouraged his brothers to send him seeds, plants and cuttings from all over the world. But this was not a show-off garden: rather, it was a place where Amschel Rothschild spent his time when weather permitted and where the family could celebrate a festival such as *Sukkot*, the fall pilgrimage festival, out of doors.[15]

II

While a select number of well-to-do British Jews owning country seats may not have done much to refashion notions of Jews and the land, later in the nineteenth century Grace Aguilar, opening up the world of working-class Jews, in part established their identity as British Jews by placing them in the domestic context of gardens. As in the real-life story of Amschel Rothschild's garden, but with an emphasis on ordinary folk, Aguilar draws a tie between cultivating the earth, domestic happiness, and Anglo-Jewish identity. These connections are most apparent in her novella *The Perez Family*, written for the Cheap Jewish Library (1843). Aguilar frames the family's life in relation to nature:

> Leading out of one of those close, melancholy alleys in the environs of Liverpool was a small cottage, possessing little of comfort or beauty in outward

appearance, but much in the interior in favor of its inhabitants; cleanliness and neatness were clearly visible, greatly in contradistinction to the neighboring dwellings. There were no heaps of dirt and half-burnt ashes, no broken or even cracked panes in the brightly shining windows, not a grain of unseemly dust or stains either on door or ledge—so that even poverty itself looked respectable. The cottage stood apart from the others, with a good piece of ground for a narrow lane, to the banks of the Mersey, and thus permitted a fresher current of air. The garden was carefully and prettily laid out, and planted with the sweetest flowers; and the small parlor and kitchen of the cottage opened into it, and so, greatly to the disappointment and vexation of the gossips of the alley, nothing could be gleaned of the sayings and doings of the inmates.[16]

Aguilar attributes middle-class respectability to this poor Jewish family, emphasizing their clean and ordered existence. But Aguilar also sets middle-class domesticity in a version of nature imagined as private or secluded space. Michael Galchinsky has argued that Aguilar "bargained" with the dominant culture and agreed to confine Jewish ritual and practice to the private world of the home, with the public lives of her characters less conspicuously Jewish.[17] This passage replicates such a bargain because it shows that the very set-up of the garden, in the tradition of more elaborate walled gardens (here the dingy alley stands in for the ancient wall), creates and endorses that private space, where the family celebrates the Jewish Sabbath with Hebrew blessings and prayers as well as traditional foods. In addition, we later learn that the father of the family has planned and laid out the garden with care in a kind of redemptive act—here it is prettily laid out, planted with the sweetest flowers—in contrast to the heaps of dirt and ashes that are evoked by their very absence from the Perez's garden.

Aguilar reiterates the situation of the garden later in story, there explaining that the garden was created after their first home was destroyed in a fire:

The most painful circumstance in their present dwelling was its low neighbourhood; and partially to remedy this evil Sarah prevailed on her uncle to employ his leisure in cultivating the little garden behind the house, making their sitting-room and kitchen open into it, and contriving an entrance through them, so as scarcely to use the front, except for ingress and egress which necessity compelled . . . Both local and national disadvantages often unite to debar the Jews from agriculture, and therefore it is a branch in which they are seldom, if ever, employed. Their scattered state among the nations, the occupations which misery and persecution compel them to adopt, are alone to blame for those peculiar characteristics which cause them to herd in the most miserable alleys of crowded cities, rather than the pure air and cheaper living of the country. Perez found pleasure and a degree of health in his new employment: the delight which it was to his poor little blind Ruth to sit by his side while he worked, and inhale the reviving scent of the newly-turned earth or budding flowers, would of itself have inspired him, but his wife too shared the enjoyment. It was a pleasure to take the twins by her side, and teach them their God was a God of love, alike through his inspired Word, and through his works; and Joseph and Ruth learned to love their new house better than their last, because it had a garden and flowers, and they learned from that much more than they had ever learned before. (97)

The first part of this passage reiterates the situation of the garden, but the narrative voice goes on to explain why cultivating a garden is so significant for Perez. Aguilar echoes the argument that Hazlitt made in "Emancipation" about Jews and agriculture. Nature and cultivation represent the establishment of roots, as well as health and spiritual well being. The garden scene is also the perfect complement to the indoor domesticity celebrated in other parts of the novella because it is the site of nurturing and education for the family, in this case an ecological joy in God's works inspired by the Bible as well as by the English Romantic poets that Aguilar knew so well. Although crowded in the city, members of the Perez family create their own refuge, an English version of the Vale of Cedars that had been essential to the Spanish-Jewish family in Aguilar's novel of that name.

In tracing the development of the Perez family, their hardships and their increasing respectability, Aguilar uses the garden as an indicator of the family's social status: "A small but most comfortably-furnished parlour of a new respectable-looking dwelling, in one of the best streets of Liverpool, . . . it was a room thrown out from the usual back of the house, opening by a large French window, and one or two steps into a small but beautifully laid-out flower garden, divided by a passage and another parlour from the handsome shop, which opened on the street" (167–168). Aguilar no longer offers us an image of the family in the garden, but instead emphasizes the architectural features and design that set it off. The large French window signifies the Perez's increased "station" (168), a mark of their taste and prosperity. Furthermore, the passage goes on to celebrate the fact that the "Perez Brothers" have set up a watchmaker's and silversmith's shop attached to their house, the perfect emblem of the harmony of their commercial life with their respectable home. Aguilar suggests that the separation of the private and public sphere is less clear-cut than one might think, and that perhaps the ideal involves more of a balance than a bargain. Aguilar implies this balance in describing the back parlour and garden as connected to the shop by "a passage and another parlour" (168). This arrangement breaks down the barriers between public and private spheres in the way that Davidoff and Hall explain was typical for a middle-class family before the workplace was separated from the home.[18]

For Aguilar, then, the celebration of domesticity involves both the indoor and outdoor world. Aguilar attempts literally to domesticate British Jews by showing them at home—cultivating their gardens even in dark corners of the kingdom and making the best of their connection to British soil. She imagines her Jewish family at home in nature, and hence capable of being naturalized into the British nation. Whereas the well-to-do Jews established their connectedness by owning property, often lavishly, Aguilar's upwardly mobile working-class family actually get their hands dirty, in defiance of Cobbett's diatribe denying that Jews ever dug anything. In fact, in one of the many eulogies written after Aguilar's untimely and tragic death at thirty-one, Anna Maria Hall ("Pilgrimage to the grave of Grace Aguilar") focuses on Aguilar's love of the English countryside—its rocks, and shells and flowers— as part of her identity: "She had made acquaintance with the beauties of English nature during a long residence in Devonshire; loved the country with her whole heart, and enriched her mind by the leisure it afforded; she had collected and arranged conchological and mineralogical specimens to a considerable extent; loved flowers as only sensitive women can love them; and with all this was deeply read in theology and history."[19] Aguilar herself corroborates this love for English land in her Frankfort diary, written when she was dying away from home. On a drive in the hills above Frankfort, Aguilar comments: "It was one of the hilliest drives we have taken & the air & the skies most delicious & the country tho' exceedingly pretty around Frankfort cannot compare in beauty and grandeur, to the scenery in Devonshire."[20] This translates into national allegiance. As Aguilar writes to Solomon Cohen, an American friend: "You must know I am heart and soul an English woman an enthusiast for my adopted country her government laws and talent—I cannot feel towards any other country as I do towards England. The love I bear Judea is a different kind of feeling . . ."[21] Although Aguilar does not explain this love for Judea, her comments about her love for England sound Wordsworthian and echo the sentiments of Wordsworth's linking of "patriotic and domestic love," in the *Prelude* and in his famous "Lucy" poem:

> I travelled among unknown Men,
>   In lands beyond the Sea;
> Nor England! did I know till then
>   What love I bore to thee.[22]

As a Jew affirming such a connection, Aguilar makes a leap not required of Wordsworth, because Jews did not have a "natural" connection to the English land.[23]

III

In one of the most interesting episodes in *Tancred, or the New Crusade* (1847), Disraeli focuses on the paradoxes of Anglo-Jewish identity: celebrating the pilgrimage festival of *Sukkot* in the Diaspora.[24] A warm celebration of the harvest and vineyard, *Sukkot* commemorates the biblical thanksgiving for the ingathering of the fruits. It is also linked to the Exodus from Egypt and the period in which the Israelites lived in tents on their journey to the Promised Land. Although Disraeli focuses on the relation- ships between Judaism and Christianity in "the Holy Land," and famously developed the idea that "Christianity was Judaism for the masses" (*Tancred*, 575), in this episode he focuses on Judaism in the Diaspora. He does so by describing the festival that links Jews to the land of Israel, or by metaphorical substitution, to *the land* in which they live. In so doing, he demonstrates the way in which Jews negotiate between their Jewish identity and British nationality, between the Promised Land and Britain: "The vineyards of Israel have ceased to exist, but the eternal law enjoins the children of Israel still to celebrate the vintage, although they have no fruits to gather, will regain their vineyards. What sublime inexorability in the law! But what indomitable spirit in the people!" (524).

In *Tancred*, Disraeli traces the spiritual quest and actual journey of the aristocratic young Christian Tancred to the Holy Land. Tancred's mentor is Disraeli's fabulously wealthy and generous Anglo-Sephardic Jew Sidonia (modeled on the non-Sephardic Rothschilds). Sidonia represents the height of cultured Anglo-Judaism; the narrator's focus in chapter 6 of book 5 is on ordinary Jews who find themselves in a cold northern climate amidst people who do not understand the Jews' commitment to the Law. Whereas the commentary on and dialogue of Sidonia often reiterates Disraeli's problematic theory of "Mosaic Arabs" and Semitic racial superiority,[25] the paean to ordinary Jews seems closest to inquiring into Anglo-Jewish identity. Disraeli's narrator turns aside from the story of Tancred for a few pages and directly addresses the reader several times in the present tense, establishing a much greater degree of intimacy than the usual narrative voice:

> It is easy for the happier Sephardim, the Hebrews who have never quitted the sunny regions that are laved by the midland Ocean; it is easy for them, though they have lost their heritage, to sympathise, in their beautiful Asian cities or in their Moorish and Arabian gardens, with the graceful rites that are, at least, an homage to a benignant nature. But picture to yourself the child of Israel in the dingy suburb or the squalid quarter of some bleak northern town, where there is never a sun that can at any rate ripen grapes. Yet he must celebrate the vintage of purple Palestine! The law has told him, though a denizen in an icy clime, that he must dwell for seven days in a bower, and that he must build it of boughs of thick trees; and the Rabbins have told him that these thick trees are the palm, the myrtle, and the weeping willow. (525)

Throughout the passage, Disraeli highlights the supposed incongruity of Jews celebrating *Sukkot* in a land and landscape that is alien to the ancient hills and vineyards of Palestine. Todd Endelman has read this passage as an indication of Disraeli's commitment to Jewish ethnicity and potential nationhood, rather than a meditation on Jewish religious practices. As Endelman argues, Disraeli is not interested in "redemptive dimension of the holiday, its commemoration of the period after the exodus from Egypt during which the Israelites dwelled in booths, and instead concentrated on its agricultural aspect, especially the harvesting of grapes and making of wine, a theme that is absent in Jewish tradition."[26] I agree that Disraeli's narrative celebration of *Sukkot* is related to his prophecy that Jews "will regain their vineyards" (524)—to his proto-Zionism. From the perspective of the return to Zion, such agricultural celebrations as *Sukkot* both fulfill the Law and remind the Jewish community of the possibility of return. Nevertheless, if Disraeli had commented on the relationship between *Sukkot* and the Exodus, he would have had additional reason to connect the festival with the hope of return to Zion. Perhaps he did not know of this dimension of the holiday, although he was probably familiar with David Levi's *A Succinct Account, of the Rites, and Ceremonies, of the Jews* (1782).[27] Paradoxically, too, while Aguilar's gardens emphasize the connection of her Jews to British land, Disraeli's focus on the incongruity between the ancient celebration and the British climate and landscape, reinscribes the difference between British Jews and their neighbors, between British and Jewish nationality. Although Disraeli's portrait is sympathetic, his Jews and their commitment to ancient rituals—their "devoted observance of Oriental customs in the heart of our Saxon and Sclavonian cities" (525)—alienates them as Britons.[28]

Extending the celebratory passage, the narrator draws us in and goes on to acknowledge the historical plight of the Jews in relation to their devotion to Judaism:

> Conceive a being born and bred in the Judenstrasse of Hamburg or Frankfort, or rather in the purlieus of our Houndsditch or Minories, born to hereditary insult, without any education, apparently without a circumstance that can develop the slightest taste, or cherish the least sentiment for the beautiful, living amid fogs and filth, never treated with kindness, seldom with justice, occupied with the meanest, if not the vilest, toil, bargaining for frippery, speculating in usury, existing for ever under the concurrent influence of degrading causes which would have worn out, long ago, any race that was not of the unmixed blood of Caucasus, and did not adhere to the laws of Moses; conceive such as being, an object to you of prejudice, dislike, disgust, perhaps hatred. The season arrives, and the mind and heart of that being are filled with images and passions that have been ranked in all ages among the most beautiful and the most genial of human experience . . . (526)

Disraeli sees these Jews as survivors of degraded circumstance who have been able nonetheless to maintain their connection to what is beautiful and life-affirming in their tradition. His analysis may strike contemporary readers as patronizing, but I would argue that sympathy outweighs condescension. Disraeli's narrative technique of appealing directly to the reader and creating a vivid scene brings warmth to what might have otherwise simply been a purple passage:

> He rises in the morning, goes early to some Whitchapel market, purchases some willow boughs for which he has previously given a commission, and which are brought, probably, from one of the neighboring rivers of Essex, hastens home, cleans out the yard of his miserable tenement, builds his bower, decks it, even profusely, with the finest flowers and fruits that he can procure, the myrtle and the citron never forgotten, and hangs its roof with variegated lamps. After the service of his synagogue, he sups late with his wife and his children in the open air, as if he were in the pleasant villages of Galilee, beneath its sweet and starry sky.

The sympathy for the devotion of this poor Jew is further heightened as the passage continues and the narrator sarcastically imagines the response of a pair of working-class Englishmen to this display of Jewish practice:

> . . . Save us! A party of Anglo-Saxons, very respectable men, ten-pounders, a little elated it may be, though certainly not in honour of the vintage, pass the house, and words like these are heard—
> "I say, Buggins, what's that row?"
> "Oh! It's those cursed Jews! We've a lot of 'em here. It is one of their horrible feasts. The Lord Mayor ought to interfere. However, things are not as bad as they used to be: they used always to crucify little boys at these hullabaloos, but now they only eat sausages made of stinking pork."
> "To be sure," replies his companion, "we all make progress." (527–528)

To this Disraelian display of sympathy and sarcasm, *Punch* responded with an article entitled "The Jewish Champion" (April 10, 1847) on the side of Buggins and the like:

> Mr. DISRAELI has written no less than three novels to further the great cause of Jewish ascendancy, and to prove that the battle of the Constitution is to be fought in Holywell Street. The clever *littérateur* anticipates a golden age, should his views be carried out, but he forgets that it is, after all, only an age of Mosaic gold that he is contending for. After reading his last work of *Tancred*, we took quite a fresh view of all the itinerant sons of Israel whom we met in the streets of the Great Metropolis. "Look at that old-clothes man," said we to ourselves, "who would think that the unmixed blood of Caucasus runs through the veins of that individual, who has just offered us nine-pence for our penultimate hat, and is refusing to give us ten-pence for our preter-plu-perfect, or rather more than finished and done for, high-lows?"[29]

Putting the prejudices of Buggins together with *Punch*, readers get a shorthand version of various charges and assumptions about Jews, from the rumored blood libel (that Jews need Christian blood in their rituals) and assumption that Jews really do crave pork, to notions of Jewish hard bargaining and treachery, catalogued in the paragraph that follows: Jewish products always fall apart, old clothes are tainted with disease, and so on. The paradox of Disraeli's project is that the more keenly he developed his myth of Jewish "Eastern" superiority, the less comfortable his superior Jews seemed on British soil. Unlike the committed Jew Aguilar, Disraeli more easily imagined Jews on the hills of Palestine than in the English countryside. In this sense he fulfilled the counterargument of the naysayer in Hazlitt's essay, who could not imagine Jews as permanent residents on or developers of British soil because of their hankering for their biblical home.

For all of the difficult balances and compromises, Aguilar's vision and her domesticated storytelling are more conducive to forming a viable Jewish–British identity and fulfilling the promise of liberal emancipation as articulated by Hazlitt. Aguilar seems implicitly to understand the message of recent feminist critiques of home: "Where we come to locate ourselves in terms of our specific histories and differences must be a place with room for what can be salvaged from the past and what can be made new."[30] Although the liberal dream of emancipation may be more fraught than either Hazlitt or Aguilar imagined, both the radical essayist and the Anglo-Jewish "authoress" place Jews firmly in the English landscape that Disraeli finds so inhospitable to the Jews in his fiction.[31]

Notes

*   I would like to thank The Bodleian Library, University of Oxford, for permission to reproduce MS. Gough Maps 177: "Bear Place," "Belvidere House," and "Prospect Place."

1. *Good Friday*, 17, quoted in David Vital, *A People Apart: The Jews in Europe, 1789–1939* (New York: Oxford University Press, 1999), 187.

2. In "Anglo-Jewish country houses from the Resettlement to 1800," Malcolm Brown explains that "rights of entitlement were uncertain" (20) for Jews, but a small number of wealthy Jews nevertheless succeeded in buying and passing down land to their heirs (*Transactions of the Jewish Historical Society of England* 28 [1984]: 20). See Brown's extended argument.

3. I borrow the expression "liberal dream of inclusion" from Laura Leavitt in *Jews and Feminism*, with the acknowledgment that her use of the term refers to America and that Leavitt offers a critique of this liberal vision ([New York: Routledge, 1997], 7). See below, note 31.

4. *The Complete Works of William Hazlitt*, ed. P. P. Howe after A. P. Waller and Arnold Glover (New York: ASM Press, 1967), 19:321.

5. R. W. Stewart, *Disraeli's Novels Reviewed, 1826–1968* (Metuchen, NJ: Scarecrow Press, 1975), 233. On the subject of Jews and conversion, see Michael Ragussis, *Figures of Conversion: "The Jewish Question" and English National Identity* (Durham: Duke University Press, 1995).

6. "Judaism and the Reviewer of 'Tancred' in the 'Times,'" Stewart, *Disraeli's Novels*, 237.

7. *Radical Assimilation in English Jewish History, 1656–1945* (Bloomington: Indiana University Press, 1990), 13.

8. *Seats of the Nobility and Gentry in Great Britain and Wales in a Collection of Select Views Engraved by W. Angus from Pictures and drawings by the most eminent artists* (London: W. Angus, Islington, 1787), n.p.

9. (London: Harrison & Co.: n.d. but ca. 1786–1788).

10. *Creating Paradise: The Building of the English Country House, 1660–1880* (New York and London: Hambledon, 2000), 354.

11. Endleman explains that Moses Ximenes retired to Bear Place after inheriting it from his father. He became friendly with his neighbor Lord Barrymore and acted in various theatricals that Barrymore staged (*Radical Assimilation*, 17).

12. See Endelman, *Radical Assimilation*, 25–27.

13. Quoted in Katie Fretwell and Judith Goodman. "The Fete of Abraham Goldsmid: A Regency Garden Tragedy" <http://www.nationaltrust.org.uk/environment/html>. See also Mark Schoenfield's analysis of the Goldsmid family estates in "Abraham Goldsmid: Money Magician in the Popular Press," in *British Romanticism and the Jews: History, Culture,*

Literature, ed. Sheila A. Spector (New York: Palgrave/Macmillan, 2002), 44–45. Schoenfield refers to David Hughson's *London: being an accurate History and Description of the British Metropolis and its Neighborhood, to Thirty Miles Extent*, 6 vols. (London: J. Stratford, 1805–1809). In *Northanger Abbey*, Jane Austen presents a more sinister view of such consumption by linking it to the tyrannical patriarch: General Tilney, "The walls seemed countless in number, endless in length; a village of hot-houses seemed to arise among them, and a whole parish to be at work within the inclosure" (ed. Claire Grogan [Peterborough, Ontario: Broadview, 1996], 178).

14. Some Jewish owners of large estates, however, did show a genuine interest in husbandry. Malcolm Brown mentions, for instance, Naphtali Franks's interest on his estate in Misterton (*Anglo-Jewish Country Houses*, 27).

15. *The House of Rothschild: Money's Prophets, 1798–1848* (New York: Viking, 1998), 164–165.

16. In Grace Aguilar, *Selected Writings*, ed. Michael Galchinsky (Peterbrorough, Ontario: Broadview Press, 2003), 87.

17. See Glachinsky on Aguilar's bargain, in his *The Origin of the Modern Jewish Woman Writer: Romance and Reform in Victorian England* (Detroit: Wayne State University Press, 1996), especially 135–151. In favoring nature in its secluded and cultivated state, Aguilar presents an English-garden version of the refuge that protects the Sephardic Jews (the Henriquez family) from the Inquisition in *The Vale of Cedars*, a novel completed in 1835. The narrator describes the vale: "A gradual hill, partly covered with rich meadow grass, and partly with corn, diversified with foliage, sloped downward, leading by an easy descent to a small valley, where orange and lime tress, the pine and chestnut, palm and cedar, grew in beautiful luxuriance. . . . a natural fountain threw its sparking showers on beds of sweet-scented and gaily-colored flowers. The hand of man had very evidently aided nature in forming the wild yet chaste beauty of the scene" (1843, reprint [New York: D. Appleton and Company, 1919], 5–6).

18. See *Family Fortunes*, especially chapter 8, 357–370.

19. Reprinted in Aguilar's *Selected Writings*, 359.

20. *Selected Writings*, 399.

21. Galchinsky, "Grace Aguilar's Correspondence,"101.

22. *The Prelude, 1799, 1805, 1850*, ed. Jonathan Wordsworth, M. H. Abrams, and Stephen Gill (New York: Norton, 1979), ii 195. For "Lucy," see *The Poetical Works of William Wordsworth*, ed. Ernest de Selincourt and Helen Darbishire, 5 vols (Oxford: Clarendon Press, 1940–1949), 2:30–31.

23. This lack of connection with the land is clear in *Ivanhoe*, for instance, a work in which Scott ostensibly attempts to create sympathy for Jews. But whereas Robin Hood and his outlaws find refuge and freedom in the old oak forest, Isaac mock-heroically suffers a night of torment at the hands of the drunken friar who wants to convert him. The English land and landscape cannot accommodate Scott's Jews, who go into voluntary exile at the end of the novel. See chapter 32, which begins with "The daylight dawned upon the glades of the oak forest" (1819; reprint, ed. A. N. Wilson [New York: Penguin Books, 1984]). On the subject of Wordsworth and the land, see my "Gender and Domesticity," in *The Cambridge Companion to Wordsworth*, ed. Stephen Gill (New York: Cambridge University Press, 2003), 125–141.

24. (New York: John Lane: The Bodley Head, 1905).

25. *Coningsby, or the New Generation* (New York: Signet, 1962), 222.

26. "'A Hebrew to the end': The Emergence of Disraeli's Jewishness," in *The Self-Fashioning of Disraeli, 1818–1851,* ed. Charles Richmond and Paul Smith (Cambridge: Cambridge University Press, 1998), 123.

27. In *Jewish Enlightenment in an English Key: Anglo-Jewry's Construction of Modern Jewish Thought,* David B. Ruderman calls Levi's handbook "the standard English guide to Jewish practice for almost four decades" ([Princeton: Princeton University Press, 2000] 246). See also 132–134 where Ruderman elaborates the connection between Issac D'Israeli (Benjamin's father) and David Levi, as well as their conflicting views on Judaism. For more information about Levi, see Michael Scrivener's "British-Jewish Writing of the Romantic Era and the Problem of Modernity: The Example of David Levi," in *British Romanticism and the Jews: History, Culture, Literature,* ed. Sheila A. Spector (New York: Palgrave/Macmillan, 2002), 159–177.

28. Historically, this was not necessarily the case. The lives of Moses and Judith Montefiore demonstrate that British national pride and proto-Zionism may be complementary allegiances, in theory as well as practice. The Montefiores were sponsors of Jewish agricultural development in Palestine. Disraeli's case was very different, though. Whereas the Montefiore's were observant Jews, Disraeli, as an apostate, emphasizes in *Tancred* the alienation caused by Jewish ritual observance. Furthermore, Disraeli's praise of Judaism often includes a philo-Semitic belief in Christianity as the fulfillment of Judaism.

29. Stewart, *Disraeli's Novels,* 231.

30. Caren Kaplan, "Deterritorializations: The Rewriting of Home and Exile in Western Feminist Discourse," in *The Nature and Context of Minority Discourse,* ed. Abdul R. JanMohamed and David Lloyd (New York: Oxford University Press, 1990), 364–365.

31. See Laura Levitt's critique of liberal emancipation in *Jews and Feminism*: "By juxtaposing the two sides of the liberal/colonial coin—sameness and difference—I want to expose some of the gaps in liberalism's narrative of Jewish emancipation. Although we remain grateful to the liberal revolutions of the late eighteenth century for bringing Jews into the dominant cultures of the West, this is not the entire story. Our acceptance remains partial" (7).

CHAPTER 8

CHARLOTTE DACRE'S ZOFLOYA: THE GOTHIC DEMONIZATION OF THE JEW

Diane Long Hoeveler

I

In 1769, an odd little chapbook made its appearance in Hull, entitled *The Wandering Jew, or, The Shoemaker of Jerusalem: Who Lived When Our Lord and Savior Jesus Christ Was Crucified, and By Him Appointed to Wander Until He Comes Again: With His Discourse With Some Clergymen About the End of the World.*[1] This anonymous pamphlet was typical of much millenarian propaganda floating around at the time. But in this work, the Wandering Jew informs the Protestant clergymen that "before the End of the World the Jews shall be gathered together from all Parts of the World, and returned to Jerusalem, and live there, and it shall flourish as much as ever, and that they, and all others, shall become Christians, and that Wars shall cease, and the whole World live in Unity with one another" (7–8). The need to believe that the *Other*, the Jew, would become "one of us" was indeed strong across Europe, and the thinking was that if they could not be converted, then they could always be killed—for their own good, of course.

The legend of Ahasuerus, the Wandering Jew, is, perhaps, one of the most overlooked archetypal figures in the gothic repertoire, overlooked, that is, by Christian literary critics who simply do not easily recognize the codes of anti-Semitism operating in literary texts. Certainly, by the time Eugène Sue published his version of the tale, *Le Juif errant* (1844–1845), the figure was well established in gothic texts, but in 1806, when Charlotte Dacre (b. Charlotte King, ca. 1772–1825) took up her pen to write *Zofloya, or the Moor: A Romance of the Fifteenth Century,*[2] the Wandering Jew was more of a floating signifier, suggesting vague political, sexual, and religious anxieties. For instance, Andrew Franklin's *The Wandering Jew, or, Love's Masquerade* (Drury Lane, 1797), has a fairly light, mocking, and satiric tone. In this work the Jew is presented as motivated by "miscegenation," his intention being to move to London in order to marry a British beauty and produce an heir to whom he can leave his wealth (shades of Dracula). But apart from the figure of the Wandering Jew, the Jew as Satan or the devil was, in fact, a much more established and pernicious trope. Certainly, since the Middle Ages, Jews had been identified with the devil through six specific associations: as the embodiment of the anti-Christ, as a sorcerer, as a poisoner, as a defiler of the sacrament of communion, as a usurer, and as a practitioner of the ritual murder of Christians.[3]

In this essay, I argue that the demon and eponymous character Zofloya is not meant by Dacre to be understood as simply a devilish black man, as I have argued elsewhere earlier in *Gothic Feminism*.[4] In fact, I think that if we take the full religious, cultural, and social contexts into account, not to mention Dacre's personal history, it is more accurate to read Zofloya as a Jew, and an abjected, demonized, and wandering Jew at that. In projecting her Jewishness onto a black devil who takes her antiheroine over a cliff with him, Dacre symbolically sent her own birthright, her Jewish identity (shameful because of its association with her father, the "Jew King" of London), into the depths, to emerge as a newly purified British matron-mother, an appropriately WASP-y wife for her respectable WASP and Tory husband Nicholas Byrne.[5] Dacre would appear, in fact, to have suffered from what Sander L. Gilman more recently has called "Jewish self-hatred," and it is the permutations of how that condition is worked out in the novel that are examined in this essay.[6]

It is hardly necessary in a collection of this kind to rehearse all manifestations of anti-Semitism in Britain, but a few are important for placing *Zofloya* into a fuller cultural context than it has previously received. In 1753, the Jewish Naturalization Bill was decisively rejected in Britain, and actually so unpopular that it was commonly referred to as the "Circumcision bill." The anonymous pamphlet *A Modest Apology for the Citizens and Merchants of London, Who Petitioned the House of Commons Against Naturalizing the Jews* (London, 1753), argued that "England was a Christian nation, 'founded upon the doctrine of Jesus Christ,' and could not admit these 'crucifiers' without becoming involved in their inherited guilt."[7] Further, as Michael Ragussis has argued, "The Jewish Question" became inextricably interwoven with "the heart of English national identity." For Ragussis, the desire to convert Jews to Christianity was part of nineteenth-century Britain's national cause and identity.[8] There were approximately 8,000 Jews in Britain in 1800, but debates about extending their civil rights were met with an overwhelmingly negative response.[9] As James Shapiro has noted, "The English turned to Jewish questions in order to answer English ones."[10]

But from the medieval period, Jews were anathema in Europe, and certainly England was no exception. The reasons for this demonization are complex, but perhaps the most important for an understanding of *Zofloya* were the associations Jews had with primitive blood rites, such as ritual slaughter of animals (with the suggestion of cannibalism), and circumcision (misunderstood as male menstruation and symbolic castration). Even more unsavory, in what was known as "the blood libel," Jews were accused of defiling the Host and killing Christians and non-Jews whose blood could be used for the Passover seder, as well as for the unnatural prolongation of Jewish lives.[11] Because of these residual traces of their supposed religious practices, Jews were coded as socially *other* and required to announce this otherness in badges worn on their clothing, badges that were mandatory for all members of the Jewish community as early as 1218 in England.[12] As Trachtenberg notes, "with a little ingenuity the Jew badge may be explained altogether as a sign of the Jew's allegiance to the devil, as medieval versifiers ultimately get around to doing" (26). The Jew was clearly associated with the devil in the popular imagination, and in several medieval engravings, Satan is depicted as wearing a Jew badge and shown participating in Jewish financial transactions. Massacres against Jews occurred in Eastern Europe in 1768, causing a large wave of Jews to emigrate to England, where yet more violent attacks on them began to occur. The Aliens Act of 1793 allowed the government to deport many Jews, as well as to place foreigners living in England under surveillance.[13]

In addition to their association with the devil, Jews were also thought to be closely tied to the practice of economic blood sucking, as usury was known at this time. Moneylending at an interest was a sin for which Catholics could be excommunicated, but Jews represented in their very being this connection between cash and blood, thought to be at the very root of Christ's betrayal (Judas's thirty pieces of silver). Later, Shakespeare's portrait of Shylock (seeking flesh in exchange for lost money) played on this very stereotype. The Hebrew word for lending money at an interest was *neshekh*, also meaning "to bite," and, as Malchow has noted, "there was always a metaphoric vampirism in the traditional image of the Jew as usurer, as bloodsucker" (160). It was not a huge metaphoric leap for the culture to move from notions of Jews as vampiric and literal bloodsuckers to Jews as agents of the devil to Jews as devils.

In 1783, Parliament passed the Irish Naturalization Act, but Jews were specifically excluded from the rights of citizenship, and ironically, they were frequently aligned in the popular press with the Irish, who were themselves presented as simians, brutish simpletons, or a lower species of humanity. But the major difference was that Jews were most typically presented as smarter, much more cunning, Svengali-types of criminals. They were also believed to be the degenerate carriers of syphilis or other diseases (certainly this type reaches its apotheosis in Bram Stoker's creation of the vampire Dracula, with his hook nose and high forehead). Ken Gelder has argued that Jews were frequently figured as "nomadic," and hence were difficult to monitor in their movements throughout Britain. For Gelder, the mobility of the foreign Jew actually produced two contradictory attitudes in British citizenry: Jews were seen on one hand as admirable since they accumulated capital, while on the other hand they became sources of national anxiety because "they drained capital by moving it elsewhere."[14]

Jews were also traditionally associated with Cain (the "cursed" wanderer who had killed his brother), and hence were believed to be part of a criminal and conspiratorial group of Christian-killers. The word "cabal" entered the public discourse sometime during the later half of the seventeenth century. The term made its way very early into gothic literature, and Davison has identified the "cabalistic" backdrop of early gothics, stating that we can recognize the cabalistic in the persistence of "the Spanish inquisition, conspiratorial anti-Christian secret societies (or cabals), secret sciences, the violation of familial bonds (e.g., patricide and incest), popular millenarian ideas, and the bastardization and demonic figuration of the Cabala as a dark mirror, or double, of the Christian New Testament" (22). All of these figurations were, according to Davison, precipitated "by fears that a secular–spiritual 'Apocalypse' like the French Revolution would occur on British soil. Many thought that such a cataclysm would signal the Last Days and would occur as a result of an intricate anti-Christian conspiracy which qualified as Gothic fiction in its own right" (22). Freemasons and Rosicrucians, believed to be controlled by Jacobin-like Jews who were scheming to advance their own economic interests, were thought to be operating at the expense of British national "progress."[15]

In fact, in what we can recognize as a species of "Jewish hysteria," Christians actually began to think that they had become the Wandering Jew. Martin Gardner sees the Wandering Jew impersonations as instigated by a pamphlet published first in Germany in the seventeenth century, in which a Jewish shoemaker named Ahasuerus claimed to be the actual Wanderer. Over the next two centuries, people claiming to be the Jew appeared all over Europe, with one appearing as late as 1868 in Salt Lake City.[16] In his *Curious Myths of the Middle Ages* (2 vols., London, 1866), the Reverend Sabine Baring-Gould tells us that "men who were either impostors claiming to be the Wandering Jew, or lunatics who actually believed they were this unhappy man, appeared in England in 1818, 1824, and 1830."[17]

Trachtenberg has argued that the negative portrait of the Wandering Jew began during the medieval period and was very quickly assigned to the entire Jewish population as a whole: "In most of the accounts, the Wandering Jew had forsaken his false faith and adopted the true faith of Jesus, in contrast to the obduracy of his fellow Jews; several versions, however, have him remain a Jew, refusing to acknowledge through baptism the truth to which his own unique career testified, and thus typifying the attitude of all Jews" (17). Further, Trachtenberg observes that "Satan's semitic features are often emphasized with grotesque exaggeration . . . [and] Mephistopheles is usually swarthy, hook-nosed, [and] curly-headed" (26). Hyam Maccoby, however, has provided a nuance to our understanding of the Jewish stereotype by observing: "The Jews were never put on the same footing as the other heretics. They were the representatives of the Old Religion, against which Christianity had rebelled, and there was a feeling of bad conscience against them. The Jews were Father-figures, and rebellion against the father is never a straightforward expression of hatred" (239). The Jew as devilish father-figure would have been all too familiar to Dacre, whose father was increasingly the source of scandal and embarrassment to her as she attempted to establish herself as both a woman writer and as a respectable wife and mother.

Maccoby also emphasizes the other, Germanic versions of the Wandering Jew, the man who was a purely negative embodiment of defiance in the face of Jesus's sufferings and death. In these darker versions of the figure, the sufferings of the Wandering Jew are seen merely as just punishment for his depravity. He is not a convert to Christianity, but an unregenerate Jew, with evil magic powers derived from his long experience of life and his association with the devil. It was this negative version that gave rise to the nineteenth-century anti-Semitic stereotype, taken up with enthusiasm by the Nazis, of the Jew as a "rootless cosmopolitan" (252). When Dacre presented Zofloya as a black man who by the conclusion of the text reveals himself as the devil, her reading audience would have instantly understood the many twisted and long-established associations: Zofloya is not simply the devil; he is also a figure of Judaism itself, the old religion that needed to be sent over the edge into the abyss before the newly nationalistic Christian Britain would be safe. Throughout the text, he provides magical powers, sleeping potions, and poisons to Victoria, while conducting mysterious financial dealings. Besides reminding contemporary readers of the devil's associations with Jews, this portrait of Zofloya is also a strange, cryptic, bitter picture of Dacre's own father, the devilish Jew in her own life.

II

The final aspects in understanding the use that Dacre makes of the Jewish devil are philosophical, metaphysical, and personal. As Daniel Jonah Goldhagen has observed:

> Antisemitisim tells us nothing about Jews, but much about anti-Semites and the culture that breeds them. Even a cursory glance at the qualities and powers that Antisemites through the ages have ascribed to Jews—supernatural powers, international conspiracies, and the ability to wreck economies; using the blood of Christian children in their rituals, even murdering them for their blood; being in league with the Devil; controlling simultaneously both the levers of international capital and of Bolshevism—indicates that anti-Semitism draws fundamentally on cultural sources that are independent of the Jews' nature and actions, and the Jews themselves then become defined by the culturally derived notions which antisemites project onto them.[18]

Similarly, Jean-Paul Sarte has observed: "It is not the Jewish character that provokes anti-Semitism but, rather, . . . it is the anti-Semite who creates the Jew." And further, he has noted that "Far from experience producing [the anti-Semite's] idea of the Jew, it was the latter which explained his experience. If the Jew did not exist, the anti-Semite would invent him." Julia Kristeva has followed Sartre's lead, stating that the anti-Semites's Jew is an abject "phantasmatic" figure representing ambivalence; he is feared and hated because he does not "respect borders, positions, rules" and "disturbs identity, system, [and] order."[19]

But most recently, Sander Gilman has provided a particularly useful way for explaining what Dacre has done by portraying the devil as both Jew and father. For Gilman, "Jewish self-hatred" is caused when Jewish people accept "the mirage of themselves generated by their reference group—that group in society which they see as defining them—as a reality." In order to be part of the community and share in that community's identity, the Jew of necessity has to subscribe to "the liberal fantasy that anyone is welcome to share in the power of the reference group if he abides by the rules that define that group. But these rules are the very definition of the Other. The Other comprises precisely those who are not permitted to share power within the society. Thus outsiders hear an answer from their fantasy: Become like us—abandon your difference—and you may be one with us" (2). If we read Zofloya as Dacre's construction of the abjected Jew, then it would appear that he carries symbolic as well as personal freight. Dacre clearly must have heard the siren song of abdicating her Jewish identity and subscribing to her culture's demonization of the Jew when she created Zofloya.

In fact, as Gilman points out, there is also a "conservative curse" to the syndrome of self-hatred: "The more you are like me, the more I know the true value of my power, which you wish to share, [then] the more I am aware that you are but a shoddy counterfeit, an outsider." The dominant group wishes both to integrate the outsider and yet also to keep him or her at arm's length, and thus "preserve the reification of its power through the presence of the powerless. Thus the liberal promise and the conservative curse exist on both sides of the abyss that divides the outsider from the world of privilege." This contradiction between the "liberal promise" of complete assimilation and the "conservative curse" of perpetual marginalization put the outsider into what Gilman calls a "classic double bind situation." But outsiders have yet one more possible move: they can "select some fragment of that category in which they have been included and see in that the essence of Otherness, an essence that is separate from their own definition of themselves and [one that] embodies all of the qualities projected onto them by the power group." It would appear that by selecting the most extreme embodiment of the Jew—as Satan, as the devil—Dacre was attempting to abject the ultimate category of otherness within herself. But Gilman observes: "for even as one distances oneself from this aspect of oneself, there is always the voice of the power group saying, Under the skin you are really like them anyhow. The fragmentation of identity that results is the articulation of self-hatred" (2–3).

Now, to Dacre's personal history: We know enough about Dacre's father, Jonathan King (1753–1824), to surmise that he would have been an embarrassment to someone as ambitious as Charlotte Dacre. King was one of the most famous Jewish self-made men in London, a banker, a pamphleteer, and a supporter of radical political causes. He was also rumored to have been the lover of Mary Robinson (based on evidence that he had financially blackmailed her); and that was one of the more favorable rumors associated with his name. In 1785, he divorced his first wife, Deborah, the mother of Charlotte and her sister Sophia, in order to marry a countess. He financially supported the defendants in the 1794 Treason Trials, and was the political ally of Charles James Fox and Thomas Paine. By 1798, however, he found himself facing bankruptcy and complete ruin. Most damning, however, were the charges of sodomy and sexual assault brought against him by two prostitutes in July 1798. In rehearsing the sensational claims that the prostitutes made against him, the newspapers of the day asserted that he had beaten his first wife, and that now he was charged with flogging and sodomizing two prostitutes and then offering to pay a small amount of money to hush them up. Not coincidentally, 1798 was the last year that Charlotte published using her father's name.[20]

But not only did Dacre want literary fame, she also wanted to marry the Tory editor of the *Morning Post*, Nicholas Byrne, the man with whom she had already had three children (b. 1806, 1807, and 1809). He, unfortunately, was already married, so they could not marry and baptize their children until 1811, the year his wife died. I would contend, although I admit that I do so solely on the basis of detecting a mass of swirling anxieties in a number of poems and novels, that Dacre suffered from a shame of being Jewish (or the Jewish daughter of an almost comically stereotypical Jewish father). Her poem "To the Shade of Mary Robinson" vaguely recalls the rumors that circulated about her father's nefarious blackmail of Robinson, while the other pieces in her *Hours of Solitude* (1805) suggest that she associated an intense, morbid anxiety with a demon lover–father figure who himself was sexualized in an unnatural, satanic manner.

In addition to marriage and respectability, however, Dacre also wanted to obtain the benefits of full citizenship that her father had written about. In his pamphlet *Oppression Deemed No Injustice* (1798?), King noted that he suffered from being "alone, isolated and abandoned" after his bankruptcy, and that all Jews were treated as he was, as "beings of another nature, the dignity of humanity is lost."[21] It is not difficult to see that in Dacre's mind, her father was a doomed, devilish, sexually compromised, financially corrupt Jew. Her portrait of Zofloya is not drawn simply from cultural stereotypes about Jews, but to some extent, must have been drawn from life.

Zofloya, or the Moor (1806) was Charlotte Dacre's second novel, written when she was twenty-four years old (or so she claimed; she was actually thirty-four) and the beautiful toast of London literary circles. Her first novel, *The Confessions of the Nun of St. Omer*, was written when she was eighteen (read twenty-eight) and in the grip of an infatuation with the excessive gothicism of Lewis's *The Monk*. By 1809, Dacre's novels were ridiculed as "lovely ROSA's prose" by Byron, who went on to mock the novels as "prose in masquerade, / Whose strains, the faithful echoes of her mind, / Leave wondering comprehension far behind."[22] Despite their improbabilities or more likely because of them, *Zofloya* was also an early influence on Percy Shelley, whose two youthful gothic novels, *Zastrozzi* (1810) and *St. Irvyne;*

or The Rosicrucian (1811), bear a number of clear resemblances to Dacre's work. She and her four novels and two-volume collection of poetry have been virtually forgotten, except by aficionados of the gothic, but all of these works—most particularly *Zofloya*—are important historical documents for understanding how literary texts participated in the larger culture's attempt to rewrite appropriate feminine behavior as passionless, passively domestic, and pious. But in creating the character of Zofloya, she also produced a strange act of self-hatred, or perhaps symbolic parricide, creating a black devil who is coded as Jewish, and then purged at the conclusion of the text, much as Dacre changed her name not once, but twice, distancing herself further and further—at least in her own mind—from her notorious Jewish pedigree.

As I have argued elsewhere, *Zofloya* is racist, xenophobic, and misogynistic— as politically incorrect as any early nineteenth-century text could be. But it is only fair to recognize the anti-Semitism in the novel, also, and given Dacre's parentage and eventual marriage to a WASP, I believe we also need to read the text as one that denigrates and demonizes Dacre's own Jewish origins. And although the action is set in late fifteenth-century Italy, the novel holds up for our view the popular consciousness of bourgeois England, circa 1806. It reveals how thoroughly this society felt besieged by the sexually and financially voracious demands of women and Jews. It reveals that this was a culture looking for someone to blame for the social, familial, political, and economic transformation it was experiencing. It chose to blame the devil-Jew, in league with a sexually demanding woman. This is not an original plotline, to be sure, but it does epitomize this culture's intense dread of maternal and feminine sexuality as so viciously evil and unnatural that it rivals the blackness of Satan's dark deeds.

Zofloya traces the gothic adventures of Laurina's daughter Victoria, and to a much lesser extent her son Leonardo. Whereas his fall is gradual and tragically familiar within the gothic universe, Victoria's is spectacular and sublimely ridiculous. Consider this scenario. Victoria is initially taken by her fallen mother and the mother's adulterous lover Ardolph to an elderly aunt's estate for safe keeping. Ever the opportunist, however, Victoria manages to escape by tricking a female servant into exchanging clothes and then leading her to the edge of the aunt's wooded estate. From there, it is nothing to walk back to Venice where Victoria quickly sets about seducing a rich aristocrat, Berenza, who decides to marry Victoria after she is stabbed trying to defend him against a dagger-wielding assassin. She should have known—the attacker was her own brother Leonardo, who was at this time living with Berenza's former mistress, Megalina Strozzi, a Florentine prostitute. Megalina, like all Italian women in this text, tends to use daggers to settle her scores, and she originally sent Leonardo to kill Berenza, not aware that Berenza would be in bed with Leonardo's sister.

But the action has barely begun. Because Victoria was willing to take a knife in the shoulder for him, she earns the undying love and trust of Berenza. He marries her and they spend the next five years in comparative harmony. But all that is shattered when Berenza's younger and more handsome brother, Henriquez, arrives for a visit. Victoria immediately suffers an intense and lustful infatuation for him, but he finds her repulsive. Indeed, on at least two occasions, he describes her as odious because she is "masculine" (190). Henriquez, instead, is enamored of his lovely little thirteen-year-old orphaned friend, Lilla, thrown into his protection by the deaths of both her parents. Lilla is as blonde as Victoria is dark. Lilla is as prepubescent, passive, good, and obedient as Victoria is the opposite. Lilla, in other words, is the new bourgeois ideal of the "civilized" domestic idol, the professionally feminine girl–woman, and her murder by Victoria would have been understood by Dacre's contemporaries as mimicking the Jewish ritual murder of a young Christian for sacrificial demon-worship. Victoria embodies the earlier, uncivilized, aristocratic woman—vain, lustful, aggressive, actively and openly sexual and violent—but she also increasingly takes on Jewish characteristics that were associated with the devil.

Before we move to Lilla's murder scene, however, it is necessary to examine the other protagonist in the novel—Zofloya, or the Moor—the titular and presumably the most important character in the work. Zofloya is initially presented to us as Henriquez's black servant, acquired in Spain after Zofloya's master was killed in a battle. Matthew Lewis had portrayed a powerful and vengeful black servant named Hassan, in his gothic drama *The Castle Spectre* (1798), and he had chosen to use Hassan to embody the dualistic characteristics that blacks (and, we might add, Italian women in gothic novels) were thought to possess: a superficial eagerness to please, combined with a tendency, when injured, to plot a violent and extreme revenge. As in Matthew Lewis's *Journal of a Residence among the Negroes in the West Indies*, about visits to his own Jamaican plantation, the gothic drama presents black slaves only too quick to flip the master–slave dialectic and deal in voodoo–Obeah and slave uprisings. Sensational press accounts of the maroon wars of the 1790s in Jamaica and the bloody revolution in Haiti made the issue all too immediate to ignore.

Significantly, when Hassan swears that he will have his vengeance, he uses language that implies the sexual threat implicit in his very presence in this society: "Am I not branded with scorn? am I not now despised? What man would accept the negro's friendship? What woman would not turn from the negro in disgust? Oh! how it joys me when the white man suffers!" (196). Dacre responded to Hassan's query by creating a white woman who embraces the negro—or the Jew—and gains supernatural powers by doing so. By the conclusion of the novel, Victoria and Zofloya are living together as lovers, Zofloya having first appeared to Victoria in her dreams the night she met Henriquez and decided that she must sexually possess Henriquez or die. Victoria's dreams, which occur throughout the novel, always accurately present the next major action of the text.

Dreams in Dacre's work, however, also suggest a new level of psychological sophistication we have not seen before in the gothic. Victoria's dreams present us with the possibility that the character we recognize as "Zofloya" is actually less a real personage than the dark, demonic, Jewish forces within Victoria's own psyche, her abject Jewishness. The confluence here of the sexually predatory woman, the Jewish devil, and the black male servant is revealing for what it says about early nineteenth-century British attitudes toward gender, religion, and race. A woman who would sexually pursue not simply one, but two men—and brothers, at that—is a woman who has to be full of the devil. And the devil is not simply represented as black, lower class, and foreign; he is literally empowered by functioning in league, as one, with the Jew, as well as with a corrupt aristocratic and foreign woman. The farcical elements of the novel revolve around the unlikely alliance of the hyperbolically white Victoria and her very black and demonic ally and lover, the Jewish devil Zofloya. The menace inherent in the text, however, is not simply the menace of white women taking black or Jewish men as illicit lovers. The deeper threat would appear to be the social and economic alliance of dispossessed populations working together, recognizing their mutual alienation and objectification, and banding as one in a maniacal and deadly pursuit of the great white father and his property. In her alliance with Zofloya, Victoria projects/rejects her demonic Jewishness only to reincorporate it back within herself. That is, she becomes the poisoner, the magician, the murderer of young blonde Christian innocence by incorporating within herself the devil Jew's powers, the very powers she despised in her father.

Victoria uses magical powers gained through her association with the devil/Jew Zofloya to poison her husband, seduce Henriquez, and then cause Henriquez's suicide. After accomplishing these dire deeds with the obliging assistance of Zofloya, Victoria then stalks her real prey, the orphan Lilla, whom Zofloya has left chained and defenseless in the stone cave. The confrontation between the two women is one of the most bizarre in the history of female gothic fiction, almost campy in its self-conscious and hyperbolic posturings, coded in stereotypical gendered terms, loaded with representations of an intermingling of feminine sexuality and perversity. When Victoria descends on the innocent Lilla, she finds Lilla sleeping on the floor of the cave, surrounded by "coarse fragments of scanty food" and clothed only in "a mantle of leopard skin, brought her by Zofloya." The leopard skin, so incongruous in fifteenth-century Italy, tropes the descent this very civilized domestic paragon has made into the animal (or black, passionate) realm: "Upon awakening, Lilla clasps her thin hands upon her polished bosom, and with some of her long tresses, still in pure unaltered modesty, essaying to veil it, she raised her eyes, of heavenly blue, to the stern and frantic countenance of her gloomy persecutor, appearing, in figure, grace, and attitude, a miniature semblance of the Medicean Venus" (218). Lilla here is presented as a virtual Christian icon, a statue of a secularized Virgin Mary, "polished," a "Medicean Venus," while at the same time, she is represented as the embodiment of domestic virtues and characteristics: modest, blue eyes, long blonde hair. Her iconic, fetishistic qualities are further accentuated as she begs Victoria not to murder her. And the fact that Lilla is killed, not by a corrupt monk or a greedy usurping uncle, but by a lustful, vengeful, and passionate aristocratic woman, suggests that by 1806, the female gothic genre had shifted sufficiently to present women as inveterate enemies of each other. But Victoria is not simply a woman; she is the reincarnation of the Jewish devil herself, sacrificing young, innocent Christian blood in order to commit unspeakable ritual acts of Satanic (read: Jewish) worship.

Victoria drags her victim to the top of a cliff, leaving Lilla's "blood red traces at every step," and announces that she will "push thee headlong" because "no art could root [thee] from the breast of Henriquez." Terrified by the view, Lilla makes her next appeal to Victoria, the sentimental one: "Oh, sweet Victoria, remember we have been friends—I loved thee! nay, even now I love thee, and believe that thou art mad!—Oh, think, think we have been companions, bedfellows!" (219). Bedfellows? Somehow, one cannot imagine any reason why Victoria would have crawled into bed with Lilla. This appeal to the cult of female friendship is scornfully rejected by Victoria, who now announces to Lilla that Henriquez is dead.

Lilla now makes her final appeal to Victoria. She asks to be killed the same way Henriquez was, by a stiletto through the heart, and to this Victoria agrees. The first plunge wounds "only her uplifted hand, and glanc[es] across her alabaster shoulder, the blood that issued thence, slightly tinged her flaxen tresses with a brilliant red" (220). As much is made of Lilla's shed blood as is made of her blonde tresses. The imagistic mingling here of the two is significant as a representation of soiled innocence. The horror of the scene has to be located in its unnaturalness, the violent murder of one woman by another. And again, we are reminded of a nightmare of Jews feeding voraciously on the flesh of young, idealized, innocent Christian flesh.

But by the conclusion of the novel, Victoria has no hope of escaping the consequences of her many crimes. Her husband's body, which Zofloya had hidden in an old casket in a deserted wing of the castle, has been discovered, as has Henriquez's. Victoria has no choice but to beg protection from Zofloya, who now makes her his mistress. Dacre's sexual and racial nausea can barely be concealed, as the two lovers find themselves living in wanton abandon in the Italian mountains with a band of banditti, led by Victoria's brother Leonardo and his dark mistress Megalena. To make the dysfunctional family circle complete, Laurina and Ardolph suddenly arrive as captives, and Leonardo quickly murders Ardolph in retaliation for Ardolph's beatings of Laurina, Leonardo's dying mother. Certainly memories of a man beating his wife would have had a particularly pertinent resonance for Dacre, who once more positions her father's crimes front and center in the text.

We are now told that the only earthly authorities feared by Victoria are the Venetian council of ten, Il Consiglio de Dieci, the powers of the Roman Catholic Church as represented by the Inquisition. Whenever Zofloya wants to threaten or intimidate Victoria, he refers to the "familiars of the holy inquisition," and Il Consiglio is the one legal force against which he could never protect or shield Victoria. Clearly, Dacre's readers would have recognized this aspect of Zofloya as devil/Jew in the Jew's traditional association with the cabal, or a secret society intending to plot the overthrow of

Christianity. Even the devil (read Jew), it would appear, hesitates to tangle with the Inquisition. But more significantly, Dacre surely must have known that the Inquisition was blatantly anti-Semitic, forcing Iberian Jews to choose between conversion and death. Historically, the Anglo-Jewish community was founded by Iberian Jews fleeing the Inquisition. Of course, these very forces descend on the mountainous hideout, and Leonardo and Megalena both kill themselves rather than risk being taken alive. Once again, Victoria asks Zofloya to save her, and this time, he announces that he can only do so if she will travel with him to his abode, hell. He strips away the appearance he has assumed on earth, and appears before her as he actually is: "a figure, fierce, gigantic, and hideous to behold!—Terror and despair seized the soul of Victoria; she shrieked, and would have fallen from the dizzying height, had not his hand, who appeared Zofloya no longer, seized her with a grasp of iron by the neck!" (254). Racism demanded a demonization of difference, and, as Malchow has suggested, the gothic offered "a language that could be appropriated, consciously or not, by racists in a powerful and obsessively reiterated evocation of terror, disgust, and alienation. But the gothic literary sensibility itself also evoked in the context of an expanding experience of cultural conflict, of the brutal progress of European nationalism and imperialism, and was in part a construct of that phenomenon" (3).

But anti-Semitism also demands a demonization of difference, and this we can see when Victoria quite literally goes to the devil. The moral which Dacre pens on her last page makes her mother's guilt and responsibility for all this clear: "Over their passions and their weaknesses, mortals cannot keep a curb too strong . . . Either we must suppose that the love of evil is born with us (which would be an insult to the Deity), or we must attribute them (as appears more consonant with reason) to the suggestions of infernal influence" (254–255). If the devil is an active presence in the world, then the Jew is its manifestation in the public sphere.

Finally, Victoria embodies Dacre's worst imagining of herself as a Jewish woman descended from a Jewish father who eerily resembled her culture's worst stereotype of a Jew. Victoria is also the representation of every vice that bourgeois Britain found itself repulsed by in Jews. Victoria is the excessive aristocratic woman who has finally waged open war on bourgeois values and received her just punishment, but she also can be read as the devilish Jew, the poisoning, conspiring, murdering force who threatened Britain as it attempted to move toward a new national identity as bourgeois, anti-French, and Protestant.

Notes

1. (Hull, 1767; reprint in *Wandering Jew. A chap-book, containing The Hull Version of the Wandering Jew Legend* [London: John Pitts, 1800–1809?]). For a historical overview of the trope, see G. K. Anderson, *The Legend of the Wandering Jew* (Providence, RI: Brown University Press, 1965), as well as his earlier "Popular Survivals of the Wandering Jew in England," *Journal of*

English and German Philology 46 (1947), 367–382, reprint in *The Wandering Jew: Essays in the Interpretation of a Christian Legend*, ed. Galit Hasan-Rokem and Alan Dundes (Bloomington: Indiana University Press, 1986), 76–104, which specifically discusses the Hull chapbook, 84–85. More recently, Frank Felsenstein includes a chapter on the wandering Jew in *Anti-Semitic Stereotypes: A Paradigm of Otherness in English Popular Culture, 1666–1938* (Baltimore: The Johns Hopkins University Press, 1995); see chapter 4, "Wandering Jews, Vagabond Jews" (58–90).

2. Ed. Adriana Craciun (Ontario: Broadview, 1997), 190. All quotations from the novel are from this edition, with page numbers in parentheses.

3. Joshua Trachtenberg, *The Devil and the Jews: The Medieval Conception of the Jew and Its Relation to Modern Anti-Semitism* (New Haven: Yale University Press, 1943), 215. Jacob Katz carries the investigation to the Holocaust in *From Prejudice to Destruction: Anti-Semitism, 1700–1933* (Cambridge: Harvard University Press, 1980).

4. See Diane Long Hoeveler, *Gothic Feminism: The Professionalization of Gender from Charlotte Smith to the Brontës* (University Park: Pennsylvania State Press, 1998), 143–158. Recently, Kim Ian Michisaw has argued that Dacre's intent in Zofloya is to "restore the dignity, self-worth and culture to the African" in contrast to "abolitionism's pathetic, dying negro." Michisaw specifically sees Dacre presenting Zofloya the Moor not as Satan, but as the "conquering African," and in his allegiance with Victoria, "the domesticated woman," the two represent a particularly frightening and culturally anxious duo: the nubile woman in league with the "enslaved African" (52). See his "Charlotte Dacre's Postcolonial Moor," in *Empire and the Gothic: The Politics of Genre*, ed. Andrew Smith and William Hughes (New York: Palgrave/Macmillan, 2003), 35–55.

5. On King, see Todd M. Endelman, "The Checkered Career of 'Jew' King: A Study in Late Eighteenth-Century Anglo-Jewish Social History," *AJS Review* 7/8 (1983): 69–100.

6. *Jewish Self-Hatred: Anti-Semitism and the Hidden Language of the Jews* (Baltimore: The Johns Hopkins University Press, 1986), passim.

7. Thomas W. Perry, *Public Opinion, Propaganda, and Politics in Eighteenth-Century England: A Study of the Jew Bill of 1753* (Cambridge: Harvard University Press, 1962), 92–93. More recently, in "Great Britain or Judea Nova? National Identity, Property, and the Jewish Naturalization Controversy of 1753," Alan H. Singer has placed the "Jew Bill" into its broader historical context (in *British Romanticism and the Jews: History, Culture, Literature*, ed. Sheila A. Spector [New York: Palgrave/Macmillan, 2002], 19–36). In *From Shylock to Svengali: Jewish Stereotypes in English Fiction* (Stanford: Stanford University Press, 1960), Edgar Rosenberg claims that "each age recreates the Wandering Jew in its own image" (188). By examining the use to which the Wandering Jew is put in literature, he claims, we can "answer the purposes of literary history more readily . . . [than the general representations of the Jew for] it changes[,] . . . adapts itself to the demands of diverse generations and diverse beliefs[, and] . . . provides a more reliable and more 'readable' barometer than Shylock to the kind of civilization, ideology, and regnant literary convention in which it flourishes" (188). Further, he states, "The history of Ahasuerus in the period between the appearance of Matthew Gregory Lewis's *The Monk* in 1796 and the publication of *Trilby* in 1894 is largely the story of

his translation from a religious figure of whom Christ made an example for the edification of other sinners, to a black magician whose sorcery was interesting on secular grounds" (206).

8. Michael Ragussis, *Figures of Conversion: "The Jewish Question" and English National Identity* (Durham, NC: Duke University Press, 1995), 188. Also, see Trachtenberg, *The Devil and the Jews*, passim; and H. L. Malchow, *Gothic Images of Race in Nineteenth-Century Britain* (Stanford: Stanford University Press, 1996).

9. Derek Cohen, "Constructing the Contradiction: Anthony Trollope's *The Way We Live Now*," in *Jewish Presences in English Literature*, ed. Derek Cohen and Deborah Heller (Montreal: McGill-Queen's University Press, 1990), 62. The most recent study of Anglo-Jewish history is Todd M. Endelmann's *The Jews of Britain: 1656–2000* (Berkeley: University of California Press, 2002). On the Romantic Period in particular, see his *The Jews of Georgian England, 1714–1830: Tradition and Change in a Liberal Society* (Philadelphia: The Jewish Publication Society of America, 1979; reprint, with a new preface, Ann Arbor: University of Michigan Press, 1999).

10. James Shapiro, *Shakespeare and the Jews* (New York: Columbia University Press, 1996), 1.

11. Trachtenberg, *The Devil and the Jews*, 215.

12. Trachtenberg, *The Devil and the Jews*, 116.

13. Carol Margaret Davison, "Gothic Cabala: The Anti-Semitic Spectropoetics of British Gothic Literature" (Ph.D. diss., McGill University, 1997), 21.

14. *Reading the Vampire* (London: Routledge, 1994), 14.

15. The most recent history of Freemasonry is Marsha Keith Schuchard's *Restoring the Temple of Vision: Cabalistic Freemasonry and Stuart Culture* (Leiden: Brill, 2002).

16. "The Wandering Jew and the Second Coming," *Free Inquiry* 15 (1995): 32. For further information, see Hyam Maccoby, "The Wandering Jew as Sacred Executioner," in *The Wandering Jew: Essays in the Interpretation of a Christian Legend*, ed. Galit Hasan-Rokem and Alan Dundes (Bloomington: Indiana University Press, 1986), 236–260.

17. Ed. Edward Hardy (London: Jupiter, 1977), 25.

18. *Hitler's Willing Executioners: Ordinary Germans and the Holocaust* (New York: Knopf, 1996), 39.

19. Jean-Paul Sarte, *Anti-Semite and Jew*, trans. George J. Becker (1948; New York: Schocken, 1965), 143, 13; Julia Kristeva, *Powers of Horror: An Essay on Abjection*, trans. Louis A. Roudiez. (New York: Columbia University Press, 1980), 180, 4. In a very similar move, Jacques Derrida, in *Specters of Marx: The State of the Debt, the Work of Mourning, and the New International*, discusses what he calls Marx's rhetorical "spectropoetics," his obsession with ghosts, specters, and spirits. Derrida defines the spectre as "among other things, what one imagines, what one thinks one sees and which one projects—on an imaginary screen where there is nothing to see" (trans. Peggy Kamuf [New York: Routledge, 1994], 100–101).

20. The best biographical source for the facts of Dacre's life can be found in Adriana Craciun, *Fatal Women of Romanticism* (Cambridge: Cambridge University Press, 2003), 111–112.

21. Craciun, *Fatal Women*, 60.

22. *English Bards and Scotch Reviewers*, in *The Poems of Lord Byron*, ed. Jerome McGann (Oxford: Oxford University Press, 1980), 1:756–758.

PART III

THE JEWS AND BRITISH ROMANTICISM
OUTSIDE OF ENGLAND

CHAPTER 9

COMMERCE, CONCERN, AND CHRISTIANITY: BRITAIN AND MIDDLE-EASTERN JEWRY IN THE MID-NINETEENTH CENTURY

Reeva Spector Simon

As the British Empire extended to the Middle East in the aftermath of the Napoleonic Wars, imperial interests created an unlikely synergy between Britain and those Jews residing in the Ottoman Empire. In contrast to domestic policy, which was largely determined by a reluctance to incorporate Jews into the body politic at home, in their Middle-Eastern policy, the British advocated citizenship, liberty, and freedom for the Jews who were under Muslim rule.

This new relationship was reflected in decisions undertaken during the term of British Foreign Minister Lord Palmerston (Henry John Temple, third Viscount; 1784–1865), whose foreign policy was chiefly concerned with British economic intrusion into and safeguarding of the political integrity of the Ottoman Empire. Political crises that emerged concerning British commercial interests, the rights of minorities under Islamic rule, demand for an Anglican presence in the Holy Land, and expansion of the evangelical mission to the cradle of Christianity led to British protection of Jews in the Middle East in the same manner that the French protected Catholics, and the Russians, Orthodox Christians. At once pragmatic and idealistic, this intersection between Britain and Middle Eastern Jewry during the first third of the nineteenth century foreshadowed British imperial realpolitik that was to follow.

In 1800, the Middle East was part of the Ottoman Empire, whose core was modern Turkey but which extended to Hungary and the Balkans in

Europe, to Persia in Asia, and to Egypt and the fringes of Arabia. But, by the end of the eighteenth century, Russian armies began chipping away at Ottoman territory in Europe and the Caucasus, and the political situation began to change. In 1798, Napoleon Bonaparte and a French army landed in Egypt—the first Christian army to do so since the end of the Crusades. Proclaiming "Liberté, Égalité, et Fraternité," the French military and scholarly expedition became not only a catalyst for Muslim self-introspection, but also reflected Europe's new interest in the Middle East.

Bonaparte was sent by the French revolutionary government to the Levant to interfere with British economic hegemony from India to the Mediterranean. In India, the British had reduced French holdings to some 143 square miles, and agents of the British East India Company moved freely throughout the Persian Gulf and Arabia. Forging treaties with local sheikhs, they suppressed piracy, tried to ban slavery and turned the Persian Gulf into a British lake.[1] In the Mediterranean, British interests were similarly represented by the Levant Company—until its dissolution in 1825—that not only dominated British commerce with the Ottoman Empire, but that also acted as a surrogate vehicle for British foreign policy. The company paid the salaries of the British ambassador and consul general in Constantinople (later Istanbul) and in other selected Ottoman cities and worked to garner economic concessions from the Turks. Christians and Jews were the middlemen who facilitated trade in the Empire.[2]

From the eighth century on, Christians and Jews had been subordinate to the Muslims who ruled the Middle East. According to Islamic law, they were protected minorities who were permitted to practice their faiths and to adjudicate matters of civil status within the parameters of their religious traditions. In exchange for physical security, they paid a special tax (*jizya*) and were required to conform to a number of discriminatory practices that were meant to be a constant reminder of their inferior status. In spite of the dress codes, limitations on the construction of churches and synagogues, and the constant threat of persecution by local rulers, minorities played a useful role in Ottoman society. They often served as financial advisors, customs agents, and tax collectors for the government. As the European powers penetrated the region commercially, they used their coreligionists—Christians, primarily, as their intermediaries with the Muslim authorities. Where they lacked Christians, they used Jews.

In the eighteenth century, much of world Jewry still lived outside of Christian Europe and were under Muslim rule. There were Jewish communities throughout the Middle East, some predating the Muslim conquest, others taking root in the Balkans and Asia Minor after the Spanish expulsion in 1492. For a century or so, Jews played key roles in Ottoman society: they were the physicians, diplomats, translators, commercial agents, and financial advisors to rulers. Thereafter, travelers to the region wrote of decline, and described the dire conditions under which most Jews lived, dominated by a small Jewish economic elite that was heavily involved in trade and competed with Christians for lucrative commercial posts.

At the same time, Christian powers began to wrest economic concessions that enabled them to set up warehouses in some Middle Eastern
cities and to hire minorities to represent their interests with the government.
As Europeans expanded their commercial ventures in the region, they
demanded the right of diplomatic protection for their employees. These "capit-
ulations," as the privileges were called, gave European governments extra-
territorial rights within the Ottoman Empire. What began as protection of
individual Christians, became a statement of foreign policy when in 1774,
the Russians proclaimed that the Tsar was the protector of Eastern Orthodox
Christians in the Ottoman Empire.[3] The French followed suit, claiming the
Catholics.

Napoleon's military expedition had unexpected consequences. Like
Alexander the Great before him, the general took with him a corps of
scholars—in this case, in concert with Enlightenment multicultural interests,
to study the area that had produced Europe's Near Eastern roots. The discovery by a French soldier in Egypt of the Rosetta Stone, which made deci-
phering Egyptian hieroglyphics possible, and a similar breakthrough by
British scholar-diplomats in Persia, for ancient cuneiform texts, resulted in a
serious study of European Middle-Eastern antecedents, and led to a century
of British and European travel to the region. These discoveries, along with a
resurgence of Protestant evangelicalism in Britain and the United States during the early part of the nineteenth century, revived European interest in the
Holy Land and in Middle-Eastern Jewry.

Napoleon's tenure in Egypt was brief: he left Egypt for Acre where he was
defeated by the Ottomans in May 1799; and in 1801, the French army in
Egypt surrendered to the British. Yet, Bonaparte's effect was far-reaching,
the ensuing French presence in the area causing the British to reconsider
their policy in the region. Out of the maelstrom of the French invasion
emerged a quasi-independent Egyptian government that looked to regional
economic and political hegemony led by an Albanian military officer,
Muhammad 'Ali who, although remaining a subject of the Ottoman Sultan,
began to redirect the Egyptian economy toward the goal of economic self-
sufficiency, as supported by a modern army and navy. While acting under
orders from Istanbul to suppress the Wahhabi religious threat in Arabia, his
forays east sparked rumors of further conquests in Mesopotamia; however,
his real interests lay in Syria. Backed by the French, Egyptian armies moved
up the coast and conquered Syria and Palestine in 1830, reaching as far as
the borders of Anatolia. Under Egyptian rule for a decade, the Syrian
Christian minority was relieved of the traditional Islamic discriminatory
regulations and forged closer relations with the French.

With Russia advocating for the rights of Eastern Christians, and with
France proclaiming itself as the historic protector of Latin Christians in the
region, Britain sought its own legitimate claim of interest. As with the suppression of piracy in the Persian Gulf and attempts to stop the slave trade,
there was a logical link between the rights of minorities in the Ottoman
Empire and British progressive values. The problem was that whereas other

European powers had their own Christian protégés, there were no Protestants in the Middle East to protect—but there *were* Jews. Back in England, at the same time that foreign policy makers were occupied with the minorities issue in the Middle East, the British at home were debating the rights of their own Jews to emancipation. British merchants used Middle Eastern Jewish middlemen to foster trade in the Ottoman Empire, but did not allow British Jews to be members Levant Company, for fear of collusion with their coreligionists to the detriment of Christians;[4] and in 1830, British Jews had no access to retail trade in London.[5] Similarly, although Jewish converts to Anglicanism were suitable for posts as missionaries abroad, Anglican authorities were wary that they would "regard missionary service as a back door to ministry and social elevation in England."[6]

Ironically, many of the same politicians who supported assurances that Britain remain a Christian country, and so opposed seating Jews in parliament, were also advocates of Jewish minority rights in the Ottoman Empire. Both Lord Palmerston and Ashley Cooper (later Lord Shaftesbury), who opposed the Jews' Bill, worked for protection of the Jews under Muslim rule, first as Jews, but more significantly, as what they hoped eventually would be as Protestant converts to Christianity.[7] Together, missions to Jewish communities in the Ottoman Empire and the focus on the Holy Land in the aftermath of Napoleon's Middle East adventure sparked interest in an Anglican presence in Jerusalem and an expansion of the evangelical mission to the cradle of Christianity. At once idealistic and pragmatic, this intersection between Britain and Middle-Eastern Jews raised foreign-policy issues regarding British protection of the Jews and conflicts between missionaries and Jews.

Termed the "Eastern Question," the essence of British foreign policy in the Middle East followed strategic, economic, and religious lines. It was, first, a corollary to the balance of power politics in Europe. Under the aegis of Lord Palmerston, who was either foreign secretary or prime minister of England for most of the period from 1830–1865,[8] the British sought to keep their erstwhile enemy, the French, at bay in the Levant, in order to prevent the Russians from making military inroads in the Black Sea toward the city of Constantinople (Istanbul) and, above all, to maintain economic dominance. British foreign policy was based on the premise that preservation of the integrity of the Ottoman Empire was paramount in order to ensure British, as opposed to either Russian or French, military and economic hegemony.[9] If the Empire fell apart, it was thought, there would be no control over who picked up the pieces. To that end, the British supported the Turks diplomatically and militarily, while seeking major inroads in Ottoman commercial markets.

With the demise of the Levant Company in 1825 and the increase of British exports to Turkey, British Foreign Secretary Lord Palmerston advocated the development of river transport on the Euphrates, with its obvious links to India, and convinced the Ottomans that opening the Middle East to British commerce would make Turkey less dependent upon France and

Russia. An Anglo-Ottoman commercial treaty (Treaty of Balta Liman), signed in 1838, resulted in a doubling of British Middle-Eastern trade and an increase in British political leverage in Istanbul.[10] The British also moved to find their own non-Muslim minorities to champion in competition with the French and Russian claims of protection of Catholics and Eastern Christians.

To that end, Palmerston used the opportunities presented by the Egyptian invasion of Syria to further British interests. Clearly, Palmerston's motives in fostering British trade abroad and Ottoman reform, especially with regard to the rights of Christian minorities, were easily understood; his policies regarding the Jews, however, have engendered scholarly debate.[11] Were these signs of an incipient British proto-Zionism, or a combination of religious romanticism and imperialism? At issue were the establishment of the Anglican bishopric in Jerusalem, plans for Jewish settlement in Palestine, and pressure for official recognition of British protection of the Jews throughout the Ottoman Empire, all of which had not only political, but religious and commercial overtones, as well. They were, in effect, the result of a coalescence of imperial policy and the resurgence of religious evangelism that ascribed key roles to the Jews in the millenarian drama.

The evangelical and millennial strains in British Protestantism, produced by the evangelical revival in England at the turn of the nineteenth century, led to an outburst of missionary activity that affected British policy toward Middle Eastern Jewry. Anticipating the forthcoming establishment of God's kingdom on earth, British evangelicals emphasized the need for and their belief in the fact of redemption in Christ; they highlighted the value of lay involvement and the possibility of creating new initiatives for evangelism and religiously motivated social action—such as the Abolitionist Movement and labor reform, and proclaimed the worth of every soul. These years marked a return to religious piety in reaction to Enlightenment rationalism, Bible reading at home, and the establishment of countless voluntary religious associations. At the same time, and often through the efforts of the same people, at the same time that Captain Cook and others voyaged to the South Seas and beyond, missions were launched to carry the Gospel to the farthest reaches of the planet.[12]

There were those among the Calvinists and Puritans who believed that the thousand-year reign of Christ on earth could not begin until the Jewish people were restored to their homeland and would then be ready to welcome Jesus as their messiah. According to this view, Jews had a unique past as the people of God and were destined for a more glorious future by playing a key role (not as witnesses according to Catholic and mainline Protestant doctrine) in the fulfillment of the destiny of Christ. The readmission of Jews to England in the seventeenth century was the first step. The French Revolution and the Napoleonic Wars were seen as omens that not only was the time ripe for the onset of the millennium, but that man could move events along rather than await divine intervention. Books such as James Bicheno's *The Signs of the Times* and *The Restoration of the Jews: The Crisis of*

Nations led to the popular belief that the critical date was now in the 1860s—1,260 years between the rise of the ("apostate") Roman Catholic Church and the end of history.[13] Napoleon's victories in Germany, Holland, and Italy, his expedition to Egypt and the Holy Land, support for the Jews' return to the Holy Land, and the emancipation of French Jewry, all intensified interest in the Jews and their portended role in the unfolding eschatological process.[14]

In England, Charles Simeon, minister of Trinity Church at Cambridge, used his position to expound upon Britain's special role as a bulwark against Rome in the millennial denouement that was certain to unfold in the wake of the French Revolution and on the special role of the Jews in the divine process. The institutionalization of missionary activity was to be the vehicle for the British, who believed themselves to have been chosen—to combat Rome, to send the light of the Gospel to the people living in darkness, and to bring the Jews into the Christian fold. "In our religious zeal, however, the Jews cannot be forgotten," Simeon wrote and preached throughout England for nearly half a century—for "in converting the Jews to Christ, we adopt the readiest and most certain way for the salvation of the whole world." Convert the Jews first and the gentile world will follow.[15]

It was in this context that such organizations such as the London Missionary Society (founded in 1795; dedicated to the bringing the Gospel to Jew and gentile alike, both at home and abroad), and the London Society for the Promoting of Christianity Amongst the Jews (1809; also known as The London Jews Society) were founded in England. The London Jews Society came under the sole auspices of the Church of England in 1815 and worked to bring indigent, mostly Ashkenazi, Jews into the Christian fold. Rabbis pronounced a ban against any Jews who read the society's literature, and in one case the Jews threw the tracts back at the missionaries.[16] Its record hardly reflected the funding and effort: by 1859, the baptism of only 829 Ashkenazim had been recorded, of whom only 367 were adults.[17] The missionaries did, however, distribute a prodigious amount of literature.

After a few years, the Society itself realized that it was making little headway, and in its *Eleventh Report* recommended that its efforts should now be directed "to the *state of the Jews abroad*."[18] As early as 1812, interest in the Near East was expressed through a letter from a missionary in Malta who suggested that emissaries be sent to the Jews in Jerusalem, Egypt, and Greece.[19] He also argued for the institution of Protestant activity in the Holy Land which, until then, had been primarily the focus of interest for romantic travelers and scientific explorers.[20]

Beginning in the 1820s, the move to convert Jews outside of England led to the establishment of missionary stations, or locations where a missionary lived on a more or less permanent basis, at least partly supported by the Society. The first were located in Berlin, Frankfort, Amsterdam, Warsaw, and other European cities where there were large Jewish communities.[21] At the same time, the Society engaged a German-speaking Swiss pastor to visit Palestine, recommended that he learn Hebrew and Arabic, and acquaint himself with the conditions of the Jews. He was also to call upon the English consuls who, at that time, were not part of the British government, but in the service of the Levant Company. A second traveler soon followed. A converted German Jew, Joseph Wolff, who had studied theology under Charles Simeon at Cambridge, set off on a tour of the Middle East where he visited Gibraltar, Malta, Alexandria, Cairo, Jaffa, Jerusalem, Beirut, Damascus, Aleppo, Mosul, Baghdad, and Basra. He distributed a few copies of the New Testament, baptized a Jew here and there, and set to paper his colorful observations, which appeared posthumously as *Travels and Adventures of the Rev. Joseph Wolff, Late Missionary to the Jews and Muhammadans in Persia, Bokhara, Cashmeer, etc.* (London 1861). Testifying to the spirit of inquiry portrayed by the local Jews, Wolff encouraged the society to set up missions in Palestine and Syria. In Syria, the reaction of the rabbis was excommunication of Jews who interacted with the missionaries.[22] In Palestine, the work of the society became part of the process instrumental in establishing a church, a British consulate, and an Anglican Bishopric in Jerusalem.

In the Middle East, the Society's primary mission was to work against the obstinate refusal of "fallen Israel" to be converted. But missionaries also prayed for the overthrow of Ottoman rule in the region, and clearly desired that the British government "protect" their work by influencing the authorities in Istanbul to tolerate the conversion to Anglican Protestantism not only of Jews and Eastern Christians but of Muslims as well, an aim that was certainly problematical in the contexts of Anglo-Ottoman relations and the conflicts that arose between the divergent goals of the missionaries and the British Empire.

In the 1830s and early 1840s, these religious and imperial interests coalesced. From the outset, the London Jews Society caught the imagination of important people active in the Church and in British politics. In addition to Charles Simeon of Cambridge, who considered Middle-Eastern Jews to be more authentic than their western emancipated coreligionists who prayed in a "temple without a Shekhinah,"[23] the Archbishop of Canterbury and most of the bishops supported the work of the Society. Other patrons and backers included the Duke of Kent, the abolitionist William Wilberforce, and Ashley Cooper, the Seventh Earl of Shaftesbury, who was president of the society from 1848 until his death in 1885. Shaftesbury's mother-in-law was married to the Foreign Minister, Lord Palmerston.

For Palmerston, the protection of minorities was both a corollary of British liberal thought that advocated abolition of slavery and the safeguarding of personal property rights, and a pragmatic instrument of foreign policy. For Christians and Jews in the Ottoman Empire, it translated to British pressure on the Empire to remove disabilities from minorities so that they could enjoy equal citizenship and opportunity while remaining loyal subjects of the Empire—a quid pro quo for British economic and political support in the face of the Egyptian occupation of Syria. The focus of the Hatt-ı Sherif of Gulhane, as the edict handed down in 1839 was called, was more toward Christians than Jews and did not go as far as Palmerston wished. In 1839,

Palmerston was occupied with Ottoman–Egyptian relations and gave little thought to the Jews; a year later, however, the crisis in Damascus became the catalyst that brought the Jews squarely into British policy. The British had found their own minority protégés.

On February 5, 1840, while Syria was still under Egyptian rule, a Capuchin friar, along with his Muslim servant, disappeared in Damascus, and local Christians instituted a "blood libel," accusing the Jews of murdering the Christian for his blood, supposedly to be used for Passover matzos. Although well known from medieval Europe, the "blood libel" was until then relatively rare in the Middle East. Because the missing friar had been under French jurisdiction, the French consul in Damascus supported the accusation against the Jews, and Damascus authorities subsequently arrested, tortured, and exacted confessions from prominent Jews, several of whom died.

What had begun as a local crisis took on international political overtones. Leaders of Western Jewry took up the cause, and Palmerston, with the support of a variety of British Christians—including the Archbishop of Canterbury, prominent members of the London Jews Society, and the commission of the general assembly of the Church of Scotland—protested Muhammad 'Ali's support of French assertions of Jewish guilt.[24] Palmerston granted special government protection to the Jewish delegation led by Moses Montifiore of Britain and Adolphe Crémieux of France that not only attempted to intercede with the Ottoman and Egyptian authorities but launched an international campaign to rescue the Jews as well.[25] Montifiore (1784–1885) was a prominent British Jew who served as president of the Jewish Board of Deputies, the organization that represented Jewish interests in Britain. Crémieux (1796–1880), a French attorney and advocate of Jewish causes, was a member of the Jewish Consistory of France, a quasi-governmental body that represented the interests of French Jews. By the end of the summer, the Jews were released, but the Egyptian authorities, backed by the French, refused to exonerate them. The Ottoman sultan, Abdulmecid I, supported by Britain which, at the same time, was actively pursuing an Egyptian retreat from Syria, denounced the blood libel and specified that the Jews were to be included in reforms that were underway in the Ottoman Empire.[26]

In this context, Lord Shaftesbury's religious views complemented Palmerston's liberal sensibilities and practical view of British political and commercial policy.[27] Palmerston's advocacy of minority rights within the Empire, at the same time that the Ottomans were reasserting control in Palestine, provided him with the opportunity to press for an active British presence in Jerusalem and the resettlement of Jews in the Holy Land, a concrete step toward Britain's role in the eschatological process. With access to a sympathetic ear, Shaftesbury and the London Jews Society worked actively for the repatriation of the Jews in Palestine and the establishment of an Anglican Church in Jerusalem.[28]

During the long summer of 1840, Shaftesbury, who had already begun lobbying for the program in 1838, discussed with Palmerston the prospects of resettling the Jews in Palestine, a view shared by Evangelicals and High Churchmen who believed that in preparation for the Second Coming, the Jews had to be restored to the Holy Land. With the backing of the London Jews Society and its director, Alexander McCaul, Shaftesbury once again floated a plan that conceived of the British protecting the Jews and of the Ottoman Sultan as the new Cyrus who would allow the Jews to return to Jerusalem. Because of diplomatic bungling by the British representatives in Istanbul, the proposal was never seriously developed; still, the British interest in establishing Jewish and Christian residence in Jerusalem foreshadowed a future role as a bulwark of European influence primed for later development. It also raised the question of British protection of Jews throughout the Ottoman Empire.[29]

Plans to establish an Anglican bishopric, however, *were* successful. The British would now have diplomatic representation in Jerusalem as part of Palmerston's strategy to establish British diplomatic missions in the major cities of the Empire. Although there was now a base for missionary activities, questions were soon raised as to how far British protection of the Jews would go in the Ottoman Empire, whose adoption of western concepts of national sovereignty would only be completed in 1856. By 1841, negotiations over the bishopric with the Ottoman authorities were worked out and a Royal Navy ship transported the new Archbishop to the Holy Land to build the church and to carry out his mission. The post was first offered to Alexander McCaul of the London Society, who declined and suggested that the post be more appropriately occupied by "a descendant of Abraham." The church decided to send a Hebrew "to lead fallen Israel to Christian truth."[30] He was Michael Solomon Alexander, a Jewish émigré from Posen to England, who had converted to Christianity in 1825 and worked for the London Society as a missionary. Alexander served as Anglican Bishop in Jerusalem until his death in 1845 and was succeeded in the position by Samuel Gobat.[31]

The Porte, the Ottoman government, was concerned about Bishop Alexander's mission; and Palmerston's successor, Foreign Secretary Lord Aberdeen (1841–1846)—a man with a more limited vision of the British role in the region, who assumed his office just as Bishop Alexander undertook his new charge—reassured the Porte that the Bishop was to receive the same privileges as any other British subject. Furthermore, in a dispatch in May 1842 to William Young, the Vice-Consul in Jerusalem, British policy regarding the Church and its work was clearly spelled out: the Church was not to "interfere into the religious concerns either of the Mahomedan, or the Christian subjects of the Porte; and not to attempt to make proselytes to the Church of England from either of these classes . . ." Alexander's mission was specifically limited to proselytizing among Jews, and more specifically, only those Jews who were Ottoman subjects. Work among Russian Jews, who were under the protection of the Russian Empire, for example, would be more problematical. Young was further enjoined to abstain "from assisting to promote any scheme of interference with the Jewish subjects of the Porte, in which Bishop Alexander may possibly engage."[32] The relationship between the diplomats and the churchmen in Jerusalem remained controversial after James Finn, who supported the goals of the London Society and the restoration of the Jews, served as British consul in Jerusalem.[33] Palmerston supported Finn's policy of protecting the Jews throughout Finn's tenure as British consul in Jerusalem.[34]

It is still debatable whether or not Palmerston wished to press for British protection of *all* Jews within the Ottoman Empire. In a series of dispatches in 1840–1841, Palmerston instructed British representatives to "afford protection to the Jews generally," and to allow the Jews of Palestine to transmit to the Porte through the British authorities any complaints which they might have to prefer against the Turkish authorities.[35] Later instructions to British representatives throughout the Ottoman Empire went a step further, authorizing them to report directly to the ambassador at Constantinople (Istanbul) any cases of Jews being subjected to oppression or injustice. The Ottoman response was predictable: the authorities would welcome representations made by the British Ambassador for clarification of issues but would not accept the British representatives as intermediaries between the Jews and the Government.[36] Despite the fact that these policies were tempered by the Aberdeen interregnum, which also reduced government support for the work of the London Society, responses to appeals for protection from missionaries by Jews to the British representative did not reach official recognition status.

A case in point is an incident that occurred in Baghdad in 1846. When the rabbis of Baghdad issued a public curse against missionaries of the London Society and an edict of excommunication against Jews who visited them, both the Jews and the missionaries appealed to the British government for protection.[37] The Jews protested the work of the missionaries in their community and the missionaries were incensed by the ban against them.

Part of the Ottoman province that the British called Turkish Arabia (later Mesopotamia) and the Jews called Bavel (Babylonia), had been ruled for three hundred years by governors (mamluks) sent out from the capital, who became more independent as Istanbul's control of the periphery weakened. The rebellion in 1831 by the last mamluk ruler, Da'ud Pasha, however, came at a time when the Ottomans were concerned with the invasion of Syria by the Egyptian army of Muhammad 'Ali. Fearful of Egyptian designs on Baghdad and the possibility of Da'ud's assistance to the Egyptians and to the Russians whose presence loomed in the north, an Ottoman general was sent out from Istanbul to Baghdad to reassert central authority. As a result, trade picked up and the Ottoman reforms began to be implemented. What had been a backwater Ottoman province now began to attract significant European interest, not only because of the revitalization of transit routes from India to Istanbul, but also due to European interest in archaeological research and the possibility of new souls to be saved. Travelers and traders came through, among them members of the London Society.[38]

In 1846, Baghdadi Jewish merchants were key commercial players in Persian Gulf/Indian Ocean trade to the Far East, an area the British had been working commercially and diplomatically for almost a century. The Sassoon family, already in residence in Bombay and Calcutta after emigrating from Baghdad by the turn of the nineteenth century, had established branches of the family business in Manchester and Singapore, and were trading partners with coreligionists back home in Iraq, who were in direct competition with British merchants now looking for inroads into markets that became available with the Ottoman–British commercial agreements.[39] When, therefore, rabbis in Baghdad issued an edict of ostracism against anyone consorting with the missionaries, the incident not only had religious ramifications, but impacted on commerce. Some of the Jews who were affected by the ban were important merchants in the city who met with the missionaries to learn English.

Members of the London Society appealed to the British representative in Baghdad for intervention with the Ottoman authorities on their behalf, and the Jews appealed both to the Ottomans and to the British for protection against missionary activity in the context of religious rights as citizens of the Ottoman Empire. Concerned about stability in a region where ethnic strife was common, both governments were loath to take overt action that would impede the flow of commerce. Although Palmerston, in London, sympathized with the religious rights of Jews to adopt measures against Christian proselytization—

I have to observe while that Gentleman [Rev Vicars of the London Jews Society] contends for religious liberty, he ought to concede it to others; and if the heads of the Jewish Church chose to denounce spiritual penalties against all Jews who may listen to Christian preaching, it would be interference with the religious discipline of the Jewish Church, to prevent them from doing so; and I do not exactly see in what way, or by what proper and legitimate authority the Turkish Government could so interfere.[40]

The British resident in Baghdad had to accede to the Ottoman solution to the problem—that the missionaries cease proselytizing and the rabbis remove the edict of ostracism, thereby maintaining civil order and the uninterrupted flow of commerce. Therefore, the Society in London decided that work in Baghdad was not really cost effective and the missionaries did not press their case with the British government. Their work throughout most of the region gradually petered out.

By the early 1850s, the Eastern Question had become central to British foreign policy in the region. Although Palmerston succeeded in thwarting the French challenge to British hegemony in the Near East, in opening new markets for British commerce, and in establishing a formal British presence in Jerusalem, the Ottoman Empire faced severe military and financial challenges that seemed to threaten its very existence. Because of local independence movements and wars with Russia, the Turks were forced to modernize militarily at such a great financial cost that they had to turn to Britain for diplomatic, military, and financial support. As a result, the British became involved even more directly in Ottoman internal affairs. While fighting together with the Turks in the Crimean War (1854–1856), the British were also busily structuring financial loans to keep the Ottoman Empire afloat, all the while pressing the Porte for more liberal political reform with regard to minorities.

Jewish resettlement plans were floated again during the Crimean War and after, but were not seriously considered until World War I. Even then, British support for Jewish homeland, as stated in the Balfour Declaration, converged with the political and religious interests advocated by some Britons a half-century or so before. Throughout his tenure in office, Palmerston created a favorable atmosphere in support of British protection of Middle-Eastern Jews and backed Sir Moses Montifiore's visits to the region, but these sensitivities were never translated into official policy. And because the Jews were not in mortal danger, the British saw no reason to interfere with Ottoman policy.[41]

By the end of the Crimean War, the internal political situation in the Ottoman Empire changed once again. On February 18, 1856, the Imperial Rescript (Hatt-ı Humayun) was handed down. Worked out by England, France, and Austria, the western allies that fought with the Empire against Russia, the proclamation reiterated the reforms of the 1839 Imperial Rescript and stressed the principle of equality between Jews, all non-Muslim and Muslim citizens of the Empire. It would take two more years before British Jews could sit in Parliament in London.

Notes

1. J. C. Hurewitz, "Britain and the Middle East up to 1914," in *Encyclopedia of the Modern Middle East*, ed. Reeva S. Simon, Philip Mattar, and Richard W. Bulliet (New York: Macmillan, 1996), 1:398–400.
2. Alfred C. Wood, *A History of the Levant Company* (London: Oxford University Press, 1934; reprint, New York: Barnes and Noble, 1964), 214–215.
3. The Russian victory over the Ottomans resulted in the treaty of Kuchuk Kaynarja (1774) by which the Russians gained land north of the Black Sea and the right to build an Orthodox church in Istanbul. The Russians then proclaimed Russian protection over all Orthodox Christians in the Empire.
4. Wood, *Levant Company*, 154–155.
5. Mel Scult, *Millennial Expectations and Jewish Liberties: A Study of the Efforts to Convert the Jews in Britain, up to the Mid Nineteenth Century* (Leiden: E. J. Brill, 1978), 129.
6. C. Peter Williams, "British Religion and the Wider World: Mission and Empire, 1800–1940," in *A History of Religion in Britain: Practice and Belief from Pre-Roman Times to the Present*, ed. Sheridan Gilley and W. J. Shiels (Oxford: Blackwell, 1994), 382–385.
7. By 1858, Shaftesbury regarded opposition to the passage of the Jews' Bill as useless (Isaiah Friedman, "Lord Palmerston and the Protection of Jews in Palestine, 1838–1851," *Jewish Social Studies* 30 [1968]: 23–41).
8. Palmerston, who was replaced by Lord Aberdeen from September 1841 to 1846, returned to the post of foreign secretary from 1846 to 1852; he served as prime minister from 1855 to 1858, and then from 1859 to 1865.

9. Frank E. Bailey, "The Economics of British Foreign Policy, 1825–50," *The Journal of Modern History* 12 (1940): 449–484; Frederick S. Rodkey, "Lord Palmerston and the Rejuvenation of Turkey, 1930–41," *The Journal of Modern History* 2 (1930): 193–225.

10. Martin Lynn, "British Policy, Trade, and Informal Empire in the Mid-Nineteenth Century," in *The Oxford History of the British Empire: The Nineteenth Century*, ed. Andrew Porter (New York: Oxford University Press, 1999), 111–112.

11. See articles by Rodkey and Friedman. See also M. Vereté, "The Restoration of the Jews in English Protestant Thought," *Middle East Studies* 8 (1972): 3–50; and Sybil M. Jack, "No Heavenly Jerusalem: The Anglican Bishopric, 1841–83," *The Journal of Religious History* 19 (1995): 181–203.

12. Williams, "British Religion," 383. Note the work of William Wilberforce in the Abolition Movement, and Ashley Cooper in factory reform. Both were supporters of the London Society for Promoting Christianity Amongst the Jews.

13. Jonathan Frankel, *The Damascus Affair: "Ritual Murder," Politics, and the Jews in 1840* (Cambridge: Cambridge University Press, 1997), 285–287.

14. Scult, *Millennial Expectations*, pp. 80–81.

15. From Charles Simeon, *Discourses on Belhalf of the Jews* (London, 1839), as quoted by Michael Ragussis, *Figures of Conversion: "The Jewish Question" and English National Identity* (Durham: Duke University Press, 1995), 5, 302.

16. Mel Scult, "English Missions to the Jews—Conversion in the Age of Emancipation," *Jewish Social Studies* 35 (1973): 7.

17. Robert Michael Smith, "The London Jews' Society and Patterns of Jewish Conversion in England, 1801–1859," *Jewish Social Studies* 43 (1981): 283.

18. From *The Jewish Expositor* (1819), as quoted by Smith, "Jewish Conversion," 290.

19. A. L. Tibawi, *British Interests in Palestine 1800–1901: A Study in Religious and Educational Enterprise* (London: Oxford University Press, 1961), 6–7.

20. Naomi Shepherd, *The Zealous Intruders: The Western Rediscovery of Palestine* (New York: Harper and Row, 1987), 37–39.

21. Note the negotiations with Czar Alexander I in 1817 to establish a colony of Jews in the Crimea (Scult, *Millennial Expectations and Jewish Liberties*, 107). See also Michael Stanislawski, *Tsar Nicholas I and the Jews: The Transformation of Jewish Society in Russia 1825–1855* (Philadelphia: Jewish Publication Society of America, 1983).

22. Tibawi, *British Interests*, 6–8; 12.

23. Quoted in Frankel, *The Damascus Affair*, 288–289.

24. There were also protests against persecution of the Jews of the island of Rhodes.

25. Rodkey, "Lord Palmerston," 203; for a detailed analysis of the Damascus case, see Frankel, *The Damascus Affair*.

26. At the London Conference of 1840, Muhammad 'Ali agreed to retreat from Syria, Lebanon, Palestine, and the Sinai in return for the title of Egyptian viceroy and a hereditary dynasty. The last ruler was King Farouk, who abdicated in 1952.

27. Edwin Hodder, *The Life and Work of the Seventh Earl of Shaftesbury, K. G.* (London: Cassell, 1888), 1:310–315.

28. The story is related in detail in Tibawi, *British Interests*, 37–57. Pertinent documents are published in Albert M. Hyamson, *The British Consulate in*

Jerusalem in Relation to the Jews of Palestine, 1838–1914, 2 vols. (London: The Jewish Historical Society of England/Edward Goldston, Ltd, 1939). From the outset, the Anglican bishopric in Jerusalem was controversial because it was a joint British–Prussian Protestant endeavor. The churches went their separate ways in 1883 (see also the article by Jack, *No Heavenly Jerusalem*).

29. Friedman, "Lord Palmerston," 23–41.
30. Tibawi, *British Interests*, 50.
31. Todd M. Endelman, *Radical Assimilation in English Jewish History 1656–1945* (Bloomington: Indiana University Press, 1990), 158–159.
32. Tibawi, *British Interests*, 55–57; Hyamson, *The British Consulate*, xxxvii–xxxviii.
33. Finn's wife Elizabeth was the daughter of Alexander McCaul. For Finn's inner conflicts of church–state issues, see Arnold Blumberg, *Zion Before Zionism 1838–1880* (Syracuse: Syracuse University Press, 1985). See also the articles by Jack and Friedman. Finn supported the goals of the London Jewish Society and the Restoration of the Jews, but also the official diplomatic representative of Britain.
34. Friedman, "Lord Palmerston," 38.
35. Friedman and Harold Temperley both interpret the dispatches as advocating British protection of the Jews (see Harold Temperley, *England and the Near East: The Crimea* [New York: Archon Books, 1965], 444–445); in contrast, Tibawi maintains that reading the documents leads to the conclusion that protection of the Jews was not to be by Britain but "by their local sovereign, the Sultan" (*British Interests*, 35).
36. Hyamson, *The British Consulate*, xxxvi ff.
37. For a complete account of the incident, see Reeva Spector Simon, "The Case of the Curse: The London Society for Promoting Christianity amongst the Jews and the Jews of Baghdad," in *Altruism and Imperialism: Western Cultural and Religious Missions in the Middle East*, ed. Eleanor H. Tejirian and Reeva Spector Simon (New York: The Middle East Institute, Columbia University, 2002), 45–65.
38. See, e.g., H. Southgate, *Narrative of a Tour through Armenia, Kurdistan, Persia, and Mesopotamia* (London, 1840); Eliezer Bashan, "Testimonies by European Travelers about the Jews of Bavel and Kurdistan from the End of the 16th Century," in *Studies in the History of the Iraqi Jews and Their Culture*, ed. Shmuel Moreh (Tel-Aviv: Center for the Heritage of Iraqi Jewry, 1981), 19–30 (Hebrew).
39. Stephen Helmsley Longrigg, *Four Centuries of Modern Iraq* (London: Oxford University Press, 1925), 294; Hala Fattah, *The Politics of Regional Trade in Iraq, Arabia, and the Gulf 1745–1900* (Albany: State University of New York Press, 1997).
40. Great Britain, Foreign Office. FO 195/257 Palmerston to Wellesley, Foreign Office, October 20, 1846.
41. The question was revisited in 1860 after massacres of Jews in Syria.

CHAPTER 10

JEWISH TRANSLATIONS OF BRITISH ROMANTIC LITERATURE (1753–1858): A PRELIMINARY BIBLIOGRAPHY

Sheila A. Spector

It has long been recognized that British Romanticism played a significant role in the development of Jewish culture. Hillel Bavli (1893–1961), Hebrew poet and Professor of Modern Hebrew Literature at the Jewish Theological Seminary of America, introduced his essay "The Modern Renaissance of Hebrew Literature" by acknowledging the importance of English Romanticism to his subject.[1] More recently, Benjamin Harshav, Professor of Hebrew and Comparative Literature at Yale University, established, in his monograph *The Meaning of Yiddish*, the importance of British Romanticism to the history of Yiddish culture.[2] Sometimes directly—as in the case of Jews who spoke English, sometimes indirectly—as with those who absorbed British romantic themes and attitudes through European (French, German, or Russian) intermediaries, Jews have consistently been exposed to British Romanticism.[3] One significant, if underappreciated vehicle through which the Jews gained access to British romantic literature has been through Hebrew and Yiddish translations. Ever since the *Haskalah* (the Jewish Enlightenment), translation has been a major component of Jewish secular education. Therefore, in order to understand the full significance of this preliminary bibliograhy of Hebrew and Yiddish translations of British romantic literature, it is necessary first to establish the broader context of Jewish culture in the West from the mid-nineteenth century to the present.

European Jewish culture developed as a hybrid of at least three linguistic traditions: Hebrew—the language of the Bible; Yiddish—the Jewish vernacular; and the European vernacular of the host country.[4] Although originally, each of these implied its own sphere of interest, their interactions together establish the full implications of Jewish culture in the post-*Haskalah* world. If Hebrew articulated the religious core, Yiddish defined the secular, especially after the eastward migrations within the Pale of Settlement, while the increased use of European languages reflected the growing impetus toward modernization, especially in conjunction with the Enlightenment. Chronologically, Jewish development tended to lag about a century behind European, but even so, intellectual movements frequently paralleled those of the West: the *Haskalah*, usually dated from the late eighteenth century, the period when philosopher Moses Mendelssohn (1729–1786) introduced the process of modernization, exerted an influence on the Jewish community comparable to that of the Western Enlightenment in Britain; the pogroms of 1881–1882, like the French Revolution in England, initiated a period of romantic reflection, in which Eastern Jews, being alienated from the larger communities, sought other means of actualizing their identity within a gentile world; the Balfour Declaration of 1917, comparable to the Reform Bill of 1832, gave the Jews the security of British protection; and finally, statehood in 1948, parallel to emancipation in 1858, granted the Jews their full rights as citizens of the world.[5]

In its most basic formulation, British Romanticism can be said to have developed as a reaction against Enlightenment rationalism. With the consolidation of the modern nation state and the obligations imposed by imperialism, and with the shift to industrialized economies and the concomitant requirement of a literate work force, the successive American and French Revolutions initiated a period of self-reflection, as the English explored the full range of intellectual faculties beyond the purely rational level, considered social problems in terms of human rights and the class system, studied science and nature, and theorized about aesthetics and the arts. Throughout the period, the British enacted a series of progressive reforms that, among other things, banned slavery, protected the rights of the working classes, emancipated the Catholics, expanded public education, and eventually, by 1858, eliminated most of the disabilities that prevented the Jews from enjoying the full rights of citizenship. While clearly, these specific acts were designed to answer to English needs,[6] the impetus behind them was universal, and the history of Jewish culture can be viewed as a transformation of the British movement to accommodate Jewish needs.

At the time of the Enlightenment, most Jews were Ashkenazim, living in Eastern Europe. Although their culture had originated in medieval Germany, many Ashkenazim, over the next few centuries, settled in Eastern Europe, where conditions were far different from those that obtained in the West. Therefore, when considering the question of acculturation, it is necessary to take into account the disparate conditions experienced by the different Jewish communities. In the West, especially in Germany and England, Enlightenment values facilitated Jewish assimilation;[7] in the East, however, throughout the nineteenth century, Jews would be confined to the Pale of Settlement, where their economic, cultural, and religious opportunities would be severely restricted until, after the pogroms of 1881–1882, they began migrating to America and *Eretz Israel*. Finally, in the mid-twentieth century, the Holocaust would effectively end the Yiddish culture, while the recently established State of Israel would create a new home for the Hebrew.

Strongly influenced by the Christian Enlightenment, the *Haskalah*, as it originated in Germany under Mendelssohn's leadership, emphasized vocational education and vernacular languages in order to facilitate Jewish assimilation into the secular society, while still permitting the retention of religious affiliation.[8] In conjunction with the intellectual movement, Reform Judaism, its religious counterpart, instituted a modernized form of worship, introduced the vernacular into religious services, and reinterpreted Jewish messianism and Zionism in terms of post-Enlightenment nationalism. Specifically, the Reform movement attempted to apply the values associated with messianism to the contemporary secular world by transforming the literal into a metaphorical belief in a return to Zion.[9] In this way, *maskilim*—advocates of the *Haskalah*—hoped that by reforming Judaism into a Christian analogue, they might demonstrate that their own religion could be as "enlightened" as the dominant faith, and therefore, that its people merited equal rights as citizens of the state. With the emphasis on the vernacular, there was little need for Jewish translations of contemporary literature, and therefore, only a small number of the translations in this bibliography come from Western Europe.

Given the fact that Poland, Russia, and the other eastern European nations themselves were slow to adopt enlightened values, it should not be surprising that eastern Jews lagged far behind their Western counterparts. In the East, the Jews were far more effectively segregated from the dominant society, so religious authorities exerted far greater control over internal Jewish matters. Consequently, Reform Judaism never really took hold there. As for education, the state controlled the schools. At first, many *maskilim* agreed to teach, hoping that consistent with Mendelssohnian principles, they might accelerate the process of acculturation so that the Jews might be integrated more smoothly into the larger community. Unfortunately, as they eventually realized, the government was interested not in assimilation, but in conversion, having established the state schools primarily for evangelical purposes. And as those who did convert would learn, even if they turned their backs on their own people, they would never be fully accepted by the Christian world, and would ultimately be relegated to the margins of both societies, neither part of the Jewish world they had abandoned, nor fully absorbed into the Christian society they aspired to be part of. By the pogroms of 1881–1882, most *maskilim* had already despaired of implementing Western reform, so instead, they adapted the *Haskalah* to their own needs.

Language was always central to Jewish Enlightenment. In the West, *maskilim* turned to the vernacular as the vehicle through which to negotiate between the competing needs to assimilate with the dominant culture and to retain a Jewish identity. But in the East, the language problem was more internal, revolving around the questions of whether or not either Hebrew or Yiddish could ever be capable of communicating Enlightenment values on a

level comparable to that of western languages. Most *maskilim* were secular-
ists who saw no need to preserve Hebrew as the medium for religious discourse. Rather, they believed that if what they viewed as the contaminating
accretions of religious literature could only be removed, pure Hebrew could
then compete with any other language. To that end, they attempted to adapt
biblical Hebrew to the needs of a modern society by revivifying what had
been virtually a *dead* language, used primarily for written communication,
into a modern vernacular. Beyond that, some ideologues attempted to
discourage completely the use of Yiddish, insisting that Jewish culture would
be elevated if the modernized Hebrew were substituted for a language they
frequently denigrated as a *jargon*, spoken by the masses. On the practical
level, however, it was obvious that many Jews barely knew enough Hebrew
to say their prayers and required Yiddish for everyday communication. But
even those who accepted the need still disputed the suitability of Yiddish for
cultural purposes. While, as some asserted, to continue writing in Yiddish
would perpetuate its use, others believed that in order to educate the lower
classes about the values and modes of behavior appropriate for an enlightened society, it was necessary to speak in the people's own language; but still
others countered that such efforts would only encourage further use of
Yiddish. The result was that purists eschewed Yiddish entirely, while for
practical reasons, pragmatists compromised ideology.

The pogroms of 1881–1882, analogous to the French Revolution in the
West, effectively ended the Jewish Enlightenment, the realities of anti-
Semitism initiating a Jewish romantic period of introspection. Comparable to
English debates over human rights, secular Jews rejected earlier attempts to
assimilate into the Russian Empire, and, instead, turned either to socialism,
advocating equality for all workers world wide, or to a renewed interest in
Jewish nationalism, with political Zionists, under the leadership of Theodor
Herzl, beginning the move toward a new Jewish homeland.[10] In the East,
where they had never had a real chance of becoming part of the establishment,
Jews retained their literal belief in messianism and Zionism, which, by the end
of the nineteenth century, manifested itself in *Hibbat Zion*, a movement that
originated among Russian Jews who advocated Jewish emigration to *Eretz
Israel*; but in contrast to Herzl's political movement, the idealistic Easterners
attempted to bypass the political exigencies of dealing with the authorities, and
simply established settlements on their own. Needless to say, their efforts
failed, though Herzl's did not. Zionism, as a movement, would eventually lead
to the Balfour Declaration, the British guarantee, in 1917, of a Jewish national
home. Not all Jews emigrated to *Eretz Israel*, however. From the 1880s on,
many Ashkenazim began moving to America, settling primarily in New York,
where they enjoyed the freedoms unavailable in Eastern Europe.[11]

Regardless of their land of settlement, and regardless of their language of
communication, Jews of the post-1881 period became more and more
interested in secular literature. At this time, a number of Jewish periodicals,
newspapers, and presses were established in major European and American
Jewish communities, and after 1918, in *Eretz Israel*, as well; and an
important focus of this renewed literary activity was translation. In the

attempt to elevate the Jews to a par with other educated cultures, the intelligentsia translated numerous works from other literatures into Hebrew and Yiddish. While the impetus was to acculturate the Jews, the choice of works to translate had less to do with the canonical interests of the language of origin than with the interests of the translators and their readers. Thus, to cite some obvious examples, different Hebrew versions of Byron's *Hebrew Melodies* were published in St. Petersburg in 1884, and in Leipzig in 1890. At the height of eastern immigration to the West, a Hebrew version of Coleridge's paean to the wandering Jew, *The Rime of the Ancient Mariner*, was published in New York in 1910, and a Yiddish *Childe Harold* was published in London in 1915.

The twentieth century witnessed the gradual dominance of Hebrew over Yiddish. In the period between the two world wars, while Yiddish matured into "a refined instrument for the expression of the profoundest thoughts and the subtlest moods of the Jewish people,"[12] modern Hebrew consolidated into the Israeli medium of communication. During this time, for example, Yiddish translations of Dickens' *Oliver Twist* and *David Copperfield* were published in 1920–1921, while Byron's *Manfred* and Shelley's *Defence of Poetry* were translated into Hebrew, in 1922 and 1927–1928 respectively. In the 1930s, as the Holocaust loomed, Yiddish versions of *Cain* (1931) and *The Prisoner of Chillon* (1937) were published in Europe; and at its aftermath, Shelley's *Prometheus Unbound*, one of the last Yiddish translations, was published in Chicago in 1953. In contrast, after the State of Israel was established, Hebrew translations flourished, with, for example, the publication of William Blake's *The Marriage of Heaven and Hell*, complete works of Jane Austen, many novels by the Brontës, and fittingly, perhaps, all culminating, at the end of the twentieth century, with a Hebrew version of Edmund Burke's *Reflections on the Revolution in France*. Although most Jews in America and Israel know English, there is no reason to assume that Hebrew translators will stop now. More than simply the transformation of a text from one language into another, translation is an act of literary transplantation that not only enriches a new culture, but also equally as important, expands the interpretive context of the work itself.

A note on the bibliographies.[13] Because the use of language reflects a cultural, as well as ideological choice, I have kept the Hebrew and Yiddish bibliographies separate from each other. I have roughly transliterated the titles of works, though given the complexities of both Hebrew and Yiddish pronunciation, I have not attempted to render their original pronunciations. I have, however, placed in brackets brief translations of those titles that are not self-explanatory. Regarding proper names, I have attempted to use standardized American English forms, either as used in the *Encyclopaedia Judaica*, or major library catalogues, especially those of the Library of Congress and the New York Public Library. Regarding publication information, wherever possible, I have included English place names and the spellings publishers used in their English-language notices. It should be noted that some publishing houses, though originally founded in Eastern or Central Europe, over time moved west, eventually to America or Israel. As far as publication dates are concerned, I have consistently used those of the Common Era. Given the inconsistencies between the solar and lunar calendars, in some cases it was necessary to indicate a range over two years. It is also important to be aware that much of this material has never been collated. Consequently, some entries lack complete bibliographical records. Still, rather than omit them, I have included whatever information I have been able to find, scanty though it may be. Finally, as I indicate in my subtitle, this is not a comprehensive, but only a preliminary bibliography. While records for translations published in book form are relatively accessible, many were published in the periodical presses for which we lack indexes or even, in some cases, extant copies. Consequently, it seems reasonable to infer that regardless of the wealth of materials I have been able to locate, much salient information is likely absent from the following bibliographies.

Hebrew Translations

Aguilar, Grace. *The Perez Family: A Tale.*
  Kur ha-nisayon: Sipur (Measure of the test: a tale). No trans. Tel-Aviv: Netsah, 1976.
Aguilar, Grace. *The Vale of Cedars; or, The Martyr.*
  Milhemet ha-emunah veha-ahavah (The war of love and truth). Trans. Yesha'yah Gelbhoyz. Mainz: Y. Brill, 1875.
  Ganon ve-hatsel: sipur mi-korot ha-anusim be-Portugal (Deliverance from the shadow: a story from the annals of the forced ones). Trans. Azriel Nathan Frenk. Warsaw: no publisher, 1893.
  'Emek ha-arazim: halakim alef u-vet. Adapted and trans. Abraham Shalom Friedberg. Calcutta: no publisher, 1895; Tel Aviv: Omanut, 1939.
  ha-Anusim: sipur mi-yeme ha-Inkvizitsyah bi-Sefarad (The forced ones: stories from the days of the Inquisition in Spain). Abridgement by Sh. Kantorovits of Abraham Shalom Friedberg's *Emek ha-arazim,* itself an adaptation of Grace Aguilar's *The Vale of Cedars.* Warsaw: Hotsa'at Barka'i, 1923; Tel Aviv: S. Sreberk, 1972; Jerusalem: Sefarim Toraniyim, 1984.
  'Emek ha-arazim: Kohah shel emunah ('Emek ha-arazim): sipur mi-tekufat ha-Inkvizitsyah bi-Sefarad. No trans. Tel Aviv: Netsah, 1970.
Austen, Jane. *Emma.*
  Emah. No trans. Tel Aviv: Ha-Kibbutz Ha-Me'uhad, 1982.
Austen, Jane. *Mansfield Park.*
  Mensfild Park. Trans. Aharon Amir. Tel Aviv: Ma'ariv, 1988.
Austen, Jane. *Northanger Abbey.*
  Minzar Nortanger. Trans. Talah Bar. Tel Aviv: Or'am, 1986.
Austen, Jane. *Persuasion.*
  Hatayat lev. Trans. No'omi Karmel. Jerusalem: Keter, 1983.
Austen, Jane. *Pride and Prejudice.*
  Ahava v'gaavah. Trans. Shoshana Shrayra. Tel Aviv: M. Newman, 1952.
  Ahavah ve-ge'avah. Trans. Talah Bar. Giv'atayim: Or'am, 1984.
  Ga'avah u-mishpat kadum. Trans. Aharon Amir. Tel Aviv: Ma'ariv, 1984.
Austen, Jane. *Sense and Sensibility.*
  Binah ve-rahashi-lev. Trans. Aharon Amir. Tel Aviv: Ma'ariv, 1984, 1994.

Blake, William. *The Marriage of Heaven and Hell.*
  Nisu'e ha-'eden veha-she'ol. Trans. Giora Leshem. Tel Aviv: Eked, 1967–1968; Tel Aviv: G. Leshem, 1997.
Blake, William. Selections.
  Mi-shire vilyam blak (From the poetry of William Blake). Trans. Joshua Kochav. Tel Aviv: Ofir, 1968.
  Od mi-shire blak ve-kits (added title page: *More from the Poetry of Blake and Keats*). Trans. Joshua Kochav. Tel Aviv: Ofir, 1980.
  Tenison, robert herik, edgar alan po, vilyam blak, vilyam ernst henli, heinrikh heine (added title page: *Alfred Tennyson, Robert Herrick, Edgar Allan Poe, William Blake, William E. Henley, Heinrich Heine: New Translations into Hebrew*). Trans. Samuel Friedman. Tel Aviv. S. Friedman, 1986.
Brontë, Charlotte. *Jane Eyre.*
  G'ein Eir. Trans. Hanah Ben-Dov. Tel Aviv: M. Newman, 1946.
  G'ein Eir. Trans. Talah Bar. Tel Aviv: Or'am, 1986.
  G'ein Eir. Trans. Li'orah Hertsig. Tel Aviv: Zemorah, Bitan, 1987.
  G'ein Eir. Trans. Semadar Kogo. Tel Aviv: Ofarim, 2002.
Brontë, Emily. *Wuthering Heights.*
  Enkat gevahim. Trans. Aharon Amir. Jerusalem: Keter, 1990.
Bulwer-Lytton, Edward. *The Last Days of Pompey.*
  Yeme Pompe ha-aharonim. Trans. Abraham Shlonsky. Tel Aviv: Omanut, 1928–1929.
  Yeme Pompe ha-aharonim. Trans. Ya'el Ron-Lerer. Tel Aviv: Ofarim, 1994.
Bulwer-Lytton, Edward. *Rienzi, the Last of the Roman Tribunes.*
  Ri'entsi: aharon ha-Tribunim. Trans. Abraham Birman. Jerusalem and Tel Aviv: Devir, 1881–1882.
Burke, Edmund. *Reflections on the Revolution in France.*
  Mahashavot 'al ha-mahapekhah ha-Tsarfatit. Trans. Aharon Amir. Jerusalem: Hotsa'at Shalem, 1999.
Byron, George Gordon. *Cain, A Mystery.*
  Kayin; melitsah bat shalosh ma'arakhot. Myster nach Lord Byron in 3 Acten. Ha'atakah hofshit be-mishkol ha-tenu'ot u-mil'el mi-meni ha-tsa'ir. Trans. Y'akov Tsevi Ben Rabi Avraham ha-Levi L'ev. Unsd'orf: Shenat Berit li-ferat katan, 1851–1852; microfilm, 1981.
  Kayin: shir hizayon 'al-pi kitve ha-kodesh. Trans. David Frishman. Warsaw: Tushiyah, 1900; Warsaw: Merkaz ("Central"), 1914. Reprinted in Frishman's *Targumim* (translations), ed. Eliezer Steinman, 207–242. Tel Aviv: M. Newman, Hotsa'at sefarim "Keneset," 1953–1954.
Byron, George Gordon. *Heaven and Earth.*
  Shamayim ve-aretz. Trans. David Frishman. Original publication data unavailable. Reprinted in Frishman's *Targumim* (translations), ed. Eliezer Steinman, 243–260. Tel Aviv: M. Newman, Hotsa'at sefarim "Keneset," 1953–1954. Reprinted in Frishman, *Kol kitve* (complete works). Jerusalem: M. Neuman, 1964. 7:5–81.
Byron, George Gordon. *Hebrew Melodies.*
  Neginot 'Ever: shirim shonim: yesodotam be-harere kodesh. Trans. Matityahu Simhah Rubener. Czernowitz: E. Igel, 1864.
  Zemirot Yisrael. Trans. Judah Leib Gordon, in his *Kol shire Yehudah Leb Gordon: yeshanim gam hadashim be-arba'ah sefarim* (Complete poems of Judah Leib Gordon . . .), 1:70–78. Warsaw and St. Peterburg: Bi-defus G. F. Pines vi-Yesha'ahu Tsederboim, 1884.

Shire Yeshurun. Trans. Shelomoh Mendelkern. Leipzig: no publisher, 1890.

Shire Yi 'srael shel Bairan. Trans. Nathan Horowitz. London: no publisher, 1930.

Manginoth 'ivriyoth. Trans. Jacob Orland. Jerusalem: Achiasaf, 1944.

Manginot 'Ivriyot/Lord Bairon. Trans. Samuel Friedman. Intro. Michael Dachau. Jerusalem: S. Friedman, 1983.

Byron, George Gordon. *Manfred.*

Manfred, po'emah dramatit. Trans. David Frishman. Warsaw: Stybel, 1922. Reprinted in his *Targumim* (translations), ed. Eliezer Steinman, 261–282. Tel Aviv: M. Newman, Hotsa'at sefarim "Keneset," 1953–1954. Reprinted in his *Kol kitve* (complete works), 7:83–168. Jerusalem: M. Newman,1964.

Byron, George Gordon. *Mazeppa.*

Mazepah. (published with *Asir Shilyon*). Trans. Y. L. Barukh. Frankfort am Mein: Omanut, 192–.

Byron, George Gordon. *Prisoner of Chillon.*

Asir Shilyon. Trans. Y. L. Brocowitz. *Achiasaf* 8 (1900): 87–96.

Asir Shilyon. (published with *Mazepah*). Trans. Y. L. Barukh. Frankfort am Mein: Omanut, 192–.

Byron, George Gordon. Selected Poems.

Selected poems in *'Arafot zahav: hemah shirim yekarim mi-gedole meshorere ha-'amim: 'asuyim bi-demutam ve-ne 'ataku li-leshon 'Ever = Gedichte von Schiller und Lord Bryon in einer Auswahl un Hebraische übertragen.* Trans. Meir Letteris. Vienna: Schmidbauer u. Holzwarth, 1852.

Selected poems in *ha-Shoshanah ha-kehulah: shirim.* Trans. Moshe Giora. Tel Aviv: Idit, 1959–1960.

Coleridge, Samuel Taylor. *Kubla Khan.*

Shirat ha-malah ha-kadmoni ve-Kublah Khan (published with *The Rime of the Ancient Mariner*). Trans. Akiva Fleishman. New York: Bi-defus A. H. Rozenberg, 1910–1911.

Coleridge, Samuel Taylor. *The Rime of the Ancient Mariner.*

Shirat ha-malah ha-kadmoni ve-Kublah Khan (published with *Kubla Khan*). Trans. Akiva Fleishman. New York: Bi-defus A. H. Rozenberg, 1910–1911.

Shirat yored-ha-yam ha-yashish: be-shiv'ah halakim. Trans. Ruth Blumert. Tel Aviv: Keshev la-shirah, 2001.

Cumberland, Richard. *The Jew.*

Ish Yehudi: mahazeh sha'ashu'im. Trans. Joseph Brill. Vilna: L. Matz, 1878.

Dickens, Charles. *The Cricket on the Hearth.*

ha-Tsartsur me'ahorey ha-tagur: sipur, shel Ts'arlz Dikens. Trans. Ya'akov Serayski. Warsaw: no publisher, 1924–1925.

Dickens, Charles. *David Copperfield.*

David Koperfild. Trans. Moses ben Eliezer. Tel Aviv: Omanut, 1900, 1928; Jerusalem: Turgeman, 1921.

David Koperfild. Trans. Yesha'ayahu Levit. Tel Aviv: M. Mizrahi, 1950.

David Koperfild. Trans. M. Harpaz. Tel Aviv: Niv, 1965–1966.

ha-Historyah ha-ishit shel David Koperfild. Trans. Meir Wieseltier. Tel Aviv: Devir, 1987.

David Koperfild. Trans. Binah Ofek. Tel Aviv: Ofarim, 1997.

Dickens, Charles. "The Haunted Man."

Etsem ha-kesamim. Trans. Uri'el Ofek. Tel Aviv: Yehoshu'a Ts'ets'ik, 1970.

Dickens, Charles. *The Life and Adventures of Nicholas Nickleby.*

Parashat hayav ve-harpatka'otav shel Nikolas Nikelbi. Trans. Yosef Luz. Tel Aviv: Am Oved, 1947–1948.

Dickens, Charles. *Little Dorrit.*
  Dorit Ketina. Trans. Tsevi Ron. Tel Aviv: J. Sreberk, 195–.
  Dorit ha-ketanah. Trans. Ofirah Rahat. Jerusalem: Mosad Bialik, 2002.
Dickens, Charles. *The Old Curiosity Shop.*
  Bet-mimkar- ʿatikot. Trans. O. Ovsey. Warsaw: Stybel, 1924–1929.
  Bet mimkar ʿatikot. Trans. Moshe ben Eliezer. Tel Aviv: Yizrael, 1942, 1980.
  Bet mimkar ʿatikot. Trans. Binah Ofek. Tel Aviv: Ofarim, 2001.
Dickens, Charles. *Oliver Twist.*
  Oliver Tvist. Trans. Hillel Bavli. Warsaw: Stybel, 1924.
  Oliver Tvist. Trans. Isaac Shoenberg. Tel Aviv: no publisher, 1934–1935.
  Oliver Tvist. Trans. Eliezer Carmi. Tel Aviv: ha-Dov, 1949; Tel Aviv: Revivim, 198–.
  Oliver Tvist. Abridged trans. Aryeh Sivan. Tel Aviv: M. Newman, 1954–1955.
  Oliver Tvist. Trans. Y. Shai. Tel Aviv: Stybel, 1960.
  Oliver Tvist. Trans. Y. Yishay. Giv'atayim: Masadah, 1979.
  Oliver Tvist. Trans. Ya'el Ron-Lerer. Tel Aviv: Ofarim, 1995.
Dickens, Charles. *Oliver Twist.* Videocassette.
  Oliver Tvist videorecording: kaletet shire ha-mahazemer: ʿibud hadash le-sifro. Trans. Menahem Golan; music by Roni Vais. Or Yehudah: Hed artsi, 199–.
Dickens, Charles. *The Pickwick Papers.*
  Ketavim me- ʿizvon bet ha-va ʿad ha-Pikviki. Trans. Israel Hayyim Tawiow. Warsaw: Stybel, 1921.
  Mo'adon ha-Pikvikim. Trans. Aryeh Sivan. Jerusalem, Tel Aviv: M. Newman, 1969–1970.
  Reshumot mo'adon ha-Pikvikim; iyurim me-et Piz. Trans. Aharon Amir. Tel-Aviv: Ma'ariv, 1990.
Dickens, Charles. Stories for Children.
  Sipure Dikens li-yeladim: Dorit ketina, Nil ha-ketanah, Pip pa'ut (Dickens' stories for children: Little Dorrit, Little Nell, Little Pip). Trans. Binah Gewirtz. Ed. Z. Ari'el. Tel Aviv: J. Sreberk, 1940, 1968.
Disraeli, Benjamin. *Alroy*
  Hoter mi-geza' Yishai, o, David Al-ro'i: sipur . . . asher be-harare erets ha-kedoshah (a fragment about the passing away of the messiah, or, David Alroy: A story in the mountains of the Holy Land). Trans. Avraham Aba Rakovski. Warsaw: L. I. Schapira, 1883–1888, 1898, 1909.
  David Alro'i: sipur histori mi-tekufat ha-ge'onim (David Alroy: an historical story on the authority of the rabbis). Trans. A. Roset. Warsaw: Barka'i, 1924; Tel Aviv: Yizrael, 192–, 1935, 1950, 1954.
  Alroi. Trans. Elihu Amikam. Tel-Aviv: S. Friedman, 1951–1952.
Disraeli, Benjamin. *Tancred.*
  Nes la-goyim, o, Tankred (miracle for the nations, or, Tancred). Trans. Judah Loeb Levin. Warsaw: A. Ginz, 1883.
  Tankred: sipur me-haye ha-atsilim ha-Angliyim ba-me'ah ha-shemoneh-'esreh (Tancred: story from the lives of the English nobility in the nineteenth century). No trans. Warsaw: Ahisefer, 1927; Tel Aviv: Yizrael, 1957.
Keats, John. Letters.
  Mivhar mikhtavim (edited letters). Trans. Dan Da'or; intro. Aryeh Zaks. Tel-Aviv: Sifriyat Po'alim: Ha-Kibuts Ha-Me'uhad, 1984.
Keats, John. Selections.
  Divre shel yafi: shirim (things of beauty: poems). Trans. Reuben Tsur. Tel Aviv: Eked, 1971.

Od mi-shire Blake ve-Keats (added title page: *More from the Poetry of Blake and Keats*). Trans. Joshua Kochav. Tel Aviv: Ofir, 1980.

Lamb, Charles and Mary. *Tales from Shakespeare.*

Mi-sipure Shekspir. Trans. Aharon Amir. Tel Aviv: Mahbarot le-Sifrut, 1948–1949; 1957–1958, 1962, 1965, 1967.

Sipure Shekspir. Trans. Aron J. Barr. Tel Aviv: Tamuz, 1985.

A Midsummer Night's Dream; The Merchant of Venice; Much Ado About Nothing; Romeo and Juliet; The Tempest; Twelfth Night; Two Gentlemen of Verona; A Winter's Tale.

Sipure Shekspir. Trans. Ayalah Rahav. Tel Aviv: Mahbarot le-Sifrut, 1988.

King Lear; A Midsummer Night's Dream; Romeo and Juliet.

Scott. Walter. *Title?*

Bat ha-nasikh ha-no'azah. Trans. M. Harpaz. Tel Aviv: Yosod, 1975.

Scott, Walter. *Ivanhoe.*

Aivenho: roman. Trans. Moshe ben Eliezer. Odessa: Turgeman, 1916; Jerusalem: Turgeman, 1920.

Scott, Walter. *Ivanhoe.* Adaptation.

ha-Sifriyah ha-klasit: Aivenho. Trans. Eliezer Carmi. Tel Aviv: Revivim, 198–.

Scott, Walter. *Quentin Durward.*

Kventin Durvard. Trans. Yitshak Levanon. Tel Aviv: Amichai, 1975.

Scott, Walter. *Rob Roy.*

Rob Roy: giborah ha-le'umi shel Skotyah (Rob Roy: the national hero of Scotland). Trans. Shtemper. Tel Aviv: Elkanah, 1995.

Scott, Walter. *The Talisman.*

Talisma: roman. Trans. Samuel Mohilewer. Tel Aviv: Omanut, 1929–1930.

Terufat ha-pela'im (miraculous cure). Trans. M. Harpaz. Tel Aviv: Niv, 1964

Shelley, Mary. *Frankenstein.*

Frankenshtain: Promete'us ha-moderni. No trans. Jerusalem: Elishar, 1983.

Frankenshtain o Promete'us ha-moderni. Trans. Iris Bar'am. Hod ha-Sharon: Astrolog, 1995.

Frankenshtain. Trans. Larry Weinberg. Jerusalem: Keter, 1996.

Frankenshtain: Promete'us ha-moderni: bi-sheloshah sefarim. Trans. Ya'arit Ben-Ya'akov. Tel Aviv: Prag, 2000.

Shelley, Mary. *Frankenstein.* Videorecording.

Frankenshtain videorecording. Or Yehudah: Hed Artsi, Wham, 1999?

Shelley, Percy Bysshe. *Adonais.*

Adonis: Elegyah 'al moto shel Jon Kits. Trans. Jacob Orland. Tel Aviv: Eked, 1976.

Shelley, Percy Bysshe. A *Defence of Poetry.*

Sanegoryah 'al ha-shirah. Trans. Simon Halkin. Tel Aviv: Hedim, 1927–1928; Tel-Aviv: Hakibbutz Hameuchad, 1982.

Wordsworth, William. Selections.

Mi-shire Shekspir Vordsvort ve-Tenison (alternate title: *Poems by Shakespeare, Wordsworth and Tennyson*). Trans. Yehoshua Kokhav. Tel Aviv: Ofir, 1969.

Yiddish Translations

Aguilar, Grace. *The Vales of Cedar.* Adaptation.

Di ungliklikha miryam; oder, die blutine geshikhte fun der inkvizitsia, ein historisher roman fun ispania (the unlucky Miriam; or the bloody history of the Inquisition, a historical novel about Spain). Trans. Yoha Trubnik. Vilna: M. Katsenelenbogen, 1888, 1910–1911.

Blake, William. "The Flea."
  "Die flieg." Trans. A. Asen.[14] *Jewish American/The American* (Yiddish periodical)
    (May 17, 1957).
Blake, William. ("Love of Home" [?]).
  "Geheime libe." Trans. A. Asen. *Jewish American/The American* (Yiddish
    periodical).
Bulwer-Lytton, Edward. *The Disowned.*
  Der Verstossene. No trans. Stuttgart: J.B. Metzler'schen Buchhandlung, 1845.
Burns, Robert. "My Love Is a Red Red Rose."
  "Mein liebste" (my love). Trans. A. Asen. *Der oyfkum: khoydesh zhurnal far liter-
    atur un kultur-inyonim* (Khoydesh-Zhurnal far literatur un kultur-inyonim)
    (The Rise: Monthly journal of literature and cultural matters) 4 (October–
    November 1929): 38.
Burns, Robert. "To John Kennedy: A Farewell."
  "A zei-gesunt tsu mein liebster" (farewell, dear friend). Trans. A. Asen.
Byron, George Gordon. *Cain, A Mystery.*
  Kain. Trans. Nathan Horowitz. London, 1925.
  Kain. Trans. Abraham Asen. Serial publication: *Der oyfkum: khoydesh zhurnal far
    literatur un kultur-inyonim* (Khoydesh-Zhurnal far literatur un kultur-inyonim)
    (The Rise: Monthly journal of literature and cultural matters) 3 (June–July
    1928): 41–53; 3 (August–September 1928): 38–53; 3 (October 1928): 26–38.
    In book form: Vilna: B. Kletskin, 1931.
Byron, George Gordon. *Childe Harold.*
  Tchild Harald, Canto 1. Trans. Ezekiel Bleicher. In *Dos neie leben* (the new life),
    journal edited by Chaim Zhitlowsky (New York) 1 (1908–1909): 155–157,
    217–220, 267–269. Also, in *Eyropeische literatur* (European literature). Ed.
    Abraham Reisen. Warsaw: Progres, no. 12 (1910): 27–32; no. 14 (1910):
    28–34; no. 15 (1910): 34–38; no. 16 (1910): 35–38; no. 17 (1910): 31–36;
    no. 20 (1910): 29–36; no. 21 (1910): 30–36. Bleicher's biographical sketch of
    Byron is in no. 12 (1910): 23–26. Also in Bleicher's *Veh un unruh* (Traveling
    and restlessness). London: Kunst, 1915: 63–101.
Byron, George Gordon. *Heaven and Earth.*
  Himmel un erd. Trans. Ezekiel Bleicher. Kiev: Darum, 1919.
Byron, George Gordon. *Hebrew Melodies.*
  Bayron's hebreishe melodyen: mit a forvort. Trans. Nathan Horowitz. London:
    "Express" Printers, 1925.
  Idishe melodies. Trans. Abraham Asen. New York: Max Yankovitch, 1928.
Byron, George Gordon. *Hebrew Melodies.* Selections.
  Trans. A. Asen. *Der oyfkum: khoydesh zhurnal far literatur un kultur-inyonim*
    (Khoydesh-Zhurnal far literatur un kultur-inyonim) (The Rise: Monthly journal
    of literature and cultural matters) 1 (1908–1909): 224; 2 (July 1927): 17;
    3 (January 1928): 44–45; 3 (January 1928). *Kavne* (February 27, 1938): 49.
  Trans. Ezekiel Bleicher. *Dos neie leben* (the new life), journal edited by Chaim
    Zhitlowsky (New York) 1 (1908–1909): 224.
Byron, George Gordon. *Manfred.*
  Manfred. Trans. Nathan Horowitz. London, 1925?
Byron, George Gordon. Occasional Pieces.
  "Euthanasia."
    "In sheinkeit shtarbn." Trans. A. Asen. *Tsuzamen* (September 1931).
  "Fill the Goblet Again."
    "Gist an vider di bekher." Trans. A. Asen.

"When We Two Parted."

"Ven mir habn zikh gesheidt." Trans. A. Asen. 1927.

Byron, George Gordon. *The Prisoner of Chillon.*

Der gefangener fun Shilon. Trans. Max Hershman. In *Der arbaytr fraynd* (the worker's friend) (1922).

Der gefangener fun Shilon. Trans. Abraham Asen. New York: Feder, 1925.

Der gefangener fun Shilon. Trans. Moisei Khashchevatskii. Krakow: Kinder-Farlag bam Ts. K. L. K. Yu. P. O., 1937.

Coleridge, Samuel Taylor. "Love."

"Libe." Trans. A. Asen. *Der oyfkum: khoydesh zhurnal far literatur un kultur-inyonim* (Khoydesh-Zhurnal far literatur un kultur-inyonim) (The Rise: Monthly journal of literature and cultural matters) 2 (September 1927): 33–34.

Dickens, Charles. *Barnaby Rudge.*

Di sreyfe in Londoner turme: roman (the fire in the tower of London). Trans. Lamed Shapiro. Vilna: Kletskin, 1924.

Dickens, Charles. *A Christmas Carol.*

Vaynakht (Christmas). Trans. Esther Kreitman. Warsaw: Helios, 1929.

Dickens, Charles. *David Copperfield.*

David ben David (Kopperfild): fray iberzetst fun English (David the son of David [Copperfield]: free translation from English). Trans. Bernard Gorin. Vilna: I. Shriftgiser and M. Katsenelenbogen, 1894.

Dovid Koperfild. Trans. Isaac Deutscher. Warsaw: no publisher, 1920–1921.

Dovid Koperfild. Trans. Itzik Kipris. Kiev: Kultur-lige, 1928.

Dickens, Charles. *Dombey and Son.*

Dombi un zun. Abridged trans. J. Chwatt. Bialystok: Dos bukh, 1922.

Dickens, Charles. *Oliver Twist.*

Oliver Tvist, di geshikhte fun an enlt kind (Oliver Twist, the history of a lonely child). Trans. Y. Ashkenazi. Warsaw: no publisher, 1920.

Oliver Tvist. Yiddish abridgement L. Reznik. Kiev: Kultur-lige, 1925.

Oliver Tvist: dos tragishe leben fun a yo'sem (Oliver Twist: the tragic life of an orphan). Trans. J. Ashkenazi, vol. 1; Shloyme Sheynberg, vol. 2. Warsaw: S. Goldfarb, 1926–1927

Oliver Tvist. Trans. Isaac Deutscher. Warsaw: no publisher, 1927.

Oliver Tvist. Trans. S. Rozenberg. Warsaw: S. Goldfarb, 1927–1930.

Oliver Tvist. Yiddish abridgement. No trans. Kiev: Kultur lige, 1930.

Disraeli, Benjamin. *Alroy.*

Dovid Elroi. Trans. Falk Halperin. Warsaw: Merkaz (Central), 1924.

Disraeli, Benjamin. *Tancred.*

Tankred. Trans. Sh. Zaks. Warsaw: S. Goldfarb, 1927.

Hunt, Leigh. "Abou ben Adhem."

"Abu ben adhem un der melekh." Trans. A. Asen. *Amerikaner/The Jewish American* (June 19, 1932).

Keats, John. *La Belle Dame sans Merci.*

La bel dame san merci. Trans. A. Asen. *Zukunft* (1927).

Keats, John. "Fancy."

"Die fantazia." Trans. A. Asen. *Der oyfkum: khoydesh zhurnal far literatur un kultur-inyonim* (Khoydesh-Zhurnal far literatur un kultur-inyonim) (The Rise: Monthly journal of literature and cultural matters) 4 (April 1929): 41–42; *Literarishe bleter,* no. 27, p. 527.

Keats, John. "Ode on a Grecian Urn."
"An ade tsu a grikhisher urne." Trans. A. Asen.
Keats, John. "Ode on Melancholy."
"An ode tsu der melankalie." Trans. A. Asen. *Der oyfkum: khoydesh zhurnal far literatur un kultur-inyonim* (Khoydesh-Zhurnal far literatur un kultur-inyonim) (The Rise: Monthly journal of literature and cultural matters) 3 (April 1928): 32–33.
Keats, John. "Ode to a Nightingale."
"An ode tsu der nakhtigel." Trans. A. Asen. *Der oyfkum: khoydesh zhurnal far literatur un kultur-inyonim* (Khoydesh-Zhurnal far literatur un kultur-inyonim) (The Rise: Monthly journal of literature and cultural matters) 4 (March 1929): 37–38.
Keats, John. "On Death."
"Oif dem toit." Trans. A. Asen. *Frei arbeiter shtime* (Free voice of labor) (August 27, 1926).
Keats, John. "To Autumn."
"Herbst." Trans. A. Asen. *Der oyfkum: khoydesh zhurnal far literatur un kultur-inyonim* (Khoydesh-Zhurnal far literatur un kultur-inyonim) (The Rise: Monthly journal of literature and cultural matters) 1 (September 1926): 17.
Keats, John. "To Hope."
"Die hafnung." Trans. A. Asen. *Der oyfkum: khoydesh zhurnal far literatur un kultur-inyonim* (Khoydesh-Zhurnal far literatur un kultur-inyonim) (The Rise: Monthly journal of literature and cultural matters) 3 (November 1928): 33.
Keats, John. "To Sleep."
"Tsum shlaf." Trans. A. Asen. *Der oyfkum: khoydesh zhurnal far literatur un kultur-inyonim* (Khoydesh-Zhurnal far literatur un kultur-inyonim) (The Rise: Monthly journal of literature and cultural matters) 6 (February–March, 1931): 37.
Lamb, Charles. "The Old Familiar Faces."
"Die alte bakante gezikhter." Trans. A. Asen. *Der oyfkum: khoydesh zhurnal far literatur un kultur-inyonim* (Khoydesh-Zhurnal far literatur un kultur-inyonim) (The Rise: Monthly journal of literature and cultural matters) 4 (December 1929): 17.
Lamb, Charles. *Tales from Shakespeare.*
Shekspier's oysgevehlte verk: mit zayn biografye un bild (Shakespeare's most popular work: with his biography and picture). Trans. D. M. Hermalin. New York: S. Drukerman, 1907; 1908; 1909; 1912.
Scott, Walter. *Ivanhoe.*
Ivanhoye: oder dos umkehrung fun dem krayts ritser (Ivanhoe: or the return of the Christian knight). Trans. Balbine Klatshke. Warsaw: A. Ginz, 1879.
Der shvartser riter (the black knight). Trans. Lamed Shapiro. Warsaw: Bikher-far-ale, 1911, 1927.
Ayvenho: roman. Trans. Moyshe Teyf. Minsk: Melukhe-farlag fun Vaysrusland, 1937.
Scott, Walter. "*Ivanhoe.*" Adaptation.
Oto da-fe oder rebeka di 18-yerike makhsheyfe (Auto-da-fe, or Rebecca the eighteen-year . . .). Adapt. Ben-Tsien Benedikt. Odessa, manuscript, 1882.
Shelley, Percy Bysshe. "Death."
"Der toit." Trans. A. Asen. *Frei Arbeiter Shtime* (Free voice of labor) (October 20, 1923); *Jewish American/The American* (October 29, 1930).

Shelley, Percy Bysshe. "Good Night" (?).
    "A gute nakht" (good night). Trans. Zusman Segalowitch. In *Eyropeische literatur*
    (European literature). Ed. Abraham Reisen. Warsaw: Progres, no. 3 (1910): 123.
Shelley, Percy Bysshe. "The Indian Serenade."
    "An indianishe serenade." Trans. A. Asen. 1933.
Shelley, Percy Bysshe. "Love's Philosophy."
    "Philazafie fun libe." Trans. A. Asen.
    "Die stramen gisen zikh tsuzamen" (the streams flow together). Trans. L. Niedus.
    In *Eyropeische literatur* (European literature). Ed. Abraham Reisen. Warsaw:
    Progres, no. 21 (1910): 14.
Shelley, Percy Bysshe. "Mutability" (?).
    "A dereinerung." Trans. A. Asen. *Chicago* (Yiddish periodical), September 1931.
Shelley, Percy Bysshe. "*The People*" (?). Adaptation.
    Der Volken (the people). Adapt. Sh. Hurvits-Zalkes. In his *Leben un visenshaft*
    2: 10 (1912): cols. 1–3.
Shelley, Percy Bysshe. "Ode to the West Wind."
    "A gezang zum vest-vint." Trans. A. Asen. *Di Feder: Zamlshrift far literatur, kunst
    un kritik* (The Pen: Miscellany of Literature, Art and Criticism).
Shelley, Percy Bysshe. *Prometheus Unbound*.
    Prometeus, der goyel (Prometheus, the savior). Trans. Moshe Blaichman. Chicago:
    L. M. Stein, 1953.
Shelley, Percy Bysshe. "To Night."
    "Die nakht." Trans. A. Asen.
Shelley, Percy Bysshe. "A Vindication of Natural Diet: Being One in a Series of Notes
    to Queen Mab, a Philosophical Poem."
    "Gedanken iber vegetarizm," in *Der vegetaryoner gedank: a zamlung fun vege-
    taryoner abhandlungen-geshrieben* (thoughts on vegetarianism, in vegetarian
    thought: a collection of written discussions on vegetarianism). Trans. Hayim
    Goldblum. Philadelphia: Filadelfier vegetaryoner fereyn, 19–.
Shelley, Percy Bysshe. "The Wanderer" (?).
    "Vanderer." Trans. A. Halevi. *Der oyfkum: khoydesh zhurnal far literatur un kultur-
    inyonim* (Khoydesh-Zhurnal far literatur un kultur-inyonim) (The Rise: Monthly
    journal of literature and cultural matters) 4 (March 1929): 38.
Shelley, Percy Bysshe. "When the Voice Dies Away" (?).
    "Ven die stim fargeyt." Trans. A. Asen.1958.
Wordsworth, William. "The Sailor's Mother."
    "Dem matraz's muter." Trans. A. Asen. *Die Feder* (The pen) (1927): 31.
Wordsworth, William. "The Solitary Reaper."
    "Die einzame shniterin." Trans. A. Asen. *Morgen Journal* (1938): 14.
Wordsworth, William. "We Are Seven."
    "Mir zeinen ziben." Trans. A. Asen. *Der oyfkum: khoydesh zhurnal far literatur un
    kultur-inyonim* (Khoydesh-Zhurnal far literatur un kultur-inyonim) (The Rise:
    Monthly journal of literature and cultural matters) 1 (October 1926): 21.

Notes

1. In *The Jews: Their Religion and Culture*, ed. Louis Finkelstein (New York:
   Schocken, 1949), 228–266.
2. For example, Harshav cites the influence of British Romanticism in general
   on the development of Yiddish poetry, of Byron in particular on Aaron

Glanz Leyeles (1889–1966) (Stanford: Stanford University Press, 1990), 157, 141.

3. For a discussion of British Romanticism and Hebrew poet Hayyim Nahman Bialik, see Lilach Lachman's contribution to this volume, "The Reader as Witness: 'City of the Killings' and Bialik's Romantic Historiography."

4. This approach to and summary of modern Jewish culture derives in large part from Harshsav's *Language in Time of Revolution* (Stanford: Stanford University Press, 1993). A good history of the Hebrew language is Angel Sáenz-Badillos, *A History of the Hebrew Language*, trans. John Elwolde (Cambridge: University Press, 1993). The standard history of Yiddish is Max Weinreich, *History of the Yiddish Language*, trans. Shlomo Noble, 2 vols. (Chicago: University of Chicago Press, 1980).

5. For an historical overview, see David Vital, *A People Apart: The Jews in Europe, 1789–1939* (Oxford: Oxford University Press, 1999).

6. On the contrast between the domestic and foreign attitudes toward the Jews, see Reeva Spector Simon's contribution to this collection, "Commerce, Concern and Christianity: Britain and Middle-Eastern Jewry in the Mid-Nineteenth Century."

7. On the *Haskalah* in England, see David B. Ruderman, *Jewish Enlightenment in an English Key: Anglo-Jewry's Construction of Modern Jewish Thought* (Princeton: Princeton University Press, 2000).

8. The most recent study of the *Haskalah* is Shmuel Feiner, *Haskalah and History: The Emergence of a Modern Jewish Historical Consciousness*, trans. Chaya Naor and Sondra Silverston (Oxford: Littman Library of Jewish Civilization, 2002). On Coleridge's response to Mendelssohn, see Frederick Burwick's "Mendelssohn and Coleridge on Words, Thoughts, and Things," in this volume.

9. The standard history of Reform Judaism is Michael A. Meyer, *Response to Modernity: A History of the Reform Movement in Judaism* (New York and Oxford: Oxford University Press, 1988).

10. David Aberbach notes that "Crisis in the Tsarist Empire led to heightened Jewish national identity" (*Revolutionary Hebrew, Empire and Crisis: Four Peaks in Hebrew Literature and Jewish Survival* [New York: New York University Press, 1998], 117). The most current information about the history of the Jews in the Middle East can be found in Reeva Spector Simon, Michael Menachem Laskier, and Sara Reguer, eds., *The Jews of the Middle East and North Africa in Modern Times* (New York: Columbia University Press, 2003). See especially, Ruth Kark and Joseph B. Glass, "Eretz Israel/Palestine, 1800–1948" (335–346).

11. On the history of Jews in America, see Howard M. Sachar, *A History of the Jews in America* (New York: Knopf, 1992).

12. Sol Liptzin, *A History of Yiddish Literature* (Middle Village, NY: Jonathan David, 1972), 426.

13. This bibliography could not have been compiled without a great deal of assistance. I was able to receive some help from earlier lists: Jacob I. Dienstag's "English–Jewish Literature in Hebrew Translation" ("targumim ivri'im mi'saphrut anglit-yehudit"), *Jewish Book Annual* 8 (1949–1950): 35–47, Hebrew section; Mayer Horowitz, "Bibliography of Yiddish Translations of English Literature," *Jewish Book Annual* 11 (1952–1953): 136–153; and Leonard Prager, "Charles Dickens in Yiddish (A Survey)," *Jewish Language*

Review 4 (1984): 158–178. Also of use is Robert Singerman's *Jewish Translation History: A Bibliography of Bibliographies and Studies*, intro. Gideon Toury, Benjamins Translation Library, vol. 44 (Amsterdam and Philadelphia: John Benjamins Publishing Company, 2002). Also, I would like to thank the staffs at the following libraries, especially their Judaica sections: Brandeis University; Harvard University; Hebrew University National Library; the Hebrew Union College; the Jewish Theological Seminary of America; the Library of Congress; the New York Public Library; the University of Pennsylvania; Yale University; and the YIVO Institute for Jewish Research. Finally, a number of individuals have contributed to this project: Michael S. Galchinsky, Nancy Moore Goslee, Robert J. Griffin, Sara Guyer, Fred Kaplan, Lilach Lackman, Kerry McKeever, Donald H. Reiman, Charles E. Robinson, Linda Stein, and Michael Weingrad.

14. Abraham Asen (1886–1958), a prolific Yiddish translator of British and American poetry, left his papers to the YIVO Institute for Jewish Research, among which are copies of undocumented poems that were published in the first half of the twentieth century. Rather than omit them, I've included citations with whatever bibliographical information there is available, though it is often incomplete.

CHAPTER 11

THE READER AS WITNESS: "CITY OF THE KILLINGS" AND BIALIK'S ROMANTIC HISTORIOGRAPHY

Lilach Lachman

The Kishinev Pogrom and the Question of Bialik's Response[1]

To the graveyard, beggars! Dig for the bones of your fathers
and of your sainted brothers and fill them with your bundles
and hoist them on your shoulders and take to the road, fated
to merchandize them at all the trade fairs;
and you will seek a stand at the crossroads where all can see,
and lay them out in sunshine on the backs of your filthy rags
and with a parched voice sing a beggar's song over their bodies
and call for the mercies of nations and pray for the kindness of goyim . . .[2]

The hundred years that have passed since the Kishinev pogrom mark an epoch in the study of "City of the Killings" by Hayyim Nahman Bialik (1873–1934), and of Hebrew Romanticism in general. Now is perhaps a good moment to approach a complex of historical and poetic problems through the discussion of a single work. The questions raised by this long poem are once again resonant, although their importance may not yet have been fully absorbed.[3] Of special interest is how the poem makes a correlation between Jewish history and the reader's role in shaping it. While centering his "City of the Killings" on an anatomy of the life and death of the nation, Bialik not only urges a revival of Jewish identity, but also requires the reader's active engagement in its construction. In the first part of my essay, I examine how Bialik's encounter with Kishinev affected his ideological and historiographic principles, which, in turn, shaped the poetics of "City of the Killings." In the second part, I propose that the question of Jewish history might be indispensable to the belatedness of Hebrew Romanticism. I account for Bialik's innovation of the Hebrew long poem by reference to the interplay between his historiographic and aesthetic principles. As much as "City of the Killings" enhanced a new paradigm of action and identity, the tensions between history and aesthetics required Bialik to sever Hebrew literature from the romantic models that his own poetry had incorporated, and to reshape the existing Hebrew tradition, pushing it forward to Modernism.

During Passover 1903, a pogrom in the Bessarabian city of Kishinev left forty-nine Jews murdered, 600 wounded, and 1500 houses and shops plundered or destroyed. After the event, the thirty-year-old poet, together with two other persons, was commissioned by the Jewish community to investigate and record the horror in detail. Bialik fulfilled his task but did not submit his report.[4] Instead of distributing his notebooks in which he had transcribed the testimonies of survivors and observers, eight months after the slaughter he published "City of the Killings," written in near-biblical Hebrew. The 272-line poem, composed chiefly of loosely rhymed couplets, invokes a journey through a city in the aftermath of a pogrom and draws its materials from the poet's investigation. Bialik's response to this pogrom made a shattering impression upon the literate, socially minded public. Bialik's treatment of the event stands in contrast to the calls for assistance heard in popular Yiddish poetry (such as in the work of Simon Frug), or the typical Russian–Jewish literary depictions of pogroms that were modeled upon earlier martyrologies (1096 and 1648), or the stylized lamentations found in Jewish American literature.[5] His poetic account also differs from the emphasis on the attackers' cruelty found in the contemporary Hebrew journal *Ha-zeman*.[6] Even more notable is the difference between the hostility displayed toward the victims in "City of the Killings" and Bialik's own identification with them in "*Al ha-shehita*" ("On the Slaughter"), a short lyric that he wrote in the immediate aftermath of the atrocity. No less striking is the gap between the poem's record and the information offered by Bialik's own official testimony. "City of the Killings" does not mention incidents of self-defense, nor does it record the support given to the killers by the army and police, nor does it distinguish what the authorities did or failed to do (facts that are documented in the report he wrote). Bialik flinches from none of the horrific details of the pogrom: skulls crushed on walls, bellies ripped apart and stuffed with feathers, bones smashed with crowbars. Yet, the attackers' brutality does not occupy the center of his address. Rather than memorializing the victims or calling for them to be avenged, as he had been expected to do, the poet chose to disparage their behavior and values. He views them as "calves slaughtered" (l. 186). Concerned with the conduct of the Jewish survivors themselves—not with that of the Moldavians or Russians—he scornfully exposes the victims' self-humiliation in the face of persecution: "They fled the flight of mice and hid like tics / And died like dogs there where they were found" (ll. 120–121).

How can we account for Bialik's decision to place the slaughter within such a grotesque and hopeless picture of Jewish existence?[7] Was this his idiosyncratic way of preaching Zionism? In what sense and in what way can his refusal to memorialize, to mourn or to accuse be seen as a purifying act that laid the groundwork for the construction of a positive identity?

The prevailing critical opinion is that the poem offered a new paradigm for responding to the catastrophe.[8] By means of its shocking and even scandalous effect, "City of the Killings" confronted contemporary Jews with a horrible mirror of their existence, thus demanding their radical self-evaluation. In order to persuade his readers of the need to detach themselves from the repressive and restrictive world of tradition, the poet takes us on a tour of the locality where the horror took place, guiding us through the wreckage scattered in the yard outside a home, through the cellar where Jewish girls were raped, across to the graveyards where the beggars trade the bones of their kin, to the desert into which the poet will flee. Leading its addressee from one site to another, the poem's spatiotemporal logic compels the reader to follow this tortuous anti-quest; it is a tour through which the reader confronts the Jews' expropriation from everything they have regarded as sacred: their "books and scrolls," their "divine labour," their grace, their lives, even their God who has "gone down in the world" and is likened now to a bankrupt householder with a broken arm. Bialik's readers were thus prompted to disassociate themselves from a whole cultural tradition around which the heart of their Jewish identity was coiled.

This ideological motive is equally relevant to the poem's key command; "Rise and go to the town of the killings" counterpoints a resolution based on religious sacrifice. Alluding both to Abraham, who offered his son on the altar, and to Isaac, who bared his throat to the knife (Gen. 22:2), Bialik parodies the value accorded to *Kidush Hashem* (literally, "sanctification of the Holy Name," meaning to die in and for God's name), which was misapplied by his contemporaries as necessitating passivity and lack of defiance.[9] Rather than praising the Jews' resistance to forced conversion, the poem takes up their quietism and exposes the degrading and self-humiliating aspects of martyrdom. We recall that in "On the Slaughter," Bialik's speaker, defying both the Hangman and God, posits himself as the victim:

> Hangman! Here's a neck—come kill . . . (2:1)
> And if there is justice—let's see it now! (3:1)

But in contrast to the poem he wrote before his visit to Kishinev, "City of the Killings" confronts us not with a poet who challenges God, but with a God who declares his own self-bankruptcy (6:13–16).[10] God's very address to his "children" demonstrates that he can no longer serve as a reference for pattern or meaning. His words are used by Bialik to undercut, not so much the authority of divinity, as the people's self-enfeebling conception of God. *Kidush Hashem* is thus emptied of its traditional values:

> Your sacrifices are sacrificed for nothing—and neither you nor I know
> Why you died,

Nor who nor what for,
And there's no point to your deaths as there was no point to your lives.
(6:16–19)

Shedding an ambiguous light on the poem's prophetic command, these lines allude to the "City of the Killings" as the place in which the meaning of both life and death are undermined. God's words are, accordingly, viewed as an ironic counterpoint to the opening imperative: "Rise and go." They reverse, in fact, the prophetic narrative modeled on the tale of Jonah: "Rise and go to Nineveh, that great city, and cry against it" (Jon. 1:2) becomes "Rise and go to the town of the killings and you'll come to the yards." Unlike the forefather Abraham (Gen. 12:1), the prophet Ezekiel (Ezek. 37:1–15) or the biblical Jonah, Bialik's prophet is not called upon to initiate a historical covenant, or to foretell future redemption, or to carry a message of doom to a great city, but to witness a disaster that has already occurred.[11] Nevertheless, "Rise and go" seems designed not merely to provoke outrage against atrocity but to impel a constructive act of some kind. The execution of this summons, however, requires a shattering of our self-presence and a complete reversal of our orientation. In this regard, the poem has a claim to a revolutionary imperative. In its historical context, "Rise and go to the town of the killings" may accordingly be read as a proposition that we contemplate "not here," "not like now," "not as you [= we] are."[12] Perhaps only by such an extreme denial of traditional existence could Bialik drive his readers to self-defense, to national action, and to a recognition of the crucial need for a change of self-identity.

However, this ideological explanation does not sufficiently account for the radical nature or for the specificity of Bialik's response to the pogrom. Another direction that I wish to pursue is the issue of a formative change in Bialik's understanding of history. Following the instructions of the historian Simon Dubnov, Bialik did indeed provide not only written records, but also a visual documentation of the wreckage: a photograph of a dead child, openmouthed against the camera; a picture of corpses wrapped in *talithes* (prayer shawls); the image of ripped Torah scrolls. But "City of the Killings," together with the poet's written testimonies and letters, in fact reveals the crisis he was undergoing regarding Enlightened ideas of history and the possibility of rendering an "objective" truth.[13] We may well assume, therefore, that Bialik's self-awareness of his role as a witness prevented him from fulfilling Dubnov's requirement to present "a complete historical picture of the entire event from its beginning up to the day in which we stand."[14] The poet who saw the bodies, witnessed the victims' distress and listened to their testimonies became an insider, a participant who could not render the event from the outside. The main challenge Bialik confronted was how to be faithful to his inner positioning as a witness—one who is committed to the constricted reality of what he perceives—and at the same time to provide his readers with the facts from which they themselves could construct a historical narrative.

Between History and Narrative Poetry

A key question for our understanding of the poet's reshaping of his materials is how this challenge affects the contract between Bialik and his audience. Most crucially, it raises the issue: To what is the poet committed? And what is the reader supposed to assume when summoned to follow the prophetic command, "Rise and go to the town of the killings"? Are we embarking on a journey that claims an historical truth, or are we mere readers of a fictional poem disguised as prophecy? Meir Sternberg views the distinction between fictional and historical narrative as conventional, not textual. In his view, the most significant difference between the two modes is that historical writing makes truth claims, whereas fictional writing is independent of such claims.[15] In "City of the Killings," this conventional boundary becomes so apparent precisely because Bialik has so effectively violated it. This produces the dual generic features in his work. The historiographic aspect surfaces in the poem's materials, in its circumstances of publication, in its dating. At another level, the text even underlines the operation of this principle through metahistorical allusions to biblical prophecy, to *Lamentations*, to the command "Rise and go," which is traditionally interpreted as a directive to remember the historic covenant between God and Israel. As to the aesthetic principle, we encounter it in the poem's textual traits (title, poetic lines, stanzaic organization, allusive system), all of which signal its status as poetry. Interestingly, however, the dynamics of the communicative transaction depend on the traffic between these polar modes. On the one hand, the command that turns the addressee into a witness ("with your eyes and your own hand feel") clearly appoints factuality as the sole authority. On the other hand, the speaker calls upon the addressee to personally bear witness to a reality to which he or she has no direct access. Due to the poem's biblical modes of address ("Rise and go," "son of man"), we are led to believe that the poem's speaker is God, who both authorizes and enforces the addressee's quest. The pattern of the telling, its richness of detail and its credibility, the metonymic sequence that constitutes its spatiotemporal progress, the additive syntax that enumerates the ruins, and the consequent assault on the sensibility of the viewer—all these blur the conventional generic difference.

Bialik's decision to re-present the Kishinev event in a manner that counters the ideological and generic expectations of his contemporaries is indispensable to this overall effect. Joseph Klausner, perhaps the most important authority on Hebrew literature at the time, noted: "The Devil knows what one is to make of it: it is not really a poem, it is not a lyric, it is more of a prophecy by Jeremiah or by Ezekiel. You have attained the uppermost peak of Hebrew poetry and perhaps of poetry in general."[16] "City of the Killings" resembles an historical narrative insofar as it makes claims to referentiality and verifiability, claims that locate it in the traditional realm of history or prophecy, rather than of poetry. Its narration revives the wrecked community with such power that it radically displaces and questions not only any common notion we might have entertained about the pogrom, but our very vision of reality as such, our sense of what Enlightenment, culture, and our life within it are about.

But the poem is not a historical document on the pogrom, nor does it share prophecy's sacred contract between God and man. By exposing God's address as nothing but a rhetorical principle and a compositional axis, the poem draws attention to its own fictionality. In this way, Bialik shifts our attention from history to its narration, from the biblical contract between God and man to the question of the romantic poet's contract with the reader, the sources of the poet's authority, the nature of his responsibility to his audience, his shaping of history.

Rather like modern historiography, which does not presume to provide a direct apprehension of the "thing itself," this poem offers a mediated perspective on reality.[17] For a miniature illustration of this duality, consider the poem's title. "*Be'ir Haharega*" (literally "In the City of the Killings") can be read as a distancing abstraction: specific geographical and historical references are effaced, the victims are anonymous. Rather than the literality of a historical event, it signals a figuration—a metonymic substitute that designates not the place's name but its defining attribute: "City of *the* Killings."[18] Concurrently, however, the preposition "in" (omitted in Hadar's English translation) underscores the perspective from which the reality is featured ("*In* the City of the Killings") rather than alluding to what exactly happened there. The event itself is beyond language's ken (as is reflected in the projective *Shekhinah* who "wants to roar and keeps quiet / and silently festers in mourning and secretly stifles" [4:26–27]). Our only access to the event is via the witnessing perspective, which conveys the devastation by depicting the aftermath of oblivion:

> and you will not stand by the carnage and pass by there on your path—and the rye blooms before you and pours perfume in your nose, and half the buds will be feathers, and their smell the smell of blood; and in your spite and against your heart you'll bring their strange incense like the tender spring to your bosom—and it will not be loathsome to it; and with a multitude of golden arrows the sun will pierce your liver and seven rays from every grain of glass will dance in your torture. (1:15–21)

The more concrete the obliteration of nature becomes, the more the challenge that confronts the witness intensifies. The poem thus becomes an exploration of the shifting points of view from which the wreckage can be inspected: from the inaccessible surface of "the fence / and . . . the trees . . . the stone . . . and plaster of the walls" in full daylight (1:2–3, 20), through "the attics of the roofs," where the poet will climb and "stand in darkness" and confront the "Ghosts of the 'martyred'" (1:33–34, 38), down to "the dark cellars," "places where they hid" and "from under the mounds of wheels, among the cracks and holes" (2:1, 3:1, 4:14). Although at the beginning, our focus is directed toward what can be viewed from each of these angles, it is the deepening crisis of the witness that increasingly occupies our attention. The repeated confrontation with the traces of the horror as well as with their effacement in each of the poem's units (organized according to a series of physical sites) directs us to perceive the simultaneity in a certain order, which has the effect of temporalizing the viewer's perception of depicted space. In the course of the poem, the witness's responsibility increases as he is led from the unrecognizable dehumanized ruins into spaces that encapsulate the heart of Jewish life: the yards, the synagogue, the cemetery. In these places, which are part of Jewish cyclical time, crisis moments now occur. Most forceful is Bialik's weaving of the socio-public aspect of Jewish life with its clandestine and even repressed side: the secrets of the attic, the stable, and the cellar. Here time is experienced as instantaneous; it is as if its duration falls outside of the normal course of lived religious routine: "Before slaughter, during slaughter and after slaughter!" The interweaving of Jewish holy rituals (such as those of purification and butchery) with the attackers' loathsome acts of rape is relayed through the eyes of the cowardly bystanders (2:81–82). As he moves through this series of physical sites, the witness audits the silent internal witnesses to the past: "the tender spring" that has obliterated the slaughter, and "the spiders" who "tell all the facts"; "Ghosts of the martyred" who witnessed the pogrom as victims; "husbands, fiancés, brothers, peeping out of holes" who witnessed the carnage as bystanders, the *Shekhinah* who "wants to roar and keeps quiet," and finally God himself who "has gone down in the world" and is presented both as a perpetrator and as a victim. But at the center of this tour is the narrator's mediation of the destructive images of the present. Rather than a view of the past, the poem offers a disorienting vision of the *now*, a forceful insight into the complex relationship between history and poetic witnessing.

"Rise and Go": Witnessing as Speech-act

While "City of the Killings" is made up of prose and poetry, it is dominated by voices that cast the reader into a variety of dramatic situations. Bialik lets the martyrs, the spiders, and the bystanders silently speak as his prophet-poet encounters a wounded God and the exhausted and depleted *Shekhinah*. In consequence, language is used not primarily to tell a story or express feelings, as it might traditionally be deployed in narrative prose or lyric poetry, but to command, protest, accuse, lament, scorn, pretend, execute, choose, call, and resist.

According to speech-act theory, such performances are enabled by accepted conventions that include the uttering of certain words by certain persons in certain circumstances.[19] In this poem, however, the poet's communication with his readers is grounded in the performative act of a divine pronouncement. "*Kum lech lecha*" ("Rise and go") is a visionary cry that differentiates the addressee from his community. In addressing his readers by defining them in terms of their past while calling upon them to relinquish the bonds that fetter them to that history, Bialik also assumes a divinely bestowed right to make such a pronouncement. Moreover, by incorporating this definition and command within the world of the poem, the poet invokes the biblical rules of communication whereby remembrance of the past bears on the present and determines the future.

Nevertheless, Bialik's imperative invites a transgression; few of the poet's readers would accord him the right to call upon them to "Rise and go to the town of the killings." Judging from his poetic strategy, no institution (such as a court of justice, the Jewish historical committee, the religious community) would grant him the right to dictate to his addressee the journey he calls upon us to make; such authority is the privilege of the martyrs, the *Shekhinah*, or God Himself, figures who are identified with the sacred laws of the Jewish community. Yet there are many verbal echoes in "City of the Killings," including the key command "Rise and go," that reflect the breakdown of institutionally sanctioned language. Bialik negotiates between religious and sociopolitical speech on the one hand, and the individual language of vision on the other, in order to establish the effectiveness of his witnessing.

Historical memory is individualized in a single addressee, and witnessing is understood according to the potential capacity of each and every hearer. Paradoxically, therefore, the very remembrance of the past is invoked to enforce a recognition of change: only by turning one's back on one's own time and looking to the past—which includes the pogroms of 1881 as well as the martyrologies of 1096 and 1648, but also biblical history, legends, prayers, and chronicles—can the reader achieve this visionary perspective. The prophet who is summoned by God, as well as the reader who is addressed by the poet, is individually invited to participate in the reconstruction of a wrecked world, in the event that caused the wreckage and in the history that may account for it. The imperative mode that underlies the poem's address conjures up a speaker who directs the action and a listener who carries out the command:

> Rise and go to the town of the killings and you'll come to the yards and with your eyes and your own hand grope the fence and on the trees and on the stones and plaster of walls the congealed blood and hardened brains of the dead (1:1–4)

Instead of referring to a documentary truth, the speaker calls upon the poet as well as the reader to personally bear witness by firsthand seeing and touching. Hence the importance, but also the danger, of the performance of sensual testimony, reliant upon sight, touch, and smell. As opposed to the addressee who is required to take responsibility for this multisensuous witnessing, the victims and bystanders are defined throughout the poem by what and how they fail to see.[20] Nature ("tender spring" and "rain") is oblivious to the slaughter ("For the Lord called the Spring and the slaughterer together: / the sun rose, rye bloomed, and the slaughterer slaughtered" [1:22–23]); it is unaffected by the carnage ("tomorrow a rain will come down, and sweep it to one of the wasteland / streams" [1:28–29]). The "Ghosts of the 'martyred'" see ("the axe found them and to this place they come / to stamp here the look of their eyes in the last moment" [1:40–41]), but fail to understand the purpose and the significance of what they see ("all the sorrow of their pointless death and all the curse of their lives / . . . silently raise their eyes to protest their disgrace and ask: why?" [1:42, 45]). The bystanders who "peeping out of holes" "lay in their shame and saw . . . / and they didn't pluck out their eyes or go out of their heads" (2:12, 16, 17) are exposed by Bialik as blind to their own disgrace, profanation, and hypocrisy, unaware of their responsibility as witnesses ("their husbands emerged from their holes and ran to the house of God / . . . And the priests among them went and asked their rabbis: 'Rabbi! / My wife, / what is she? Allowed or not allowed?'" [2:22, 24–25]). The *Shekhinah*, despite being aware of her responsibility toward the "martyred," is nevertheless figured as a "single black Presence," a metonymic extension of mourning; she is so overwhelmed by "suffering and great torment," "weary with sorrow and exhausted," that she is literally blinded by her empathy. And God himself, a witness to His own bankruptcy, ironically does not understand the purport of what He sees and, in fact, overlooks His responsibility toward His children. This witnessing crisis explodes the prophetic mode itself when, at the end of his journey, the poet's wrath finally bursts out, only to be drowned by the storm that obliterates any possibility of communication.

As opposed to the failures of all his internal witnesses, including the poet himself, Bialik commands his addressee to physically see, interiorize, record, and not to be blinded by empathy ("and I will stop your eyes so that you will not shed a tear" [6:7]). In this manner the poem shifts the responsibility of history from God and his prophet-poet to each reader. Instead of describing the precise historical facts, the command that organizes the poem requires of the viewer factual accuracy and commits him or her to sensuous engagement. Rather than requiring of his reader an ideological response, be it objection or consent, Bialik demands active witnessing. The performative utterance— "Rise and go . . . and you'll come . . . feel . . . and pass by . . . and your feet will sink . . . and you will not stand by the carnage" (1:1–15)—creates a world that circumvents the existing one, allowing the poet some degree of imaginative independence from the particular historical circumstances about which he is writing. At the same time, however, the addressee's first-hand witnessing moves the viewer closer to the horror, requiring us not to recall an event, but to conjure up a picture.

This aesthetic choice shifts our focus from the scene's horror to our perceptions of it, both emotive and cognitive. The images that arrest the viewer's attention are eye-opening, jarring, and clamorous. Bialik uses them as a way of apprehending but also memorizing the abominable reality. The reader is compelled to contemplate not the event itself, but rather its traces and effects: the blood-splattered walls, the shattered ovens, the filthy pillow-case, and blushing pillow.[21] On the one hand, inanimate objects ("black stone and shears of brick all burned" [1:8]) are compared to animate ones

("and they'll look like the open mouths of black and mortal wounds" [1:9]),
negatively exposing the absence of the human, but also giving the witness's
perspective a diagnostic, almost clinical angle. On the other hand, when the
recorded images show corpses so mangled that they could be those of a dead
dog, a pig, or the flesh of donkey, one understands that the scale of the
carnage has destroyed that which identifies people as individuals, or even
as human beings. In this manner, too, the collective myth of sacrifice is
undercut and estranged by the concrete, corporeal image.

While each image is an invitation not only to look but to bodily engage
in the horror, the terse references to the addressee's silent bodily gestures
(climbing, standing, gnashing his teeth, going down, shutting the gate,
gripping, baring his chest, etc.) insist on the difficulty of doing just that.
A voice, presumably God's or the poet's, badgers the viewer: can you bear
to look at this any longer? And the addressee is compelled to pursue the
journey, to enter "the out house, the pigpen and the other places smeared
with shit" (3:2), cross into "the stable of the killing" (4:2) across to the
"graveyard" (6:1) digging up further manifestations of Jewish shame, until
he or she has not only utterly appropriated them, but his own soul is
bankrupt and estranged.

In this regard, "City of the Killings" seems to undermine the phenomenal
manifestation traditionally demanded by the romantic *Bildung*. Whereas in
British Romanticism the itinerary of *Bildung* consists of the aesthetic unveil-
ing of Man and of making the world's one own, the process of auto-
production that is materialized here as a series of *Bilden* (which can mean
both image and model) obliterate the process of acculturation commonly
manifested in a historically specific site.[22] As opposed to Wordsworth's journey in *The Prelude*, which has been described by Hartman and others as a
process of cultivating both the imagination and nature, in "City of the
Killings" Bialik deploys nature to uncover the destruction of the very idea of
human cultivation. The darkest aspects of the represented scene are not
those that allude to the specific historical event, as one might expect both
from Bialik's testimonial task and from his speaker's documentary gesture.
Instead, the horror is primarily revealed in the ways by which the scene is
diagnosed (recall the poem's opening with its powerful clinical perspective)
as a site that displays the utter ruin of man's humanity and sovereignty, a ruin
that undercuts the Enlightened dream of *Bildung* both in culture and in
nature. In parallel to Wordsworth who, in *The Prelude*, historicizes his past
in order to engage the poetic imagination anew, Bialik historicizes his
people's past in order to engage his audience in a new beginning. If
Wordsworth's summons of a new Heaven is burdened by his literary debt to
Milton, Bialik's call paradoxically confronts his reader with the contaminated
burden of Jewish history. The reader who is supposedly called to *Bildung*,
("Rise and go") is in fact disabled by his encounter with the nation's corpses,
burnt books, and unconscious malady.

By choosing this mode with which to engage his reader, Bialik achieves a
double effect: First, he resists the discourse that might be associated with legal

and social institutions (such as those found in history books, courts of justice, political committees, all of which could have been possible contexts for his report) and, firmly in the tradition of romantic poetry, displaces the authority from institutions to individual visionary consciousness; second, he stakes his utterance on a claim to divine inspiration. This claim—which only has meaning insofar as he persuades his audience to obey the command "Rise and go"—is modified through the reading process; during the journey in which the poet-witness encounters the voices of other witnesses and bystanders, he becomes uncertain whether he is really perceiving what he believes himself to be perceiving or if he is in effect speaking in his own voice. Perhaps that is why the addressee is required to maintain his silent distance and stifled outrage.

Further, the reader gradually discovers that forms of address derived from law, economics, and politics accumulate to undercut the theological and prophetic mode set up by the poem. The victims themselves are presented as ruins of men who exploit their catastrophes for commerce, beg for rewards from their kin and pray for the mercy of *goyim*. Moreover, the speech act that begins by echoing the sacred command "Arise and go" turns into an address to a nation of beggars who dig up the bones of their fathers and offer them for sale. Most extreme is the reversal of the hierarchical roles of God and the prophet; here the poem's speaker is a God who undermines His own authority, and His addressee is the poet-prophet who is doomed to witness and keep silent. The bankruptcy of God and the shrewd realization of the mirroring effect of His misery—"Beggars of the world, your God is as poor as you / Poor he is in your living and so much more so in your deaths" (4:13–14)—not only empty the poem's central speech act of its traditional content, but also parody its romantic assumptions.

Jewish History, Hebrew Romanticism, and *Bildung*

Even though the poem presents a history of destruction that culminates in an anti-*Bildung*, on another level a historical recuperation is proposed. As part of Bialik's formative role in Hebrew revival, "City of the Killings" can be taken as a central experiment in the recovery of Hebrew poetry as a dynamic and interactive system that demands, receives, and modifies the full development of its historical strata. Only by adapting European romantic models to new ends and by the innovation of earlier Hebrew models could the poem fulfil its new historical role.[23]

In order to reassess the cultural significance of Bialik's understanding of his task, this attempt at recuperation should be viewed in light of the long dependency of Jewish history and literature on European culture. To emphasize this perspective, consider the following admission by Yudke, a kibbutz member in Hayim Hazaz's (1898–1973) famous short story, "The Sermon": "Because we didn't make our own history, the *goyim* made it for us."[24] In Yudke's explanation of his opposition to that *goyish*/gentile version of Jewish history, he questions its very legitimacy.

Certainly, the narrative leading to Jewish self-formation was, as it is radically represented in Bialik's "City of the Killings," very much circumscribed by waves of pogroms and persecutions. Similarly, Jews had been the cultural target of Western and Central Europe's civilizing mission for centuries. Because Jews were depicted as the assimilated *Others* of European culture, the traditional historiography of modern Hebrew literature is closely interwoven with European history. Accordingly, Hebrew Enlightenment (*Haskalah*), which coexists with European Romanticism but extends a full century after it, is conventionally held to have begun with the Austrian Emperor Joseph II's 1782 edict, which made elementary education in German compulsory for Jewish children, thus assimilating them into the dominant Austrian culture. Moreover, the Renaissance period of Hebrew literature (*Sifrut Hatehiya*), which began in Odessa at the turn of the twentieth century with the writings of Bialik himself, as well as with the work of the Hebrew essayist and philosopher Ahad Ha'Am and of the historian Simon Dubnov, and which dominated Hebrew literature until about 1920, is usually epitomized by the writing known as "Storms in the Negev" that emerged after the 1883 pogroms in Russia—pogroms that abruptly dashed the Enlightened hopes of Eastern European Jewish intellectuals for Jewish existence in the Diaspora. The telling shift from *Sifrut Hahaskalah* (Enlightenment literature) to *Sifrut Hatehiya* (Modern Hebrew literature) that is thus located around the end of the 1880s and the beginning of the 1890s, is accordingly considered to have been a direct outcome of the historical events of the 1880s.[25]

In continuity with this European narrative, standard historical accounts of modern Hebrew literature argue that the transition from the Enlightenment to Revival brought to Hebrew literature, after a delay of about a hundred years, the romantic sensibility toward nature, the imagination and myth.[26] The appearance of romantic Hebrew poetry almost a century after the heyday of European Romanticism has been represented by contemporary Israeli critics as almost anachronistic: "Hebrew Romanticism appeared in Hebrew literature a long time after it had lost favor in Europe, where it had been replaced by Neo-Romanticism, Symbolism and other new trends."[27] In the 1970s and 1980s, Israeli critics who deployed historical and theoretical models from their study of British Romanticism saw Bialik as the moving force behind the shift in Hebrew poetry from the Enlightenment to Romanticism.[28] As Hamutal Bar-Yosef points out, however, this merely entrenched the image of Bialik as the author responsible for introducing into Hebrew literature a mode that was already considered outdated in European literature. He was viewed as a poet who belonged to the nineteenth century.[29]

But this external narrative of Jewish history and Hebrew Romanticism is complicated and significantly modified by the emergence of modern Jewish historiography. While the European perspective on the Jews established a Christo-centricism in which the Jews were defined as the quintessential *Other*, Jewish historians such as Heinrich Graetz (1817–1891) and Dubnov, from their post-Romantic vantage point, delineated the space in which the Jews could construct their own narrative. In *Zachor*, Yerushalmi offers a new model that replaces the narrative of the decaying organism of Judaism with an internalized meta-historical approach. This model requires an engaged reader who will participate in the subjective reconstruction of his or her own history.[30] Akin to Yerushalmi, who highlights the internalization that pertains to the shaping of modern historiography, Benjamin Harshav, in *Language in Time of Revolution*, emphasizes the internalized process regarding the actual forming of modern Jewish history; according to Harshav, although European history did indeed determine the conditions of Jewish survival, Jewish modern culture resulted from *internal responses* to world history from within Jewish society itself. In this sense, it is the Jews who made their own history.[31] Indicative of this duality, I think, is Bialik's complex response to the pogrom. First, as the head of a committee that arrived in Kishinev days after the pogrom to investigate and document, in detail, the horror of the carnage, he does not set out to address the gentiles and indict the murderers. Instead, he chooses to transform testimonies into Hebrew poetry and thereby to make an internal address to Jewish society. Second, by appealing to the future via models of the past, he reshapes a European model and endows it with new functions: The long poem thus changes from a narrative at whose center is a hero, to a narrative of the individual; from the national narrative authorized by the poet-prophet to a history reconstructed by the individualized "you"—that is, the poet as well as the reader.

This attempt at recuperation occurred at a crucial juncture of Jewish history, specifically at a time when the entire enterprise of European Jewry, in the face of anti-Semitism and assimilation, and already in the process of being destroyed, was viewed by Zionism as no longer viable. Enlightenment ideology was, accordingly, being replaced by nationalistic trends that were to lead to the Hebrew literary revival. Moreover, the 1881 pogroms, which were a rehearsal for those of 1903–1906, accelerated the processes that prompted the late nineteenth-century migration of Jews from villages and towns to cities, and strengthened the Jews' national awareness and cultural awakening. Historically, this awakening—which coincided with the Hebrew revival and its extensive literary output—enabled the belated transition from Hebrew Neoclassicism to Romanticism a full century after it had occurred elsewhere. On the one hand, the Jewish national renaissance, which has been commonly defined as a linear progression from Jewish Enlightenment to Revival, echoes (despite ideological and historical differences) the tenets of European Romanticism.[32] On the other hand, in the value and behavioral shift that it entails, it also parallels in time and nature the revolution that occurred in Modernist art and literature.

Accordingly, typical of this internal narrative of Jewish history is its partial and highly precarious association with a cluster of conflicting trends. Note, for example, how the heavy burden laid on the individual (an offspring of both Enlightenment and romantic thought) as a mediator of the shifting values, the revived language and the new history (of culture, of literature and of the self in his or her relation to a new territory) highlights the ambivalent relationship of modern Jewish secular identity to both Enlightenment and Romanticism. The promises of civil rights and entry into universal engagements, as part of the legacies of these traditions, indeed enabled the liberation of the Jews from the constraints of an orthodox identity and encouraged the process of Jewish national normalization; at the same time, as an Enlightenment legacy, the terms of these promises, which focused on the state rather than on the individual, in fact constrained the evolution of the individualized Jew and modern subject. No wonder, therefore, that within the Hebrew Revival, Romanticism acquired different and often opposing values.[33] In the essays of Ahad Ha'Am, and in some of Bialik's narrative poems (*Mete Midbar* [The Dead of the Wilderness] 1902; *Ha-Matmid* [The Talmud Scholar], 1896–1897), romantic models were deployed to enhance the identification of the writer with his nation. In other literature, such as the fictional prose of Berdichevsky, and in many of Bialik's own lyrics, romantic models were borrowed to explore and realize the autonomy of individual expression, which often opposes national identity and stands in continuity with the subject's world of dream, imagination and perception.[34]

The propheticism of Bialik benefited from both trends. On the one hand, it fitted well with the distinctive characteristics of Romanticism, such as positing the self as the center of experience and knowledge, having faith in nature as a healing force, turning to myth as an expression of the individual and national psyche, and elevating the status of the imagination to a supreme spiritual level. On the other hand, whereas the romantic writer was expected to identify with his nation, Bialik's identity was founded on a set of conflicts between the *I* and the collective. The need to establish this identity explains the gap between the expected historical task that Bialik encountered in Kishinev and the *poema* (long poem) he ended up writing. My reading of the poem underscores the dramatization of these conflicts both in the poem's generic interplay and in its communicative situation. In one sense, "City of the Killings" can be read as a rewriting of the myth of the romantic poet's self-isolation, as we know it from Wordsworth or Byron; but the shift of focus from the poet to the reader, or in M. H. Abrams' terms, from the expressive to the pragmatic function, significantly modifies those models that Bialik had interiorized primarily through the mediation of Russian and German literature.[35] The prophet's vocation, for Bialik, is to replace expressive, impulse-driven speech acts with a code of witnessing, where witnessing is the epitome of a legitimated Hebrew linguistic practice. When the witness detects the Jews' responsibility for their own history, we discover that most of their offenses consisted of speech acts: They prayed for their safety instead of caring for their kin; they uttered blessings instead of protests; they declared their wives' purity; they professed their betrayal of their fathers; and they called for the mercy of nations.

By offering allusions to daily social practices (such as prayer, purification, and commerce) together with his subversive and perceptual biblical idiom, as a challenge to the sanctioned language of law and homiletic interpretation, Bialik historicizes Hebrew. The genre, too, is historicized as the poem partly recalls the conventions of the romantic *Bildung* and of the traditional high lyrical mode (that of the ode and formal elegy), but above all, it constitutes a modern variation on the brief epic or the romantic long poem.[36] Furthermore, the poem presents a crucially different approach to that of the official historiography of the nineteenth and early twentieth century, such as that proposed by Graetz or Dubnov, who conceived of history as a grand, continuous narrative: Bialik enforces a more radical concept of history, constructing his innovative *poema* as a present-tense citation of the past: "Rise and go."[37]

As we have seen, this performative utterance, original and responsive at once, summons to mental action and yet invokes the reader's engagement in his or her history. The poem's imperative mode focuses attention on the positions from which the speaker addresses his reader, on the authority behind his words, and on the way these positions shift over the course of the poem. As such, speaking is not only an act of "positing" (i.e., creation), but also an act of responding to the vision invoked. By structuring his encounter with Kishinev around a speech act, Bialik questions the Enlightened positivistic view of history. Instead, he calls attention to its social, mental, and linguistic construction by the reader. For him, history—both as poetry and as narrative—is apprehended in its individualized cognitive and bodily perception. Furthermore, this speech act, in commanding both inner and outer addressee to become active witnesses, becomes a historical event in itself. On yet another level, Bialik also uses the speech act to account for historical change. He applies language to modify both the prophetic and romantic idioms that he borrows, to position his reader via the horror, to both estrange and deepen his or her perception, and thereby to arouse him or her to action.

In all these ways and from all these perspectives, Bialik's project in "City of the Killings" is no less than the radicalization of his readers' perception of history, of community and of selfhood, both in relation to the identity of the individual and to his or her place within history. The complex interaction between the three, bound by experience no less than by the restrictions of language and faith, provides a position from which we can constitute our narrative while at the same time laying it open to self-critique.

Notes

1. This essay originated in a paper given in Ontario at the 2002 Conference of the North American Society for the Study of Romanticism. I would particularly like to thank Sheila Spector who provided the context for this essay. Her persistence and interest have been vital for its writing.
2. Hayim Nahman Bialik, "City of the Killings," 10:1–8. "City of the Killing," in Hebrew *Be-'ir ha-hareiga*, meaning "In the city of the slaughter," was first published with the Hebrew title *Massa Nemirov* ("The vision of Nemirov"), in *Ha-Zeman*, ed. Ben Zion Katz (St. Petersburg, 1908), vol. 3. The title, which

refers to the 1648 pogrom, answered the censor's demand for non-topicality, while certain lines were omitted so as to ensure the censor's approval. The poem was only published in full three years later, when it was entitled "In the city of the slaughter." The Yiddish version (*In a shkhite shtot*) was written by Bialik in 1906. Here and elsewhere in the essay, unless otherwise noted, extracts from the poem are cited from *Songs from Bialik*, edited and translated from the Hebrew by Atar Hadari (Syracuse: Syracuse University Press, 2000).

3. For a variety of critical perspectives over five decades, see Uzi Shavit and Ziva Shamir, eds., *Bi-mvoey 'ir ha-hareiga: mivhar ma-amarim al shiro shel Bialik* (At the gates of Kishinev: Essays on Bialik's poem "In the City of Slaughter") (Tel Aviv: Hakibbutz Hameuchad, 1994). More recent are Dan Miron's discussion of Bialik's modernization of the biblical prophetic mode, in *H. N. Bialik and the Prophetic Mode in Modern Hebrew Poetry* (Syracuse: Syracuse University Press, 2000); Boaz Arpali's emphasis on the denial of Jewish existence in "City of the Killings" ("'For hundreds of years these abhorred [Gentiles] spat in our face, and we wiped away the saliva': Bialik, Brener, Uri Zvi Grinberg," [*Haaretz*, October 10, 2003]); and Michael Gluzman's reading of the poem's role in the evolution of the "New Jew" ("The Lack of Power—The Most Shameful Disease: Bialik and the Kishiniev Pogrom," *Theory and Criticism: An Israeli Forum* no. 22 [spring 2003]: 105–132). My own reading underscores the relationship between Bialik's historiographical principles and his poetic choices.

4. Some of the testimonies that Bialik transcribed have been published by Israel Halpern, ed., *Sefer hagevurah: antologyah historit-sifrutit (The Book of Heroism: An historical-literary anthology)*, 3 vols. (Tel Aviv: Am Oved, 1951), 3:4–14. This document was later published in Hebrew by Ya'akov Goren, ed. *'Eduyot nifge 'e Kishinov, 1903: kefi she-nigbu 'al-yede H. N. Byalik va-haverav* (Testimony of the 1903 Kishinev Pogrom as Written down by Ch. N. Bialik and others) (Tel Aviv: Hakibbutz Hameuchad and Yad Tabenkin, 1991). See also Hayim Shurer, ed., *Ha-pogrom Be-Kishinov* (The Kishinev pogrom of 1903) (Tel Aviv: World Federation of Bessarabian Jews, 1963).

5. While Jewish writers such as S. F. Frug, David Frishman, Y. L. Perez and Shay Imber have provoked strong reactions and deeply influenced the literary perception of the pogrom, Bialik's writing has had the strongest cultural impact. See Alan Mintz, *Hurban: Responses to Catastrophe in Hebrew Literature* (1984; Syracuse: Syracuse University Press, 1996), 130–132.

6. Pesach Aurbach, in *Ha-zeman* 29 (1903): 11.

7. This question was raised by Hamutal Bar-Yosef, in *Haaretz*, December 2, 1994.

8. See, for example, Mintz, *Hurbon*, 154; Anita Shapira, *Herev Hayona: Hatzionut vehakoach 1881–1948* (The Dove's Dagger: Zionism and Power 1881–1948) (Tel Aviv: Am Oved, 1992), 63; and Gluzman. In "The Lack of Power," Gluzman emphasizes the impact of the manifesto of the Hebrew writers (published on April 20, 1903, about two weeks after the pogrom, and signed, among others, by Ahad Ha'Am (Asher Hirsch Ginsberg; 1856–1927), Simon Dubnov (1860–1941), and Bialik himself, on the change in Bialik's response to the pogrom. Miron significantly makes a correlation between Bialik's ideological and generic innovation (*H. N. Bialik*, 15–21).

9. Discussing Bialik's violation of "*Kidush Hashem*," Miron emphasizes the absolute importance of this norm for traditional Judaism.

10. Menakhem Perry, who identifies God as the speaker, was the first to address the complexity of the poem's rhetorical situation (*Hamivneh hasemanti shel shirei Bialik* (*Semantic Dynamics in Bialik's Poetry*) (Tel Aviv: Porter Institute, 1977), 147–154. See also Mintz, *Hurban*, 140–143.

11. Various scholars have detected allusions to Jeremiah, Ezekiel, and Jonah; see, e.g., Yeruham Fishel Lahower, in *Bialik: hayyav vi-yzirotav* (Bialik: his life and his works) (Tel Aviv: Dvir, 1944–1947), 2:430–431); Mintz, *Hurban*, 141–142; and especially Shavit, "Intertextual Parody," 169–172. With different emphases, Mintz, Shavit, and Miron (*H. N. Bialik*, 9–15) all underscore the parodic role of the intertextual patterns.

12. In *Language in Time of Revolution*, Benjamin Harshav defines the modern Jewish literary revolution as a governing semiotics based on the three deictic negations that refer to the speaker, to the time and to the place of the discourse (Berkeley: University of California Press, 1993), 17–18.

13. According to Lahower, Bialik followed Dubnov's instructions in interviewing and photographing available witnesses, attending trials of those perpetrators who were brought to justice, visiting cemeteries and hospitals, examining registers and collecting relevant documents (*Bialik*, 2:424–226). The possible effects of this historical task on Bialik's sense of history should be considered, however, within the framework of his larger historiographical outlook. As opposed to the brilliant and influential essayist Ahad Ha'Am, who believed that the "national will for survival" was a historical given, Bialik, together with Micha Josef Berdichevsky (later Ben Gurion; 1865–1921), believed in the need for a historical reconstruction. Accordingly, unlike Ahad Ha'Am, who privileged non-belletristic writing, Bialik believed in the role of the Hebrew language and literature, with all its genres and intercalated biblical, Mishnaic, medieval, and now modern layers, in shaping Jewish history.

14. Lahower, *Bialik*, 2:424.

15. Sternberg more specifically distinguishes between truth-claim and truth-value; the former refers to commitment to facts, the latter to factual accuracy. For an extended discussion of these distinctions, see Meir Sternberg, *The Poetics of Biblical Narrative: Ideological Literature and the Drama of Reading* (Bloomington: Indiana University Press, 1985), 26–31.

16. As quoted by Lahower, *Bialik*, 2:437–438.

17. The view that history-telling is mediated is shared by Hayden White, in *Metahistory: The Historical Imagination in Nineteenth-Century Europe* (Baltimore: The Johns Hopkins University Press, 1973), Sternberg and others. Modern historiography carries this point to the extreme by claiming that there is a connection between such mediation and a new consciousness of historical time. See, e.g., Ian Balfour's discussion in *The Rhetoric of Romantic Prophecy* (Stanford: Stanford University Press, 2000), 1–18, and Yosef Hayim Yerushalmi's examination of the dilemma of modern Jewish historiography in *Zakhor: Jewish History and Jewish Memory* (New York: Schocken Books, 1989), 101–132.

18. *Be'ir* means "house-beast" in Hebrew; hence the second meaning of the poem's title *Be'ir ha-hareiga* is "Beast of Slaughter," thereby alluding not to the place but to its victims, or to a world in which the two have become synonymized.

19. I am thinking of J. L. Austin's first condition of the performative (*How to Do Things with Words*, ed. J. O.Urmson and Marina Sbisa, second ed.

[Cambridge: Harvard University Press, 1975], 14). I have also benefitted from Angela Esterhammer's informative discussion of the opposition between the performance of vision and sociopolitical speech in Blake (see *Creating States: Studies in the Performative Language of John Milton and William Blake* [Toronto: University of Toronto Press, 1994], especially 119–173).

20. In this regard, Bialik's strategy anticipates the post-*shoah* emphasis on the blindness of witnessing. See the exploration of multiple points of view in Claude Lanzman's *Shoah*, as analyzed by Shoshana Felman in "The Return of the Voice: Claude Lanzmann's *Shoah*," in *Testimony: Crises of Witnessing in Literature, Psychoanalysis and Theory*, ed. Felman and Dori Laub (New York: Routledge, 1992), especially 207–208.

21. For a discussion of the poem's metonymic strategy, see Mintz, *Hurban*, 143–147.

22. In *Natural Supernaturalism: Tradition and Revolution in Romantic Literature*, M. H. Abrams discusses *Bildung* in Wordsworth's *Prelude* and Hegel's *Phenomenology* as presenting a theodicy of the human spirit based on an evolutionary teleology (New York: Norton, 1971), 95–122, 183–195. For a different—anti-redemptive—model of *Bildung*, see Geoffrey Hartman's reading of *The Prelude (Wordsworth's Poetry 1787–1814* [New Haven: Yale University Press, 1964], 31–69; 208–259). Elaborating on Philippe Lacoue-Labarthe and Jean-Luc Nancy, in *The Literary Absolute: The Theory of Literature in German Romanticism*, trans. Philip Barnard and Cheryl Lester (New York: State University of New York Press, 1988), Marc Redfield, who likewise offers a subversive reading of *Bildung*, points to the genre's mirroring and prefiguring of its own fulfillment in history (see "Romanticism, *Bildung* and the Literary Absolute," in *Lessons of Romanticism: A Critical Companion*, ed. Thomas Pfau and Robert F. Gleckner [Durham and London: Duke University Press, 1998], 41–54). In my view, Bialik's "City of the Killings" can be seen as a reversal of the redemptive model described by M. H. Abrams: a process of crisis and self-recognition that culminates in a stage of self-coherence and assured power that is its own reward; at the same time, Bialik's poem can be described, in accordance with Redfield's sense, as a poem that "forms and informs pedagogical and historical process" by its self-production (45).

23. For Bialik's role within the history of the Hebrew long poem in kinship to its European and English models, see Judith Bar-El, *The Hebrew Long Poem from its Emergence to the Beginning of the Twentieth Century: A Study in the History of a Genre* (Jerusalem: Bialik Institute, 1995). Miron, who emphasizes Bialik's new nationalistic uses of the genre, makes a correlation between the genre's evolution and the transition from Enlightenment ideology to Zionism (see *H. N. Bialik*, especially 18–21).

24. This passage from Hazaz's "Sermon 1946" is taken as a paradigm by Robert Alter, in *Modern Hebrew Literature* (New York: Berman House, 1975), 274; by Yerushalmi, *Zakhor* (125–127); and by Harshav, *Language* (7).

25. See, e.g., Gershon Shaked, *Hasiporet haIvrit 1880–1970* (Hebrew narrative fiction 1880–1970) (Tel Aviv: Keter and Hakibbutz Hameuchad, 1977), 25.

26. See Baruch Kurzweil's emphasis on the *I*'s relationship with nature (*Bialik and Tschernichovski* [in Hebrew] [Tel Aviv: Schocken, 1963], 52–89); Yosef Ha-Ephrati's historical reading of Bialik's representation of nature ("Changes in Landscape Description in Poetry as a Paradigm of Literary Transition"

[in Hebrew with an English summary], *Ha-sifrut-literature* 17 [1974]: 50–54); Miron's anatomy of the evolution of Bialik's romantic self, in both his *H. N. Bialik and the Prophetic Mode in Modern Hebrew Poetry*, and "*Ha-preida min ha-ani ha-a-ni*" (Taking leave of the impoverished self: H. N. Bialik's early poetry 1891–1901) (Tel Aviv: Hauniversita Haptuha, 1986); David Aberbach's discussion of romantic influences on Bialik (*Bialik* [London: Peter Halban, 1988]); and Hamutal Bar-Yosef's highlighting of Bialik's adaptation of symbolism (*Decadent Trends in Hebrew Literature: Bialik, Berdychevski, Brener* [in Hebrew] [Jerusalem: Mosad Bialik, 1997], 33–41).

27. Shaked, *Hasiporet*, 104.
28. Ha-Ephrati ("Changes," 167–175) and Miron ("*Ha-preida min ha-ani ha-a-ni*," 210; 308–310) both read Bialik's nature poetry in the context of British romantic models. Aberbach (*Bialik*, 48–50; 108–111) discusses the role of foreign influences (Lessing and Schiller, together with Pushkin, Goethe, Heine, Lermontov, and Byron).
29. Arguing for Bialik's kinship with *fin de siècle* decadence and modernist symbolism, Bar-Yosef herself opposes this very consensus which she cites (*Decadent Trends*, 45–57).
30. Yerushalmi attributes this change in the individual's role in the shaping of history both to the cleavage in continuity of Jewish life and to the dwindling of Jewish collective memory, leading to an increased emphasis upon the individual's reconstruction of history (*Zakhor*, 110–132).
31. Harshav's integrative historiographical model is, accordingly, defined by analogy to the speaker's relation to his speech situation, as a governing semiotics.
32. As they are presented in René Wellek's "The Concept of Romanticism in Literary History," in his *Concepts of Criticism* (1963; New Haven: Yale University Press, 1973), 128–198.
33. In this regard, Hebrew Romanticism repeats the ambivalent relationship of British Romanticism to its Enlightened tradition. See Marshall Brown, "Romanticism and Enlightenment," in *The Cambridge Companion to British Romanticism*, ed. Stuart Curran (Cambridge: Cambridge University Press, 1993), 25–47.
34. Berdichevsky's faith in the construction of a national Subject as contingent on the sovereignty of the individual is encapsulated in his well-known formulation: "Let us mold the life of a single individual, and the rest will follow" (41). For the ideological milieu of the conflicting values between Ahad Ha'Am and Berdichevsky within the emerging Hebrew canon, see the discussion of the cultural debate between Ahad Ha'Am and Micha Yosef Berdichevsky in Hanan Hever's *Producing the Modern Hebrew Canon: Nation Building and Minority Discourse* (New York and London: New York University Press, 2002).
35. Whereas Abrams locates the Romantic paradigm in the shift from imitation to expression (*The Mirror and the Lamp: Romantic Theory and the Critical Tradition* [Oxford: Oxford University Press, 1953], 47–69), "City of the Killings" seems to shift the emphasis from the poet to the role of the reader. For Russian and German influences on Bialik and for his knowledge of Byron, see, e.g., Aberbach (*Bialik*, 48). For his ambivalence toward earlier Romantic models (including the British models), see Miron (*H. N. Bialik*, 10–13) and Bar-Yosef (*Decadent Trends*, 48–55).
36. For a comprehensive introduction to the history of the modern long poem, see Michael Bernstein, *The Tale of the Tribe: Ezra Pound and the Modern Verse*

Epic (Princeton: Princeton University Press, 1980), 3–28. In *Bialik and the Prophetic Mode in Modern Hebrew Poetry*, Miron delineates how Bialik's long poem differs from its tradition in its parodic role (1–15). My own analysis emphasizes the reconstruction of history as both an aim and a means for individualizing and activating the reader. For temporalized space as the focus of the shift in the composition of the long poem, see my "Keat's *Hyperion*: Time, Space, and the Long Poem," *Poetics Today* 22:1 (spring 2001): 89–127.

37. An analogous model for the relationship between prophecy and history can be found in Walter Benjamin's "Theses on the Philosophy of History," in his *Illuminations*, ed. Hannah Arendt, trans. Harry Zohn (1969; New York: Schocken, 1978), 253–267. In Ian Balfour's words, for Benjamin "to prophesy the present is, typically, to cite the past" (*Rhetoric*, 16).

PART IV

CODA: COLERIDGE AND JUDAICA

CHAPTER 12

COLERIDGE'S MISREADING OF SPINOZA

Stanley J. Spector

Henry Crabb Robinson characterized Coleridge's peculiar attitude toward Benedict (Baruch) Spinoza (1632–1677) fairly accurately in a diary entry from 1812, where he described the following encounter with Coleridge:

> In the course of a few minutes, while standing in the room, Coleridge kissed Spinoza's face at the title page, said his book was his gospel, and in less than a minute added that his philosophy was, after all, false. Spinoza's system has been demonstrated to be false, but only by that philosophy which has at the same time demonstrated the falsehoods of all other philosophies. Did philosophy commence in an IT IS instead of an I AM, Spinoza would be altogether true; and without allowing a breathing-time he parenthetically asserted: "I, however, believe in all the doctrines of Christianity, even of the Trinity."[1]

Three points from this entry highlight Coleridge's odd relationship with Spinoza. The first peculiarity is that Coleridge declared Spinoza's *Ethics* "his gospel," even though he believed it to be false.[2] Second, Coleridge seemed to accept Kant's analysis in showing that Spinoza's philosophy is false in the way that all other philosophies are false, and yet, in the face of the Kantian critique, he nevertheless accepted the "doctrines of Christianity" as being true.[3] The third is an inconsistency in Coleridge's objections about Spinoza's philosophy, as found in various places throughout Coleridge's work. In his remarks to Robinson, he indicated that a major problem was Spinoza's beginning the philosophic system of the *Ethics* from the perspective of an "IT IS" rather than an "I AM." However, as we shall see below, Coleridge, though emphatic, was mistaken when he perceived Spinoza's discourse of God beginning with an "IT IS," that is, with God as an object.

From Robinson's account alone, we could conclude that Coleridge was both confused and ambivalent about Spinoza, an uncertainty that appears elsewhere in Coleridge's work. For example, in the weekly lectures on the history of philosophy delivered during the winter of 1818–1819, Coleridge devoted very little attention to a systematic discussion of Spinoza in general, or *The Ethics* in particular,[4] limiting himself to positive comments about Spinoza's strong character or rigorous philosophical system. The part of Coleridge that admired Spinoza and caused him, according to Robinson, to kiss Spinoza's picture is the same characteristic that identified the *Ethics* as one of the three "greatest Works since the introduction of Christianity."[5] Yet, even in his *Biographia Literaria*, Coleridge avoided a systematic philosophical discussion with Spinoza.[6] He commented mostly about the rigor of Spinoza's system, the kind of life Spinoza lived, and the horrible, but undeserved, criticism that was commonly made about Spinoza's being an atheist and living a non-Christian life. Ironically, Coleridge defended Spinoza the man while simultaneously asserting the falsity of Spinoza's philosophy, specifically the analysis of God. It seems strange, given his deep admiration for Spinoza, that Coleridge did not engage *The Ethics* in either his public lectures or his written works to reconcile his ambivalent attitude.

The ambivalence might be summarized this way. On the one hand, Coleridge admired the tenacity and rigor of Spinoza's system; he appreciated the geometric method that Spinoza employed throughout the *Ethics*, and he defended Spinoza against charges of atheism. However, he had difficulty reconciling Spinoza's account of God with his own understanding of God as culled from the Gospels. Or, as he put it in *Biographia Literaria*, "my head was with Spinoza, though my whole heart remained with Paul and John" (*BL* 1:201). So, while at the same time praising Spinoza's method, Coleridge denied what he perceived to be Spinoza's conclusions, asserting that Spinoza erred in the way he began building and articulating his system.

More significantly, further confusion in the way that Coleridge articulated his objections suggests that Coleridge had not actually read *The Ethics* very closely. In the following pages, I review the substance of Coleridge's objections and show how a careful reading of *The Ethics* either meets his objections or shows them to be misguided.[7]

The most succinct statement that Coleridge made about Spinoza appears in what had been an unpublished note found in the British Museum, subsequently published in 1960 by Lore Metzger.[8] Coleridge's aim in this note was to defend Spinoza from those who slandered or dishonestly misinterpreted his system. To Coleridge's credit, what Metzger calls his "vindication" was not so much a defense of Spinoza's system, as it was a polemic against those who illegitimately criticized Spinoza's system. Nonetheless, in his opening paragraph, Coleridge elaborated his primary objection to Spinoza:

> "*Unica Substantia infinitis Attributis*": the well known words of Benedict Spinoza, whose (most grievous) error consisted not so much in what he affirms, as in what he has omitted to affirm or rashly denied:—not that he saw God in the Ground, i.e. in that which scholastic theology is called Natura naturans in distinction from Natura naturata; but that he saw God in the ground *only and exclusively*, in his *Might* alone and his *essential* Wisdom, and not likewise in his moral, intellectual, existential and personal Godhead. (283)

Coleridge understood the God of Spinoza's *Ethics* to be limited in His power; this God could not interfere with the actions of human beings or the course of history. Spinoza's God, according to Coleridge, did not stand outside of nature and the world of experience; He was not a judge, watching or evaluating or even answering the prayers of supplicants. No, Spinoza's God, Coleridge wrote in *Aids to Reflection*:

> . . . would not longer be the God, in whom we *believe* . . . (but) the World itself, the indivisible one and only substance (*substantia una et unica*) of Spinoza, of which all *Phœnomena*, all particular and individual Things, Lives, Minds, Thoughts, and Actions are but modifications.[9]

Ironically, even though Coleridge's assessment was correct, he was still dissatisfied with his conclusion. The irony apparently stems from Coleridge's confusion about much of Spinoza, from the *Ethics*' beginning to its very end, of which Coleridge remarked that one would not find "passages as thoroughly *Pauline*, as completely accordant with the doctrines of the established Church" as the last proof (*BL* 2:245). I believe that Coleridge's confusion stemmed from his inability to suspend his belief in the premises that he accepted from Scripture. To those who accept the view of God as commonly understood in both the Jewish and Christian traditions of the seventeenth century, Spinoza's ideas are, indeed, blasphemous. However, one of Spinoza's achievements in the *Ethics* was to correct what he considered to be the confusions and irrationalities about God that were current in the domain of philosophic discourse. Therefore, despite Coleridge's professions of deep admiration, he was still being rather perverse when he criticized Spinoza's reasoning on the basis of premises in fact introduced not by Spinoza, but by Coleridge himself; at the very least, those premises must be suspended if one is to work with Spinoza through the series of definitions and theorems that constitute his geometric method. In other words, Coleridge's criticism of Spinoza is analogous to someone's claiming, after having finished a course in geometry, his appreciation of the rigor of the method, while still insisting that triangles have four sides.

Specifically, Coleridge makes at least three mistakes in his interpretation of Spinoza: (1) his interpretation of the concept of God; (2) the distinction between *natura naturans* and *natura naturata*; and (3) his reading of the last proposition as an example of Pauline theology. These are not, however, three separate and distinct issues in the philosophy of Spinoza; rather, when taken together, they articulate the interconnectedness and relatedness of distinct elements of his system.

Spinoza's Concept of God

Spinoza's *Ethics*, a systematic and interrelated demonstration of metaphysics, epistemology, and ethics, is divided into five parts: (1) "Concerning God," (2) "Of the Nature and the Origin of the Mind," (3) "On the Origin and

Nature of the Emotions," (4) "Of Human Bondage or the Strength of the Emotions," and (5) "On the Power of the Understanding, or of Human Freedom." Considering the fact that Spinoza used the geometric method to show how the nature of reality and the human condition are very closely connected, that which he said about God cannot be separated from his assertions about what we can know and how we are to live. In other words, the proofs of the propositions in the later parts rely on what was established earlier; and the entire system rests on the set of eight definitions and seven axioms that open Part I. Consequently, what Spinoza had to say about God is closely related to his comments about Nature, and, at the end of the *Ethics*, to his claim about Blessedness.

The confusion that Spinoza set about correcting was not solely part of theological discourse, but was actually the subset of a larger confusion in the philosophical literature, one that had been festering for centuries, dealing with an ultimate metaphysical ground or first principle. Before the Western intellectual tradition came into contact with Scripture, Plato had identified a first principle in terms of the unchanging Form of the Good. Aristotle also identified a first principle, in his case in terms of motion, which he called an Unmoved Mover. When Constantine converted to Christianity, the Scholastics attempted to merge Aristotelian Philosophy with Scripture, yielding the emergence of God as the ultimate first principle of reality. By the beginning of the sixteenth century, philosophers recognized that the Scholastic project of integrating Aristotle and Scripture had failed. The new generation of empirical scientists that applied scientific method to their observations and mathematized nature discovered that neither Aristotelian Philosophy nor Scripture could explain natural phenomena. It was also during this period that what had been a unified study of philosophy was beginning to be compartmentalized into the different sciences.

A paradigmatic example of the new thinker to emerge in the seventeenth century is René Descartes (1596–1650), the French philosopher and mathematician who struggled to demonstrate the existence of God and the distinction between the mind and the body, much the way he could demonstrate the properties of a right triangle and the workings of the eye. Descartes understood both that he was studying different phenomena and that each demarcated area of study was still an expression of the divine principle. Nevertheless, he still hoped to give a coherent explanation of the natural, mathematical, philosophical, and theological worlds. Unfortunately, he was somewhat hindered, having inherited from Aristotle and the Scholastics a metaphysical vocabulary that included such concepts as substance and mode, essence, infinite and eternal, and God. By the time that Descartes began working with these concepts, each of them had already had a history dating back to Aristotle, who had originally defined them and used them coherently within his metaphysics. As these concepts continued to be used by the Scholastics, definitions were transformed to reflect a new metaphysical use in Christian philosophy. When Descartes attempted to demonstrate the existence of God, for example, he used this vocabulary, and consequently, derived absurd conclusions. He believed that he had delivered on his promise to demonstrate the existence of God and the distinction of the mind from the body, but in the end, he merely demonstrated a confusion about the notion of substance by asserting not only that there are both infinite and finite substances, but also that there are three types of infinite substances, as well. He certainly did not convince Spinoza, who believed that part of Descartes' problem was his lack of precision with definitions. Otherwise, Descartes would not have concluded that there are many different substances: a God substance, mental and physical substances, infinite substances, and finite substances.

In order to eliminate this kind of confusion, Spinoza carefully defined his key terms—"self-caused," "finite after its own kind," "substance," "attribute," "mode," "God," "free," and "eternity"—on the very first page of the *Ethics*, and through a series of thirty-six propositions, he demonstrated first that there can only be one infinite substance, signified variously by the names "God" and "nature." With Spinoza, we get an identification of the subject matters of theology, philosophy and natural science. These sciences do not study different phenomena; rather, it is the same one, only called by different names. Because this substance, also known as God, or nature, is infinite, it has infinite attributes expressing its essence; however, human beings can only recognize two of these—extension and thought. So, in reply to Descartes, who claimed that minds and bodies have independent existences as mental and physical substances, Spinoza responded that minds and bodies are modifications, or modes, of the single infinite substance, each expressing an essential attribute of that substance. In addition, it is only that substance, also known as God, and also known as nature, that is free, for only it "exists solely by the necessity of its own nature, and of which . . . [its] action is determined by itself alone" (*Ethics*, Part I: Def VII).

Spinoza's Distinction between *Natura Naturans* and *Natura Naturata*

Although Coleridge understood correctly that Spinoza identified God with Nature, he misunderstood in what sense, erroneously believing that Spinoza identified God with *natura naturata*, nature viewed as passive. Spinoza, however, clearly identified God with *natura naturans*, active nature. By *natura naturans*, Spinoza understood

> . . . that which is in itself, and is conceived through itself, or those attributes of substance, which express eternal and infinite essence, in other words (Prop xiv., Coroll, i, and Prop. xvii, Coroll, ii) God, in so far as he is considered as a free cause.
> By nature viewed as passive I understand all that which follows from the necessity of the nature of God, that is, all of the modes of the attributes of God, in so far as they are considered as things which are in God, and which without God cannot exist or be conceived. ("Note" to Proposition XXIX)

Coleridge was correct in that his picture of God and his interpretation of nature, as derived from the Gospels, was radically different from Spinoza's, but he did not understand why. He failed to recognize the importance of the recurring phrase "insofar as," that Spinoza employed in every significant distinction he made throughout the *Ethics*. When, for example, Spinoza distinguished the different ways nature can be viewed, he demarcated them from particular perspectives. When nature is viewed from God's perspective, that is, insofar as God perceives nature, it is active; however, when viewed from the perspective "of the modes of the attributes of God . . . insofar as they are considered as things which are in God," then it is passive. Coleridge seems to have equivocated on the term *thing* here. Spinoza clearly differentiated the kind of thing that is self-existing from the kind that is not. According to Spinoza, when one views nature as passive, it appears as though it is populated with many different things. However, these things are not self-existing, but have external causes. When one views nature as active, on the other hand, nature is only a single, self-existing thing, namely, "Substance," also called "God" and "nature." Human beings are not self-existing things; we exist as modifications, or modes, of the single, infinite substance, understood as either bodies or minds. Each of these—body and mind—is one of the only two attributes, from among the infinite number of attributes that express God's essence, that human beings are capable of grasping, namely, extension and thought.

Part I of the *Ethics*, "Concerning God," makes the case for a single infinite and eternal substance. In other words, having explicated the reality of God, also known as active nature, Spinoza next takes up questions concerning human activity against the backdrop of that reality. A human being is not a substance; he is not "conceived through itself: in other words, . . . a conception can (not) be formed independently of any other conception" (*Ethics*, Part I, Def. III). For example, the classic Greek definition of a human being "as a rational animal" first places us in the genus of animals and then differentiates our species as being rational. However adequate or inadequate this definition may be, it still serves as a model for forming conceptions about human beings. It is only the concept of God that "is conceived through itself" (*Ethics*, Part I, Def. III), without reference to any other concept, for God is "a being absolutely infinite—that is, a substance consisting in infinite attributes, of which each expresses eternal and infinite essentiality" (*Ethics*, Part I, Def. IV). So, throughout the *Ethics*, Spinoza alternated between the two perspectives, those of God and of human beings, inserting the expression "insofar as" to remind his readers of this distinction. Nature, then, insofar as it is conceived through itself, is active, and, insofar as it follows from the necessity of something else, is passive.

Coleridge understood God to be an independent cause residing outside of a natural order, which had been created by Him. In Coleridge's view, had God wanted to, He could have created any number of worlds since God's will, freedom, and power are infinite, and God can interact in the created world whenever and wherever He wants to. This view, Spinoza showed, is self-contradictory. To understand that God could have an external desire or be affected by an external cause is to deny God freedom, in the sense of acting according to the necessity of His own nature. God is not constrained or determined to act by anything or anyone; God is the sole free cause in that all that God does follows directly from His nature alone, which in Spinoza's philosophy is the active nature, *natura naturans*. In addition, because from the perspective of *natura naturans*, time and place do not exist, there can be no "whenever" or "wherever" as a time and place in which God could act. God is eternal and infinite: eternal, not in the sense of everlasting, but in the sense of atemporality; and infinite, not in the sense of possibilities, but in the sense of absence of negations and limitations, leaving no place or space (to use a spatial metaphor) not filled by Him. In contrast, Spinoza's passive nature, *natura naturata*, is the physical universe that is studied as an object by the natural sciences. It has laws that govern the movement of the bodies that compose it, but those bodies are not free. They do not act spontaneously according to their own nature, but are put in motion by the limiting boundaries of other bodies, all of which are modifications of substance understood under the attribute of extension. When viewed as discrete bodies in motion, nature is passive; but those same bodies viewed all together and at once constitute active nature.

Coleridge, missing this distinction, thought he was giving glory to God by postulating a living God, though he was actually anthropomorphizing Him into a God of limitation, negation, and finitude, a God who, being less than infinite, could have acted otherwise. In Spinoza's view, there is no difference between God and God's creation, if we are even to speak the language of creation. That is, from the perspective of God, or active nature, the idea of an act of creation at a given time is absurd. God is eternal, without a beginning in time, and so God and God's creation are not two separate entities. What we understand as creation is equivalent to Spinoza's passive nature. Insofar as God is active nature, passive nature does not exist. It is only from the confused perspective of finite modes that one can consider nature as passive nature at all; from the perspective of God, there is no passive nature, for from God's perspective there is no discreteness, no time or space. There is just a single substance with infinite attributes expressing its essential, infinite nature.

From the context of this reality, Spinoza then demonstrated how human beings fit into this picture. The only two attributes that we grasp of the infinite attributes expressing God's essential nature are extension and thought. In terms of ourselves, we can say that we are body, and we can say that we are mind, but not in the same way that Descartes did. Descartes argued that thought and extension are substances in their own right and that human beings are essentially minds that have bodies attached to them. There is a slew of problems connected with this view, not least of which is how these two completely separate things can causally interact. Spinoza's response is to show that thought and extension, while not being substances themselves, express the nature of the single, eternal, and infinite substance in what we perceive as particular bodies and ideas. This notion, of course, led to charges of blasphemy, for suggesting that God is a body as well as a mind.

God, being infinite, has an infinite number of attributes expressing His essence, but we can only recognize these two. The body of God is made up of the order and connection of all bodies viewed in passive nature, taken together and at once, thus constituting active nature. Similarly, God's mind is the order and connection of all ideas taken together and at once. In so far as both of these attributes express God's essential nature, Spinoza argued, "The order and connection of ideas is the same as the order and connection of things" (*Ethics*, Part II, Prop. VII). Spinoza did not have the same problem as Descartes, who tried to give an account of causal interaction between bodies and minds. For Spinoza, the answer was simple: there is no causal interaction. Instead, the order and connection of ideas parallel exactly the order and connection of bodies. According to Spinoza, then, an account of human experience can be given either solely in terms of the attribute of extension, or else solely in terms of the attribute of thought; and it would be a mistake to confuse one approach with the other.

Spinoza and Pauline Theology

By focusing on human beings both as modes who think and as modes who are bodies, Spinoza, through the bulk of the *Ethics*, first showed how we become enslaved by the emotions and then demonstrated how we might subsequently become free. In the middle of Part V, "Of Human Freedom," Spinoza shifted his focus to declare: "It is now, therefore, time to pass on to those matters, which appertain to the duration of the mind, without relation to the body" (Prop XX, note). In his proof to the last of this set of twenty-two propositions—a passage Coleridge considered "thoroughly *Pauline*" (*BL*, II:245)—Spinoza wrote:

> Again, in proportion as the mind rejoices more in this divine love or blessedness, so does it the more understand (V. xxxii); that is (V iii Coroll.), so much the more power has it over the emotions, and (V xxxviii) so much the less is it subject to those emotions which are evil; therefore, in proportion as the mind rejoices in this divine love or blessedness, so has it the power of controlling lusts. And, since human power in controlling the emotions consists solely in the understanding, it follows that no one rejoices in blessedness, because he has controlled his lusts, but, contrariwise, his power of controlling his lusts arises from this blessedness itself. Q.E.D. (Part V, Prop. XLII, Proof)

Here, again, Coleridge seems to have misinterpreted what Spinoza was saying about blessedness and man's relation to God. What emerges immediately when interpreting this passage in the spirit of Paul and the Gospels is a picture of human beings reflecting on, or even basking in, God's divine love, as if there were a separate entity, named God, who emanates love to lesser creatures. While it is true that human beings are lesser creatures insofar as they are not substances, it is not true, at least according to Spinoza, that they are separate from God, or, indeed, that they are even creatures at all. Because Spinoza defined God as the total order and connection of bodies or minds, both and at the same time, he did not conceive of a God who stands outside of nature, shining his light or love from a vantage point outside of the total system. God is the *totality* of the system, seen all together and at once. At the same place where Spinoza clarified the relationship between human beings and the divine, that is, in the last twenty-two propositions of the *Ethics*, he also explicitly defined blessedness, showing how human beings, through the exercise of knowledge, can achieve that state.

In Part II, Prop. XL, Note II, Spinoza differentiated among three kinds of knowledge. "*Knowledge of the first kind, opinion, or imagination*" results in two ways. The first occurs when we look at things or understand them "fragmentarily, confusedly, and without order through our senses." These are "perceptions," which Spinoza called "by the name of knowledge from the mere suggestions of experience." To Spinoza, then, memory and imagination comprise the second variety of knowledge, while fragmentary and confused perception, along with memory and imagination, constitute only opinion, but not knowledge. We know, for example, that it would be incorrect to claim simply on the basis of its appearance when we look up into the sky, that the sun is about the size of a basketball; if, however, we were to make that claim, we would be demonstrating the so-called knowledge of the first kind, which actually is not knowledge at all. For Coleridge to claim a discrete existence for human beings, or a separateness of human beings from each other and from God, is to understand the totality of nature only "fragmentarily, confusedly, and without order through our senses."

The second kind of knowledge, that which Spinoza called "*reason*," arises "from the fact that we have notions common to all men, and adequate ideas of the properties of things." This is the knowledge of mathematics and the new scientific method of the sixteenth and seventeenth centuries. This kind of knowledge corrects the images derived solely on the basis of sense experience, and demonstrates, for example, that the sun's actual size is much greater than a basketball's. It demonstrates in a way that leaves no room for any other possibility the relationship between the hypotenuse of a right triangle and the length of the other sides. It is a systematic method whose every successive step can be trusted because the previous step had been discovered according to ironclad rules of reasoning. Thus, one of the differences between these two types of knowledge is that the first kind cannot be used to establish truth or falsity. There is no measure for determining the veracity of a sense perception, not even further sense perception, because judgments based on them may or may not be true. However, by following the steps of a rational proof, we can determine if something is true or false.

Another difference between these two levels of knowledge is that the second relies on "adequate ideas," a concept which Spinoza defined in the beginning of Part II (Def. IV):

> By *an adequate idea*, I mean an idea which, in so far as it is considered in itself, without relation to the object, has all the properties or intrinsic marks of a true idea.

Explanation.—I say *intrinsic*, in order to exclude that mark which is extrinsic, namely, the agreement between the idea and its object (*ideatum*).

For an idea to be true, it must agree with its object, that is, with what the idea refers to in the world. For example, our idea that "a regulation basketball court is ninety-four feet long" is true because a regulation basketball court really is ninety-four feet long. This notion that truth corresponds to its object seems obvious and correct. However, given his ontology of God/substance/nature, Spinoza needed to find a way to ground truth within the totality of his system. To do that, he introduced the notion of an adequate idea, one whose mark of truth is contained wholly within itself, without reference to an external object. Such an idea would be complete in itself and would necessarily have to be eternal in the sense of atemporality. It would be God's only idea, His idea of himself. The fact that human beings are modifications of God/substance/nature allows us to understand human beings as having a connection with the infinite and eternal. As minds, that is, as modifications of God/substance/nature understood under the attribute of thought, we can switch our perspective from the discreteness of passive nature to the totality of active nature, and thus understand ourselves under the aspect of eternity, which we are insofar as we are modifications of the eternal substance understood under the attribute of thought. That is, it is clear that human beings are temporal; and the exercise of reason, the second way of knowing, is a temporal process in which we proceed from one step in time to the next. Grasping an adequate idea, however, is atemporal; this means that there is some part of a human being that can access what is eternal. Insofar as we are modifications of eternal substance understood under the attribute of thought, we are eternal in the sense of not being a particular, discrete thing, but in the sense of comprising, with all other modes taken together and at once, the eternal substance. So, insofar as human beings are temporal, we have inadequate ideas, some of which may be true and some of which may be false, all gathered through the first way of knowing. In addition, our ideas resulting from the second way of knowing are also inadequate, although they are true—we can demonstrate their truth through a process of reasoning which happens in time. However, in order to initiate such a process, we need first to recognize an adequate idea, something that is possible only insofar as human beings are understood as an expression of the eternal, under the form of eternity.

We access such an idea by way of the third kind of knowledge, that which Spinoza called intuition:

> Besides these two kinds of knowledge, there is, as I will hereafter show, a third kind of knowledge, which we will call intuition. This kind of knowledge proceeds from an adequate idea of the absolute essence of certain attributes of God to the adequate knowledge of the essence of things. (Prop. XL, Note II)

This note of Spinoza's misleadingly implies that this kind of knowledge is also durational. It seems more likely, though, that as with a note appearing in

Part II, where Spinoza was exemplifying the second way of knowing, he had no other way to introduce his topic. He explained intuition in more detail in Part V, where it becomes clear that this kind of knowledge is possible because there is a sense of our actually being eternal. Now, insofar as I am writing these words and you are reading them, we are both temporal, as one word follows the other. Yet, insofar as we, together with all other modes, are grasped at once, we are eternal, and the understanding of ourselves as temporal is a false idea that we have "represented to our intellect fragmentarily, confusedly, and without order through our senses" (Prop. XL, Note II).

The exercise of the third kind of knowledge involves the simultaneous recognition of the essence of things and the absolute essence of God. For example, when someone perceives his body under the form of eternity, he does not perceive one particular thing existing in space and time with other particular things. Instead, he perceives his body, along with all other bodies, as a single extended thing, that is, as a single system comprising the order and connection of all things taken together and at once. He does not perceive this totality of relations by constructing the system in time, but, rather, by apprehending it at once. The point at which one recognizes the interrelated system of bodies, while simultaneously viewing oneself under the form of eternity, is precisely the recognition of the absolute essence of God as the attribute of extension. At that moment, the individual is no longer himself in the sense of a discrete, particular modification of substance, but part of the substance itself. That is, from the perspective of modes, for short intervals he is God/ substance/nature; and as he gets better at exercising this kind of knowledge, that is, as he increases his adequate ideas, those intervals increase.

So, the act of perceiving adequately entails the recognition that man is an expression of God's intellect insofar as the total order and connection of minds is what God is thinking. God's thinking, though, is absolutely complete; there is no external object of thought because God's thought, essentially, is a thought thinking itself. God's thinking, being complete and real, is also perfection itself.[10] The human being's state of perfection depends on the extent to which he grasps adequate ideas by this third way of knowing. The more a human being thinks adequately, the greater his state of perfection, since the more adequately he thinks, the more he expresses God as thought. A human being's greatest perfection comes about, then, with his greatest understanding of the eternality of God, which is the atemporal simultaneous knowledge of how the absolute essence of things is the absolute essence of one of God's attributes. For those moments, human beings are not finite and temporal, but simulate the infinite and eternal aspects of God; and it is in those moments when human beings exercise the third kind of knowledge that they experience their highest "salvation, or blessedness, or freedom" (*Ethics*, Part V, Prop. 36, Note). It is in those moments of grasping the eternal aspect of human nature that one simultaneously grasps the loss of a discrete existence and the complete identification with God as God, not insofar as people are discrete, particular individuals, but as they, together with all other minds, are precisely what God is.

Thus, Coleridge's claim that Spinoza shared an affinity with the doctrines of the Gospels is erroneous. The problem was that Coleridge was incapable of distinguishing Spinoza's language from his own, and he apparently failed to check the precise definitions that Spinoza developed throughout the *Ethics*. Although Spinoza did discuss a separation of human beings from each other and from God, as is found in Pauline theology, his discussion was used to highlight his notion that this claim of separation can only be made insofar as we inadequately view human beings from the perspective of the first kind of knowledge. Yet, when viewed from the perspective of the adequacy of the third kind of knowledge, human beings are God, because they then instantaneously understand and grasp reality as the total order and connection of things or ideas.

Notes

1. Edith J. Morley, ed., *Henry Crabb Robinson on Books and Their Writers* (London: J. M. Dent, 1938), 1:112.
2. Although Spinoza completed the *Ethics* by 1674, its publication was prevented by theologians who claimed he denied the existence of God. The treatise was published posthumously in the *Opera Posthuma* (Amsterdam, 1677). For this essay, I am using the translation by R. H. M. Elwes (New York: Dover, 1955).
3. One of the ironies of Coleridge's ambivalent attitude toward Spinoza is that the Kantian critique of transcendental philosophy is enough to refute absolutely Spinoza's discussion of God and active nature. Coleridge, however, never used Kant's analysis in any of his specific objections.
4. *The Philosophical Lectures of Samuel Taylor Coleridge*, ed. Kathleen Coburn (New York: Philosophical Library, 1949).
5. The comment is found in a note on the front flyleaf of F. W. J. Schelling, *Philosophische Schriften* (Landshut, 1809), I, British Museum MS. Egerton 2801, fol. 1–10. The note was first published by Lore Metzger in her "Coleridge's Vindication of Spinoza: An Unpublished Note," *Journal of the History of Ideas* 21 (1960): 279–293.
6. *Biographia Literaria, or, Biographical Sketches of My Literary Life and Opinions*, ed. J. Engell and W. J. Bate (Princeton: Princeton University Press, 1983), 1:201. References to *Biographia Literaria* are to the Engell-Bate edition, abbreviated *BL*.
7. This is not to say that Coleridge was alone in this regard. In "The Spinozistic Crescendo," the second chapter of *Coleridge and the Pantheist Tradition*, Thomas McFarland describes the Spinoza-mania that occurred in the Romantic Period, especially on the Continent, noting that Goethe, among others, while at one point claiming to be "reading and reading" Spinoza, at another confesses, "I cannot say that I ever read Spinoza straight through" ([Oxford: Clarendon Press, 1969], 83, 86).
8. British Museum MS. Egerton 2801, fol. 1–10. Watermark: Ruse & Turners 1817. This appeared in Metzger, "Coleridge's Vindication," 279–293.
9. (London, 1825), as quoted by Metzger.
10. *Ethics* Part II, Def. VI; I use the terms *reality* and *perfection* synonymously.

CHAPTER 13

MENDELSSOHN AND COLERIDGE ON
WORDS, THOUGHTS, AND THINGS

Frederick Burwick

In his marginalia to *Morgenstunden* (1785), Samuel Taylor Coleridge
(1772–1834) was especially intrigued with the way in which Moses
Mendelssohn (1728–1786) challenged the interaction between language
and perception.[1] The latter provides an empirical ground through sensory
experience; the former a means for describing and communicating. Neither
is reliable. *Morgenstunden*, of course, is not about language per se, but about
proving the existence of God. As Mendelssohn's final work, it was intended
as a companion to his *Phaedon* (1767), on the immortality of the soul.[2]
Bound together with Coleridge's copy of *Morgenstunden* was Mendelssohn's
Jerusalem (1783), a work that cleverly undermined claims of spiritual authority.[3] Although addressing Judaism, Mendelssohn implicated the concept of
religious power at large and demonstrated the essential disjuncture between
spiritual and material claims to strength. A passage from *Jerusalem* on might
and right, transcribed into Coleridge's notebook in the summer of 1809, was
accompanied by a commentary on the Hobbesian thesis on law and power
subsequently published in Coleridge's *Omniana* (1809–1816) (*CN* 3548
and 3548n; *LR* 1). Coleridge added a few notes to *Jerusalem* at the time he
was also reading Friedrich Heinrich Jacobi's *Werke* and revising *The Friend*
(1818). Coleridge read and annotated *Morgenstunden* sometime during the
period that he was writing essays for the *Courier*, lecturing on literature, and
reissuing *The Friend* (1812–1814), perhaps even during the time that he was
assembling his *Biographia Literaria* (1815–1816) (*M* 3:846–862).[4]

On the problems of language and perception, to which he continued to
dedicate his attention in his lectures on Shakespeare, Coleridge had already
adapted ideas from David Hartley, George Berkeley, Immanuel Kant, and
Friedrich Schelling. That he had also already made up his mind on how a

proof of God's existence must be constructed is evident in his very first note to *Morgenstunden*:

> The unspeakable importance of the Distinction between the Reason, and the Human Understanding, as the only Ground of the Cogency of the Proof a posteriori of the Existence of a God from the order of the known Universe—[5] Remove or deny this distinction, and Hume's argument from the Spider's proof that Houses &c were spun by Men out of their Bodies becomes valid. (*M* 3:848)[6]

Although Mendelssohn did indeed distinguish between *reason* and *understanding*, he did not adopt the Kantian distinction between *Vernunft* and *Verstand*; rather, he referred to *reason* as the process of deliberation and *understanding* as the product of deliberation. In the divine *alpha* and *omega*, the means and end are already synthesized. Coleridge may well have been surprised to discover that Mendelssohn grounded his proof of God's existence in the rational process itself, in the conceivability of God (*MS* 161–162; *GS* 3.2:100).[7] Astonished at this argument, Coleridge wrote in the margins: "can this be asserted by a Disciple of Leibniz, Wolf, Baumgarten?"

Mendelssohn had indeed learned from the great German rationalist, Gottfried Wilhelm Leibniz (1646–1716) and from his followers, Christian Wolff (1679–1754) and Alexander Gottlieb Baumgarten (1714–1762). But he had honed his philosophical principles in debate with more immediate contemporaries—Gotthold Ephraim Lessing, Friedrich Nicolai, Johann Kaspar Lavater, Immanuel Kant, and Friedrich Heinrich Jacobi. Further, he held fast to his early talmudic education.[8] With his work on the ritual laws of the Jews, his translation and dual-language edition of the Pentateuch, Mendelssohn became a leading exponent of the Jewish Enlightenment (*Haskalah*) in Europe.[9] With major works on the immortality of the soul and the existence of God, he was foremost a philosopher of religion, but that philosophy attempted to embrace broad cultural concerns with education and the arts, with tolerance and the integration of the Jews.[10]

Together with Lessing and Nicolai, Mendelssohn discussed literary theory and the province of practical criticism, and established himself as a shrewd and polemical spokesman on aesthetic problems. He joined Nicolai as founding editor of the *Bibliothek der Schönen Wissenschaften und der Freyen Künste*, and with both Nicolai and Lessing he contributed to *Briefen die neueste Litteratur betreffend*. He later wrote for Nicolai's *Allgemeiner Deutscher Bibliothek*. His contributions are brief but penetrating, written with stylistic verve and a witty polemical edge. As literary critic, he centered his analysis in philosophical issues. While he allied himself with Lessing's views on the drama, he nevertheless maintained his own aesthetic criteria. Although he modified his earlier position on the role of the emotions in aesthetic experience,[11] he refused to accept the definition of *sympathy* that Lessing had adapted from English criticism, but resorted, instead, to the German sense of *Mitleid*.[12] Mendelssohn's account of illusion and an internalized mimesis, however, anticipate key attributes of Coleridge's theory of the drama.

Because he was responding to similar philosophical concerns, there is something proto-Coleridgean in Mendelssohn's emphasis on individual perception of beauty and participation in the divine creative process. Mendelssohn distinguished beauty from metaphysical perfection. The latter perfection is absolute "unity in manifold" ("die Einheit im Mannigfaltigen"); the former beauty in art is merely a contrived "unity in manifold," substituting an artificial uniformity into the fragmentary perceptions of the whole.[13] First formulated in his "Observations on the Origins and the Connections of the Fine Arts and the Sciences" (*Betrachtungen über die Quellen und die Verbindungen der schönen Künste und Wissenschaften*, 1757), Mendelssohn went on to apply his concept of "unity in manifold" in his *Morgenstunden*, where he informed his discrimination of the artistic imitation of absolute unity with the idea of sameness and difference (*MS* 84; *GS* 3.2:53–54), the *Idem et Alter* that Coleridge claimed to have derived from Philo, the Jew of Alexandria.[14] But it is not the incidental echoing of "die Einheit im Mannigfaltigen" in such Coleridgean topoi as "unity in multëity" or *idem et Alter* that is pertinent here, but rather that a poetic theory is contained within a theological one.

The theological ground is obvious enough in Coleridge's definition of the primary imagination as the participation of "the Finite I am in the Infinite I AM." In his well-known formulation of "that willing suspension of disbelief for the moment which constitutes poetic faith" (*BL* 1:304 and n3 and n4; 2:6 and n2), Coleridge implicates the very tension of disbelief *vs.* faith that he had also discussed in *Statesman's Manual* and *Aids to Reflection*. Mendelssohn precedes Coleridge in linking human creative endeavor to the divine act of creation. The godlike power of the artist, of course, is an age-old concept, evident in the myth of the fire that Prometheus stole from the gods and gave to man, in the belief of divine inspiration in the *furor poeticus*. Plato, unfolding the Eleusinian Mysteries, and Augustus, describing the City of God, went further than mere analogy, and sought to clarify the mental steps by which individual consciousness could participate in the divine. Mendelssohn and Coleridge translated that endeavor in terms supported by contemporary philosophy. Defined as a mediation of divine power, the work of art becomes subject to a theologized aesthetic.

That the poet participated in the divine act of creation Coleridge affirmed in defining the primary imagination as "a repetition in the finite mind of the eternal act of creation in the infinite I AM." That same "living Power," Coleridge also stated, is not achieved exclusively in the lofty flights of the mind, but is in fact "the prime Agent of all human perception." The very moment of sensory apprehension is a threshold revelation of divine creative power. When Mendelssohn, in Lecture X, similarly argued the coincidence of the finite and infinite, he insisted that idealism and common sense are matters of perspective, both relying on the same facilities of sensory perception (*MS* 130–136; *GS* 3.2:81–87). If the imagination mediates divine power, what holds that power in check? What restraint, or constraint, keeps the work of art from fostering mass hallucination (*MS* 130–136; *GS* 3.2:81–87)?

Mendelssohn's answer, subsequently elaborated by Coleridge, Keble, and the critics of the Oxford Movement, was that the divine power keeps itself in check.[15]

Mendelssohn began his *Morgenstunde* with a modest jest at Kant's presumption of cosmos-altering power. He can resist the "works . . . of the all-becrushing Kant" ("die Werke . . . des alles zermalmenden Kants"), Mendelssohn confesses, only because he knows them only through the reviews and the reports of friends (*MS* 2; *GS* 3.2:3). Although mocked by Jacobi,[16] Mendelssohn's phrase was happily adopted by Coleridge, first in describing his own theory of the supernatural, and then in appraising Wordsworth's theory of poetic style as "the real language of men." Not as radically disparate as they might seem, "alles zermalmenden" in all three contexts refers to a theory that totally reconstructs perception. Just as Kant had declared that his *Kritik der reinen Vernunft* had brought about a Copernican revolution of the mind,[17] Coleridge's theory of apparitions decentered the phenomena of ghosts, attributing their origin to bodily cramps and pains as a species of somnambulism.[18] In describing Wordsworth's theory of poetic language, Coleridge is also prompted to think of "the striking but untranslatable epithet, which the celebrated Mendelssohn applied to the great founder of the Critical Philosophy '*Der alleszermalmende* Kant', i.e., the all-becrushing, or rather the *all-to-nothing-crushing Kant*" (*BL* 2:89).

How all-becrushing is Wordsworth's theory? By referring to John Milton and drawing example from Thomas Gray, Wordsworth seemed to extend his theory far beyond his own poetic experiment of adapting "subjects from low and rustic life." The poet could not have intended, Coleridge immediately adds, to mandate a theory thus "over-whelming in its consequences." In advocating a "language of nature," free of "false and showy splendour," Wordsworth's "predilection, at first merely comparative, deviated for a time into direct partiality." His "real object," however, is the language of "apt expression of thought." With Campbell and Blair, the advocates of "natural language" did not hold that a primal Adamic link between words and things might be restored; however, they did believe that an associative use of words might attain a closer bond between words and thoughts.[19] Not the arguments of the associationist rhetoricians, but rather the critical principles of Christian Garve, professor of philosophy at Leipzig, inform Coleridge's exposition on affirmation of lucidity in expression as desideratum (*BL* 2:90). But even here, he raises doubts about any reliable bridge between thoughts and their objects, between signs and things signified.

This is essentially the same skepticism that Mendelssohn had voiced about the attempt to define truth as the coincidence, or relative agreement, of word, concept, and thing: "Since our thoughts correspond to a certain extent to their objects in the same way as signs to things signified, some have tried to apply this explanation universally and to define truth as the agreement of words, concept, and things" (*MS* 7; *GS* 3.2:10). Coleridge's marginal note to this passage not only elaborates on Mendelssohn's reservations about the efforts of "some . . . to apply this explanation universally," but he goes on to anticipate the alternative that Mendelssohn was to propose:

> Instead of Things and Matters of Fact put Ideas and the Verities of Reason on the one hand, and (on the other) the Perceptions and the Forms of Sense, under the conditions taught by Experience—and the correspondence of Words to Conceptions, and of these to the Realities of Sense and Reason is no bad answer to the question What is Truth?, i.e. relatively to the Human Mind. Relatively to God the Question has no Meaning or admits but of one reply— viz. God himself. God is the Truth—i.e. the Identity of Thing and Thought, of *Knowing* and *Being*. (*M* 3:848–849)

In "What Is Truth?," the first lecture of *Morgenstunden*, Mendelssohn discusses how appearances and misapprehensions (*Schein und Irrtum*) distort perception and reason. If Coleridge has not read the entire work before writing his marginalia, he is remarkably prescient about the structure of Mendelssohn's argument. Coleridge in his earlier note, before Mendelssohn formulated his distinction between reason as the process and understanding as the product of divine knowing, had already asserted that the distinction between reason and understanding were crucial to any argument on God's existence. In Mendelssohn's formulation, the division between reason and understanding arose from human limitations, while the two are ever synthesized in divine consciousness. Granting the divine "Identity of Thing and Thought, of *Knowing and Being*" before Mendelssohn proposes it, Coleridge readily endorses the argument that he was to elaborate in Chapter 12 of the *Biographia Literaria* (1:285–286).

To be sure, Coleridge gives his version a Kantian spin by invoking the discrimination of *Vernunft* and *Verstand*. Nevertheless, he shifts the ground of "Things and Matters of Fact," precisely as Mendelssohn was to do, from the realm of objects to the phenomenal realm of "Perceptions and the Forms of Sense." Words relate not to objective things, Coleridge argues, but to the perceptions and conceptions formed through reason and experience. Thus, in a postscript to his note, he also observes that as mental phenomena the "Realities of Reason" have a coequivalent status with the "Realities of Sense." Both are the "Things" of deliberation:

> I see no sufficient cause, why the Realities of Reason might not be called Things as well as the Realities of Sense, in this connection at least. If so, the coincidence of the Word, the Thought, and the Thing would constitute Truth, in its twofold Sense of Insight, and the adequate Expression of the same. (*M* 3:849)

The coequivalence of "Realities of Reason" and "Realities of Sense" may seem to allow the one to confirm the other. Neither, however, is infallible. Coleridge, in his *Logic*, reviews David Hume's account of the speculative ground of inductive reason and goes on to describe the always inadequate comprehension of causality that baffles what is "brought together by luck or chance during the hunt of induction while the mind is beating about for *most general* turns—or (what it may please to consider) *pure* conceptions—without any ground of certainty that the induction is complete" (*Logic* 195–197; 267). Mendelssohn's second lecture, on Cause and Effect, Ground and Force, similarly traces the inherent fallibility of inductive reasoning, with the significant difference that Mendelssohn places less trust in causal association and more in rational induction. Learning by association is commonplace in training animals: even pigs or chickens learn to respond to the farmer's call. Because not all apparent links between cause and effect are necessary links, it is the task of induction to determine which sequentially associated factors are more permanently binding. To dismiss induction altogether would undermine science; at the other extreme, too generous an acceptance of inductive propositions would turn logic into the plaything of sophists. An informed induction seeks to discriminate factors of sequential with an understanding of how the apparent causal relationship might operate. The link between cause and effect must be informed by discerning the operative laws (e.g., of mechanics, or chemistry, or medicine). Those laws are what Mendelssohn comprehends as Ground and Force—as in the laws of gravity or magnetic attraction (*MS* 21–24; *GS* 3.2:18–19).

Coleridge mistrusts even the relative confidence that Mendelssohn places in induction. When Mendelssohn claims that the argumentative force (*Ueberführungskraft*) of induction provides a "ground for conviction" (*Grund der Ueberzeugung*), Coleridge objects that Mendelssohn has confused logical persuasion with "certainty." Mendelssohn writes:

> Not that this incomplete induction lacks persuasive power or evidence; in many cases, on the contrary, it completely suffices to provide full certainty and remove all doubts. Each of us expects with indubitable certainty, for example, that he will die, although the certainty is grounded only on incomplete induction. (*MS* 26–27; *GS* 3.2:21)

In his response to this passage, Coleridge notes that "induction is always incomplete!" But his main objection is to Mendelssohn's claim for "full certainty":

> I do not at present recollect any German word fully answering to our "Positiveness"—"I am positive"—but I suspect that my beloved Mendelsohn has here confounded Positiveness with CERTAINTY: or rather the Twilight between both with the full Light of the Latter. (*M* 3:849)

The English use of "positive," as derived from the literal sense of the Latin *posituus*, meant "settled" "agreed or decided upon," and thus in common usage a synonym for "certain." Coleridge insists upon desynonymizing, not simply because the Latin sense of positing implicated an arbitrary imposition, but also because the term was anchored in deliberative process. He was quite willing, therefore, to accept a "positive" status for "matters of fact," for facts, as determined by the observation and understanding of objective circumstances, have useful but tentative reliability in the progress of science. "Certainty" is a word that Coleridge wishes to use exclusively for the intuitive truths of the mind.[20] Thus in his annotations to *Colloquia mensalia* (1652), he approves Martin Luther's assertion that "the Holie Spirit is the certaintie in the Word towards God, that is, that a man is certain of his own mind and opinion." Doctor Hennage objects that, were this true, then "all Sects have the H. Ghost, for they will needs bee most certain of their Doctrine and Religion." Coleridge suggests that Luther might well have replied: "*positive*, you mean—not *certain*."

For Mendelssohn, "positive" referred to a correspondence between the individual and the divine consciousness.[21] Even if "positive" could also have meant "settled" or "decided upon" in Mendelssohn's vocabulary, it would not have led him to formulate the contrast that is so important to Coleridge. Mendelssohn argues that because of the limits of human reason, we must be content with that degree of proof that can be provided by "incomplete induction":

> Upon what do we ground our undoubting certainty? Not upon the knowledge of scientific reasoning, but rather upon incomplete induction, which however comes so close to completeness that it is adequate for full conviction. (*MS* 26–27; *GS* 3.2:21)

In moral and spiritual matters, Mendelssohn argues, our reasoning is pushed beyond the objective realm of empirical observation into a mixed venture of seeking correspondences between the real and the not real, so that our knowledge must be of a mixed composition (*MS* 27; *GS* 3.2:21).

Coleridge, too, had occasion to acknowledge that his "facts" were not as empirically accurate as he had supposed: thus he altered his footnote on the electricity of the marigold in his poem, "Shurton Bars," and also the line, the "furrows followed free," in *The Rime of the Ancient Mariner*. His concern with "matter of fact" had been altered not only by Hume's stance on inductive reasoning, but also by Hume's challenge to the reliability of "testimony" and "witness."[22] As he noted in his essay "On Certainty," the "matter of Fact" tended to retreat under scrutiny. It became a noumenal "Ding-an-sich" that could be posited only tentatively. His desynonymization of "Positiveness" and "Certainty," of "Belief" and "Faith" are attributes of his persistent anxiety about truth-claims (e.g., *CN* 3592n.).[23] In attempting to establish a scale of possible factuality or degrees of truth, he finds the distinction between "Positiveness" and "Certainty" crucial. Even after he explains the distinction, as in his marginalia to Luther and to Mendelssohn, not the terms but the phenomena they describe seem to shade into each other. Coleridge's desynonymization of "Positiveness" and "Certainty" is grounded on the discrimination of *Verstand* and *Vernunft*. What Coleridge called "Matters of Fact" were those experiences derived from "the Perceptions and the Forms of Sense" that enabled one to declare, "I am positive"; they had no relation whatsoever to those "Verities of Reason" that empowered one to say, "I am certain."

In distinguishing "the feeling of postiveness from the sense of certainty," "the blessedness of Certainty contrasted with the Bubble-bubble of *Positiveness*," Coleridge aligns "postiveness" with ephemeral physical sensation and feeling, "certainty" with an abiding intuitive sense. Those who have "seen, felt, & known the Truth" necessarily know, too, that "reality is a phantom, & virtue & mind the soul actual & permanent Being." Disputation and proselytism, Coleridge asserts, undermine "certainty" by stirring the emotions: "I might lose my Tranquillity, & in acquiring the *passion* of proselytism lose my *sense* of conviction / I might become *positive*! Now I am *certain*! I might have the *Heat* of Fermentation, now I have the warmth of Life."[24] From "eloquent books" one can be led to feel "all the fermenting & busy heat of utmost positiveness," but the shallow ephemerality of that positiveness is revealed when the same person is "made to demonstrate a problem of geometry, feels the sense of *certainty*, & finds no difficulty save in words to distinguish it infallibly from the sensation of postiveness."[25] As he formulated the distinction in a letter to Thomas De Quincey, "I can affirm with a *sense* of *certainty* intuitively distinguished from a mere delusive *feeling of Positiveness*."[26] In his Lectures on Philosophy, it was Coleridge's particular praise for Socrates that his "great object was to withdraw men from vain speculations beyond their powers to the practical duties of life, but to prevent especially that feverish positiveness that so often deludes minds under their best impulses into the worst actions, to teach men what a difference there is between positiveness and certainty."[27] Even though he emphasizes "how distinct and different the sensation of positiveness is from the sense of certainty," and insists that it is a difference not in degree but "a difference in *kind* between the *sense* of certainty and the *sensation* of positiveness," Coleridge nevertheless confesses that "certainty" eludes him: "how many years I have been toiling thro' mist and twilight; but I have not a fuller conviction of my own Life than I have of the Truth of my present convictions."[28]

In spite of his distinction, then, Coleridge is still left with the inherent tentativeness of both "Positiveness" and "Certainty." The truth-claims are always speculative and provisional. Hume argued that the connection between cause and effect could be demonstrated, repeatedly demonstrated, but never conclusively proven to be always and everywhere valid. Much of the assurance that arises from our experience of cause and effect derives from assumptions of probability; indeed, because of the fallibilities of memory and reasoning, all knowledge degenerates into probability.[29] Hume thus undermined the binding validity of inductive reasoning. Once it was observed that an inductive premise was often contained within a deductive syllogism, deduction, too, was pushed into the margins of conditional speculation.[30] Coleridge wanted to escape Humean skepticism by claiming an intuitive ground for certainty. Mendelssohn was content play to the game of chance and ground his knowledge on the accumulation of corroborative evidence:

> Out of the abundance of correspondences that I have experienced, I anticipate in similar cases similar correspondence, with more or less evidence in relation

to greater or fewer cases in which I experience the correspondence. (*MS* 20; *GS* 3.2:17)

Mendelssohn did not abandon the efforts of apodeictic reasoning; he simply adopted a degree of Humean skepticism:

> Is a system of final causes subject to an apodeictic proof? That is, may a single fact be adequate to direct us along a scientific path that is grounded on a final cause? Or, whether an abundance of single cases must not be gathered to an apparent induction and thus provide us with certainty?[31]

Mendelssohn was reconciled to a relative rather than an absolute certainty because human reason had no available alternative: it could lead us to an awareness of divine reason in the universe, but it would take divine reason itself to comprehend divine reason (*MS* 86–87, 189; *GS* 3.2:55, 115).

In his marginalia, Coleridge persists in questioning Mendelssohn's assumptions about the "degree of certainty" available through the inductive process. Citing as example the observation that iron expands when exposed to heat, Mendelssohn concludes:

> Having seen bodies expand every time they are brought nearer to the fire, we connect the cause of the expansion with the constant properties of fire; we attribute to fire a power to expand bodies; and we expect from fire and bodies just that effect which we have never experienced before. The degree of certainty increases the more instances we observe; and when the number of instances is quite large [. . .] it is hardly distinguishable from complete evidence. (*MS* 33; *GS* 3.2:25)

Coleridge counters with an opposite case to demonstrate that experience might lead us to assume a false inductive premise:

> and yet still in the Dark! Thus, the Heat that expands Iron, contracts Clay, even in its purest state, and after it has been deprived of all accidental moisture: & without any answering ponderable Results which might account for its Shrinking in magnitude by its diminution in Quantity—It is possible, that Experiments have not been duly instituted, but I speak of our present knowledge as dependent on INDUCTION. (*M* 3:850)

The quarrel, however, is not simply with the reliance on inductive logic, but with Mendelssohn's effort to build an analogical argument upon inductive premises. To Mendelssohn's example of an ability to deduce the quality (not only its freshness, but also its taste and nutritional value) from the exterior appearance, color, and feel of a loaf of bread (*MS* 33–34; *GS* 3.2:25), Coleridge objects that Mendelssohn is confounding the deliberative process:

> But surely this is a false Creation of a *Thing* out of an aggregate of Effects— and what more does the sane Idealist plead for, than 1. an X Y Z for the

Objects, or Things in themselves—and 2. the analogy from the one thing known (Life, Consciousness) to the Unknown?

When Mendelssohn goes on to discuss ways in which various kinds of evidence from the senses may produce in the mind degrees of conviction approaching certainty, Coleridge reiterates his distinction between "Postiveness" and "Certainty":

> Still I find the confusion between a *sensation* & a *sense*. The *Sensation* I call Positiveness: the *Sense* Certainty—Now between these the difference is not only perceptible but I have an insight into their essential disparity. In problems of the absolute Infinite the *sense*, or Insight, is directly opposed to the Sensation. (*M* 3:850)

Although "*Sense* Certainty" sounds as if it might be akin to Hegel's "sinnliche Gewißheit," actually it is just the opposite. It was Coleridge's "Positiveness," acquired through reliance on sensory evidence, that approximated what Hegel meant by "sinnliche Gewißheit." For Coleridge, "Sense Certainty" was a matter of intuitive reason. Implicated in Coleridge's contrast between Positiveness and Certainty is the equally important contrast between Sensation and Sense, and in the above note he emphasizes that contrast: *Sense* leads to Certainty, which is Insight, and is therefore "directly opposed to the Sensation."

While it would not be proper to assume that Coleridge annotated only those ideas in Mendelssohn with which he disagreed, it must be noted that he inserts no notes at all in many of the chapters which would seem close to his own ideas. Coleridge leaves no marginalia on chapter 3 (on evidence—of sensation and of reason), chapter 4 (on Truth and Illusion), chapter 5 (on Being, Waking, Dreaming, Ecstasy), chapter 6 (Association of Ideas and Idealism), chapter 7 (Debate between Idealists and Dualists—drive for truth as opposed to drive to approve or confirm). There are a few interspersed notes to chapter 8 and to chapters 12 and 13, but none to chapter 9 (Evidence in Physics compared to Evidence in the Proof of God's Existence), chapter 10 (Reason and Common Sense; Proof of God's Existence by the Idealists from our own existence; ideal being and objective world of the senses), or chapter 11 (Epicurianism; Accidence; Cause and Effect; Infinitude, forwards and backwards; Timeless, without beginning or end or continuation).

The first seven chapters are the series of lectures on "Foreknowledge of Truth, Appearance, and Error." The second section of *Morgenstunden*, chapters 8 through 27, are the lectures expounding Mendelssohn's proof, his "Scientific Exposition of the Being of God." Chapter 8, the introductory lecture to this section, argues the importance of the endeavor to affirm a divine Creator and appeals, perhaps with a deliberate sense of the controversial implications, to the unorthodox theology of Johann Bernhard Basedow (1723–1790), who postulated the "Duty of Faith" as a necessary condition of human happiness. In this lecture, too, Mendelssohn develops his argument for "positive thinking" as an alignment of human thought with divine consciousness.[32] At the close of this lecture, Mendelssohn appends seven axioms that assert that Truth can only be determined through "positive thinking." As his culminating example, Mendelssohn gives as analogy the universality of gravity:

> If, for example, matter can just as well have or not have universal gravity, then the statement "All matter has gravity" can be true only in so far as, thus and not otherwise, without regard to time and place, it [gravity] is recognised and confirmed as the best [explanation]. Thus Gravity becomes a general law of nature. (*MS* 120; *GS* 3.2:75)

Coleridge apparently supports Mendelssohn's argument for his gloss to the final axiom is an attempt to make it stronger. The weakness in the argument is the continued reliance on induction, as if the Truth of gravity was ratified by repeated experience and by consensus of opinion:

> How is Matter conceivable without or rather, what is Matter but, the synthesis of its essential component Powers, Attraction and Repulsion? Take A. as Thesis and R. as Antithesis; and again Rep. as Thesis and Attraction as the Antithesis: the Synthesis, (= Gravity, is) of ~~of~~ ideal (& therefore, if matter exist, no less of physical) necessity. Its existence has its cause in the will of God; but its essence has its ground in his Being or Nature. (*M* 3:851)[33]

Rather than opposing Mendelssohn's analogy, Coleridge sought to give it greater relevance by shifting from the matter-based physics of the eighteenth century to the more current energy-based physics. He confirms a pervasive energy both as a manifestation of the infinite will and as the ground for all material appearance.

An eighteenth-century philosopher should not be faulted for persisting in an eighteenth-century mode of thought. But Coleridge may have felt a degree of frustration in Mendelssohn's conformity to the truisms of his age. In discussing probability and chance (chapter 12), Mendelssohn seems to reduce to mere verbal quibbles the apparent disruption of causal necessity by the unpredictability of "accidence." Chance, he argues, occurs somewhere and sometime; necessity prevails always and everywhere. Chance is an aberration of a particular time and place; causal necessity is the operative scheme of the best and most perfect. This, of course, leads Mendelssohn to reiterate Voltaire: "Dans ce meilleur des mondes possibles [. . .] tout est au mieux."[34] Because all existence is the manifestation of divine will, "Alles was ist, ist das Beste" (*MS* 153; *GS* 3.2:75). This unbounded optimism prompts Coleridge to demur. When Mendelssohn declares that he recognizes "no other freedom either for man or for God himself than that which depends on the knowledge and choice of the best," Coleridge wonders how Mendelssohn might account for evil: "The power to perceive, to sanction, and to choose this best is true freedom, and a power to act contrary to this knowledge, sanction, and choice is, in my opinion, an utter impossibility" (*MS* 158; *GS* 3.2:98). Even if "Satan & his Crew" were nothing but a myth, Coleridge counters, there are in this "best of all possible worlds" perpetrators of vile crimes:

> But, dear and revered Mendelsohn! what were the result, if instead of applying this Position to God, and to good & wise men, you had considered it in its relations to wicked Intelligences? Satan & his Crew you perhaps would have non suited with a good-natured Smile of Unbelief; but Caesar Borgia, or (for you are still alive in my mind, dear Mendelsohn!) Talleyrand, Buonaparte?— Would it not end in reducing Guilt to innocent error? (*M* 3:851)

Coleridge may be right to chide Mendelssohn's optimism, but he is wrong in assuming that Mendelssohn would absolve guilt as mere "innocent error." Mendelssohn does indeed recognize evil, not as innocent error but as ignorant perversity. The key term here is "Freedom," which he applies only to acts based on "knowledge, sanction, and choice." Such acts are inevitably benevolent. In acts of evil or malevolence, one of those three factors is faulty or inadequate.[35]

The grounds for affirming identity were much debated in contemporary philosophy. Descartes's *cogito ergo sum* provided one formulation for positing material being through the activity of the conscious self; Berkeley's *esse est percipe* turned that formulation around so that material being was equated with the activity of the perceiving mind. Hume challenged the philosophical assumption that personal identity, an essential self, was available through consciousness. Coleridge, who in chapter 12 of the *Biographia Literaria* constructed from a pastiche of quotations from Schelling an elaborate argument on how perception leads to apperception, was clearly disappointed that Mendelssohn in chapter 12 of the *Morgenstunden* seemed to construct the self on a simple act of self-predication and to neglect the process of emergent self-consciousness. Mendelssohn wrote:

> If the conspicuously [sensorily] evident statement "An external world really exists" or . . . the statement "I myself really exist" must be objectively true, then I as subject of this statement must be connected with existence, its predicate, and that which I am, with all my individual characteristics, cannot be conceived without this predicate, for every truth must be capable of apprehension through the positive in the power of thought. (*MS* 160; *GS* 3.2:99)

Coleridge responded:

> Not convincing to me. The "I" is assumed as the Material, and its Existence as the Form. Can any thing be more arbitrary? What if the I be the phaenomenon of the inner Sense? And *I*ing or Self-ponence be as Running, Writing &c? (*M* 3:852)

Coleridge expected Mendelssohn to argue against Hume's denial of an essential self, or Kant's argument that the noumenal self was inaccessible to phenomenal awareness.[36] Perhaps because his own distinction between the "positive" and the "certain" has gotten in the way, Coleridge has missed what he claimed to be looking for: an affirmation of the "I" as "the phaenomenon of the inner Sense." That affirmation is implicated in Mendelssohn's assertion that "every truth must be capable of apprehension through the positive in the power of thought." As already noted, "das Positive der Denkungskraft" was Mendelssohn's version of the "replication in the finite mind of the eternal act of creation in the infinite I AM" (*BL* 1:304). Of Mendelssohn's statements, Coleridge asserts that "The 'I' is assumed as the Material, and its Existence as the Form." He apparently misses Mendelssohn's explanation that the formulation cannot be affirmed in material being. The truth of the above statements are found *not* in the Material, but in the Formal; not in the conceivability of the subject, but in the goodness and perfection that it seeks to comprehend. Were the "I" bound to material form it would be static rather than dynamic. As the mind consciously pursues the "positive," it participates in the process. It is the constant mercurial change that defines (and baffles attempts at fixed definition) conscious identity (*MS* 160–161; *GS* 3.2:99–100).

After Mendelssohn confirms "the subjective consciousness of my changeability," he goes on to assert that "a being who is conscious of its change must actually be changeable." What is important in this argument is not simply the "immediate consciousness" of the inner process of change, but more importantly the growing awareness of the direction of that change (*MS* 161–162; *GS* 3.2:100), a direction freely chosen that brings the finite self in closer accord with the infinite:

> Now, this relative goodness of an accidental being can acquire its reality in no other way but in so far as it serves the purpose of a free cause and thus can be sanctioned by it . . . This free cause cannot itself be accidental. . . . In the end we must therefore return to a necessary being whose reality lies in the conceivability of the subject itself, to a being . . . that exists because it can be conceived. (*MS* 161–162; *GS* 3.2:100)

Coleridge does indeed acknowledge Mendelssohn's argument about the changeability of the self, but "das Positive der Denkungskraft" is dismissed reductively as "moral Determinants":

> Even here I believe myself to detect an equivocation—"That which I was (i.e. felt and did) yesterday, I am not today—but in the position in Time does not diminish the conceivability of the former state. Reverse the position—and the two States remain equally conceivable—Therefore, some other cause must be supposed, and this can be found only in the moral Determinants, for final Causes." Such is M's argument. (*M* 3:853)

Although Mendelssohn clearly stated that the truth was not to be sought in the conceivability of the subject, but in the moral direction of the change, Coleridge glosses the argument as if it were somehow the equivalent of presuming the watch-maker from the watch, the Divine Mechanist from the wondrous complexity of the Machine:

> But (I reply) by *whom* is it conceivable? ~~Or far rather~~ At least *negatively*—i.e. not-*in*conceivable? By *me*. Who know and overlook but a few links in the vast Chain, and these but imperfectly? Be it so. The same would hold good of every ignorant person with respect to the works of a complex Machine. But by the Mechanist? But by an omniscient Mind? And can this be asserted by a Disciple of Leibnitz, Wolf, Baumgarten? And <what becomes> of their favorite Principium indiscernibilium? And after all, is this Denkbarkeit (conceivability) any thing more than the power of repeating the Conceptions, Lung + Heart in the order, H. + L.? (*M* 3:853)

This passage, it will be recalled, was earlier cited as revealing Coleridge's perplexity about Mendelssohn's philosophical position. He has assumed that in Mendelssohn's *Phaedon* and *Morgenstunden* he would encounter a rationalist philosophy akin to Leibniz's *Theodicy* (1710). He is in the hold of this misapprehension when he questions Mendelssohn's apparent disregard for Leibniz's "principium identitatis indiscernibilium," which postulated the impossibility of absolute identity: there are no two things without any difference.[37] Implying that for Mendelssohn "Denkbarkeit" (conceivability) is an act of mental replication or mirroring, Coleridge again misses Mendellssohn's insistence on freedom and choice.

As might be expected, Coleridge exhibits a keen interest in the next lecture (chapter 13), in which Mendelssohn addresses Spinozism, Pantheism, and attempts a refutation of the Spinozan "All is One and One is All." Coleridge is forced here to recognize that Mendelssohn had distanced himself from Leibniz's "Principium indiscernibilium." In the *Biographia Literaria* (chapter 8), Coleridge traces the history of dualism and the doctrine of a preestablished harmony (Harmonia præstabilita) from Descartes, to Spinoza, and then to Leibniz. Although he cautioned "That the system is capable of being converted into an irreligious PANTHEISM," he could not believe that pantheism was "in itself and essentially [. . .] incompatible with religion." He was uncertain, too, whether Spinoza had propagated irreligion in his *Ethics*. His escape from that dilemma of Spinozan pantheism he attributed first to Kant's *Critique of the Pure Reason* and then to Fichte's *Doctrine of Science*.

Mendelssohn distinguishes his own position from Spinoza's by asserting that in addition to the causal purpose of Divine Will, accidence, too, contributes to the manifold substance of the universe. Chaos interpenetrates the Cosmos. The finite being exists only through a dependence on the Infinite, and would be inconceivable without the Infinite, but its subsistence is not necessarily unified with the Infinite. Participation in the Infinite depends on free choice, an act of positive thought: "We live, and toil, and exist, as created by God, but not in God" (*MS* 171; *GS* 3.2:105). The Spinozist, on the other hand, maintains that there is only one Infinite substance: "One is All; or rather the Spinozist says that the whole essence of infinitely many finite things and infinitely many thoughts constitutes *one* single infinite *whole*, infinite in extension and infinite in thought: *all in one*" (*MS* 172; *GS* 3.2:106). Coleridge declares flatly that Mendelssohn "did not understand Spinoza," and he specifically denies Mendelssohn's argument: "that God is the collective or *gesammte Inbegriff*" is a point that "Spinoza repeatedly and earnestly guards against" (*M* 3:854.)[38] When Coleridge describes in *Biographia Literaria* (chs. 8, 9, 10, 22, and 24) his own wrestling with Spinoza, the two key problems are: (1) Spinoza's exclusion of godhead, God a conscious entity; and (2) Spinoza's insistence on the difference between divine and human nature.[39] These are issues that he accuses Mendelssohn of misunderstanding. On the first point Mendelssohn wrote:

> In order to become as closely acquainted with this system as possible, let us not for the moment censure Spinoza for seeming to confuse infinite power with infinite extension. From infinitely many finite thoughts he constructs, so to speak, the infinite in thought. (MS 173; GS 3.2:106)

Coleridge denies "the infinite in thought" that Mendelssohn attributes to the Spinozan Universe:

> All this is false as attributed to Spinozism. M. has confounded with it a quite different System, that of the Anima Mundi, non per se sed ex Harmonia omnium cum omnibus [*World Soul*, <existing> *not through itself but from the harmony of all things with all things*]—a mind the result of an organized Universe—in which God is a coeternal Effect: than which nothing can be more opposite to Spinoza's System. (*M* 3:854)

Mendelssohn is wrong, Coleridge declares. An affirmation of universal consciousness is precisely what is absent from Spinoza's *Ethics*. Mendelssohn goes on to explain the identity and difference in the human relationship with the divine. The absolute All is *self-sustaining*; the individual who participates in this absolute All is merely *self-subsistent*:

> We too admit that such a self-sufficient substantiality can be attributed only to the infinite and necessary being and cannot even be communicated by it to any finite being. Only we distinguish the *self-sustaining* from the *self-subsistent* being. The former is autonomous and needs no other being for its existence. It is, therefore, infinite and necessary; but the self-subsistent being can be dependent in its existence and still be one of the infinite separate beings; that is, one can conceive of beings that do not consist of modifications of another being, but have their own permanence and [capacity for] self-modification. (*MS* 174; *GS* 3.2:106–107)

Coleridge objects that Mendelssohn has failed to define his distinction, and that he errored in attributing consciousness to the Spinozan Absolute:

> Would Mendelssohn have been able to give a distinct Conception of his Fursichbestehende [*self-sustaining*], that was yet not Selbstständige [*self-subsistent*], in any sense different from that in which Spinoza himself admits

it—. Why dwell wholly on one of Spinoza's metaphors, Modification? Does he not admit, that God thinks the Human Soul as [?is] abiding & progressive? Does he deny, that A is A and not B?—Above all, does he not establish an infinite Chasm between God and all finite things?—Assuredly, the defect in Spinoza's System is the impersonality of God—he makes his only Substance *a Thing*, not *a Wil*—a *Ground solely*, & at no time a *Cause*. Now this Mendelssohn has left untouched—The Question which Sp. would put to *M* would be—"If God were to suspend his Power, would that, which now is, still continue to be just as a House after the Death of the Builder?" If he answered, Yes! then indeed there would exist an essential difference between them respecting the aggregate of finite Existents. But then M. would be in opposition to all Philosophers, Jewish & Christian, as well as to Spinoza. (*M* 3:855–856)

Coleridge is certainly right in asserting that Spinoza established a "Chasm between God and all finite things" by emphasizing the difference between the divine and human nature, between infinite substance and finite things.[40] Spinoza does indeed assert that the intellect and will are human properties and do not belong to the essence of God; while individual things cannot be conceived without God, God does not belong to their essence.[41] Mendelssohn interprets Spinoza's discrimination to mean that intellect and will are the peculiarly human endowments necessary to minds that do not possess infinite consciousness, do not know all things, must therefore grapple with error and must make choices. It is precisely this difference which enables Mendelssohn to distinguish the absolute and autonomous divine as *self-sufficient* and the limited and dependent human as nevertheless capable of being *self-sustaining*. Thus Mendelssohn not only answers the Spinozan question whether the universe might continue if the divine power were suspended. In the self-sustaining dependency of individuals, Mendelssohn confirms Spinoza's assertion that "God is not only the cause of things' beginning to exist, but also of their persevering in existing, or (to use a Scholastic term) God is the cause of the being of things."[42] He also avoids Coleridge's own difficulty with the apparently contradictory crux in which Spinoza describes the existence of finite individual things as contingent upon other finite individuals.[43]

What is apparent here is not that Mendelssohn was right and that Coleridge was wrong, but rather that each approached Spinoza from his own philosophical vantage and provided his own interpretation of Spinoza. They differed fundamentally in their discrimination of divine and human nature. Jacobi, far more vigorously than Coleridge, took Mendelssohn to task for his errors in reading Spinoza.[44] Mendelssohn persists in arguing that Spinoza actually meant "substance" to mean "mind":

We have reason to believe that a substantiality of the second order can be attributed to finite contingent beings. . . . If Spinoza does not want to call these substance, because of their half-dependence, then he is merely quarrelling with words. Once the difference in the object is admitted, one should invent a different name for the essence of dependent beings, in order not to leave unperceived a difference that resides in the object; and the dispute is settled. (*MS* 174–175; *GS* 3.2:107)

"Ay! but here is the Rub," says Coleridge (*M* 3:856)—Spinoza did *not* invent a different name. Mendelssohn's discrimination between the *self-subsistent* Absolute and the *self-sustaining* individual allowed him to attribute mind to the latter, and thus posit a human community established through "positive power of thought." But try as he might, he could not ground his own philosophy in Spinoza's *Ethics*. "Instead of proving that all self-subsistent things are only One, Spinoza merely establishes in the end that all self-sustaining things are only One" (*MS* 175; *GS* 3.2:107). Coleridge rightly observes that here it is Mendelssohn, not Spinoza, who "plays with words":

> What does M. mean by Eins? Sp. meant by one, that which being conceived all other things are conceived in it: that which must be conceived, whenever one thing is conceived. Thus, my Thoughts & my Mind are *one*: not that I therefore think my Mind the mere Aggregate or generic Term of all my Thoughts. (*M* 3:856)

Mendelssohn, of course, meant this sort of Oneness, but he could not, nor could Coleridge, find in Spinoza the affirmation that the finite mind participated in the infinite mind. Human beings, as "self-sustaining things," could form only the Oneness of community.

Mendelssohn continues the debate on pantheism in chapter 14, to which Coleridge adds no annotations. Mendelssohn concludes that pantheism need not be at odds with theism as long as consciousness is granted. In chapter 15, he turns to Lessing's interpretation of pantheism, which sustains the Logos as expression of divine consciousness and grants, too, the filiation of the divine Son, and thus meets the Athanasian expectations of a divine Trinity in which the Holy Spirit is the pantheistic presence on the One in the All (*MS* 221; *GS* 3.2:134).[45] Coleridge responds:

> I should like to hear, what the objections are to this metaphysical Proof of the eternal Filiation of the Logos, a self-comprehending Creator having been assumed. Not surely that the adequate & therefore substantial Idea of God would think a third Idea, and so on ad infinitum? This the co-existence of the Ideat[u]m or Father would preclude: for we suppose a living Intelligence & supreme Wisdom, not a blind Power. (*M* 3:856)

With the negation, "Not surely," Coleridge at once raises and denies the objection to this Trinity-engendering pantheism: "what if it keeps on engendering, think a third Idea, and so on ad infinitum?" Coleridge grants, with Mendelssohn, a divine consciousness continually expressing its own creation, naturing its own nature, but he adds that the chaos of unlimited fecundity would be precluded by the inherent sense of wise economy that must belong to "supreme Wisdom."

In chapter 16, Mendelssohn continues his argument on "positive power of thought" as a progressive alignment between individual and divine consciousness. The very fact that the individual mind must struggle to overcome ignorance and the incompleteness of self-knowledge becomes a ground for positing a complete and perfect knowledge in God. Coleridge's attention in this chapter seems focused on Mendelssohn's interpretation of language as a human reenactment of the divine creative force. Arguing that "everything that is real must also be able to be thought," Mendelssohn follows Philo's exegesis of Genesis on Adam's giving names to all that God created (*MS* 228; *GS* 3.2:138).[46] Truth must be recognizable through the positive force of our faculty of thought. The senses, however, are not less positive force, than the reason. Both rational and sensory knowledge derive from the same source, and all sensory knowledge is absorbed into rational knowledge (*MS* 229; *GS* 3.2:138–139). The problem, as Coleridge sees it, is that Mendelssohn seems to assume also the converse of his proposition: "everything that is thought must also be real." That is, in affirming the correspondence between word, thought, thing, Mendelssohn seeks to construct a proof of God from the idea of God.

Mendelssohn proposes this thesis:

> A concept must correspond to a thing; every object must be represented in some subject; every model will be reflected in some mirror. A thing without a concept has no reality; reality, unless some being is certain of it, carries not the least degree of evidence and is therefore no reality at all. (*MS* 236; *GS* 3.2:142)

As Coleridge notes, Mendelssohn's rationalism seems to lapse into idealism, and he also seems to confirm Berkeley's *esse est percipe*:

> M. does not defend Idealism: & yet every where I find the Idea identified with the Ideatum, the Begriff (conceptio) with that, of which we have the conception—I can not know A but by the Notion, a—if there were no percipient or thinking Beings, A would not be known—but this of itself proves only that A + a would not exist, not that A would not *be*. There may be other proofs of this; but M's is not. (*M* 3:857)

Coleridge is not incorrect in his appraisal here, but he provides a more accurate appraisal when he recognizes that, for Mendelssohn, language provides the necessary mediation between the *esse* and *percipe* of Berkeley's dictum. But in chapter 16, Mendelssohn does not clarify the role of mediating language. He writes, rather, of perception as providing an apparently unconditioned mediation between thing and thought, object and subject:

> All possibilities thus have their ideal existence in the thinking subject, which ascribes them to the object as conceivable. A possibility that is not conceived [by a subject] is an utter absurdity. . . . Therefore all real things must not only be *conceivable* but also must be *conceived* by some being. Each real existence has a corresponding ideal existence in some subject; each thing has a

corresponding conception. Without being perceived nothing is perceptible; without being observed there can really be no mark, and without a concept no object. (*MS* 241–242; *GS* 3.2:145)

Coleridge objects that relation between concept and object is far more complex than Mendelssohn grants:

> Mend. evidently grounds his Position on the inherence of the Thing in the Thought: for supposing them separate, & simply correspondent, as my face to the Image in the Looking-glass, it is absurd to say that my face would not exist or be if there were no Looking-glass. Instead of being an argument therefore from Realities, it is in fact only an argument against them, in any other sense than as modes of mind. For the whole amounts to no more than the impossibility of conceiving a thing per se unconceived—i.e. conceived and not conceived. It would have been far better therefore to have begun with the thesis—We can attach no meaning to the term, *Thing, separated* from Thought—or that all *possibility* (or by the bye, the German seems to have led M. into an Equivoque, for I should have said, *Potentiality*) is the mere application of Time and Space to Objects—I know Iron, I know Caloric—They are now together & there is a Fluid. I withdraw the latter—there is a solid. I apply to the Objects before me future Time—& imagine the same space to both—and say, Fusion is a potentiality of this Iron.—But Time & Space are forms of Perception—ergo, &c.—But a plain man would answer: Tho' we cannot know any thing but by knowing it, yet having thus known its existence we at the same time learn that it would have been tho' we had not known it. (*M* 3:858)

Coleridge's point is that knowledge does not spring full-blown like Athena from the head of Zeus, but involves tentative conjectures, speculations and probings. On the other hand, it is Coleridge, not Mendelssohn, who upholds intuitive "Certainty."

Although Mendelssohn does not refer to intuition, and speaks only in passing of the possibility of having a rational presentiment (*MS* 24; *GS* 3.2:20), he does argue in chapter 17 that the existence of God as perfect, necessary, and independent Being, is an *a priori* concomitant of the same self-recognition of imperfection, accidence, and dependency that gives rise to the possibility of a "positive force in thinking." Mendelssohn cites Descartes's proof:

> In place of the necessary being he [Descartes] put the infinite, the perfect being. It is evident that the necessary being cannot have changeable bounds and therefore must possess all perfections in the highest degree. In the idea of a necessary being thus resides the essence of all perfect qualities with which a being can be endowed. Now, Descartes further concludes, existence is really a perfect quality of things; thus the concept of the necessary being must also include the perfection of existence; thus the necessary being must really exist. (*MS* 247; *GS* 3.2:149)

In the previous chapter, he acknowledged the word *dependent* (*abhängig*) carried with it an inherent metaphor of *dangling* from some higher being, and the word necessary (*notwendig*) from its metaphor of *Not*—a dire need that imposes compelling force. Liberated from their etymological origins, the words become synonymous, and must again be differentiated (*MS* 229; *GS* 3.2:138). Mendelssohn wants to keep the metaphors operative, yet grant to both conditions, *Abhängigkeit* and *Notwendigkeit*, an awareness of, and a freedom to strive toward, their contrary conditions. Coleridge's response is that the Cartesian Proof is merely a verbal play with the two words:

> I could never discover in the Cartesian Proof more than this: If I have a clear conception of a necessary Being, i.e. that which cannot be thought of otherwise than as existing: then I must conceive his Existence.—But what compels me to assume a necessary Being? Whatever that be, must, methinks, have anticipated this Proof. If there be any thing at all, it must be either dependent or independent: if the former, there must be the latter, for omne quod dependet, dependet *ab* aliquo ["Everything that is dependent is dependent on <*from*> something"; the preposition *from*, because "depend" means literally "hang down from"] if the latter, it is of itself. What does the Cartesian Proof add to this; but a Verbal Interpretation of a Necessary Being?—or substitute "all-perfect"—"God has all perfections; but Existence is a Perfection; therefore, God exists." Yes! if it be first proved, 1. that every clear idea has its correspondent Ideatum or Reale ["object" or "realization"], and 2. that we have a clear *idea* of an all-perfect Being, and that what is so called is not a mere series of Ideas abstracted from this and that, and then asserted collectively. (*M* 3:859)

Having already objected that Mendelssohn oversimplified the relation between concept and object, Coleridge again emphasizes the disparity between words, things, and thoughts. A degree of coincidence is possible, sometimes apprehended intuitively, often evolved only through the trial-and-error of learning. Having the concept of a thing, does not mean that the thing exists. Coleridge thus modifies the Cartesian Proof, but dismisses the modification as well:

> it would seem that the Position ought to run thus:—The Idea of God implies all perfections: ergo, Existence as being a perfection. Consequently, in the Idea of God I have the Idea of his Existence. But the BELIEF therefore? Does that necessarily follow?—I have a distinct Idea, whenever I chuse to have it, of a Chain of Mountains in the planet Jupiter 8 times higher than the Andes—the *Idea* of its being there is of course the *Idea of its* being there; but not the Belief. (*M* 3:859)

Discriminating the act of *believing* from the act of *knowing*, Coleridge reopens his own case for Certainty as opposed to Positiveness:

> if by Idea be meant a clear perception of the Actuality of the Thing, then again it is a mere lazy Truism.—The thing to be proved is, not that the Idea of God involves the Idea of his Existence, but that the Idea of God contains in itself the Belief in that Idea. Now this seems to contradict the essential meaning of

> Belief: which is always a something added to, not contained in, an Idea or Conception.—Again, it would require proof that Intellect & Will were Perfections—i.e. positive Attributes, and not (as Spinoza believed himself to have demonstrated) the result of Limitation & Modification[47]—It would require Proof that the Universe is any thing but its constituent Laws—& that these Laws are not the necessary Being. (*M* 3:859)

Mendelssohn, as previously observed, did not make the mistake of trying to define Intellect or Will as attributes of the Absolute Perfection. Not God, but the dependent and fallible human being needs Intellect to discern and understand the surrounding world; not God, but the capricious human being needs Will to choose goals and actions.

Coleridge's more serious charge, however, is that Mendelssohn is inconsistent in arguing the relationship of thoughts, words, and things. The idea of a thing often becomes confounded in Mendelssohn's argument with the thing itself. Further, Mendelssohn gives credit to a verbal affirmation of being as ratification. "I see a tree" is a statement of sensory experience. An alternate phrasing, "Here is a tree," transforms the statement into a rational deduction that comprehends time, place, and essence (the nature of the tree) (*MS* 230; *GS* 3.2:139). That ratification is compromised if the declarative sentence is transformed into a conditional one: "There may be a tree here" (to be determined when the sun rises, or when we can see on the other side of this large rock), or "This tree may bear fruit" (the tree is affirmed; the fruit is only a possibility). Mendelssohn implicates language to escape the limitations of *esse est percipe*. Language can posit the possibility of being beyond perception. The Berkeleyan question "If a tree falls in the woods" implicates a possibility rather than a negation.[48] Statements of possibilities, even though they may approach the truth, remain possibilities. Some statements, however, may pose as mere possibilities a real and actual predicate: "This tree may bear fruit" is immediately ratified when closer inspection reveals the apples hidden in the leaves (*MS* 237–238; *GS* 3.2:143–144).

When Mendelssohn argues that a being could not exist as "a concept without an object," Coleridge agrees. But he also counters that the *idea* of a being might well exist without an object. Mendelssohn wants the words, the verbal predication, to serve as confirmation of reality:

> If then the union of all affirmative predicates or perfections is not inconceivable, and if existence manifestly belongs to the essence of all perfections, it can be correctly inferred that ∧ existence is inseparably linked to the concept of the infinite or the supreme perfection. (*MS* 248–249; *GS* 3.2:150)

Coleridge inserts a hatchet into Mendelssohn's text before word "existence," and supplies the necessary modification: "∧ The concept of existence, not existence" (∧ der Begriff der Existenz, nicht die Existenz) (*M* 3:860). The word may express the concept, but neither the word nor the concept validates the thing. Mendelssohn persists in arguing the substantive validity of word and thought:

> I can conceive a limited being as a modification of myself without ascribing a real existence to it. . . . The necessary being, on the other hand, either cannot be thought of, can have no reality even as modification of myself, or else I must at least think of it as really existing. (*MS* 250; *GS* 3.2:150–151)

Coleridge expresses his dismay that Mendelssohn holds so stubbornly to his equation of idea and being:

> Still the same (to me almost in(con)ceivable) Sophism. The necessary Being cannot be a modification of my mind; but the Idea of a necessary Being may. Is a Poker and the Idea of a Poker the same? (*M* 3:860)

At this point the dialogue that Coleridge has carried on with Mendelssohn in his annotations to *Morgenstuden* has reached an impasse. Mendelssohn repeats his equation,

> It is utterly impossible that this being should be merely a concept without an object; this being cannot be thought of as mere modification of our thinking power. (*MS* 250; *GS* 3.2:151)

and Coleridge repeats his denial: "Certainly not; but the idea of this Being may" (*M* 3:861).

Coleridge's reception of Mendelssohn's philosophy seemed doomed to end on a negative note, but then he browsed through Mendelssohn's addenda and discovered an idea that he must applaud. The "6th page of the Anmerkungen," he declares, is "excellent" (*M* 3:861).

Mendelssohn has attached the note to a passage in chapter 9, where he first began to argue that the relation of subject to predicate confirms the relation of concept to reality. His examples are the "sentences" of the mathematician:

> Things that are not conceivable at the same time can also not be at the same time really present. Therefore the sentences of the mathematician in relation to actually existing things, under the assumption of their reality, allow that reality to be confirmed with certainty. When the subject is really at hand, then the predicate that provides the confirming sentence, must also arrive at the objective reality; just as the predicate of a negative sentence can also not be attributed to reality. (*MS* 123; *GS* 3.2:76–77)

Here Mendelssohn's claims for the relation of "sentences" to reality is confined to the sign-system of numbers. It is clear that he looks upon the subject–predicate relationship as a logical demonstration: the subject is a subjective concept; the predicate is the assumption or claim of its truth. He then gives the example of the geometrist's use of figures:

> Should a practical use and application be made of his conditional sentences, so must the geomtrist transfer his subject through his sensory knowledge of the

actual being, so that he can confirm his predicate with certainty. If his figure represents a triangle, so it must have the attributes of a triangle; if a sphere is properly represented, it must therefore cast from all sides the same shadow. That the represented triangle is an actual triangle, or that the represented figure an actual sphere, must be accepted by the evidence of the senses. The certainty with which the geometrist proceeds in the exercise of his science is not merely the evidence of pure reason, it is mixed with the reliability of sensory knowledge. (*MS* 123; *GS* 3.2:76–77)

Coleridge also cited how the demonstration of "a problem of geometry" brought about "the sense of certainty."[49] Kant, too, grounded the concepts of geometry in pure reason, and argued that the confirmation had to be "synthetic," relying on sensory experience.[50]

Thus far Coleridge is in complete accord with Mendelssohn. He rejects the argument only when Mendelssohn puts aside the "evidence of the senses" and presumes that the "positive power of thought" alone suffices to confirm the predicate. Although he denies Mendelssohn's willingness to accept the word as the thing, Coleridge fully endorses Mendelssohn's argument on the power of language to alter concepts. It is Mendelssohn's "Anmerkung" to the above passages on the geometrist sentences that Coleridge finds "Excellent." Mendelssohn acknowledges concepts without language. One might have the concept "triangle" as a very clear mental image without having the word "triangle." Mendelssohn also gives the example of having a melody in mind, without knowing musical annotation or having any experience playing a musical instrument. But knowing the words, the language, the relevant sign-system, gives clarity to concepts. The same melody in the mind of a trained musician will be informed by the mastery of musical composition and instrumentation. The triangle in the mind of the geometrist will be informed by the mastery of Euclidian proofs. Concepts may exist without words, but words add determinant boundaries and specificity:

> What do words contribute to abstraction or to clear thinking that makes them seem so necessary? My opinion is that words place every individual concept, otherwise in undetermined abeyance, within specific boundaries, so that mode, kind, degree, class, quality, relation etc. can be distinguished and determined. (*MS* 264–266; *GS* 3.2:160–161)

To the extent that the relationship between the sign and the thing signified is understood as the relationship between the word and the thought, then Mendelssohn's argument for a coequivalency has Coleridge's approval. Words, like the mathematician's numbers and the geometrist's figures, enable the reason to act upon the individual concepts, to give predicates to subjects, to compare and contrast, to formulate connections, relations. From this interaction of words and thoughts, the individual acquires the ability to develop and to communicate positive thinking.

In spite of his frustration with Mendelssohn's insistence that divine Being is proven in the act of verbal predication, and his rejection of Mendelssohn's interpretation of Spinoza, Coleridge maintains an open response to the arguments of *Morgenstunden*. Coleridge is astonished to find that Mendelssohn has expanded his rationalist foundation to appropriate many of the ideas from the idealists, dualists, and pantheists against whom he argues. Mendelssohn's quest for rational certainty prompts Coleridge to engage his own discrimination of "Certainty" and "Positiveness," with the unfortunate consequence that it leads him to overlook the implications of Mendelssohn's crucial formulation of "the positive power of thought." Although sometimes cavalier in his presumption of the naiveté of his "dear and revered Mendelssohn," Coleridge is attentive and, for the most part, reliable in his commentary on the *Morgenstunden*. Mendelssohn may not have exercised any significant influence on Coleridge's own thinking, but he did provide him with a key epithet for the "alles-zermalmenden Kant."

Notes

1. For convenience, a number of abbreviations are used in this chapter. The following indicate works by Samuel Taylor Coleridge.

   AR   *Aids to Reflection*, ed. John Beer, The Collected Works of Samuel Taylor Coleridge, 9 (Princeton: Princeton University Press, 1993).

   BL   *Biographia Literaria*, or, *Biographical Sketches of My Literary Life and Opinions*, 2 vols., ed. J. Engell and W. J. Bate, The Collected Works of Samuel Taylor Coleridge, 7 (Princeton: Princeton University Press, 1983).

   C&S   *On the Constitution of the Church and State*, ed. John Colmer, The Collected Works of Samuel Taylor Coleridge, 10 (London: Routledge, and Princeton: Princeton University Press, 1976).

   CL   *Collected Letters of Samuel Taylor Coleridge*, 6 vols., ed. Earl Leslie Griggs. (Oxford: Clarendon Press, 1956–1971).

   CN   *The Notebooks of Samuel Taylor Coleridge*, ed. Kathleen Coburn and Anthony Harding, 5 vols. (London: Routledge & K. Paul, 1957–1961).

   LS   *Lay Sermons*, ed. R. J. White, The Collected Works of Samuel Taylor Coleridge, 6 (London: Routledge, and Princeton: Princeton University Press, 1972).

   LHP   *Lectures 1818–1819 on the History of Philosophy*, 2 vols., ed. J. R. de J. Jackson, The Collected Works of Samuel Taylor Coleridge, 11 (Princeton: Princeton University Press, 2000).

   LR   *Literary Remains of Samuel Taylor Coleridge*, 4 vols., ed. Hartley Nelson Coleridge (London, 1836–1839).

   M   *Marginalia*, 5 vols., ed. George Whalley and H. J. Jackson, The Collected Works of Samuel Taylor Coleridge, 12 (London: Routledge, and Princeton: Princeton University Press, 1980–2000).

   P Lects *The Philosophical Lectures of Samuel Taylor Coleridge*, ed. Kathleen Coburn (New York: Philosophical Library, 1949).

   PW   *Poetical Works*, 3 vols. in 6, ed. J. C. C. Mays, The Collected Works of Samuel Taylor Coleridge, 16 (Princeton: Princeton University Press, 2001).

SWF   *Shorter Works and Fragments*, ed. H. J. Jackson and J. R. de J. Jackson, The Collected Works of Samuel Taylor Coleridge, 8 (London: Routledge, and Princeton: Princeton University Press, 1995).

The following abbreviations are used for works by Moses Mendelssohn:

GS   *Gesammelte Schriften*, 7 vols. in 9, ed. G. B. Mendelssohn (Leipzig: Brockhaus, 1843–1845).

MS   *Morgenstunden: oder, Vorlesungen über das Daseyn Gottes* (Berlin: Christian Friedrich Voß, 1786).

For these works, citations are indicated parenthetically in the text.

2. *Phaedon: oder, Über die Unsterblichkeit der Seele, in drey Gesprächen* (Berlin: Friedrich Nicolai, 1767).
3. *Jerusalem, oder über religiöse Macht und Judentum* (Berlin: Friedrich Maurer, 1783).
4. The two volumes of Mendelssohn's *Philosophische Schriften* (1780), also reported to have Coleridge's marginal notes, have not been located. For information on the marginalia, as well as the transcriptions, I am indebted to the commentary and notes by Lore Metzger and Raimonda Modiano (*M* 3:846–861).
5. *M* 3:848 n11: "The distinction between reason and understanding, the cornerstone of Coleridge's philosophy, is expounded especially in *Friend* (CC) 1:154–61 and *AR* (1825) 207–28; the connection between this distinction and proofs of the existence of God is made explicitly in *BL* ch 10 (CC) 1:200–3."
6. *M* 3:848 n12: "In Hume's Dialogues Concerning Natural Religion pt 7, one speaker demonstrates the absurd consequences of the argument from design by suggesting that it validates the ancient Indian theory 'that the World arose from an infinite Spider, who spun this whole complicated Mass from his Bowels. . . . And were there a Planet wholly inhabited by Spiders, (which is very possible) this Inference wou'd there appear as natural and irrefragable as that which in our Planet ascribes the Origin of all things to Design and Intelligence'" (*The Natural History of Religion and Dialogues Concerning Natural Religion*, ed. A. Wayne Colve [Oxford: Clarendon, 1976], 207. Coleridge alludes to this argument in *P Lects*, Lect. 13, 373).
7. Translations are those provided in *M* 846–861.
8. In 1735, Mendelssohn began his studies at the Talmud school in Dessau taught by Rabbi David Frankel, whom he followed to Berlin in 1743, and there pursued a self-directed study in philosophy, mathematics, and languages (Latin, Greek, French, English). See Michael Albrecht, *Moses Mendelssohn 1729–1786. Das Lebenswerk eines jüdischen Denkers der deutschen Aufklärung* (Weinheim: VCH, 1986) [= Ausstellungskataloge der Herzog-August-Bibliothek; 51].
9. In addition to Mendelssohn's *Jerusalem*, his translation, *Die fünf Bücher Mose zum Gebrauch der jüdischdeutschen Nation* (Berlin: Nicolai, 1780) was addressed to German-speaking Jews, and his *Ritualgesetze der Juden: betreffend Erbschaften, Vormundschaftssachen, Testamente und Ehesachen, in so weit sie das Mein und Dein angehen* (Berlin: Voß, 1778) explained Jewish customs to the non-Jewish public. See Allan Arkush, *Moses Mendelssohn and the Enlightenment* (Albany: State University of New York Press, 1994).

10. Coleridge, Marginalia to *Jerusalem*. In his note to a passage in which Mendelssohn discriminates actions vs. beliefs as the grounds for civil punishment, Coleridge asks: "But is not the Propagation of principles subversive of Society itself an Act? Are there none but manual actions? I am convinced that no Theory of Toleration is possible; but that the Practice must depend on Expedience & Humanity." In his discussion of tolerance in *Friend*, 1:96–97, Coleridge asserts "that the only true spirit of Tolerance consists in our conscientious toleration of each other's intolerance"; see also "Treatment of the Jews," *Courier* (June 18, 1814), in *Essays on His Times* 3:144–145.

11. Mendelssohn, *Über die Empfindungen* (Berlin: Christian Friedrich Voß, 1755).

12. Gotthold Ephraim Lessing, Moses Mendelssohn, Friedrich Nicolai, *Briefwechsel über das Trauerspiel*, ed. Jochen Schulte-Sasse (München: Winkler, 1972); see also: Frederick Burwick, "Illusion and the Audience: Lessing, Mendelssohn, and Schiller," in *Illusion and the Drama: Critical Theory of the Enlightenment and Romantic Era* (University Park, PA: Pennsylvania State University Press, 1991), 83–94, 109–116.

13. Mendelssohn, *Betrachtungen über die Quellen und die Verbindungen der schönen Künste und Wissenschaften* (Berlin: Friedrich Voß, 1758), 11–12; *GS* 1:172–173.

14. *BL* 1:279; *M* 1:690 (marginalia to Jacob Boehme); *M* 2:33 (on Arianism); *Opus Maximum* 91–92, 205–208, 233–236, 361–364.

15. The Tractarian doctrine of "reserve" was crucial to the literary criticism of John Keble (1792–1866), who used it to explain the psychology of poetic composition and aesthetics of complementation. Just as God did not declare himself fully in nature but "held back," so poetry could lead to revelation only by indirection. This "holding back," or "reserve," meant that the fullness of creation was "realized" only in the participation of human awareness or consciousness of the creation. Aesthetic complementation, the process of engaging the reader/viewer in the aesthetic process, is deliberately exercised on the tropes of litotes or understatement, but also in hyperbole which open the possibility of endless exaggeration. See Keble, *Di Poeticae Vi Medica* (1844), translated by Edward Kershaw Francis as *Lectures on Poetry, 1832–1841*, 2 vols. (Oxford: Clarendon, 1912), 1:44–48.

16. Friedrich Heinrich Jacobi, *Wider Mendelssohns Beschuldigungen, betreffend die Briefe über die Lehre des Spinoza* (Breslau, 1786), 90: "Wenn doch nur auch Kant, der alles zermalmende, die Morgenstunden lesen, und es einmal mit sich zum Durchbruch kommen lassen wollte!—Ach, und der alte Moses, wenn der doch anstatt seiner Gesetze und unausführlichen Reisebeschreibung Morgenstunden herausgegeben hätte!"

17. Immanuel Kant, "Vorrede zur zweiten Auflage," *Kritik der reinen Vernunft*, in *Werke*, 6 vols., ed. Wilhelm Weischedel (Darmstadt: Wissenschaftliche Buchgesellschaft, 1975), 2:25.

18. *CN* 4046 (January 25, 1811): "Elucidation of my all-zermalming argument of the subject of ghosts & apparitions." Coleridge had read John Ferriar's *The Theory of Dreams: in which an inquiry is made into the Powers and Faculties of the Human Mind* (London: Printed for F. C. and J. Rivington, 1808), but his physiological exposition precedes that proposed by Ferriar in *An Essay Towards a Theory of Apparitions* (London: Cadell and Davies, 1813).

19. See George Campbell, *The Philosophy of Rhetoric* (1776), ed. Loyd Bitzer (Carbondale, IL: Southern Illinois University Press, 1963); Hugh Blair, *Lectures on Rhetoric and Belles Lettres* (1783), 2 vols., ed. Harold Harding (Carbondale, IL: Southern Illinois University Press, 1965); John Cleland, *The Way to Things by Words, and to Words by Things: being a sketch of an attempt at the retrieval of the antient Celtic, or, primitive language of Europe, to which is added a succinct account of the Sanscort, or learned language of the Bramins* (London: Printed for L. Davis and C. Reymers, 1766). Recent commentaries: James McKusick, *Coleridge's Philosophy of Language* (New Haven: Yale University Press, 1986); Jerome Christiansen, *Coleridge's Blessed Machine of Language* (Ithaca, NY: Cornell University Press, 1981); and Robert Essick, *William Blake and the Language of Adam* (Oxford: Clarendon Press, 1989).

20. David Vallins, *Coleridge and the Psychology of Romanticism: Feeling and Thought* (Basingstoke: Macmillan, and New York: St. Martin's Press, 2000). In addressing Coleridge on the unity of thought and feeling, Vallins gives close attention to Coleridge's discrimination of "certainty" and "positiveness" in relation to epistemic judgments and affective responses.

21. The word "positiv" occurs twenty-nine times in *Morgenstunden*; with two exceptions, it is an adjective modifying mental or sensory power ("Kraft," "Sinneskraft," "Erkentnißkraft," "Denkungskraft," "Vernunftkräfte," "Seelenkräfte," "Vermögen"). One exception is a reference to "positive Religion," in contrast to pantheism; the other is a distinction between the positive and negative predicates in logic.

22. Burwick, "Coleridge and De Quincey on Miracles," *Christianity and Literature* 39, 4 (summer 1990): 387–421.

23. Seamus Perry, "Romantic Poetry and the Matter of Fact," unpublished paper delivered at the annual conference of the North American Society for the Study of Romanticism (NASSR), New York, August 2003.

24. *CN* 1:1410 (June 1803); *CN* 2:2643 (August1805); *CN* 2:2196 (October 1804).

25. *CN* 2:3095 (1807); see also *CN* 3:3592 and n.

26. *CL* 3:48; 25, letter of January 1808; see also *CL* 4:571, 750.

27. *LHP* 260, 720. See also: *C&S* 21n; *SWF*: "History of Logic" (1803) 132; and "Summary of the Development of Philosophy" (1818) 696.

28. *Friend* 2:7, 76n.

29. David Hume, *A Treatise of Human Nature*, ed. L. A. Selby-Bigge (Oxford: Clarendon, 1965), 104, 70–73, 153, 180.

30. See Willard Van Orman Quine, "Two Dogmas of Empiricism," *Philosophical Review* 60, 1 (January 1951): 20–43; reprint, *From a Logical Point of View: 9 Logico-Philosophical Essays*, rev. ed. (Cambridge, MA: Harvard University Press, 1961); and "Necessary Truth" (1963), reprint *The Ways of Paradox*, rev. ed. (Cambridge, MA: Harvard University Press, 1976).

31. *An die Freunde Lessings* (Berlin: Nicolai, 1786), 56 [cf. Mauthner-Spinoza, 237].

32. See note 21 above on Mendelssohn's use of the word "positive."

33. The conception of matter as the synthesis of the powers of attraction and repulsion is discussed in a letter of September 1817 to C. A. Tulk (*CL* 4:775) and in Coleridge's Marginalia to Kant, *Metaphysische Anfangsgrunde* (see especially 9 and n1).

34. Voltaire [François-Marie Arouet], *Candide, ou, L'optimisme,* ed. Lester G. Crocker (London: University of London Press, 1958), ch. 1.

35. For a similar argument on the benevolence of freedom, see William Hazlitt's essay "On the Principles of Human Action" (1805), in *The Complete Works of William Hazlitt,* ed. P. P. Howe (London: Dent & Sons, 1930), 1:1–91.

36. Hume, *A Treatise on Human Nature,* 25: "For my part, when I enter most initimately into what I call *myself,* I always stumble upon some particular perception or other . . . I never can catch myself at any time without a perception, and can never observe anything but the perception"; cf. Kant on "Das: Ich denke," *Kritik der reinen Vernunft,* § 16; *Werke* 3:136.

37. Leibniz, "On the Principle of Indiscernibles," in *Leibniz: Philosophical Writings,* ed. and tr. G. H. R. Parkinson and M. Morris (London: Dent, 1973). Leibniz's law is repeated by Alexander Gottlieb Baumgarten in his *Metaphysica* (1757), trans. Georg Friedrich Meier (Halle im Magdeburgischen: C. H. Hemmerde, 1776), Ch. III, Section 2, §§ 270–271.

38. The editors of *M* note that Coleridge makes the same argument against the concept of "die unendliche Eizige Substanz" as posited in Jacobi, *Ueber die Lehre des Spinoza:* "I cannot agree with Jacobi . . . If Insight or Intuition be the highest in the Finite because it passes out of the Finite & partakes of the Infinite, it is impossible that Sp. Should not have regarded the Infinite as identical with it eminenter tho' not formaliter. Nothing does Spinoza more zealously forbid, than the conception of God as an Abstraction or Aggregate or mode of conception or perception" (3:854). The editors also note that Coleridge's dismissal of Mendelssohn's presentation of Spinoza is shared by Harry Wolfson, who declares that "a conception of substance as merely the aggregate sum of the modes is contrary to all the uttered statements of Spinoza" (*The Philosophy of Spinoza* [1934; reprint New York: Meridian Books, 1958], 73; cf. Coleridge in *LHP,* 539, on Kant, Mendelssohn Jacobi).

39. See in this volume the chapter by Stanley J. Spector on "Coleridge's Misreading of Spinoza." In *Biographia Literaria,* Coleridge describes his difficulties with Spinoza's *Ethics:* "I could not reconcile personality with infinity; and my head was with Spinoza, though my whole heart remained with Paul and John" (*BL,* Chapter 10); "in no system is the distinction between the individual and God, between the Modification, and the one only Substance, more sharply drawn, than in that of Spinoza" (*BL,* Chapter 22).

40. *M* 3:855. The editors note that Coleridge reiterated his objections to Spinoza's philosophy in his Marginalia: "Spinoza in common with all the Metaphysicians before him (Bohmen, perhaps, excepted) began at the wrong end—commencing with God as an *Object*" (annotated 1812–1813); also in the 1817–1818 note on Spinoza in BM MS Egerton 1801 f 11, in *SWF:* "he saw God in the ground only and exclusively . . . and not likewise in his moral, intellectual, existential and personal Godhead."

41. Baruch Spinoza, *Ethics,* trans. R. H. M. Elwes (New York: Dover, 1955), pt. 1 prop. 17 cor. 2 scholium, and pt. 2 prop. 10.

42. *Ethics,* pt. 1 prop. 24.

43. *Ethics,* pt. 1 prop. 28; cf. Coleridge's 1812–1813 annotations on Crabb Robinson's copy of Spinoza (*M* 4:382).

44. Kurt Christ, *Jacobi und Mendelssohn. Eine Analyse des Spinozastreits* (Würzburg: Königshausen & Neumann, 1988), 16–19.

45. Mendelssohn cites from Lessing, "Das Christenthum der Vernunft" [aus dem Nachlaß]; see: *Theologischkritische Schriften*, ed. Helmut Göbel, vols. 7 and 8 of *Werke*, ed. Herbert P. Göpfert et al. (Munich: Carl Hanser Verlag, 1970–1979), 8:278–281. Long attributed to St. Athanasius (293–373 C.E.), archbishop of Alexandria, the Athanasian Creed is a concise exposition of the doctrines of the Trinity and the Incarnation of Christ.

46. Philo, of Alexandria, *Questionun et solutionum in Genesin*, in *Philonis Alexandrini Opera quae supersunt*, 7 vols. in 8, ed. Leopold Cohn and Paul Wendland (Berlin: George Reimer, 1896–1915), 2:47.

47. In *M* (3:859), the editors document Coleridge's references to Spinoza: "finite existence involves a partial negation, and infinite existence is the absolute affirmation of the given nature . . ." (*Ethics*, pt. 1 prop. 8); Will and Intelligence do not appertain to the essence of God but "stand in the same relation to the nature of God as do motion, and rest, and absolutely all natural phenomena . . ." (*Ethics*, pt. 1 prop. 32).

48. This question, popularly attributed to Berkeley, does not actually occur in his writings. See, however, his reference to trees in *Principles of Human Knowledge*, Part I, 23; more relevant is this passage from the first of the *Dialogues between Hylas and Philonous*: "*Phil.*: How then came you to say, you conceived a house or tree existing independent and out of all minds whatsoever? *Hylas*: That was I own an oversight; but stay, let me consider what led me into it.—It is a pleasant mistake enough. As I was thinking of a tree in a solitary place, where no one was present to see it, methought that was to conceive a tree as existing unperceived or unthought of; not considering that I myself conceived it all the while. But now I plainly see that all I can do is to frame ideas in my own mind. I may indeed conceive in my own thoughts the idea of a tree, or a house, or a mountain, but that is all. And this is far from proving that I can conceive them" (*A Treatise concerning the Principles of Human Knowledge* [1710]; *Three Dialogues between Hylas and Philonous*, ed. with intro. G. J. Warnock [La Salle, IL: Open Court, 1986], 183).

49. *CN* 2:3095 (1807); see also *CN* 3:3592 and n.

50. Kant, *Kritik der reinen Vernunft*, in *Werke*, 3:57.

CHAPTER 14

STANDING AT MONT BLANC:
COLERIDGE AND *MIDRASH*

Lloyd Guy Davies

Introduction

In the summer of 1802, Samuel Taylor Coleridge hiked in solitude through the mountains of northern England's Lake District for several days. Soon thereafter he composed a poem, based in part on a prior poem, "Chamounix beym Sonnenaufgang," by Friederika Brun (1765–1835), which describes the experience of seeing the rising sun illuminate the alpine peak of Mont Blanc. On September 11, Coleridge published his poem in the *Morning Post*, entitling it "Hymn before Sun-rise, in the Vale of Chamouni."[1] Originally well received (though even then with important criticisms from Charles Lamb and William Wordsworth), it has fallen, in modern times, into disrepute. And indeed, from most contemporary critical perspectives, it is difficult to read "Hymn before Sunrise" with appreciation, sympathy, or understanding. This critical antagonism is, in part, the ideological residue of a modernist antipathy against religious faith, and more specifically, against the biblical faith that the poem so fervently celebrates. But it is nevertheless undeniable that the poem suffers from a number of critical problems, chief among them its plagiarism of Brun's poem, its artificial staging in a location Coleridge had never actually seen, and its forced religious enthusiasm and strident expression of faith. Why did Coleridge transfer the scene from northern England to Switzerland? Why did he not acknowledge his debt to Brun? Why such "hectic rhetoric" in his expressions of religious faith?[2] Why, in sum, the striking lack of personal authenticity in Coleridge's poem?

These questions arise not so much as evidence of a defective or failed poem but rather because they point to legitimate interpretive problems that lie at the heart of Coleridge's poetic strategies. The way toward a resolution of these issues lies in a contextual poetics that can illuminate the appropriate religious, literary, and personal concerns relevant to the poem. "Hymn before Sunrise" should be engaged on its own terms and within its own frames of reference, not subjected to critical categories that Coleridge was deliberately resisting. Too many hostile critics, rather than encountering the poem's problems directly, have simply pronounced a hasty judgment, condemning those problems as defects and finding only failure in the poem's strategies of appropriation. They generally do so by forcing "Hymn before Sunrise" into the aesthetic constraints of an eighteenth-century naturalistic empiricism that Coleridge rejected and that his poem itself subjects to critical skepticism.

The aesthetic empiricism of the eighteenth century arose as English poets increasingly found their subject matter in the outdoor world of gardens and estates, and, beyond them, in valleys, mountains, and other natural formations. This poetic interest in landscape was not far removed from the newly developed scientific interest in geology, as Barbara Maria Stafford, among others, has shown, with poets and scientists (as well as landscape painters) sharing many of the same motivations and many of the same standards for observation and recording.[3] The poet, like the scientist, was supposed to be a keen and accurate observer of the natural world, and further, was expected to record his observations in a language that would be true to his vision. In this tradition it was understood that the loco-descriptive poem of nature would capture the experience of the observer by faithfully recording his impressions of geology, geography, architecture, and local color. Herein lie some of the obvious and conventional roots for a romantic "poetry of nature," whether that nature be conceived of as picturesque, beautiful, or sublime. Such a poetics insists upon the authenticity of an empirically verifiable personal experience as a supreme value; its philosophic roots lie in English empiricism and develop logically toward a naturalism that excludes any mediation—such as religion—coming between the individual and nature. It is a poetics that, despite the theoretical developments of the past generation, remains with us today.

We may witness the presence of this poetics, for instance, in *Coleridge: Early Visions*, in which Richard Holmes criticizes Coleridge for transferring, through the mediation of Brun's poem, the poetic scene of "Hymn before Sunrise" from its original location on Scafell in the Lake District to an imagined Vale of Chamouny.[4] Coleridge, according to Holmes, is "trying to play the role of the inspired bard of popular conceptions, while actually suppressing his own poetic vision" (334). With his own eyes Coleridge had seen Scafell and Corrock, Moss Force and Lodore, *not* Mont Blanc, and we are led to understand that he would have done better to remain focused on what his eyes had actually seen. Holmes thus objects to Coleridge's "cutting himself off from his own true sources in nature." "This foreign rhetoric," we are told, "weakens the borrowed verse by comparison with his own prose" (334–335). Holmes' primary objection to the poem is therefore the familiar one first mentioned by Wordsworth: "he never was at Chamouni, or near it in his life."[5] It is interesting to recall that Wordsworth also complained of

Lord Byron's so-called plagiarisms, accusing Byron, in his Alpine poetry, of not taking his "feeling of natural objects . . . from nature herself, but from [Wordsworth], and spoiled in the transmission."[6] What is striking here is Wordsworth's implicit claim that *his* feeling for nature, unlike that of Byron or Coleridge, is sincere and direct: in a word, *unmediated*. This is surely one of the points of origin for the modern critical bias that rejects any kind of literary mediation, measuring the achievement of poetry not in reference to other poems, but in reference to the genuineness, the authenticity, and the sincerity of the individual whose experience prompted the poem.[7] This bias in favor of a "native" and "natural" language arising out of the authenticity of an empirically verifiable experience is something that Coleridge's poem, which is about that very relation between language and experience, puts under intense skeptical pressure.

Skepticism, of course, is *not* one of the things for which "Hymn before Sunrise" is noted. Instead, it is commonly characterized, again in the words of Holmes, as a "conventional and overtly religiose poem full of booming Teutonic piety" (334). Or, as Ronald Tetreault says, "Coleridge strains to wring a confession of faith from the mountain, and ends by proclaiming 'God' like a poetic ventriloquist, demanding that the natural scene echo the divine monosyllable."[8] Leighton, who is even more extreme, mocks what she calls the "aching for faith which lies behind the hectic rhetoric" of the poem, while noting approvingly that "Wordsworth rightly detected in it a straining for effect which is false" (58–59). Leighton comments further, with a positive reference to Shelley's *Mont Blanc* (a conventional feature of these attacks on Coleridge),

> It is the ease with which Coleridge personifies the object of his address which above all differentiates it from Shelley's object. The landscape . . . is quickly transmuted into a living presence that can be known by faith. . . . The poem exorbitantly proclaims the resolution of all uncertainty and doubt in this litany of faith. (59)

Obviously, we are to understand, Shelley's experience of nature is the correct response to these questions of faith, vision, and voice. Finally, Leighton complains that "The obsessive naming of God exacts belief by verbal force, not by imaginative conviction" (60). Such comments are the legacy of a hostile Enlightenment skepticism that substitutes for traditional religion a romantic faith in personal conviction and authenticity; it is a faith rooted in the immediacy of experience, as opposed to what Leighton condescendingly calls Coleridge's "second-hand spontaneity" (58). In such efforts to discredit Coleridge's faith, his poem *about* faith can hardly be expected to survive intact.

Against those readings, it seems to me that the poem's critical problems are the very features that constitute its special strengths; when "Hymn before Sunrise" is freed from the constraints of a poetics to which it does not belong, its audacity and brilliance will be apparent. And, while the poem may then show itself to be deserving of our critical respect and admiration, it will also reveal that there is, indeed, something withheld and hidden—a repressed anxiety, a secret fear, an absence—that Coleridge cannot admit to, yet cannot entirely mask. Therein, I argue, lies the poem's true failure: not of authenticity, but of imagination. But to bring this out into the open, one's own critical imagination must not fail; what is needed is a poetics that will bring the unseen into visibility and give voice to the unexpressed.

Since the single most crucial context for framing our understanding of "Hymn before Sunrise" is Coleridge's participation in what I call Romantic Hebraism—the turn away from a neoclassical, Greco-Roman tradition of aesthetics and metaphysics, and toward a poetic orientation rooted in the Hebrew Scriptures—it should not be surprising that the poetics most suited to this poem should derive from the traditional practices of Jewish textual study, especially as represented in *midrash*, Judaism's typical mode of reading and interpretation.[9] *Midrash* is rooted in the reading of Scripture, so in it we do not encounter built-in objections to a poem about religious faith. *Midrash* is at the same time adroit in uncovering textual *problems*, precisely because it respects the essential integrity of the original biblical text, in which seeming errors and inconsistencies can reveal a divinely inscribed meaning. It should also be noted that *midrash* is often audaciously creative in finding solutions to textual problems. I intend to test here the interpretive power of a particular form of *midrashic* literary criticism—covenantal hermeneutics— to resolve questions of meaning and intention within the poem, reading "Hymn before Sunrise" as itself a *midrash* on creation, that is, a self-reflective poem about the creative imagination, linking the poem not only to the creation account of Genesis, but also—and here I follow traditional Judaic tradition—to the parallel account in Exodus, when the Israelites receive the Torah at Mount Sinai. In "Hymn before Sunrise," Coleridge, above all, is seeking a place to stand in the landscape of the world and of his poem, and his desire, enacted at the base of Mont Blanc, recalls two biblical mountains: Eden, where, according to Milton, "God had thrown / That Mountain as his Garden,"[10] and where humans first stand up from nature, and Mount Sinai, where the children of Israel first stand before God as a people. But in "Hymn before Sunrise," it is Mont Blanc that bears the burden of grounding human creativity and subjectivity; it is at Mont Blanc that Coleridge seeks for a human posture of freestanding being.

Context: Romantic Hebraism

During the summer of 1802, when Coleridge composed "Hymn before Sunrise," he was thinking deeply about Hebrew poetics and the nature of the creative imagination. Those thoughts are clearly connected to his poem, in which a solitary Coleridge exhorts all of creation to praise God, and which was composed, as he wrote to a friend, "in the manner of the *Psalms*."[11] However, it would be a mistake to localize or personalize this effort as a purely individual instance of poetic piety; that he consulted and made use of a German poem for his own work suggests not only the deliberateness of his effort—this was not a spontaneous effusion made in a moment of religious "enthusiasm"—but also its international character. "Hymn before Sunrise," in fact, participates in a widespread embrace of a hebraic model for poetics which can be traced first to Brun's own "Chamounix beym Sonnenaufgange" (with its explicit references to the book of Job), and, through that poem's dedication, to Friedrich Gottlob Klopstock and his crucial poem of 1759, "Frühlingsfeier" ("Spring Celebration"). All three poems insistently invoke the name of God—that "divine monosyllable" of current critical disfavor—though Brun's multisyllabic "*Jehovah*" has its clear stylistic advantages over Coleridge's "God," and Klopstock's repeated use of "*Herr*" with its rolling German *r*'s invoking a thundering storm, is a brilliant means of revealing the divine presence in natural phenomena.

Klopstock's proto-Romanticist project to appropriate the Hebrew Scriptures for German poetry finds strong support in the polemics of J. G. Hamann, a founder of the *Sturm und Drang* movement in German literary æsthetics and the Königsburg friend and intellectual opponent of Emmanuel Kant. Hamann, in a series of provocative and revolutionary essays, pamphlets, and books, waged a fierce, Blakean "mental fight" against the classical æsthetic tradition, calling upon German writers to reject the hegemony of French neoclassical rules rooted in Hellenism and to adopt instead a hebraic style; in opposition to a scholastic rationalist theoretical tradition, he articulated a new, poetic understanding of the world as a radically contingent created order in which humans are the imaginative cocreators of the world's meaning. Hamann's opposition to Enlightenment values was first articulated in reply to the orientalist Johann David Michaelis (1717–1791) and his 1757 publication, *Criticism of the Means Employed to Understand the Extinct Hebrew Language*.[12] Michaelis' work amounted to a rejection of Hebrew poetry because of its supposed primitive, figurative language; to him the use of imagery in the Hebrew Scriptures was contrary to sound reason.[13] Hamann's response to this rationalistic contempt for what he considered the very language of revelation was his *Æsthetica in Nuce* (Aesthetics in a Nutshell), published in 1762. With its subtitle—"A Rhapsody in Cabbalistic Prose"—and its opening quotations from Judges and Job in the original Hebrew, the *Æsthetica in Nuce* provocatively flaunts a defiant Hebraism. It begins with the promise "die Tenne heiliger Literatur zu fegen!" with "Nicht Leier!—noch Pinsel!—eine Wurfschaufel für meine Muse"—to sweep the floor of sacred literature, not with a lyre or a painter's brush for my muse, but a winnowing shovel.[14] Here Hamann turns away from the conventional, refined iconology of the Greek aesthetic tradition, symbolized most clearly by the harp, and takes up instead a common work tool—a shovel—as the emblem of *his* muse, one referred to, and thus legitimated, by the biblical prophets. He then boldly proclaims, "Poesie ist die Muttersprache des Menschlichen Geschlecht"—poetry is the mother-language of the human race. Against Enlightenment claims for a rationalized language, Hamann insists on its essentially figurative nature.

Hamann's basic assumptions about the cosmos are rooted in an essentially hebraic understanding of the world as Creation through God's Word and thus as a system of linguistic signification. Creation has an ontology of meaning rather than being, as he wrote in a letter to Friedrich Jacobi (April 30, 1779): "Was in deiner Sprache das Sein ist, möchte ich lieber das Wort nennen" ("What is Being in your language I would rather call the word").[15] Everything is referential beyond itself, and ultimately to God. Thus, the question of the origin of language—a matter of serious concern to Etienne Bonnot de Condillac (1714–1780), Jean Jacques Rousseau (1712–1788), Johann Gottfried von Herder (1744–1803), and countless others of the period—is nonsensical for Hamann, because *everything* is linguistically constituted, and so there could have been no point prior to meaning or signification. Hamann thus writes, in "Des Ritters von Rosencreuz letzte Willensmeinung" ("The Last Testament of the Red Cross Knight") concerning the original creation: "Jede Erscheinung der Natur war ein Wort. . . . Mit diesem Worte im Mund und im Herzen war der Ursprung der Sprache so natürlich, so nahe und leicht, wie ein Kinderspiel" ("Every appearance of nature was a word. With these words in the mouth and in the heart the origin of language was as natural, near and easy as a children's game").[16] This picture of human origins is one in which language is not supplemental—language neither mirrors an independent reality nor deviates from it—but rather is completely integral; humanity and language are inseparable. There is no moment before which speech comes into play. Thus, if Creation is the revelation of God, but nevertheless a veiled revelation, a sign to be read or a word to be heard, then the mode of existence appropriate for humanity is *interpretive*, requiring acceptance of the world not as a Kantian *Gegenstand* to be analyzed or interrogated, but rather as a signifying reality, as speech addressing us and calling forth a response.

It is possible to construct a link from Hamann in 1760 to Coleridge forty years later through another German, Friedrich Klopstock (1724–1803), whom Coleridge actually met during his 1799 stay in Germany. In 1759, at the same time that Hamann and Michaelis were disputing over the value of Hebrew poetry, Klopstock published "Frühlingsfeier" ("Spring celebration"), a hymn in free rhythm in clear imitation of the biblical psalms—the very poetry that Michaelis was condemning. Hamann praises Klopstock in the *Æsthetica in Nuce* and, against the criticism of Gotthold Ephraim Lessing (1729–1781), defends Klopstock's unconventional poetry as an imitation of "the enigmatic mechanics of the sacred poetry of the Hebrews."[17] "Frühlingsfeier" is a superb example of German poetry freeing itself from the cultural hegemony of French neoclassical norms by turning to the Hebrew Scriptures for inspiration and alternative models.[18] The poem seems, in fact, to have provided a model for Brun's "Chamouni beim Sonnenaufgange," dedicated explicitly to Klopstock in later editions of her poetry, which forms the structural core of Coleridge's own poetic essay in the Hebrew style, "Hymn before Sunrise."

The filiation of Coleridge's poems with those of Brun and Klopstock is of particular significance when seen in light of other key developments in Coleridge's thinking at the time of the poem's composition. His efforts to write in the Hebrew mode occurred at the same time that he was formulating, in several crucial letters, his preference for Hebrew poetry over Greek, his theoretical split with Wordsworth, and his developing concept of the imagination. In a letter to William Sotheby on July 13, Coleridge notes that he and Wordsworth "begin to suspect, that there is, somewhere or other, a *radical* Difference [in our] opinions" (*CL* 2:812). A few days later, in another letter to Sotheby, he criticizes the affectations and false literary refinement of the Swiss-German poet Salomon Gessner (1730–1787), contrasting Gessner's style with what he called the "matronly majesty—of our Scriptures" (July 19, 1802, *CL* 2:814). A week later, in a letter indicating his growing interest in Jewish theology, Coleridge asks John Prior Estlin to provide "a real History . . . of all that can be collected of the opinions of the Jews, & Jewish Doctors, concerning the Messiah/antecedent to the time of Christ, & since that time" (July 26, *CL* 2: 822). On July 29, he writes to Robert Southey, confessing,

> [I] have not had my doubts solved by Wordsworth/On the contrary, I rather suspect that some where or other there is a radical Difference in our theoretical opinions respecting poetry—/this I shall endeavor to go to the Bottom of—and acting the arbitrator between the old School & the New School hope to lay down some plain, & perspicuous, tho' not superficial, Canons of Criticism respecting Poetry. (*CL* 2:830)

During this same period he apparently was studying the poetics of the Hebrew Scriptures because, on August 26, he announces in a letter to Sotheby, "I have discovered, that the poetical Parts of the Bible . . . are little more than slovenly Hexameters—" (*CL* 2:857). Finally, by September 10, this remarkable summer of reflection and writing culminates in yet another letter to Sotheby that contains his only written reference to Friederika Brun in these veiled comments about the provenance of "Hymn before Sunrise":

> When I was on Sca'fell—I involuntarily poured forth a Hymn in the manner of the *Psalms*, tho' afterwards I thought the Ideas &c disproportionate to our humble mountains—& accidently lighting on a short Note in some swiss Poems, concerning the Vale of Chamouny, & it's Mountain, I transferred myself thither, in the Spirit, & adapted my former feelings to these grander external objects. (*CL* 2:865)

What Coleridge calls here an "involuntary" effusion nevertheless seems to have had a deliberate rationale, for in his actual composition, he intentionally imitates Hebrew poetry in conscious contrast to the traditions of classical Greece. As the letter continues, he characterizes the Greeks as poets of mere fancy, while the Hebrews are poets of the imagination *par excellence*:

> [T]he Greeks in their religious poems address always the Numina Loci, the Genii, the Dryads, the Naiads, &c &c—All natural Objects were dead—mere hollow Statues—but there was a Godkin or Goddessling *included* in each—In

the Hebrew Poetry you find nothing of this poor Stuff—as poor in genuine Imagination, as it is mean in Intellect—/At best, it is but Fancy, or the aggregating Faculty of the mind—not *Imagination*, or the *modifying*, and *co-adunating* Faculty. This the Hebrew Poets appear to me to have possessed beyond all other—& next to them the English. In the Hebrew Poets each Thing has a Life of it's own, & yet they are all one Life. In God they move & live & *have* their Being. (*CL* 2:866–867)

Here, with "Hymn before Sunrise" in his thoughts, we see Coleridge's first written attempt to distinguish imagination from fancy: the Greek model of "nature" only engages the fancy, while the Hebrew model, in which "each Thing has a Life of it's own, & yet they are all one Life," engages the imagination. Fifteen years later, in his *Lay Sermons* (1817), Coleridge would refer to the people of the Old Testament as "living educts of the imagination,"[19] and he would give his embryonic theory of the imagination its classic formulation in the *Biographia Literaria* (1815–1817), which retains residual traces of this early interest in a biblically informed poetics. For instance, the quotation from the Apostle Paul in the Sotheby letter of September 10 reappears in a footnote in chapter XII, where Coleridge uses the writings of Friedrich Wilhelm Joseph Schelling (1775–1854) to elucidate the ungrounded ground of being in the "I Am." The dominant discourse here may well be the language of German idealist philosophy, but beneath the surface, as the footnote reveals, is a strongly biblical understanding of the utter contingency and dependence of the creature on the Creator, in Whom "we live, and move, and have our being."[20] In the following chapter Coleridge proceeds to define the "Primary Imagination" as "the living power and prime agent of all human perception, and as a repetition in the finite mind of the eternal act of creation in the infinite I AM" (167). Human imagination is here explicitly linked to God's continual creative activity—first described in Genesis—as well as to God's self-disclosure to Moses on Sinai, the Mount of God, where "God said unto Moses, I AM THAT I AM."[21] To see and experience the world as Creation is contingent upon an encounter with the I AM of God, an encounter in which the human "I" can then also emerge. Here, Coleridge, like Hamann, understands the world to be a created order, in which we play a key role in response to God's "eternal act of creation," a role based upon our own creative, imaginative powers rather than the powers of the merely analytic mind.

Historically, it is clear that British Romanticism ultimately provided little fertile soil in which a distinctive theory of literature derived from the Hebrew Scriptures could take root and flourish.[22] Certainly the pervasive presence of anti-Judaic attitudes in British and European culture cannot be ignored. Intellectually, the dominant tradition of Greek logo-centric thought and onto-theology, against which a hebraic poetics must contend, proved stronger than the individual efforts of such figures as Hamann and Coleridge; it had not yet run its course, nor met its match, as it eventually would, in the successive waves of critiques issuing from Friedrich Nietzsche,

Martin Heidegger, and Jacques Derrida. While Coleridge's own interest in a hebraic poetics, so evident in 1802, was somewhat eclipsed by other concerns (like so many of his unfinished projects), it is of note that he maintained a long friendship with Hyman Hurwitz (1770–1844), the first Jewish Professor of Hebrew Language and Literature at University College, London, and author of *Hebrew Tales* (1826); in 1817, Coleridge translated Hurwitz's "Israel's Lament," "A Hebrew Dirge, chaunted in the Great Synagogue, St. James's Place, Aldergate, on the day of the Funeral of her Royal Highness the Princess Charlotte," from the original Hebrew into English verse.[23] However, by the end of the century, under the cultural authority wielded by Matthew Arnold in *Culture and Anarchy* (1869), the term "Hebraism" had become a mere description for a literary style of moral earnestness and "strictness of conscience," in contrast to the "sweetness and light" and "spontaneity of consciousness" Arnold found in Greek literature.[24] Romantic Hebraism was effectively transformed, reduced to a set of moral laws that echoed, ironically, the neoclassical rules against which Hamann and Coleridge had rebelled, each in his own way, but each from a specifically hebraic perspective.

Meanwhile, on the margins of the Christian West, and with only a passing participation in the West's long historical entanglement with Greek philosophical thought, a specifically Jewish mode of textual engagement with the Hebrew Scriptures developed into a rich independent tradition. As Susan Handelman claims in *The Slayers of Moses*, Judaism consistently opposed "the entire classical tradition of Western metaphysics."[25] She notes that, in the rabbinic view, since the world was created out of nothing through an act of God's will,

> all of creation was contingent, including all premises. Nothing was *necessary*, there were no *natural laws* that were logically deducible or rationally self-evident, and no unquestioned principles that formed the basis of reality. Everything could have been otherwise; even reason itself was not necessary. An important consequence of this perspective was that reason, too, became subject to relentless probing in a way which was anathema to the Greeks. (28)

This Judaic understanding of the world as Creation—explored by Hamann in 1760 and Coleridge in 1802—challenges Greek philosophic principles of essentialism and the autonomy of theoretical thought with a deep skepticism, a "relentless probing." Released in the modern period from its accustomed environment of *yeshiva* and synagogue, this Jewish tradition offers a fresh perspective on texts beyond Torah and Talmud, texts that, in the West, we have conventionally called literature.

Critical *Midrash*: Covenantal Hermeneutics

The possibility of a distinctive approach to literary hermeneutics based upon a Judaic understanding of God, world, and mankind, begins with the model of the Torah as both written and oral: the interplay between the Hebrew Scriptures (written Torah) and Talmud (oral Torah) constitutes a structural unity of signification and interpretation. This model is dependent upon a presumed bond of writer and reader, essentially a *covenantal* bond of mutual obligations. Harold Fisch (1923–2001), for many years Professor of British Literature at Bar-Ilan University, has given the name "covenantal hermeneutics" to this interpretive model of reading derived from the Jewish tradition of *midrash*, wherein one posits a contractual relationship between reader and writer, between reader and text.[26] As Fisch says in *Poetry with a Purpose*,

> The biblical text as a whole is founded in relationality. It demands an audience, actively participating not merely in understanding but even in constituting the text. This is of course classical Jewish doctrine. The written law . . . cannot stand alone: it is validated by the . . . oral Torah, or continuing tradition of interpretation. This is a "community of interpreters" from whom the written text receives its meaning and its generic character.[27]

This kind of textual situation, in which interpretation occurs under what Fisch calls "conditions of prior relationality" ("Power and Constraint," 6), has been eloquently described by Gerald Bruns as "the mutual belonging of the text and those who hear it"; such interpretive acts assume a "common accord between ourselves and what is written."[28]

The first requirement of such a hermeneutics is a certain receptivity; the *Sh'ma*, Judaism's fundamental confession of faith in one God ("Hear [*Sh'ma*], O Israel! The LORD is our God, the LORD alone" [Deut. 6:4; JPS]), is the model for the covenantal moment. It is, according to Fisch, not so much a confession or declaration as

> an invitation, a summons to "Israel" to *hear*, to apprehend, to interpret. What it tells us is that the divine unity is realized only when there is a community of hearers to achieve that perception, to make that affirmation; it is a perception that has to be striven for, created in the act of reading, hearing, and understanding. Nor are the words [Sh'ma Israel] a form of apostrophe, a mere rhetorical gesture: they imply rather a genuine partnership, the invocation, as a necessary presence, of a hearing ear and a perceiving intelligence in the constitution of meaning. We have in short a covenantal encounter in which the very mode of the utterance is governed by the categories of covenant. The willingness to hear, to understand, to cooperate is here declared to be a prior condition for the affirmation to which the sentence moves. And it is that willingness which the sentence solicits. Relationality, in short, precedes pronouncement and precedes command. (*Poetry with a Purpose*, 48)

Here Fisch is identifying a normative mode of human receptivity that extends beyond the specific requirements of fidelity toward a sacred text or obedience to an authoritative utterance. Covenantal hermeneutics can be usefully compared at this point with Jean-François Lyotard's understanding of the hermeneutic position as fundamentally relational: "Someone speaks to me; he places me under an obligation."[29] "No maker of statements, no utterer, is ever as autonomous," claims Lyotard. "On the contrary, an utterer is always someone who is first of all an addressee. . . . He is someone who, before he is the utterer of a prescription, has been the recipient of a prescription" (31).

Covenantal hermeneutics recognizes the contextual, relational, and prescriptive character of human interpretive life. Avivah Zornberg, working within the Jewish tradition and practicing what she calls a "dialectical hermeneutics," writes of "an opening of the ear, eye, and heart to a text that reflects back the dilemmas and paradoxes of the world of the reader."[30] "To read," she says, "is to call out for response to a text that itself calls out, summons, and addresses the reader" (xvii). Within that mutuality of text and reader there emerges what Ellen Spolsky has called "a practice of reading which is at once bound and open."[31] We are bound to the text because we find ourselves constituted by its call to us. We are, in the suggestive term used by Louis Althusser, "interpellated" as subjects: we are hailed, summoned, called-forth.[32] We awake to the world, not, as in our dreams, autonomous masters of ourselves and of the texts we read, but in the humility of creatures who must stand at attention and *listen* simply because that is our fundamental mode of existence. Yet our practice of reading is also open and free; we are obligated not only to listen but also to create meaning. We are called upon to construct the meaning of the text, to bring into the open, into that covenantal space between text and reader the hidden and unintelligible things of the world, our "fears and longings and questionings."[33] Empowered with an interpretive freedom to penetrate to the core of a text, to hear those unspoken questions to which the text constitutes an answer, we read the gaps in the text and fill them with significance. Interpretation becomes, then, as Zornberg points out, "similar to the creative act" (xix), or, in Coleridge's formulation, a "repetition in the finite mind of the eternal act of creation in the infinite I AM."

Poetic *Midrash*: "Hymn before Sunrise"

Let us return to "Hymn before Sunrise," taking our initial cue from the September 10, 1802 letter to William Sotheby, and read Coleridge's poem as a *midrash* on creation, a self-reflective poem about the creative imagination, an interpretive response to the creation account of Genesis. Much is at stake in Coleridge's effort to imitate Hebrew poetry; more than a mere stylistic exercise, "Hymn before Sunrise" is Coleridge's attempt to revive his creative muse, to bring to life those lost "genial spirits" over which his "Dejection Ode" had grieved just months before. He does so by invoking the God whose creative power Coleridge desires to share, and through whom there exists the possibility of real being—the possibility of his "I am" face to face with the I AM of God. Markus Barth has written that "The root of the biblical (Old Testament) concept of faith, *emunah*, denotes a firm stand on solid ground,"[34] that is to say, an observable stance in a verifiable landscape. Coleridge himself defines faith as "fidelity to our own being—so far as such being is not and cannot become an object of the senses."[35] It is this two-fold sense of faithful standing that Coleridge desires—the standing upon solid ground of a being that cannot be observed—and against the backdrop of the Genesis creation account we can see this drama of faith at Mont Blanc begin to unfold.

While "Hymn before Sunrise" is set, as the title announces, "In the Vale of Chamouni," at the foot of Mont Blanc and overlooking the Arve and Arveiron Rivers, the poem captures a moment just prior to their perceived existence, as Coleridge anticipates the world coming into being. "Where were you when I laid the earth's foundations?" God asks Job out of the whirlwind, and Coleridge's implicit answer to that question is that *he* was there, as a necessary, albeit imagined, spectator and participant. Standing at the foot of Mont Blanc is, for Coleridge, similar to the symbolic "standing at Mount Sinai," the "*ma'amad har Sinai*," for Jews.[36] At that time God told the Israelites, "I make this covenant, with its sanctions, not with you alone, but both with those who are standing here with us this day before the LORD our God and with those who are not with us here this day" (Deut. 29:13, JPS). Just as Jews throughout history have imagined themselves standing at Sinai with Israel during the original moment of covenant with God, so too Coleridge pictures himself present at Mont Blanc at the moment of creation: Coleridge is cocreator of the world, responsible with God for calling it into significant being. Thus Coleridge's imaginative representation of the scene in the poem is dependent precisely on the *absence* of the landscape, its invisibility. That invisibility is signaled historically by Coleridge's having never actually seen Mont Blanc; it is figured in the poem by the dark, night-time setting; even if Coleridge *had* been there, the visibility of the landscape would still be dependent upon the rising of the sun as an unseen source, like God, or the imagination. If "Hymn before Sunrise" had described a landscape based upon Coleridge's actual experience in the Lake District, hiking around Scafell, it would have played readily into empiricist assumptions about the immediacy and authenticity of an eye-witness account; it would have been acceptable to the critics. His poem, however, is deliberately mediated; it is transparently a construction of landscape as an imaginative act, producing the world of the seen only through the creativity of the spoken word.

"Hymn before Sunrise" opens, in a preconscious dream world of dark and silent night before the world materializes, with a question: "Hast thou a charm to stay the morning-star / In his steep course?" Stuart Curran relates this interrogative mode to the formal characteristics of the British hymn tradition—a Protestant impulse toward self-justification and the related need to explore the psychological motivations for hymn-making—and finds that "the question immediately raises doubts about the quality and extent of the speaker's faith."[37] This question would normally be put to God in a moment of doubt: does God indeed have the power and authority to govern the movements of the cosmos? We discover in the next line, however, that

Coleridge is not addressing God, but rather "O sovran Blanc," thus deflecting questions away from the deity and toward a representation that, having (already) taken the place of God, implicitly stands for Him. Coleridge's question is not so much an expression of doubt as of *desire*: he is tempted to see the mountain as a fit figure for the creative power of God, to be an *image* of God. This is the first in a series of displacements by which the poem explores the problem of representation; a problem that will only be resolved by Coleridge himself, made in God's image, becoming His representative as cocreator of the world.

We may read in these opening lines an initial temptation to aesthetic idolatry; Coleridge momentarily desires to worship this grand and god-like appearance, to make a part of the creation equivalent to the Creator, though by line 16 Coleridge will have turned away from the visible world to worship "the Invisible alone." But we also must recognize that Coleridge re-situates the visible shape appearing before him: in the first moment the silent form of Mont Blanc is surrounded by air which is "dark, substantial, black, / An ebon mass," but upon looking again, he recognizes the air as Mont Blanc's "own calm home," its "habitation from eternity!" Coleridge passes from a moment prior to the experience of the world, when all is doubtful—the dark night of the perceptual soul—to the state of certainty sufficient to engender a hymn. This brief sequence is rooted in the natural passage from night to day as the sky slowly brightens, but it parallels a *psychological* passage as Coleridge moves from an overwhelming or incomprehensible moment of perception, which engenders fear, to a sense of his own ability to fill that form of perception with meaning and thus place it in a context, domesticate it, make it his own. The early doubt, the moment of perceptual confusion in the gloom of early morning, is figured by Coleridge in the morning star's arrested movement above Mont Blanc, with the sky itself appearing as that "ebon mass" which Mont Blanc pierces like a wedge. Coleridge's uncertainty is emphasized by the opening question, "hast thou a charm to stay the morning-star / In his steep course?" addressed to a mountain that remains silent. In this moment Coleridge feels temporarily estranged from the familiar world; his question, seeking to make the mountain equivalent to God, is an effort to orient himself in the dark, to find a stable referent around which to organize his world, to bring an absent God into full presence. His confusion is the result, not only of visual illusion, but also of mental doubt, of not knowing where to place objects of sense within a signifying reality.

The doubt is only momentary, of course; as Coleridge looks again, he sees the mountain transfigured through its position in a meaningful context, situated in "thine own calm home, thy crystal shrine, / Thy habitation from eternity." His confusion is doubly resolved, with the sun's light bringing a visual clarity that is itself symbolic of Coleridge's conceptual clarity. Even as the yet invisible sun sheds its light on Mont Blanc and the surrounding sky, so Coleridge's invisible thoughts blend with a sensually visible form to produce a mountain that is fully present to him. Coleridge's awareness of these absent sources—the sun's rays and the mind's thoughts—as representations of divinity causes the mountain to vanish from his consciousness as he worships "the Invisible alone." The sun is an absence that this poem insistently invokes, using it as a symbol of God in His invisible efficacy and of the human mind in its world-illuminating function. The real question resonating from the opening query—"who or what has the power to represent that absence?"—resolves as Coleridge realizes that Mont Blanc merely holds and reflects the light shining upon it; worship is reserved for the ultimate source of light itself.

Coleridge's fascination with this mental process does not allow him to remain, head bowed in prayer and worship, in an Augustinian disavowal of the aesthetic; instead, in the second stanza he succumbs to the "sweet beguiling melody" (which functions as the musical prelude before the hymn itself begins) and explores the interaction by which human thought combines with natural forms to render the world. He realizes that during the experience he has just described, Mont Blanc "wast blending with my Thought"; that is, his thoughts were fusing with the form of the mountain and hence functioning analogically to the sun's light on the mountain. Coleridge himself, like the sun, serves as a source of significance, and hence *also* represents an absent divinity. This recognition of the productive part played by the imaginative consciousness is, of course, a familiar theme in both Coleridge and his friend William Wordsworth. Wordsworth's "Tintern Abbey" (1798) is a long meditation on the interplay of the forms of nature with human sensibility, with eyes and ears that half create and half perceive the world. Coleridge's "Lines . . . in the Hartz forest" (1799) profess "That outward forms, the loftiest, still receive / Their finer influence from the Life within;— / Fair ciphers else."[38] In a more somber tone, "Dejection: An Ode" (1802) affirms that "in our life alone does Nature live," that the soul must be the source of both light and a "sweet and potent voice," empowered by Joy, a "beautiful and beauty-making power," which "wedding Nature to us gives in dower / A new Earth and new Heaven."[39] In "Hymn Before Sun-rise," written only a few months after "Dejection" had mourned the loss of his "shaping spirit of Imagination," Coleridge seeks to demonstrate that his gift is not entirely lost.

These opening stanzas of the hymn portray Coleridge as imaginatively present at the creation of the world, an active participant with God in bringing the world into being: "Awake, my soul!" Coleridge urges, "not only passive praise / Thou owest!" Coleridge assumes the obligation to reveal the natural world in its essential meaning, not as mere being, but rather as Creation, as an embodied, tangible response to God's original creative speech. By accepting his responsibility as God's representative, Coleridge affirms the covenant God made with Creation. For, besides the voice of God, there is also a unique *human* capacity and obligation to speak, to endow the world with signification, constituting it as meaningful while at the same time constituting humans as free producers of meaning. The Alpine landscape functions as the place where this ongoing process rises to consciousness, as the sun rises over the Vale of Chamouni. As Mont Blanc is gradually illuminated, made visible by the still invisible sun rising from behind him, Coleridge is struck by the perception of two contrary motions: the horizontal motion of nature, represented by the rivers—incoherent and formless, which "rave ceaselessly" at Mont Blanc's base—and a vertical movement: Mont Blanc, that "most awful Form!" which, Coleridge apostrophizes, "Risest from forth thy silent sea of pines." These are the opposing alternatives before Coleridge: will he find a place to stand in the horizontal spread of the swarming multiplicity of nature, of water seeking its depths, or in the "sovran," vertical movement of the solitary mountain rising above the earth?

There are important antecedents for Coleridge's position at Mont Blanc, for he stands on ground previously occupied by Israel at Mt. Sinai and by Adam in Eden. Zornberg, in her reading of the Genesis creation account, uses these modes of being—the vertical rise and the horizontal spread—to describe the possibilities open to Adam in the Garden of Eden. Adam, the last work of Creation, is blessed with the position of domination; he is to rule *over* the other creatures. This implies a vertical relationship; Adam looks down upon the rest of Creation from an almost divine perspective. Yet he is also told to be fruitful and multiply, to fill the earth. This horizontal image of swarming is characteristic of animal life and implicit in the blessing of human fertility. The double blessings of domination and fertility describe the possible range of motion for man within Creation; they constitute what Zornberg calls the "imperative of his duality" (12). *Midrashic* literature portrays these human modalities through the image of Adam standing—a glorious but difficult physical posture—poised between heaven and earth. In one *midrash*, the standing, god-like posture of Adam causes the other creatures to worship him mistakenly. Adam also manifests his dominion over creation in the act of naming the animals; as Walter Benjamin (1892–1940) observes, "God's creation is completed when things receive their names from man."[40] Creation is a work in progress in which humans participate through their unique capacity to name.

The moment of naming the animals occurs after God, noting that Adam is alone in a newly created world, proclaims, "It is not good for man to be alone; I will make a fitting helper for him" (Gen. 2:18, JPS). These words, which Zornberg says are "perhaps the first 'God said' that has no direct effect on reality" (14), reveal the intentions of God but, unlike the earlier "let there be" declarations of God, do not bring the desired reality into immediate existence. The fulfillment waits upon Adam's own awareness, following the naming of the animals, that within the goodness of creation there is, paradoxically, an absence, there is something missing—a fitting helper capable of standing up with him, face to face. Zornberg comments, "The powerful implication here is that God's original intention can be consummated only by Adam's free perception and desire. Only when Adam comes to feel the solitude of the angelic, unitary existence is he split into two separate beings" (16). Adam must first become conscious of lack before the final separation within creation can occur, before man and woman become differentiated. Only thus can man fulfill his twofold task: to have dominion over the earth (like God, in Whose image he is made), and, with the rest of creation, to be fruitful and multiply.

Of course, Adam and Eve are unable to maintain the difficult posture of freestanding humanity given to them in Eden; the Fall is precisely a loss of stature before God, a failure to stand face to face with the Creator. At the end of Milton's *Paradise Lost*, Adam and Eve must descend the Hill of Paradise, led by "the hast'ning Angel, . . . down the Cliff as fast / To the subjected Plain" (12:637–640). The Fall is represented here as a literal loss of elevation; this sense of descent, a downward slide into chaos and nonbeing, opens up a fearful perspective on the undoing of Creation. An important *midrashic* tradition comments on the tenuous, disintegrated quality of Creation after the Fall, claiming that the solidity of Creation was ultimately dependent *all along* upon Israel accepting the Torah at Sinai; otherwise, it would have fallen back into primal chaos. As Zornberg says, "There is a provisional quality to the reality of the world. . . . The world, till Sinai, awaits its true creation" (27). The crucial source text is *Pesikta Rabbati*, a medieval *midrash* on the festivals of the year:

> "Earth and all its inhabitants dissolve: it is I who keep its pillars [*amudeha*, standing supports] firm" (Psalms 75:4). The world was in the process of dissolving. Had Israel not *stood* before Mount Sinai and said, "All that God has spoken, we will faithfully do" [lit., we will do and we will listen (Exodus 20:7)] the world would already have returned to chaos. And who made a foundation for the world? "It is I—*anokhi* who keeps its pillars firm"—in the merit of "I—*anokhi*—am the Lord your God who brought you out of the Land of Egypt."[41]

Zornberg comments:

> What saves the world, indeed what in a real sense *creates* the world, is the capacity of the people to encounter the terror of the *anokhi*. . . . One perspective emphasizes the *anokhi* of God—the transcendent and only reality. But another—audacious and difficult—emphasizes the *anokhi* of—human beings. It is man's ability to meet the voice of God out of the void, and to respond with his own *anokhi*: "We will do, we will *make* the world." . . . In this perspective, Israel creates the world, simply by finding a place to *stand* at Sinai. (32)

In Zornberg's reading of these texts, Creation depends upon the "I" of the human self standing up from nature in fear and trembling having as its only foundation neither ontological being nor essence, but only a voice, the voice of God saying, "*Anokhi*—I am" (31). Reality rests upon the vertiginous awareness that "there is nothing, nothing to stand on" but the "I am" spoken in response to the "I am" of God. The *anokhi*, the selfhood of human life, must find its standing, not only in the sovereign unity of God-like Oneness, but in relationship with other selves: thus Adam's desire for Eve, a fellow creature with whom to stand face to face, and thus Israel as the people of God, standing together at Sinai.

Like Adam in the Garden of Eden and Israel at Sinai, Coleridge in the Vale of Chamouni faces the dual imperative to recognize his unique stature: while God-like, man is not to be alone. This realization highlights a haunting ambiguity to the concluding phrase of the first stanza, "entranced in prayer / I worshipped the Invisible alone": does he worship *only* the Invisible, or is he *alone* when he worships? "The Invisible alone" invokes the words of the *Sh'ma*: "Hear, O Israel! The LORD is our God, the LORD alone." *Adonai Echad* can be translated as "the Lord alone" or "the Lord is one"; the invisible God is the one and only God, and all physical appearances, no matter how sublime, are but images. For Coleridge this is the moment when the God-like appearance of Mont Blanc "didst vanish from my thought" and when his "I" stands face to face with the "I" of God—precisely because the imagination can rise beyond "bodily sense" to commune with the Divine. Coleridge recognizes the power of what he would later call the Primary Imagination, "the living power and prime agent of all human perception, and . . . a repetition in the finite mind of the eternal act of creation in the infinite I AM." But in saying that he "worships the Invisible alone," Coleridge also reveals that *he*, too, is alone, that he is a "one"—he worships in the solitude of his individual subjectivity. In the second stanza, the self continues to find its verticality as perception blends with thought, and the soul swells "vast to Heaven." The swarming earth and its scenery cannot contain man; the soul dilates, is enrapt and transfused as Coleridge experiences the vertical, solitary movement toward a divine and singular overlook upon Creation. Yet the creation account of Genesis makes clear that "it is not good for man to be alone," for oneness belongs to God. Man is rather to proliferate and be many. To worship God alone is right and proper, but to worship in lonely solitude is problematic, for it reveals a failure to achieve that horizontal mode of being appropriate to God's creatures.

Once Coleridge's soul is focused on God, he can awaken toward active, willed speech: "Not alone these swelling tears, / Mute thanks and secret ecstasy! Awake, / Voice of sweet song! Awake, my heart, awake!" It is precisely the productive activity of the soul, the fact that it possesses a "voice of sweet song," that confers upon humanity a signifying freedom in relation to nature: only *after* Coleridge becomes cognizant of his standpoint as God's representative does he find his own voice; only then does he break forth into the hymn proper, calling the mountain landscape out of its silence into articulate speech. What is foregrounded here is the place of the human in the landscape of the world, for Coleridge a standpoint secured through his confession that the source of all representation is the voice of the biblical God. *That* Voice is always the prior text for Coleridge, a text that he can only repeat.

As we have seen, what a critic like Richard Holmes hears and objects to is precisely a *foreign* voice, the Germanic voice of Friederika Brun, and its repetition in Coleridge's poem. That voice represents to Holmes the intrusion of something alien and unnatural into a "native" language, a language in which Coleridge's "best passages" lie "closest to his own observations" (334).

Yet, if there is always a voice prior to my own, an "other" summoning me into my own selfhood, an "I" to meet my "I," that voice will always be "foreign"; it will always be other, to the degree that it is not mine. If there is always a prior word mediating my experience of the world, there is also no possibility of a purely "native" language to capture such an experience. Coleridge's poem is true to the condition of language because it draws upon a hebrew poetic model that assumes the priority of God's word—the priority of signification over perception. Brun's poem functions in "Hymn before Sunrise" as the necessarily prior text and prior voice; Coleridge's appropriation of Brun is a figurative appropriation of the Word and Voice of God as a necessary act of the imagination: the human repetition of the divine "I AM."

The remaining stanzas of Coleridge's poem—the "hymn" proper—find him at the same moment as Adam, waking alone in a newly created world. At that moment in Eden, God said, "It is not good that the man should be alone; I will make a help meet for him" (Gen. 2:18, AV). But unlike Adam, who took stock of God's newly created world and found it incomplete—for "there was not found an help meet for him" (Gen. 2:20)—Coleridge finds only abundance and plenitude. Coleridge has moved from worshipping the Invisible alone, with its ambiguity, to denying his loneliness ("Not alone these swelling tears"), and claiming companionship as he asks the "Green vales and icy cliffs" to "join my Hymn." Next we see Coleridge as choirmaster of Creation, calling all the world to join in his hymn-making. In a systematic recapitulation of the days of creation in Genesis, Coleridge catalogues the rich diversity of the created world, exhorting all the earth to praise God. But in all the goodness of Creation he does not see, or is unwilling to admit that he sees, that something is missing in the landscape, that there is a lack. He cannot see what isn't there; in other words, his imagination fails.

Coleridge first addresses Mont Blanc, which earlier in the poem he had compared to himself. He exhorts it as the "sole sovereign of the Vale"— clearly a strong paternal image—to awaken, asking who it was that "sank thy sunless pillars deep in Earth?" These lines of the poem's core come directly from Brun's "Chamouni beim Sonnenaufgange"; Coleridge's phrase, "Who sank thy sunless pillars deep in Earth" translates Brun's "Wer senkte den Pfeiler tief in der erde Schoos," but his words mask a clear sense of sexual penetration in the original, which might be more strongly translated as "who plunged thy pillars deep into the *lap* of the Earth?" Mont Blanc, a masculine figure in the landscape of creation, is a virile, creative force of nature, companion of stars and lover of the Earth, driving his pillar deep into her lap, and, as "parent of perpetual streams," fathers the "wild torrents" of the next stanza. Mont Blanc is not so alone after all—not as alone as Coleridge.

From the stable, fixed character of the mountain, Coleridge shifts his atttention to the "wild torrents" of water. These streams emphasize again the "swarming," horizontal nature of Creation on the verge of chaotic, frenzied formlessness. And yet this wild water is called into formal being by God, who commanded, "Here let the billows stiffen, and have rest." In a similar way,

Zornberg's commentary on Genesis pictures Creation coming into being as a "kind of Jelling process" in response to God's "let there be" pronouncements (6). She quotes Rashi (Solomon ben Isaac, 1040–1105), the medieval Talmudist: "To come into real being is to be strengthened, hardened into specific form: '[the waters] stood in dryness and strength—like a man who is astounded and stands [*omed*] in one place'" (Rashi, Job 26:11). Zornberg comments: "Finding one place to stand: this is Rashi's definition of being,"—in contrast to natural phenomena, that "can only freeze into place, assume their necessary posture in space" (7). Coleridge cannot simply blend into the scenery, for humans have been called to stand up from nature; with *human* being, finding a place to stand is a difficult and demanding task.

The "Hymn" next turns to the rest of creation: after the sun, the moon and the stars, and following the earth and the waters, Coleridge calls into existence flowers, pine-groves, and then animals: "wild goats sporting round the eagle's nest," and eagles, who are "play-mates of the mountain-storm." Noteworthy in this scene, from the perspective of Adam in Eden, is the sense of an idealized, perfect world in which everything is in the plural, with goats sporting and eagles playing; even Mont Blanc is in the company of the stars. Only Coleridge is alone. If he were to find his authentic place in God's created order, this would be the moment in which he would recognize his solitude as a primal lack that cries out for remedy. He would recognize, as Adam had to recognize, that "God's original idea of the human good has not yet been implemented. It is achieved only when man himself comes to recognize the pains of solitude."[42] Coleridge certainly knew the pains of solitude, as his later poem "Work without Hope" (1825) so eloquently and poignantly reveals; in a world in which "All Nature seems at work" Coleridge laments his loneliness: "And I the while, the sole unbusy thing, / Nor honey make, nor pair, nor build, nor sing." While nature retains its creative energy and fecundity in this poem, Coleridge is conscious that *he* no longer sings or pairs; he is excluded from Paradise. But in "Hymn before Sunrise," he masks that essential solitude in a forced and ultimately false hymn of divine plenitude and creative unity, through which he hopes to lose his singular voice among Earth's "thousand voices."

As the major critical problem of the poem—its "inauthenticity" in setting and voice—disappears, what then emerges into visibility in the landscape of the poem is a woman, made visible through her very absence. Of Adam, God said, "It is not good for man to be alone; I will make a fitting helper for him." The Jewish Publication Society's idiomatic English translation loses the sense maintained in the more literal rendering of the Authorized Version: "I will make him an help meet for him." The crucial Hebrew word here, *kenegdo*—"as his opposite," or "corresponding to him"—is built on the root *ngd*, which forms the verb in the *hiphil* (causative) stem, "to cause to tell, report, or make known." As an adverb its meaning is to be "in front of, in sight of, opposite to." One of the verb's primary meanings, "to be conspicuous," is related to an Arabic term for "*high land*." But the woman who should be opposite Coleridge, directly in front of him, making herself known to him, and as obvious as the looming peak of Mont Blanc at sunrise—that woman is conspicuous only in her absence.

Where is she? The absence haunting the poem, the Eve to Coleridge's Adam, is hard to find, but she is not entirely invisible. We know that at the time of the poem's composition, Coleridge was newly reconciled to his wife Sarah but also deeply in love with Sarah Hutchinson, the sister of Wordsworth's wife; it would seem that either woman could have found her place in the landscape of Coleridge's imagination.[43] But a different approach to that illusive female figure is through the poem's borrowings and rhetoric, for in them a female presence opposite to Coleridge is revealed. Friederica Brun's foreign, Germanic, and female voice, an alien intrusion into Coleridge's own "native" male language, opens the poem's otherwise lonely rhetoric toward the mutuality and intersubjectivity always inherent in human discourse. Within the fullness of Coleridge's Creation—that is to say, within the horizon of his poem—there is simply no space for his counterpart except in the repressed appropriation of Brun's prior voice.

"Hymn before Sunrise," which celebrates the creative imagination, leaves no room in the landscape for absence, and thus, ironically, no ground for that desire we call imagination. And yet the imagination is aroused, absence made visible; in the interstices of language, though the eye cannot see it, desire may be found. Ultimately there is no ground of being at Mont Blanc, only a moment of vertigo in which we see, with Israel at Sinai, *nothing* upon which to stand; this Nothing, invisible and immaterial, calls forth imagination and desire—creatio ex nihilo!—and grounds us in our selfhood. Here we may find our standing, with Coleridge, as we discover the "I Am" reverberating through the universe and through our selves, the very foundation of the world.

Notes

1. "Hymn before Sunrise," like many of Coleridge's poems, went through various revisions in its publishing history. I follow the later, revised text given in Ernest Hartley Coleridge's edition of the collected poems, *Poetical Works* (1912; Oxford: Oxford University Press, 1969), 376–380. "Chamounix beym Sonnenaufgang" ("Chomounix at Sunrise") was first published in *Gedichte von Friederike Brun, geb. Münter* (Zürich: Friedrich Matthisson, 1795), 1–3. For a study of the complex relationship between the two poems, see Angela Esterhammer's "Coleridge's 'Hymn before Sun-rise' and the Voice Not Heard," in *Samuel Taylor Coleridge and the Sciences of Life*, ed. Nicholas Roe (Oxford: Oxford University Press, 2001), 224–245.
2. The phrase is Angela Leighton's, in *Shelley and the Sublime* (Cambridge: Cambridge University Press, 1984), 58.
3. See Stafford's *Voyage into Substance: Art, Science, Nature, and the Illustrated Travel Account, 1760–1840* (Cambridge, MA: The Massachusetts Institute of Technology Press, 1984).
4. (New York: Viking Penguin, 1990), 335.
5. William Wordsworth, *Prose Works*, ed. Alexander Grosart, 3 vols. (London: Edward Moxon 1876; New York: AMS Press, 1967), 3:442. Wordsworth's

remark about Coleridge, while often quoted as an attack against Coleridge's supposed deception, is, in context, more ambiguous. Wordsworth's statement comes while explaining why Coleridge had once told him that "a visit to the battle-field of Marathon would raise in him no kindling emotion." Wordsworth comments, "Coleridge was not under the influence of external objects. He had extraordinary powers of summoning up an image or series of images in his own mind, and he might mean that his idea of Marathon was so vivid, that no visible observation could make it more so." Then, as "a remarkable instance of this," Wordsworth mentions the poem "said to be 'composed in the Vale of Chamouni,'" noting that Coleridge "never was at Chamouni, or near it, in his life." Wordsworth is arguing for the power of Coleridge's imagination to conjure up a scene as vivid as that produced by actual observation; here he is a more sympathetic and understanding reader of his friend's poetry than his disciples might want us to believe.

6. Thomas Moore, *Memoirs, Journal and Correspondence of Thomas Moore*, ed. Lord John Russell (London: Longman, Brown, Green, and Longmans, 1853–1856), 3:161.

7. Lionel Trilling discusses Wordsworth in the context of these concepts in his *Sincerity and Authenticity* (Cambridge: Harvard University Press, 1972), 90–95.

8. Ronald Tetreault, "Shelley and Byron Encounter the Sublime: Switzerland, 1816," *Revue des Langues Vivantes* 41 (1975): 149.

9. For a contemporary collection exploring the relation of *midrash* to literature, see Geoffrey H. Hartman and Sanford Budick's *Midrash and Literature* (New Haven: Yale University Press, 1986). In their glossary, Hartman and Budick define *midrash* both as "specific interpretations produced through midrashic exegesis," and as "the literary compilations in which the original interpretations, many of them first delivered and transmitted orally, were eventually collected" (365).

10. *Paradise Lost*, ed. Merritt Y. Hughes (Indianapolis: Odyssey Press, 1962), 4:225–226.

11. Samuel Taylor Coleridge, *Collected Letters*, ed. Earl Leslie Griggs (Oxford: Clarendon, 1956), 2:865; hereafter cited parenthetically as *CL*.

12. Michaelis was strongly influenced by the English Bishop Robert Lowth of Oxford (1710–1787), whose *De sacra poesi Hebræorum* (Oxford: Clarendon, 1753; English translation, *Lectures on the Sacred Poetry of the Hebrews*, trans. G. Gregory [London: J. Johnson, 1787]) instigated a fierce debate over Hebrew poetry and language that involved, among others, Johann Gottfried von Herder (1744–1803) and his *Vom Geist der ebräischen Poesie* (Dessau: Rudolstadt, 1782–1783; English translation, *The Spirit of Hebrew Poetry*, trans. James Marsh [Burlington, VT: E. Smith, 1833]). See Terence J. German's *Hamann on Language and Religion* (Oxford: Oxford University Press, 1981), 24–25, and James C. O'Flaherty's *Johann Georg Hamann* (Boston: Twayne-G.K. Hall, 1979), 63–81, 115.

13. O'Flaherty, *Johann Georg Hamann*, 69.

14. Johann Georg Hamann, *Sämtliche Werke*, ed. Josef Nadler (Vienna: Herder, 1949–57), 2:197. See also O'Flaherty, *Johann Georg Hamann*, 65.

15. Friedrich Heinrich Jacobi (1743–1819), leading representative, with Hamann, of the philosophy of feeling and a major critic of Kant; Hamann, *Briefwechsel*, ed. Walther Ziesemer and Arthur Henkel (Wiesbaden: Insel, 1955), 7:175.

16. *Sämtliche Werke*, 3:32. The full title of the essay is "The Last Testament of the Knight of the Red Cross concerning the Divine and Human Origin of Language."

17. O'Flaherty, *Johann Georg Hamann*, 80.

18. For the text of the poem, including critical commentary on Klopstock, see Robert M. Browning's *German Poetry: A Critical Anthology* (Englewood Cliffs, NJ: Prentice-Hall, 1962), 52–61.

19. S. T. Coleridge, *Lay Sermons*, ed. R. J. White. (London: Routledge & Kegan Paul, 1972), 29.

20. S. T. Coleridge, *Biographia Literaria*, ed. George Watson (London: J. M. Dent & Sons, 1975), 152.

21. Exodus 3:14, Authorized Version (AV). Hereafter scriptural references are cited parenthetically, either as AV (Authorized Version) or JPS (Jewish Publication Society).

22. An excellent source for understanding the broader context of Anglo-Judaica during this period is David B. Ruderman's *Jewish Enlightenment in an English Key: Anglo-Jewry's Construction of Modern Jewish Thought* (Princeton: Princeton University Press, 2000).

23. For more on Hurwitz, see Judith W. Page's "Hyman Hurwitz's *Hebrew Tales* (1826): Redeeming the Talmudic Garden," in *British Romanticism and the Jews: History, Culture, Literature*, ed. Sheila A. Spector (New York: Palgrave/Macmillan, 2002), 197–213. Coleridge's translation of Hurwitz's poem, "Israel's Lament," is included in *Coleridge: Poetical Works*, 433–435.

24. See chapter 4, "Hebraism and Hellenism," in Matthew Arnold's *Culture and Anarchy*, ed. Samuel Lipman (1869; New Haven: Yale University Press, 1994).

25. *The Slayers of Moses: The Emergence of Rabbinic Interpretation in Modern Literary Theory* (Albany: State University of New York Press, 1982), 27.

26. "Power and Constraint: Covenantal Hermeneutics in Milton," in *Summoning: Ideas of the Covenant and Interpretive Theory*, ed. Ellen Spolsky (Albany: State University of New York Press, 1993), 6.

27. (Bloomington: Indiana University Press, 1988), 48.

28. "Midrash and Allegory," in *The Literary Guide to the Bible*, ed. Robert Alter and Frank Kermode (Cambridge, MA: Harvard University Press, 1987), 634.

29. Jean-François Lyotard and Jean-Loup Thébaud, *Just Gaming* (Minneapolis: University of Minnesota Press, 1985), 35.

30. *The Beginning of Desire: Reflections on Genesis* (New York: Doubleday, 1996), xii.

31. "Introduction," xiv.

32. Louis Althusser, "Ideology and Ideological State Apparatuses," in *Lenin and Philosophy and Other Essays*, trans. Ben Brewster (London: New Left Books, 1971), 174.

33. Zornberg, *Desire*, xviii.

34. *Israel and the Church: Contribution to a Dialogue Vital For Peace* (Richmond, VA: John Knox Press, 1969), 39.

35. *Confessions of an Inquiring Spirit*, ed. Henry Nelson Coleridge (London: W. Pickering, 1849), 103.

36. Zornberg, *Desire*, 32.

37. *Poetic Form and British Romanticism* (New York: Oxford University Press, 1986), 60.

38. *Coleridge's Poetical Works*, 315–316.
39. *Coleridge's Poetical Works*, 362–368.
40. "On Language as Such and on the Language of Man," in *Reflections: Essays, Aphorisms, Autobiographical Writings*, trans. Edmund Jephcott (New York: Harcourt Brace Jovanovich, 1978), 319. Benjamin, a German Jew, shows a strong affinity in this essay to the ideas of Hamann, whom he quotes twice in support of his views.
41. 21 (100a); quoted in Zornberg, *Desire*, 27.
42. Zornberg, *Desire*, 13.
43. See Holmes, *Coleridge*, chapters 12 and 13, "Lover," and "Metaphysical Mountaineer."

BIBLIOGRAPHY

Aberbach, David. *Bialik*. London: Peter Halban, 1988.

——. *Revolutionary Hebrew, Empire Survival*. New York: New York University Press, 1998.

Abraham, James Johnston. *Lettsom: His Life, Times, Friends, and Descendants*. London: William Heinemann, 1933.

Abrams, M. H. *The Mirror and the Lamp: Romantic Theory and the Critical Tradition*. Oxford: Oxford University Press, 1953.

——. *Natural Supernaturalism: Tradition and Revolution in Romantic Literature*. New York: Norton, 1971.

Addison, Joseph and Richard Steele. *The Spectator*. 5 vols. Edited by Donald F. Bond. Oxford: Clarendon Press, 1965.

Adelard, John. *The Sports of Cruelty: Fairies, Folk-songs, Charms & Other Country Matters in the Work of William Blake*. London: C. & A. Woolf, 1972.

Aguilar, Grace. *Selected Writings*. Edited by Michael Galchinsky. Ontario: Broadview Press, 2003.

——. *The Vale of Cedars; or, the Martyr*. 1843. Reprint, New York: D. Appleton and Company, 1919.

Albrecht, Michael. *Moses Mendelssohn 1729–1786. Das Lebenswerk eines jüdischen Denkers der deutschen Aufklärung*. Ausstellungskataloge der Herzog-August-Bibliothek; 51. Weinheim: VCH, 1986.

[Allingham, John]. *Transformation; or, Love and Law*. Baltimore: J. Robinson, 1814.

Alter, Robert, ed. *Modern Hebrew Literature*. New York: Berman House, 1975.

—— and Frank Kermode, eds. *The Literary Guide to the Bible*. Cambridge, MA: Harvard University Press, 1987.

Althusser, Louis. "Ideology and Ideological State Apparatuses." In his *Lenin and Philosophy and Other Essays*, translated by Ben Brewster. London: New Left Books, 1971.

Altick, Richard. *Punch: The Lively Youth of a British Institution 1841–1851*. Columbus: Ohio State University Press, 1997.

Anderson, Benedict. *Imagined Communities: Reflections on the Origin and Spread of Nationalism*. London: Verso, 1983.

Anderson, G. K. *The Legend of the Wandering Jew*. Providence, RI: Brown University Press, 1965.

——. "Popular Survivals of the Wandering Jew in England." *Journal of English and German Philology* 46 (1947): 367–382. Reprint, in *The Wandering Jew: Essays in the Interpretation of a Christian Legend*, edited by Galit Hasan-Rokem and Alan Dundes, 76–104. Bloomington: Indiana University Press, 1986.

Anon. "Epistolary Correspondence of the Earlier Members of the Church." *Monthly Observer and New Church Record* 3 (1859): 281.

——. "The Reverend Jacob Duché." *The Monthly Observer* 1 (1857): 81.

Arkush, Allan. *Moses Mendelssohn and the Enlightement.* Albany: State University of New York Press, 1994.

Armstrong, Karen. *The Battle for God.* New York: Ballantine, 2000.

Arnold, Matthew. *Culture and Anarchy.* Edited by Samuel Lipman. New Haven: Yale University Press, 1994.

Arpali, Boaz. "'For hundreds of years these abhorred (Gentiles) spat in our face, and we wiped away the saliva': Bialik, Brener, Uri Zvi Grinberg." *Haaretz*, October 10, 2003.

Atwood, Craig. "Blood, Sex, and Death: Life and Liturgy in Zinzendorf's Bethlehem." Ph.D. diss., Princeton University, 1995.

——. "Sleeping in the Arms of Jesus: Sanctifying Sexuality in the Eighteenth-Century Moravian Church." *Journal of the History of Sexuality* 8 (1997): 34–44.

Auerbach, Eric. *Mimesis: The Representation of Reality in Western Literature.* Translated by Willard R. Trask. Princeton: Princeton University Press, 1953.

Aurbach, Pesach. *Ha-zeman* 29 (1903): 11.

Austen, Jane. *Mansfield Park.* Edited by James Kinsley. Oxford and New York: Oxford University Press, 1998.

——. *Northanger Abbey.* Edited by Claire Grogan. Ontario: Broadview, 1996.

Austin, J. L. *How to Do Things with Words.* Edited by J. O. Urmson and Marina Sbisa. Second ed. Cambridge: Harvard University Press, 1975.

Baer, Marc. *Theatre and Disorder in Late Georgian London.* Oxford: Clarendon Press, 1992.

Bailey, Frank E. "The Economics of British Foreign Policy, 1825–50." *The Journal of Modern History* 12 (1940): 449–484.

Bakker, Egbert J. "Mimesis as Performance: Rereading Auerbach's First Chapter." *Poetics Today* 20, 1 (spring 1999): 11–26.

Balfour, Ian. *The Rhetoric of Romantic Prophecy.* Stanford: Stanford University Press, 2000.

Balleine, G. R. *Past Finding Out: The Tragic Story of Joanna Southcott and Her Successors.* New York: Macmillan, 1956.

Bar-El, Judith. *The Hebrew Long Poem from its Emergence to the Beginning of the Twentieth Century: A Study in the History of a Genre.* Jerusalem: Bialik Institute, 1995.

Baring-Gould, Sabine. *Curious Myths of the Middle Ages.* Edited by Edward Hardy. London: Jupiter, 1977.

Barnett, Gerald. *Richard and Maria Cosway.* Tiverton: West Country Books, 1995.

Barth, Markus. *Israel and the Church: Contribution to a Dialogue Vital For Peace.* Richmond, VA: John Knox Press, 1969.

Bar-Yosef, Hamutal. "Be'ir Haharega." *Haaretz*, December 2, 1994.

——. *Maga-im shel Decadence: Bialik, Berdichevsky, Brener* (Decadent Trends in Hebrew Literature: Bialik, Berdychevski, Brener). Jerusalem: Mosad Bialik, 1997.

Bashan, Eliezer. "Testimonies by European Travelers about the Jews of Bavel and Kurdistan from the End of the 16th Century" (Hebrew). In *Studies in the History of the Iraqi Jews and Their Culture.* edited by Shmuel Moreh, 19–30. Tel-Aviv: Center for the Heritage of Iraqi Jewry, 1981.

Baumgarten, Alexander Gottlieb. *Metaphysica* (1757). Translated into German by Georg Friedrich Meier. Halle im Magdeburgischen: C. H. Hemmerde, 1766.

Bavli, Hillel. "The Modern Renaissance of Hebrew Literature." In *The Jews: Their Religion and Culture*, edited by Louis Finkelstein, 228–266. New York: Schocken, 1949.

Bell, John. *Travels from St. Petersburgh in Russia to Various Parts of Asia. Illustrated with Maps.* London: W. Creech, 1788.

Benjamin, Walter. *Reflections: Essays, Aphorisms, Autobiographical Writings.* Translated by Edmund Jephcott. New York: Harcourt Brace Jovanovich, 1978.

——. "Theses on the Philosophy of History." In his *Illuminations,* ed. Hannah Arendt, trans. Harry Zohn. New York: Schocken Books, 1968.

Bentley, Gerald E., Jr. *Blake Records.* Oxford: Clarendon Press, 1969.

——. "Mainaduc, Madness, and Mesmerism: George Cumberland and the Blake Connection." *Notes and Queries* 236 (September 1991): 294–296.

——. *Stranger from Paradise: A Biography of William Blake.* New Haven: Yale University Press, 2001.

Berdichevsky, Micha Yosef. *Kitvei Micha Yosef Ben Gurion (Berdichevsky): Maamarim* (The Writings of Micha Yosef Berdichevsky: Articles). Tel Aviv: Dvir, 1960.

Berkeley, George. *A Treatise concerning the Principles of Human Knowledge* (1710); *Three Dialogues between Hylas and Philonous.* Edited with an introduction by G. J. Warnock. La Salle, IL: Open Court, 1986.

Berman, Israel. "With H. N. Bialik in Kishinev." In *Hapogrom Bekishinov: bimlot shishim shana* (The Kishinev Pogrom of 1903), edited by Hayim Shurer, 75–80. Tel Aviv: World Federation of Bessarabian Jews, 1963.

Bernstein, Michael. *The Tale of the Tribe: Ezra Pound and the Modern Verse Epic.* Princeton: Princeton University Press, 1980.

Berquist, Lars. *Swedenborg's Dream Diary.* Translated by Anders Hallengren. West Chester, PA: Swedenborg Foundation, 2001.

Beswick, Samuel. *The Swedenborg Rite and the Great Masonic Leaders of the Eighteenth Century.* New York: Masonic Publishing Company, 1870.

Biale, David. *Eros and the Jews.* New York: Basic Books, 1992.

Bialik, Hayim Nahman. *Shirim: 1890–1898.* Edited by Dan Miron. Tel Aviv: Dvir and the Katz Institute of the University of Tel Aviv, 1990.

——. *Songs from Bialik: Selected Poems of Hayim Nahman Bialik.* Edited and translated from the Hebrew by Altar Hadari. Introduction by Dan Miron. Syracuse: Syracuse University Press, 2000.

—— and Yehoshua Hana Ravnitsky, eds. *The Book of Legends = Sefer Ha-Aggadah: Legends from the Talmud and Midrash.* Translated by William G. Braude. New York: Schocken Books, 1992.

Bible. *The Anchor Bible. Psalms I. 1–50.* Edited by S. J. Mitchell Dahood. Garden City: Doubleday, 1966.

——. *The Holy Bible.* Nashville: Thomas Nelson Publishers, 1972.

——. *JPS Hebrew-English Tanakh.* Second ed. Philadelphia: Jewish Publication Society, 2000 (1999 on title page).

——. *The JPS Torah Commentary, Numbers: The Traditional Hebrew Text with the New JPS Translation.* Edited by Jacob Milgrom. Philadelphia and New York: Jewish Publication Society, 1990.

——. *The Pentateuch and Haftorahs.* Edited by J. H. Hertz. Second ed. London: Soncino Press, 1971.

Bin Gorion, Micha Joseph, coll. *Mimekor Yisrael: Classical Jewish Folktales.* Edited by Emanuel bin Gorion. Translated by I. M. Lask. Introduction by Dan Ben-Amos. Bloomington and London: Indiana University Press, 1976.

Black, Eugene C. "The Anglicization of Orthodoxy: The Adlers, Father and Son." In *Profiles in Diversity: Jews in a Changing Europe, 1750–1870,* edited by Frances Malino and David Sorkin, 295–325. Detroit: Wayne State University Press, 1998.

Reprint of *From East and West: Jews in a Changing Europe, 1750–1870*. London: Basil Blackwell, 1991.

Blair, Hugh. *Lectures on Rhetoric and Belles Lettres* (1783). 2 vols. Edited by Harold Harding. Carbondale, IL: Southern Illinois University Press, 1965.

Blake, William. *The Complete Poetry and Prose*. Edited by David V. Erdman. Commentary by Harold Bloom. Newly revised ed. New York: Doubleday/ Anchor Press, 1988.

——. *The Poems of William Blake*. Edited by W. B. Yeats. London: Lawrence & Bullen, 1893.

——. *The Works of William Blake*. Edited by Edwin Ellis and William Butler Yeats. London: Quaritch, 1893.

Bloch, R. Howard and Stephen G. Nichols, eds. *Medievalism and the Modernist Temper*. Baltimore: The Johns Hopkins University Press, 1996.

Blumberg, Arnold. *Zion Before Zionism, 1838–1880*. Syracuse: Syracuse University Press, 1985.

Bogen, Nancy. "The Problem of William Blake's Early Religion." *The Personalist* 49 (1968): 509–520.

Bregman, Ahron. *Israel's Wars: A History Since 1947*. Second ed. London and New York: Routledge, 2002.

Bremmer, Jan N. "Erich Auerbach and His Mimesis." *Poetics Today* 20, 1 (spring 1999): 3–10.

Brewer's Dictionary of Phrase and Fable. Revised and enlarged. Fifth ed. London: Cassell, 1959.

Breymayer, Reinhard. "Ein unbekannter Gegner Gotthold Ephraim Lessings: Der ehemalige Frankfurter Konzertdirektor Johann Daniel Müller aus Wissenbach/ Nassau (1716 bis nach 1785)." In *Pietismus-Herrnhuterum-Erweckungsbewegung: Festschrift für Erich Beyreuther*, edited by Dietrich Meyer, 180–237. Köln: Rheinland-Verlag GmbH, 1982.

——. "'Élie Artiste': Johann Daniel Müller de Wissenbach/Nassau (1716 jusqu'a après 1785), un aventurier entre le piétisme radicale et l'Illuminisme." In *Actes du Colloque International Lumières et Illuminisme*, edited by Mario Matucci, 66–84. Université de Pisa: Instituto di Lingua e Letterature Française, 1985.

——. "Von Swedenborg zu Elias Artista: Der 'Prophet' Johann Daniel Müller aus Wissenbach/Nassau (1716 nach 1785), Gegner Moses Mendelssohn und Lessings, kritischer Freund Emanuel Swedenborg." In *Emanuel Swedenborg, 1688–1772. Naturforscher und Kundiger der Überwelt*, edited by Horst Bergmann and Eberhard Zwink, 89–92. Stuttgart: Württenbergischen Landesbibliothek, 1988.

Brown, Malcolm. "Anglo-Jewish Country Houses from the Resettlement to 1800." *Transactions of the Jewish Historical Society of England* 28 (1984): 20–38.

Brown, Marshall. "Romanticism and Enlightenment." In *The Cambridge Companion to British Romanticism*, edited by Stuart Curran, 25–47. Cambridge: Cambridge University Press, 1993.

Brumore, Abbé [L. G. Guyton de Morveau]. Letter. *Journal Encyclopédique* (December 1, 1785): 295.

Brun, Friederike. *Gedichte von Friederike Brun, geb. Münter*. Zürich: Friedrich Matthisson, 1795.

Bruns, Gerald L. "Midrash and Allegory." In *The Literary Guide to the Bible*, edited by Robert Alter and Frank Kermode, 625–646. Cambridge, MA: Harvard University Press, 1987.

Bryan, William. *A Testimony of the Spirit of Truth Concerning Richard Brothers.* London, 1795.

Burwick, Frederick. "Coleridge and De Quincey on Miracles." *Christianity and Literature* 39,4 (summer 1990): 387–421.

——. "Illusion and the Audience: Lessing, Mendelssohn, and Schiller." In his *Illusion and the Drama: Critical Theory of the Enlightenment and Romantic Era.* University Park, PA: Pennsylvania State University Press, 1991.

——. *Illusion and the Drama: Critical Theory of the Enlightenment and Romantic Era.* University Park, PA: Pennsylvania State University Press, 1991.

Bynum, W. F. and Roy Porter. *William Hunter and the Eighteenth-Century Medical World.* Cambridge: Cambridge University Press, 1985.

Byron, George Gordon. *English Bards and Scotch Reviewers.* In *The Poems of Lord Byron,* edited by Jerome McGann. Oxford: Oxford University Press, 1980.

Cambridge, Richard. *An Elegy Written in an Empty Assembly Room.* London: R. and J. Dodsley, 1756.

Campbell, George. *The Philosophy of Rhetoric* (1776). Edited by Loyd Bitzer. Carbondale, IL: Southern Illinois University Press, 1963.

Carlebach, Elisheva. *Divided Souls: Converts from Judaism in Germany, 1500–1750.* New Haven: Yale University Press, 2001.

Castle, Terry. *Masquerade and Civilization: The Carnivalesque in Eighteenth-Century English Culture and Fiction.* Stanford, CA: Stanford University Press, 1986.

A Catalogue of the . . . Library of Richard Cosway. London: Mr. Stanley, 1821.

Chastanier, Benedict. *Tableau Analytique et Raisonée de la Doctrine Céleste.* London, 1786.

——. *A Word of Advice to a Benighted World.* London, 1795.

Christ, Kurt. *Jacobi und Mendelssohn. Eine Analyse des Spinozastreits.* Würzburg: Königshausen & Neumann, 1988.

Christiansen, Jerome. *Coleridge's Blessed Machine of Language.* Ithaca, NY: Cornell University Press, 1981.

Cleland, John. *The Way to Things by Words, and to Words by Things: Being A Sketch of an Attempt at the Retrieval of the Antient Celtic, or, Primitive Language of Europe, to Which is Added a Succinct Account of the Sanscort, or Learned Language of the Bramins.* London: Printed for L. Davis and C. Reymers, 1766.

Cobbett, William. *Good Friday; or the Murder of Jesus Christ by the Jews.* London, 1830.

——, ed. *Parliamentary History of England.* 36 vols. London: T. C. Hansard, 1806–1820.

Cohen, Derek. "Constructing the Contradiction: Anthony Trollope's *The Way We Live Now.*" In *Jewish Presences in English Literature,* edited by Derek Cohen and Deborah Heller, 61–75. Montreal: McGill Queen's University Press, 1990.

—— and Deborah Heller, eds. *Jewish Presences in English Literature.* Montreal: McGill Queen's University Press, 1990.

Coleridge, Samuel Taylor. *Aids to Reflection.* Edited by John Beer. The Collected Works of Samuel Taylor Coleridge, 9. Princeton: Princeton University Press, 1993.

——. *Biographia Literaria.* Edited by George Watson. London: J. M. Dent & Sons, 1975.

——. *Biographia Literaria, or, Biographical Sketches of My Literary Life and Opinions.* 2 vols. Edited by J. Engell and W. J. Bate. The Collected Works of Samuel Taylor Coleridge, 7. Princeton: Princeton University Press, 1983.

Coleridge, Samuel Taylor. *Collected Letters of Samuel Taylor Coleridge*. 6 vols. Edited by Earl Leslie Griggs. Oxford: Clarendon Press, 1956–1971.

——. *Confessions of an Inquiring Spirit*. Edited by Henry Nelson Coleridge. London: W. Pickering, 1849.

——. *Essays on His Times*. 3 vols. Edited by David V. Erdman. The Collected Works of Samuel Taylor Coleridge, 3. London: Routledge, and Princeton: Princeton University Press, 1978.

——. *The Friend*. 2 vols. Edited by Barbara Rooke. The Collected Works of Samuel Taylor Coleridge, 4. London: Routledge, and Princeton: Princeton University Press, 1969.

——. *Lay Sermons*. Edited by R. J. White. The Collected Works of Samuel Taylor Coleridge, 6. London: Routledge, and Princeton: Princeton University Press, 1972.

——. *Lectures 1818–1819 on the History of Philosophy*. 2 vols. Edited by J. R. de J. Jackson. The Collected Works of Samuel Taylor Coleridge, 11. Princeton: Princeton University Press, 2000.

——. *Literary Remains of Samuel Taylor Coleridge*. 4 vols. Edited by Hartley Nelson Coleridge. London: W. Pickering, 1836–1839.

——. *Marginalia*. 5 vols. Edited by George Whalley and H. J. Jackson. The Collected Works of Samuel Taylor Coleridge, 12. London: Routledge, and Princeton: Princeton University Press, 1980–2000.

——. *The Notebooks of Samuel Taylor Coleridge*. 5 vols. Edited by Kathleen Coburn and Anthony Harding. London: Routledge & K. Paul, 1957–1961.

——. *On the Constitution of the Church and State*. Edited by John Colmer. The Collected Works of Samuel Taylor Coleridge, 10. London: Routledge, and Princeton: Princeton University Press, 1976.

——. *Opus Maximum*. Edited by Thomas McFarland, with the assistance of Nicholas Halmi. The Collected Works of Samuel Taylor Coleridge, 15. Princeton: Princeton University Press, 2002.

——. *The Philosophical Lectures of Samuel Taylor Coleridge*. Edited by Kathleen Coburn. New York: Philosophical Library, 1949.

——. *Poetical Works*. Edited by Ernest Hartley Coleridge, 1912. Oxford: Oxford University Press, 1969.

——. *Poetical Works*. 3 vols. in 6. Edited by J. C. C. Mays. The Collected Works of Samuel Taylor Coleridge, 16. Princeton: Princeton University Press, 2001.

——. *Shorter Works and Fragments*. Edited by H. J. Jackson and J. R. de J. Jackson. The Collected Works of Samuel Taylor Coleridge, 8. London: Routledge, and Princeton: Princeton University Press, 1995.

Colley, Linda. *Britons: Forging the Nation 1707–1837*. New Haven: Yale University Press, 1992.

Collins, Kenneth. "Jewish Medical Students and Graduates in Scotland." *Transactions of Jewish Historical Society of England* 29 (1982–1986): 75–96.

Colman, George the Younger. *Love Laughs at Locksmiths: A Musical Farce*. In *Lacy's Acting Edition of Plays*. London: Thomas Hailes Lacy, n.d.

Costa-Lima, Luiz. "Auerbach and Literary History." In *Literary History and the Challenge of Philology: The Legacy of Erich Auerbach*, edited by Seth Lerer, 50–60. Stanford: Stanford University Press, 1996.

The Covent Garden Journal. Edited by John Joseph Stockdale. 2 vols. London: J. J. Stockdale, 1810.

Cowen, Ann and Roger ed. *Victorian Jews through British Eyes*. London and Portland, OR: Littman Library of Jewish Civilization, 1986. Reprint, 1998.

Cowley, Hannah. *The Belle's Stratagem*. London: Longman, Hurst, Rees, and Orme, n.d.

Craciun, Adriana. *Fatal Women of Romanticism*. Cambridge: Cambridge University Press, 2003.

Cream, Naomi. "Isaac Leo Lyon: The First Free Jewish Migrant to Australia?" *Journal of Australian Jewish Historical Society* 12, 1 (1993): 3–16.

———. "Revd Solomon Lyon of Cambridge, 1755–1820." *Jewish Historical Studies* 36 (1999–2001): 31–69.

Critical Review 2 n.s. (August 1812): 216.

Curran, Stuart. *Poetic Form and British Romanticism*. New York: Oxford University Press, 1986.

———, ed. *The Cambridge Companion to British Romanticism*. Cambridge: Cambridge University Press, 1993.

Dacre, Charlotte. *Hours of Solitude. A Collection of Original Poems, now first published*. 1805. 2 vols. in 1. New York: Garland, 1978.

———. *Zofloya, or the Moor: A Romance of the Fifteenth Century*. Edited by Adriana Craciun. Ontario: Broadview, 1997.

Dallaway, James. *Constantinople Ancient and Modern, with Excursions to the Shores and Islands of the Archipelago and to the Troad*. London: Cadell and Davies, 1797.

Dalman, Gustaf. "Documente eines Christlichen Geheimbundes unter den Juden im achtzehnten Jahrhundert." In *Saat auf Hoffnung. Zeitschrift die Mission der Kirche an Israel*. Leipzig: B. Faber, 1890.

——— and Diakoms Schulze. *Zinzendorf und Lieberkuhn: Studien in der Geschichte der Judenmission*. Leipzig: Hinrich, 1903.

Damon, S. Foster. *A Blake Dictionary: The Ideas and Symbols of William Blake*. Revised edition with a new foreword and annotated bibliography by Morris Eaves. Hanover and London: University Press of New England for Brown University Press, 1988.

Danilewicz, M. L. "'The King of the New Israel': Thaddeus Grabianka (1740–1807)." *Oxford Slavonic Papers*, n.s. 1 (1968): 49–75.

Davidoff, Lenore and Catherine Hall. *Family Fortunes: Men and Women of the English Middle Class, 1780–1850*. Chicago: University of Chicago Press, 1987.

Davies, Keri and Marsha Keith Schuchard. "Recovering the Lost Moravian History of Blake's Family." *Blake: An Illustrated Quarterly* 38,1 (summer 2004): 36–43.

Davison, Carol Margaret. "Gothic Cabala: The Anti-Semitic Spectropoetics of British Gothic Literature." Ph.D. diss., McGill University, 1997.

Deghaye, Pierre. *La Doctrine Ésotérique de Zinzendorf (1700–1760)*. Paris: Klincksieck, 1969.

Derrida, Jacques. *Specters of Marx: The State of the Debt, the Work of Mourning, and the New International*. Translated by Peggy Kamuf. New York: Routledge, 1994.

Dienstag, Jacob I. "Targumim ivri'im mesafrut anglit-yehudit" (English-Jewish Literature in Hebrew Translation). *Jewish Book Annual* 8 (1949–1950): 35–47 (Hebrew sect.).

Disraeli, Benjamin. *Coningsby; or, the New Generation*. London: Longmans, 1900.

———. *Coningsby, or the New Generation*. Foreword by Asa Briggs. 1870. New York: Signet, 1962.

———. *Tancred, or The New Crusade*. Introduction by the Earl of Iddesleigh. New York: John Lane: The Bodley Head, 1905.

D'Israeli, Isaac. *A Defence of Poetry [and] Specimens of a New Version of Telemachus*. London: Stockdale, 1790.

D'Israeli, Isaac. "Farther Account of the Family of Nonsense." *The Wit's Magazine: or, Library of Momus: Being a Compleat Repository of Mirth, Humour, and Entertainment* 1 (1784): 177–79.

——. *Flim-flams!: or, The Life and Errors of my Uncle, and the Amours of my Aunt!* 3 vols. London: Printed for John Murray, 1805.

——. *The Genius of Judaism.* London: Edward Moxon, 1833.

——. "Letter from Nonsense with Some Account of Himself and Family." *The Wit's Magazine* 1 (1784): 145–147.

——. *Mejnoun and Leila.* In *Romances by I. D'Israeli. To Which Is Now Added a Modern Romance.* 1799. Philadelphia: Samuel F. Bradford, 1803.

——. *Narrative Poems.* London: John Murray, 1803.

——. "On the Abuse of Satire: An Epistle Addressed to the Poet Laureat, 1788." *Gentleman's Magazine* 59,2 (1789): 648–649.

——. *Romances by I. D'Israeli. To Which Is Now Added a Modern Romance.* 1799. Philadelphia: Samuel F. Bradford, 1803.

——. *Vaurien: or, Sketches of the Times, Exhibiting Views of the Philosophies, Religions, Politics, Literature, and Manners of the Age.* 2 vols. London: T. Cadell, 1797.

Dithmar, Christiane. *Zinzendorfs nonkonformistische Haltung zum Judentum.* Heidelberg: Universitäts Verlag C. Winter, 2000.

Dole, George. "Philosemitism in the Seventeenth Century." *Studia Swedenborgiana* 7 (1990): 5–17.

Dortort, Fred. *The Dialectic of Vision: Contrary Readings of William Blake's "Jerusalem."* Barrytown, NY: Station Hill Arts, 1998.

Draffen, George. "Some Further Notes on the Rite of Seven Degrees in London." *Ars Quatuor Coronatorum* 68 (1956): 94–110.

Dubnov, Simon. *Nationalism and History: Essays on Old and New Judaism.* Edited and translated by K. S. Pinson. Philadelphia: Jewish Publication Society, 1958.

Duschinsky, Charles. "Jacob Kimchi and Shalom Buzaglo." *Transactions of Jewish Historical Society of England* 7 (1915): 282–289.

——. *The Rabbinate of the Great Synagogue, London, from 1756–1842.* London: Oxford University Press, 1921. Reprint, with a new bibliographical note by Ruth P. Lehmann. Farnborough, Hants: Gregg, 1971.

Edgeworth, Maria. *Harrington. Tales and Novels,* vol. 9. New York: AMS Press, 1967.

Elsky, Martin. "Church History and the Cultural Geography of Erich Auerbach: Europe and Its Eastern Other." In *Opening the Borders: Inclusivity in Early Modern Studies, Essays in Honor of James V. Mirollo,* edited by Peter C. Herman, 325–349. Newark: University of Delaware Press, 1999.

Endelman, Todd M. "The Checkered Career of 'Jew' King: A Study in Late Eighteenth-Century Anglo-Jewish Social History." *AJS Review* 7/8 (1983): 69–100. Reprint in Frances Malino and David Sorkin, ed., *From East and West: Jews in a Changing Europe, 1750–1870,* 151–181. Oxford: Basil Blackwell, 1990.

——. "'A Hebrew to the end': The Emergence of Disraeli's Jewishness." In *The Self-Fashioning of Disraeli, 1818–1851,* edited by Charles Richmond and Paul Smith, 106–130. Cambridge: Cambridge University Press, 1998.

——. *The Jews of Britain: 1656–2000.* Jewish Communities in the Modern World. Edited by David Sorkin. Berkeley: University of California Press, 2002.

——. *The Jews of Georgian England, 1714–1830: Tradition and Change in a Liberal Society.* Philadelphia: The Jewish Publication Society of America, 1979. Reprint, with a new preface, Ann Arbor: University of Michigan Press, 1999.

——. *Radical Assimilation in English Jewish History, 1656–1945*. Bloomington: Indiana University Press, 1990.

—— and Tony Kushner, ed. *Disraeli's Jewishness*. London: Valentine Mitchell, 2002.

"Epistolary Correspondence of the Earlier Members of the Church." *Monthly Observer and New Church Record* 3 (1859): 281.

Erdman, David V. *Blake: Prophet Against Empire*. Revised ed. Princeton: Princeton University Press, 1969.

Essick, Robert. *William Blake and the Language of Adam*. Oxford: Clarendon Press, 1989.

Esterhammer, Angela. "Coleridge's 'Hymn before Sun-rise' and the Voice Not Heard." In *Samuel Taylor Coleridge and the Sciences of Life*, edited by Nicholas Roe, 224–245. Oxford: Oxford University Press, 2001.

——. *Creating States: Studies in the Performative Language of John Milton and William Blake*. Toronto: University of Toronto Press, 1994.

Fattah, Hala. *The Politics of Regional Trade in Iraq, Arabia, and the Gulf 1745–1900*. Albany: State University of New York Press, 1997.

Fay, Elizabeth. "Grace Aguilar: Rewriting Scott Rewriting History." In *British Romanticism and the Jews: History, Culture, Literature*, edited by Sheila A. Spector, 215–234. New York: Palgrave/Macmillan, 2002.

Feiner, Shmuel. *Haskalah and History: The Emergence of a Modern Jewish Historical Consciousness*. Translated by Chaya Naor and Sondra Silverton. Oxford and Portland, OR: Littman Library of Jewish Civilization, 2002.

—— and David Sorkin, eds. *New Perspectives on the Haskalah*. London and Portland, OR: Littman Library of Jewish Civilization, 2001.

Felman, Shoshana. "The Return of the Voice: Claude Lanzmann's *Shoah*." In *Testimony: Crises of Witnessing in Literature, Psychoanalysis and Theory*, edited by Felman and Dori Laub, 204–283. New York: Routledge, 1992.

Felsenstein, Frank. *Anti-Semitic Stereotypes: A Paradigm of Otherness in English Popular Culture, 1666–1830*. Baltimore: The Johns Hopkins University Press, 1995.

——. "Caricature." In *Encyclopedia of Antisemitism, Anti-Jewish Prejudice and Persecution*. Edited by Richard Levy. New York: ABC-Clio, scheduled for publication, 2004–2005.

——. "Punch." In *Encyclopedia of Antisemitism, Anti-Jewish Prejudice and Persecution*. Edited by Richard Levy. New York: ABC-Clio, scheduled for publication, 2004–2005.

Ferguson, James. "Prefaces to *Jerusalem*." In *Interpreting Blake: Essays*, edited by Michael Phillips, 164–195. London, New York and Melbourne: Cambridge University Press, 1978.

Ferguson, James, ed. *The British Essayists*. London: Barnard and Farley, 1819.

Ferguson, Mungo. *The Printed Books in the Library of the Hunterian Museum in the University of Glasgow*. Glasgow: Jackson, Wylie, 1930.

Ferguson, Niall. *The House of Rothschild: Money's Prophets, 1798–1848*. New York: Viking, 1998.

Ferriar, John. *An Essay towards a Theory of Apparitions*. London: Cadell and Davies, 1813.

——. *The Theory of Dreams: in which an inquiry is made into the Powers and Faculties of the Human Mind*. London: Printed for F. C. and J. Rivington, 1808.

Finkelstein, Louis, ed. *The Jews: Their Religion and Culture*. New York: Schocken, 1949.

Fisch, Harold. *Poetry with a Purpose: Biblical Poetics and Interpretation.* Bloomington: Indiana University Press, 1988.

——. "Power and Constraint: Covenantal Hermeneutics in Milton." In *Summoning: Ideas of the Covenant and Interpretive Theory,* edited by Ellen Spolsky, 1–24. Albany: State University of New York Press, 1993.

Frankel, Jonathan. *The Damascus Affair: "Ritual Murder," Politics, and the Jews in 1840.* Cambridge: Cambridge University Press, 1997.

Franklin, Andrew. *The Wandering Jew: or, Love's Masquerade.* London: George Cawthorn, 1797.

Franklin, Caroline. "'Some Examples of the Finest Orientalism': Byronic Philhellenism and Proto-Zionism at the Time of the Congress of Vienna." In *Romanticism and Colonialism: Writing and Empire, 1780–1830,* edited by Tim Fulford and Peter J. Kitson, 221–242. Cambridge: Cambridge University Press, 1999.

Franklin, Jacob. "Judaism and the Reviewer of 'Tancred' in the 'Times.'" In *Disraeli's Novels Reviewed, 1826–1968,* edited by R. W. Stewart, 237. Metuchen, NJ: The Scarecrow Press, 1975.

Fretwell, Katie and Judith Goodman. "The Fete of Abraham Goldsmid: A Regency Garden Tragedy." http://www.nationaltrust.org.uk/environment/html.

Frick, Karl. *Die Erleuchteten.* Graz: AkademischeDruck-u. Verlagsanstadt, 1973.

Friedman, Isaiah. "Lord Palmerston and the Protection of Jews in Palestine, 1838–1851." *Jewish Social Studies* 30 (1968): 23–41.

Frost, Murray. "The Edict of Tolerance and the Jews." *Deep Background: Delving Deeper into Jewish History on Stamps.* http://www.goletapublishing.com/jstamps/0102deep.htm (March 16, 2004): 1–3.

Fulford, Tim, and Peter J. Kitson, eds. *Romanticism and Colonialism: Writing and Empire, 1780–1830.* Cambridge: Cambridge University Press, 1998.

Fullenwider, Henry F. "Friedrich Christoph Œtinger, Theophil Friedrich Œtinger, und die Spätrosenkreutzer." *Blätter für Wurttembergische Geschichte* 7 (1975): 53.

Funk & Wagnalls Standard Dictionary of Folklore Mythology and Legend. Edited by Maria Leach. New York: Funk & Wagnalls, 1972.

Galchinsky, Michael. "Grace Aguilar's Correspondence." *Jewish Culture and History* 2 (summer 1999): 88–110.

——. *The Origin of the Modern Jewish Woman Writer: Romance and Reform in Victorian England.* Detroit: Wayne State University Press, 1996.

Gardner, Martin. "The Wandering Jew and the Second Coming." *Free Inquiry* 15 (1995): 32.

Garrett, Clarke. *Respectable Folly: Millenarians and the French Revolution in France and England.* Baltimore: The Johns Hopkins University Press, 1975.

——. "The Spiritual Odyssey of Jacob Duché." *Proceedings of the American Philosophical Society* 119 (1975): 143–155.

——. "Swedenborg and the Mystical Enlightenment in Late Eighteenth-Century England." *Journal of the History of Ideas* 45 (1984): 67–81.

Gelder, Ken. *Reading the Vampire.* London: Routledge, 1994.

Gerber, Jane S. *The Jews of Spain: A History of the Sephardic Experience.* New York: Free Press, 1992.

German, Terence J. *Hamann on Language and Religion.* Oxford: Oxford University Press, 1981.

Gilam, Abraham. *The Emancipation of the Jews in England 1830–1860.* New York and London: Garland Publishing, Inc., 1982.

Gillingham, S. E. *The Poems and Psalms of the Hebrew Bible*. Oxford: Oxford University Press, 1994.

Gilman, Sander L. *Jewish Self-Hatred: Anti-Semitism and the Hidden Language of the Jews*. Baltimore: The Johns Hopkins University Press, 1986.

——. *The Jew's Body*. New York: Routledge, 1991.

Gluzman, Michael. "The Lack of Power—The Most Shameful Disease: Bialik and the Kishiniev Pogrom." *Theory and Criticism: An Israeli Forum*, no. 22 (spring 2003): 105–132.

Goldhagen, Daniel Jonah. *Hitler's Willing Executioners: Ordinary Germans and the Holocaust*. New York: Knopf, 1996.

[Goldney, Edward]. *Epistles to Deists and Jews*. London: printed for the author, 1759.

——. "Friendly Address to the Jews." *Gentleman's Magazine* 29 (1759): 269–270.

Goren, Ya'akov, ed. *'Eduyot nifge 'e Kishinov, 1903: kefi she-nigbu 'al-yede H. N. Byalik va-haverav* (Testimony of the 1903 Kishinev Pogrom as Written down by H. N. Bialik and others). Tel Aviv: Hakibbutz Hameuchad and Yad Tabenkin, 1991.

Graupe, Heinz Moshe. "Mordechai Shnaber-Levison: The Life, Works, and Thought of a Haslakah Outsider." *Leo Baeck Institute Yearbook* 41 (1996): 3–20.

Greenstein, Edward L. "Sources of the Pentateuch." In *Harper's Bible Dictionary*, gen. ed. Paul J. Achtemeier, 983–986. San Francisco: Harper & Row, 1985.

Gubar, Susan and Sandra Gilbert. *The Madwoman in the Attic: The Woman Writer and the Nineteenth-Century Literary Imagination*. New Haven: Yale University Press, 1979.

Ha-Ephrati, Yosef. "Changes in Landscape Description in Poetry as a Paradigm of Literary Transition" (in Hebrew with an English summary). *Ha-sifrut-literature* 17 (1974): 50–54.

Häll, Jan. *I Swedenborgs Labyrint: Studier i de Gustavianska Swedenborgarnes liv och tänkande*. Stockholm: Atlantis, 1995.

Halpern, Israel, ed. *Sefer hagevurah: antologyah historit-sifrutit (The Book of Heroism: An historical-literary anthology)*. 3 vols. Tel Aviv: Am Oved, 1951.

Hamann, Johann Georg. *Briefwechsel*. Edited by Walther Ziesemer and Arthur Henkel. 6 vols. Wiesbaden: Insel, 1955–1979.

——. *Sämtliche Werke*. Edited by Josef Nadler. 6 vols. Vienna: Herder, 1949–1957.

Hampe, John Henry, F. R. S. *An Experimental System of Metallurgy*. London: J. Nourse, 1777.

Handelman, Susan. *The Slayers of Moses: The Emergence of Rabbinic Interpretation in Modern Literary Theory*. Albany: State University of New York Press, 1982.

Harshav, Benjamin. *Language in Time of Revolution*. Stanford: Stanford University Press, 1993.

——. *The Meaning of Yiddish*. Stanford: Stanford University Press, 1990.

Hartman, Geoffrey. *Wordsworth's Poetry, 1787–1814*. New Haven: Yale University Press, 1964.

—— and Sanford Budick, eds. *Midrash and Literature*. New Haven: Yale University Press, 1986.

Hasan-Rokem, Galit and Alan Dundes, eds. *The Wandering Jew: Essays in the Interpretation of a Christian Legend*. Bloomington: Indiana University Press, 1986.

Haskell, Francis and Nicholas Penny. *Taste and the Antique: The Lure of Classical Sculpture 1500–1900*. New Haven and London: Yale University Press, 1981.

Hazaz, Hayim. *Avanim Rothot* (Seething stones). Tel Aviv: Am Oved, 1946, 1968.

Hazlitt, William. *The Complete Works of William Hazlitt.* Edited by P. P. Howe after A. P. Waller and Arnold Glover. 21 vols. New York: ASM Press, 1967.

——. "On the Principles of Human Action" (1805). In *The Complete Works of William Hazlitt.* Edited by P. P. Howe. London: Dent & Sons, 1930.

Helms, Randall. "Why Ezekiel Ate Dung." *English Language Notes* 15 (June 1978): 280–281.

Henry, Michael. Letter to James Picciotto, June 12, 1874. MS 116/59, University of Southampton Library, Archives and Manuscripts.

Herder, Johann Gottfried von. *The Spirit of Hebrew Poetry.* Translated by James Marsh. Burlington, VT: E. Smith, 1833.

——. *Vom Geist der ebräischen Poesie.* Dessau: Rudolstadt, 1782–1783.

Herman, Peter C., ed. *Opening the Borders: Inclusivity in Early Modern Studies, Essays in Honor of James V. Mirollo.* Newark: University of Delaware Press, 1999.

Hever, Hannan. *Producing the Modern Hebrew Canon: Nation Building and Minority Discourse.* New York: New York University Press, 2002.

Hills, Gordon P. "Notes on Some Contemporary References to Dr. Falk, the Baal Shem of London, in the Rainsford Manuscripts at the British Museum." *Transactions of the Jewish Historical Society of England* (1918): 122–128.

——. "Notes on the Rainsford Papers in the British Museum." *Ars Quatuor Coronatorum* 26 (1913): 93–130.

[Hindmarsh, Robert, ed.] *The New Jerusalem Journal* 2 (September 1792): 50.

Hodder, Edwin. *The Life and Work of the Seventh Earl of Shaftesbury, K. G.* 3 vols. London: Cassell, 1888.

Hoeveler, Diane Long. *Gothic Feminism: The Professionalization of Gender from Charlotte Smith to the Brontës.* University Park: Pennsylvania State University Press, 1998.

Hogan, Charles Beecher. *The London Stage, 1776–1800: A Critical Introduction.* Carbondale and Edwardsville: Southern Illinois University Press, 1968.

Hogarth, William. *Hogarth's Graphic Works.* Compiled and with a commentary by Ronald Paulson. 2 vols. New Haven and London: Yale University Press, 1965.

Holmes, Richard. *Coleridge: Early Visions.* New York: Viking Penguin, 1990.

Hook, Theodore Edward. *The Invisible Girl.* London: C. and R. Baldwin, 1806.

Horowitz, Mayer. "Bibliografia fun yidishe iberzetzungen fun der englisher literatur" (Bibliography of Yiddish translations of English literature). *Jewish Book Annual* 11 (1952/53): 136–153.

Horowitz, Yehoshua. "Horowitz, Phinehas (Pinhas) Ben Zevi Hirsch Ha-Levi." *Encyclopaedia Judaica.* Jerusalem: Keter, 1972. 8: 999–1001.

"How the Jews Got Their Names." www.geocities.com/buddychai/Religion/Names.html. (March 13, 2004): 1–3.

Hughson, David. *London: Being an Accurate History and Description of the British Metropolis and its Neighborhood, to Thirty Miles Extent.* 6 vols. London: J. Stratford, 1805–1809.

Hume, David. *The Natural History of Religion and Dialogues Concerning Natural Religion.* Edited by A. Wayne Colver. Oxford: Clarendon Press, 1976.

——. *A Treatise of Human Nature.* Edited by L. A. Selby-Bigge. Oxford: Clarendon Press, 1965.

Hurewitz, J. C. "Britain and the Middle East up to 1914." In *Encyclopedia of the Modern Middle East,* edited by Reeva S. Simon, Philip Mattar and Richard W. Bulliet, 1: 398–400. 4 vols. New York: Macmillan, 1996.

Hutton, J. E. *A History of the Moravian Missions.* London: Moravian Publication Office, 1922.

Hyamson, Albert M. *The British Consulate in Jerusalem in Relation to the Jews of Palestine, 1838–1914.* 2 vols. London: The Jewish Historical Society of England/Edward Goldston, Ltd., 1939.

Jack, Sybil M. "No Heavenly Jerusalem: The Anglican Bishopric, 1841–83." *The Journal of Religious History* 19 (1995): 181–203.

Jackson's Oxford Journal, Dec. 28, 1753.

Jacobi, Friedrich Heinrich. *Über die Lehre des Spinoza in Briefen an den Herrn Moses Mendelssohn.* Breslau, 1785.

——. *Wider Mendelssohns Beschuldigungen, betreffend die Briefe über die Lehre des Spinoza.* Breslau, 1786.

Jermingham, Edward. *Abelard to Eloisa: A Poem.* London: J. Robson, 1792.

The Jews Free School Governors Committee Minutes 1818–1831, March 23, 1824.

Joly, Alice. "La 'Sainte Parole' d'Avignon." *Les Cahiers de la Tour Saint-Jacques* 2–4 (1960): 98–116.

Jones, Edwin. *The English Nation: The Great Myth.* Phoenix Mill: Sutton, 1998.

Jones, William, Sir. *Grammar of the Persian Language.* Third ed. London: J. Murray, 1783.

Kant, Immanuel. *Werke.* Edited by Wilhelm Weischedel. 6 vols. Darmstadt: Wissenschaftliche Buchgesellschaft, 1975.

Kaplan, Caren. "Deterritorializations: The Rewriting of Home and Exile in Western Feminist Discourse." In *The Nature and Context of Minority Discourse,* edited by Abdul R. JanMohamed and David Lloyd, 357–368. New York: Oxford University Press, 1990.

Kark, Ruth and Joseph B.Glass. "Eretz Israel/Palestine, 1800–1948." In *The Jews of the Middle East and North Africa in Modern Times,* edited by Reeva Spector Simon, Michael Menachem Laskier and Sara Reguer, 335–346. New York: Columbia University Press, 2003.

Katz, David S. *The Jews in the History of England, 1485–1850.* Oxford: Clarendon Press, 1994.

——. *Philo-Semitism and the Readmission of the Jews to England, 1603–1655.* Oxford: Clarendon Press, 1982.

Katz, Jacob. *From Prejudice to Destruction: Anti-Semitism, 1700–1933.* Cambridge: Harvard University Press, 1980.

——. *Jews and Freemasons in Europe, 1723–1939.* Cambridge: Harvard University Press, 1970.

Katz, Yaakov. *Leumiyut yehudit: Masot vemehkarim (Jewish nationalism: Essays and studies).* Jerusalem: HaSifria HaZionit, 1979.

Keble, John. *Lectures on poetry, 1832–1841.* [= *Di Poeticae Vi Medica,* 1844]. Translated by Edward Kershaw Francis. 2 vols. Oxford: Clarendon Press, 1912.

Kershen, Anne J. and Jonathan A. Romain. *Tradition and Change: A History of Reform Judaism in Britain, 1840–1995.* London: Vallentine Mitchell, 1995.

King, John N. "Religious Writing." In *The Cambridge Companion to English Literature, 1500–1600,* edited by Arthur F. Kinney, 104–131. Cambridge: Cambridge University Press, 2000.

Kinney, Arthur F., ed. *The Cambridge Companion to English Literature, 1500–1600.* Cambridge: Cambridge University Press, 2000.

Kitson, Peter. "Romantic Displacements: Representing Cannibalism." In *Placing and Displacing Romanticism,* edited by Kitson, 204–225. Aldershot: Ashgate, 2001.

Klopstock, Friedrich Gottlieb. "Die Frühlingsfeier." In *German Poetry: A Critical Anthology*, edited by Robert M. Browning, 52–61. Englewood Cliffs, NJ: Prentice-Hall, 1962.

Kowaleski-Wallace, Elizabeth. *Their Fathers' Daughters: Hannah More, Maria Edgeworth, and Patriarchal Complicity.* New York: Oxford University Press, 1991.

Kristeva, Julia. *Powers of Horror: An Essay on Abjection.* Translated by Louis A. Roudiez. New York: Columbia University Press, 1980.

Kurzweil, Baruch. *Bialik and Tschernichovski* (in Hebrew). Tel Aviv: Schocken, 1963.

Lachman, Lilach. "Keat's *Hyperion*: Time, Space, and the Long Poem." *Poetics Today* 22,1 (spring 2001): 89–127.

Lacoue-Labarthe, Philippe and Jean-Luc Nancy. *The Literary Absolute: The Theory of Literature in German Romanticism.* Translated by Philip Barnard and Cheryl Lester. New York: State University of New York Press, 1988.

Lahower, Yeruham Fishel. *Bialik: hayyav vi-yzirotav* (*Bialik: His life and his works*). 3 vols. in 2. Tel Aviv: Dvir, 1944–1947.

——. *Toldot ha-sifrut ha-'Ivrit ha-hadashah: 'im dugma'ot shel vetav ha-sifrut le-talmidim ule-mitlamdim* (A history of modern Hebrew literature). Tel Aviv: Dvir, 1963.

Lamb, Charles and Mary. *The Works.* Edited by E. V. Lucas. 5 vols. New York: AMS Press, 1968.

Landry, Donna Landry. *The Muses of Resistance: Laboring-Class Women's Poetry in Britain, 1739–1796.* Cambridge: Cambridge University Press, 1990.

Leibnitz, Gottfried Wilhelm. "On the Principle of Indiscernibles." In *Leibniz: Philosophical Writings*, edited and translated by G. H. R. Parkinson and Mary Morris. London: Dent, 1973.

Leighton, Angela. *Shelley and the Sublime.* Cambridge: Cambridge University Press, 1984.

Lerer, Seth. "Erich Auerbach and the Institutions of Medieval Studies." In *Medievalism and the Modernist Temper*, edited by R. Howard Bloch and Stephen G. Nichols, 308–333. Baltimore: The Johns Hopkins University Press, 1996.

——, ed. *Literary History and the Challenge of Philology: The Legacy of Erich Auerbach.* Stanford: Stanford University Press, 1996.

Lessing, Gotthold Ephraim. "Das Christenthum der Vernunft" (aus dem Nachlaß). In *Theologischkritische Schriften*, edited by Helmut Göbel. Volumes 7 and 8 of *Werke.* Edited by Herbert P. Göpfert et al. Munich: Carl Hanser Verlag, 1970–1979.

——. Moses Mendelssohn and Friedrich Nicolai. *Briefwechsel über das Trauerspiel.* Edited by Jochen Schulte-Sasse. München: Winkler, 1972.

Levi, David. *A Succinct Account, of the Rites, and Ceremonies, of the Jews . . . In which, their religious principles, and tenets, are clearly explained: particularly, their doctrine of the resurrection, predestination and freewill: and the opinion of Doctor Prideaux concerning those tenets, fully investigated, duly considered and clearly confuted. Also an account of the Jewish calendar, to which is added, a faithful and impartial account of the Mishna.* London, J. Parsons, 1782.

Levison, Mordechai Gumpertz. *An Account of the Epidemical Sore Throat.* London: printed for B. White, J. Bew, and W. Sharp, 1778.

——. *An Essay on the Blood.* London: T. Davies, 1776.

——. *Utkast til Physica Anmärkningar öfver Lefnadstattet I Stockholm . . . af en Engelsk Läkare.* Stockholm, 1780.

Levitt, Laura. *Jews and Feminism.* New York: Routledge, 1997.

Liebes, Esther (Zweig). "Dov Baer (The Maggid) of Mezhirech." *Encyclopaedia Judaica*. Jerusalem: Keter, 1972. 6:180–184.

Liebes, Yehudah. "A Crypto Judaeo-Christian Sect of Sabbatean Origin" (Hebrew, with an English abstract). *Tarbiz* 57 (1988): 110, 349–384.

Lindsay, Jack. *William Blake: His Life and Work*. London: Constable, 1978.

Liptzin, Sol. *A History of Yiddish Literature*. Middle Village, NY: Jonathan David Publishers, 1972.

Lister, Raymond. *George Richmond: A Critical Biography*. London: Robin-Gorton, 1981.

Lloyd, Stephen. *Richard and Maria Cosway: Regency Artists of Taste and Fashion*. Edinburgh: Scottish National Portrait Gallery, 1995.

Lockwood, J. P. *Memorials of the Life of Peter Boehler, Bishop of the Church of the Moravian Brethren*. Introduction by Thomas Jackson. London: Wesleyan Conference Office, 1868.

London, Grand Lodge. Atholl Register, Lodge #38.

——. MS. BE 166—Livre des délibérations de la loge de l'Union, #70 (ca. 1772–1790).

London, Moravian Church Library. MS. C/36/158–159; Congregation Diary, V (1751), 61, 80; Petitions for Membership—"John Blake."

London, Wellcome Institute of History of Medicine. Lalande MS. 1048 (C. G. Salzmann to P. J. Willermoz, December 31, 1781).

London Times, September 16, 1812.

Longrigg, Stephen Helmsley. *Four Centuries of Modern Iraq*. London: Oxford University Press, 1925.

Lowery, Margaret. *Windows of the Morning: A Critical Study of William Blake's Poetical Sketches, 1783*. New Haven: Yale University Press, 1940.

Lowth, Robert. *Lectures on the Sacred Poetry of the Hebrews*. Translated by J. Gregory. London: J. Johnson, 1787. Boston: Joseph T. Buckingham, 1815.

——. *De sacra poesi Hebræorum*. Oxford: Clarendon Press, 1753.

Lynch, James J. *Box, Pit, and Gallery: Stage and Society in Johnson's London*. Berkeley and Los Angeles: University of California Press, 1953.

Lynn, Martin. "British Policy, Trade, and Informal Empire in the Mid-Nineteenth Century." In *The Oxford History of the British Empire: The Nineteenth Century*, edited by Andrew Porter, 101–121. New York: Oxford University Press, 1999.

Lyon, Emma. *Miscellaneous Poems*. Oxford: J. Bartlett, 1812. Reprint on-line through the University of California at Davis "British Women Romantic Poets" project, http://www.lib.ucdavis.edu/BWRP/Works/#L.

Lyotard, Jean-François and Jean-Loup Thébaud. *Just Gaming*. Translated by Wlad Godzich. Minneapolis: University of Minnesota Press, 1985.

Maccoby, Hyam. "The Wandering Jew as Sacred Executioner." In *The Wandering Jew: Essays in the Interpretation of a Christian Legend*, edited by Galit Hasan-Rokem and Alan Dundes, 236–260. Bloomington: Indiana University Press, 1986.

Malchow, H. L. *Gothic Images of Race in Nineteenth-Century Britain*. Stanford: Stanford University Press, 1996.

Massey, Irving. "Yiddish Poetry of the Holocaust." *Find You the Virtue: Ethics, Image, and Desire in Literature*. Fairfax, VA: George Mason University Press, 1987.

Matthews, John. *Eloisa en Dishabille, Being a New Version of That Lady's Celebrated Epistle to Abelard*. London: J. Wright, 1801.

Maxted, Ian. *The London Book Trades, 1775–1800.* London: Dawson, 1977.

McFarland, Thomas. *Coleridge and the Pantheist Tradition.* Oxford: Clarendon Press, 1969.

McIntosh, Christopher. *The Rose Cross and the Age of Reason.* Leiden: Brill, 1992.

McKusick, James. *Coleridge's Philosophy of Language.* New Haven: Yale University Press, 1986.

Mee, Jon. *Dangerous Enthusiasm: William Blake and the Culture of Radicalism in the 1790s.* Oxford: Clarendon Press, and New York: Oxford University Press, 1992.

Mendelssohn, Moses. *An die Freunde Lessings.* Berlin: Nicolai, 1786.

——. *Betrachtungen über die Quellen und die Verbindungen der schönen Künste und Wissenschaften.* Berlin: Friedrich Voß, 1758.

——. *Die fünf Bücher Mose zum Gebrauch der jüdischdeutschen Nation.* Berlin: Nicolai, 1780.

——. *Gesammelte Schriften.* Edited by G. B. Mendelssohn. 7 vols. in 9. Leipzig: Brockhaus, 1843–1845.

——. *Jerusalem, oder über religiöse Macht und Judentum.* Berlin: Friedrich Maurer, 1783.

——. *Morgenstunden: oder, Vorlesungen über das Daseyn Gottes.* Berlin: Christian Friedrich Voß, 1786.

——. *Philosophische Schriften.* Berlin: Christian Friedrich Voß, 1780.

——. *Ritualgesetze der Juden: betreffend Erbschaften, Vormundschaftssachen, Testamente und Ehesachen, in so weit sie das Mein und Dein angehen.* Berlin: Christian Friedrich Voß, 1778.

——. *Über die Empfindungen.* Berlin: Christian Friedrich Voß, 1755.

Metzger, Lore. "Coleridge's Vindicaiton of Spinoza: An Unpublished Note." *Journal of the History of Ideas* 21 (1960): 279–293.

Meyer, Michael A. *Response to Modernity: A History of the Reform Movement in Judaism.* New York and Oxford: Oxford University Press, 1988.

Michisaw, Kim Ian. "Charlotte Dacre's Postcolonial Moor." In *Empire and the Gothic: The Politics of Genre,* edited by Andrew Smith and William Hughes, 35–55. New York: Palgrave/Macmillan, 2003.

Milton, John. *Paradise Lost.* Edited by Merritt Y. Hughes. Indianapolis: Odyssey Press, 1962.

——. *The Riverside Milton.* Edited by Roy Flannagan. Boston, New York: Houghton Mifflin, 1998.

Mintz, Alan. *Hurban: Responses to Catastrophe in Hebrew Literature.* 1984. Syracuse: Syracuse University Press, 1996.

Miron, Dan. *H. N. Bialik and the Prophetic Mode in Modern Hebrew Poetry.* Syracuse: Syracuse University Press, 2000.

——. *"Ha-preida min ha-ani ha-a-ni"* (Taking leave of the impoverished self: H. N. Bialik's early poetry 1891–1901). Tel Aviv: Hauniversita Haptuha, 1986.

Moncrief, William Thomas. *Rochester: or, King Charles the Second's Merry Days.* London: John Lowndes, 1819.

La Monde Maçonnique 15 (1873–1874).

Monthly Review 70 (February 1813): 213–214.

Moore, Thomas. *Memoirs, Journal and Correspondence of Thomas Moore.* Edited by Lord John Russell. 8 vols. London: Longman, Brown, Green, and Longmans, 1853–1856.

Morley, Edith J., ed. *Henry Crabb Robinson on Books and Their Writers.* London: J. M. Dent, 1938.

Nathan, Isaac. *A Selection of Hebrew Melodies, Ancient and Modern, and* [*text by*] *Lord Byron*. Edited by Frederick Burwick and Paul Douglass. Tuscaloosa: University of Alabama Press, 1988.

Nichols, John. *Literary Anecdotes of the Eighteenth Century*. 1812–1815. Reprint, New York: AMS, 1961.

Nicoll, Allardyce. *A History of English Drama 1660–1900*. 6 vols. Cambridge: Cambridge University Press, 1952.

Niebuhr, Carsten. *A Collection of Late Voyages and Travels . . . Concerning the Present State of Society and Manners, of Arts and Literature, of Religion and Government, the Appearances of Nature, and the Works of Human Industry in Persia, Arabia, Turkey, &c.* London: J. Hamilton, 1797.

Nineteenth-Century Short Title Catalogue. Series 1, 1801–1815, vol. 6. Newcastle upon Tyne et al.: Avero, 1984.

[Nordenskjöld, Augustus]. *A Plain System of Alchymy*. Inscribed by the author. London, Soho Square, December 1, 1779.

Nordenskjöld, C. F. Letter to C. B. Wadström. (January 31, 1784). In *Academy Collection of Swedenborg Documents*. Bryn Athyn: Academy of New Church, no date.

Œtinger, Friedrich Christoph. *Swedenborgs und andere Irrdische und Himmlische Philosophie*. Frankfurt und Leipzig, 1765.

O'Flaherty, James C. *Johann Georg Hamann*. Boston: Twayne-G. K. Hall, 1979.

Ogden, James. *Isaac D'Israeli*. Oxford: Clarendon Press, 1969.

Oueijian, Naji B. "Orientalism: The Romantics' Added Dimension; or, Edward Said Refuted." *EESE* (*Erfurt Electronic Studies in English*). http://webdoc.gwdg.de/edoc/ia/eese/artic20/naji/3_2000.html (January 10, 2003): 1–9.

Ouseley, William. *Persian Miscellanies: An Essay to Facilitate the Reading of Persian Manuscripts with Engraved Specimens, Philosophical Observations, and Notes Critical and Historical*. London: Richard White, 1795.

Page, Judith W. "Gender and Domesticity." In *The Cambridge Companion to Wordsworth*, edited by Stephen Gill, 125–141. New York: Cambridge University Press, 2003.

———. "Hyman Hurwutz's *Hebrew Tales* (1826): Redeeming the Talmudic Garden." In *British Romanticism and the Jews: History, Culture, Literature*, edited by Sheila A. Spector, 197–213. New York: Palgrave/Macmillan, 2002.

Pagés, Pierre Marie François de. *Travels around the World in the Years 1767, 1768, 1769, 1770, 1771*. Dublin: P. Byrne, W. McKenzie, 1791.

Paley, Morton D. *The Apocalyptic Sublime*. New Haven: Yale University Press, 1986.

———. *The Continuing City: William Blake's "Jerusalem."* Oxford: Clarendon Press, 1983.

———. "William Blake, the Prince of the Hebrews, and the Woman Clothed with the Sun." In *William Blake: Essays in Honour of Sir Geffrey Keynes*, edited by Paley and Michael Phillips, 260–293. Oxford: Clarendon Press, 1973.

Partington, James. *A History of Chemistry*. London: Macmillan, 1962.

Pelli, Moshe. *Mordechai Gumpel Schnaber: The First Religious Reformer of the Hebrew Haslakah in Germany*. Beer-Sheva: University of Negev, 1972.

Perry, Menakhem. *Hamivneh hasemanti shel shirei Bialik* (*Semantic Dynamics in Bialik's Poetry*). Tel Aviv: Porter, 1977.

Perry, Seamus. "Romantic Poetry and the Matter of Fact." Unpublished paper delivered at the annual conference of the North American Society for the Study of Romanticism (NASSR), New York, August 2003.

Perry, Thomas W. *Public Opinion, Propaganda, and Politics in Eighteenth-Century England: A Study of the Jew Bill of 1753*. Cambridge: Harvard University Press, 1962.

Peterfreund, Stuart. "Not for 'Antiquaries,' but for 'Philosophers': Isaac D'Israeli's Talmudic Critique and His Talmudical Way with Literature.'" In *British Romanticism and the Jews: History, Culture, Literature*, edited by Sheila A. Spector, 179–196. New York: Palgrave/Macmillan, 2002.

Philo, of Alexandria. *Questionun et solutionum in Genesin*. In *Philonis Alexandrini Opera quae supersunt*, edited by Leopold Cohn and Paul Wendland. 7 vols. in 8. Berlin: George Reimer, 1896–1915.

Picturesque Views of the Principal Seats of the Nobility and Gentry, By the most Eminent British Artists, with A Description of each Seat. London: Harrison & Co.: n.d. but c. 1786–1788.

Plaut, W. Gunther, ed. *The Torah: A Modern Commentary*. New York: Union of Hebrew Congregations, 1981.

Podmore, Colin. *The Moravian Church in England, 1728–1760*. Oxford: Clarendon Press, 1998.

Pope, Alexander. *Alexander Pope*. Edited by Pat Rogers. New York: Oxford University Press, 1993.

Porter, Andrew, ed. *The Oxford History of the British Empire: The Nineteenth Century*. New York: Oxford University Press, 1999.

Prager, Leonard. "Charles Dickens in Yiddish (A Survey)." *Jewish Language Review* 4 (1984): 158–178.

The Protester, on Behalf of the People, "by Issachar Barebone, one of the People," 10:58.

Public Advertiser, December 14, 1771.

Quine, Willard Van Orman. "Necessary Truth." 1963. Reprinted in *The Ways of Paradox*. Revised ed. Cambridge, MA: Harvard University Press, 1976.

———. "Two Dogmas of Empiricism." *Philosophical Review* 60,1 (January 1951): 20–43. Reprinted in *From a Logical Point of View: 9 Logico-Philosophical Essays*. Revised ed. Cambridge, MA: Harvard University Press, 1961.

Ragussis, Michael. *Figures of Conversion: "The Jewish Question" and English National Identity*. Durham and London: Duke University Press, 1995.

———. "Jews and Other 'Outlandish Englishmen': Ethnic Performance and the Invention of British Identity under the Georges." *Critical Inquiry* 26 (summer 2000): 773–797.

Raine, Kathleen. *The Human Face of God: William Blake and the Book of Job*. New York: Thames and Hudson, 1982.

Rathmell, J. C. A., ed. *The Psalms of Sir Philip Sidney and The Countess of Pembroke*. New York: New York University Press, 1963.

Redfield, Marc. "Romanticism, *Bildung* and the Literary Absolute." In *Lessons of Romanticism: A Critical Companion*, edited by Thomas Pfau and Robert F. Gleckner, 41–54. Durham and London: Duke University Press, 1998.

Report and State of the Society of Friends of Foreigners in Distress. London: W. Marchant, 1816.

Ribeiro, Aileen. *The Dress Worn at Masquerades in England, 1730–1790, and Its Relation to Fancy Dress in Portraiture*. New York and London: Garland, 1984.

Richardson, John. *A Dictionary. Persian, Arabic and English, by John Richardson, to Which There Is Prefixed a Dissertation on the Languages, Literatures, and Manners of Eastern Nations*. 2 vols. Oxford: Clarendon Press, 1777–1780.

——. *A Grammar of the Arabic Language, in Which the Rules Are Illustrated by Authorities from the Best Writers, Principally Adapted for the Use of the Honourable East India Company.* London: J. Murray, 1776.

Rodkey, Frederick S. "Lord Palmerston and the Rejuvenation of Turkey, 1930–41." *The Journal of Modern History* 2 (1930): 193–225.

Rosenberg, Edgar. *From Shylock to Svengali: Jewish Stereotypes in English Fiction.* Stanford: Stanford University Press, 1960.

Roskies, David G. *Against the Apocalypse: Responses to Catastrophe in Modern Jewish Culture.* Cambridge and London: Harvard University Press, 1984.

Roth, Cecil. "The Amazing Clan of Buzaglo." *Transactions of the Jewish Historical Society of England* 23 (1971): 11–22.

——. "The King and the Cabalist." In his *Essays and Portraits in Anglo-Jewish History.* Philadelphia: Jewish Publication Society of America, 1962.

Rubens, Alfred. "Early Anglo-Jewish Artists." *Transactions of the Jewish Historical Society of England* 14 (1935–1939): 10.

Ruderman, David B. *Jewish Enlightenment in an English Key: Anglo-Jewry's Construction of Modern Jewish Thought.* Princeton: Princeton University Press, 2000.

——. *Jewish Thought and Scientific Discovery in Early Modern Europe.* New Haven: Yale University Press, 1995.

Rumney, J. "Anglo-Jewry as Seen Through Foreign Eyes, 1730–1830." *Transactions of the Jewish Historical Society of England* 13 (1932–1935): 323–340.

Runkel, Ferdinand. *Geschichte der Freimaurer in Deutschland.* Berlin: Reimar Hobbing, 1932.

Sachar, Howard M. *A History of the Jews in America.* New York: Knopf, 1992.

Sachse, Julius. *The German Sectarians of Pennsylvania, 1742–1800.* 1899–1900. Reprint, New York: AMS, 1971.

Sáenz-Badillos, Angel. *A History of the Hebrew Language.* Translated by John Elwolde. Cambridge: Cambridge University Press, 1993.

Said, Edward. *Orientalism.* 1978. New York: Vintage, 1979.

Salbstein, M. C. N. *The Emancipation of the Jews in Britain: The Question of the Admission of the Jews to Parliament, 1828–1860.* East Brunswick, NJ: Fairleigh Dickinson University Press, 1982.

Sandler, Florence. "'Defending the Bible': Blake, Paine, and the Bishop." In *Blake and His Bible*, edited by David V. Erdman, with and introduction by Mark Trevor Smith, 41–70. West Cornwall, CT: Locust Hill Press, 1990.

Sartre, Jean-Paul. *Anti-Semite and Jew.* Translated by George J. Becker. 1948. New York: Schoken, 1965.

Schatzky, Jacob. *The History of the Jews of Warsaw* (in Yiddish). New York: Yiddish Scientific Institute, 1947–1953.

Schechter, Solomon. "The 'Baalshem'—Dr. Falk." *Jewish Chronicle*, March 9, 1888.

Scheinberg, Cynthia. *Women's Poetry and Religion in Victorian England: Jewish Identity and Christian Culture.* Cambridge: Cambridge University Press, 2002.

Schelling, F. W. J. *Philosophische Schriften.* Landshut, 1809.

Schoenfield, Mark L. "Abraham Goldsmid: Money Magician in the Popular Press." In *British Romanticism and the Jews: History, Culture, Literature*, edited by Sheila A. Spector, 37–60. New York: Palgrave/Macmillan, 2002.

Schoeps, Hans Joachim. *Barocke Juden, Christen, Judenchristen.* Bern und München: Francke, 1965.

——. "Läkaren och Alkemisten Gumpertz Levison: Ett Bidrag till den Gustavianska Tidens Kulturhistoria." *Lychnos* (1943): 23–48.

Scholem, Gershom G. *Du Frankisme au Jacobinisme.* Paris: Le seul Gallimard, 1981.

Schuchard, Marsha Keith. "Blake's Healing Trio: Magnetism, Medicine, and Mania." *Blake: An Illustrated Quarterly* 23 (1989): 20–31.

——. "Jacobite and Visionary: The Masonic Journey of Emanuel Swedenborg." *Ars Quatuor Coronatorum* 115 (2002): 230–248.

——. "Leibniz, Benzelius, and Swedenborg: The Kabbalistic Roots of Swedish Illuminism." In *Leibniz, Mysticism, and Religion,* edited by Allison Coudert, Richard Popkin, and Gordon Weiner, 84–106. Dordrecht: Kluwer Academic, 1998.

——. *Restoring the Temple of Vision: Cabalistic Freemasonry and Stuart Culture.* Leiden: Brill, 2002.

——. "The Secret Masonic History of Blake's Swedenborg Society." *Blake: An Illustrated Quarterly* 26 (1992): 40–51.

——. "Why Mrs. Blake Cried: Swedenborg, Blake, and the Sexual Basis of Spiritual Vision." *Esoterica: The Journal for Esoteric Studies* 2 (1999): 1–58. <http://www.esoteric.msu.>.

——. *Why Mrs. Blake Cried: William Blake and the Sexual Basis of Spiritual Vision.* London: Random House, forthcoming.

——. "William Blake and the Promiscuous Baboons: A Cagliostroan Séance Gone Awry." *British Journal for Eighteenth-Century Studies* 18 (1995): 185–200.

——. "Yeats and the Unknown Superiors: Swedenborg, Falk, and Cagliostro." In *Secret Texts: The Literature of Secret Societies,* edited by Hugh Ormsby-Lennon and Marie Roberts, 114–168. New York: AMS, 1988.

Scott, Walter. *Ivanhoe.* 1819. Reprint. Edited by A. N. Wilson. New York: Penguin Books, 1984.

Scrivener, Michael. "British-Jewish Writing in the Romantic Era and the Problem of Modernity: The Example of David Levi." In *British Romanticism and the Jews: History, Culture, Literature,* edited by Sheila A. Spector, 159–177. New York: Palgrave/Macmillan, 2002.

Scult, Mel. "English Missions to the Jews—Conversion in the Age of Emancipation." *Jewish Social Studies* 35 (1973): 3–17.

——. *Millennial Expectations and Jewish Liberties: A Study of the Efforts to Convert the Jews in Britain, up to the Mid-Nineteenth Century.* Leiden: E. J. Brill, 1978.

Seats of the Nobility and Gentry in Great Britain and Wales in a Collection of Select Views, Engraved by W. Angus from Pictures and drawings by the most eminent artists. London: W. Angus, Islington, 1787.

Shaftsley, John. "Jews in English Regular Freemasonry, 1717–1860." *Transactions of the Jewish Historical Society of England* 25 (1977): 150–209.

Shaked, Gershon. *Hasiporet haIvrit 1880–1970 (Hebrew narrative fiction 1880–1970).* Tel Aviv: Keter and Hakibbutz Hameuchad, 1977.

Shamir Ziva and Shavit Uzi, eds. *Bi-mvoey ʿir ha-hareiga: mivhar ma-amarim al shiro shel Bialik* (At the gates of Kishinev: Essays on Bialik's poem "In the City of Slaughter"). Tel Aviv: Hakibbutz Hameuchad, 1994.

Shapira, Anita. *Herev Hayona: Hatzionut vehakoach 1881–1948* (The Dove's Dagger: Zionism and Power 1881–1948). Tel Aviv: Am Oved, 1992.

Shapiro, James. *Shakespeare and the Jews.* New York: Columbia University Press, 1996.

Shavit, Uzi. "The Model of Intertextual Parody as a clue to 'Be-ir Ha-harega.'" In *Bi-mvoey Bi-mvoey ʿir ha-hareiga: mivhar ma-amarim al shiro shel Bialik* (At the Gates of Kishinev: Essays on Bialik's Poem "In the City of the Slaughter"), edited by Uzi Shavit and Ziva Shamir, 160–173. Tel Aviv: Hakibutz Hameuchad, 1994.

———, and Ziva Shamir, eds. *Bi-mvoey Bi-mvoey 'ir ha-hareiga: mivhar ma-amarim al shiro shel Bialik* (At the Gates of Kishinev: Essays on Bialik's poem "In the City of the Slaughter"). Tel Aviv: Hakibutz Hameuchad, 1994.

Shepherd, Naomi. *The Zealous Intruders: The Western Rediscovery of Palestine*. New York: Harper and Row, 1987.

Sheridan, Richard Brinsley. *The Dramatic Works of Richard Brinsley Sheridan*. Edited by Cecil Price. 2 vols. Oxford: Clarendon Press, 1973.

Shurer, Hayim, ed. *Hapogrom Bekishinov: bimlot shishim shana* (The Kishinev Pogrom of 1903). Tel Aviv: World Federation of Bessarabian Jews, 1963.

Sidney, Philip. *An Apology for Poetry*. In *Critical Theory Since Plato*, edited by Hazard Adams, 142–162. Revised ed. New York: Harcourt Brace Jovanovich, 1992.

Sigstedt, Cyriel Odhner. *The Swedenborg Epic*. London: Swedenborg Society, 1981.

Sigstedt, Sigrid. "Chronological List of Swedenborg Documents." Typescript in Swedenborg Society London 2 (1943): #2876, 2154, 2265–2266.

Simon, Reeva Spector. "The Case of the Curse: The London Society for Promoting Christianity amongst the Jews and the Jews of Baghdad." In *Altruism and Imperialism: Western Cultural and Religious Missions in the Middle East*, edited by Eleanor H. Tejirian and Simon, 45–65. New York: The Middle East Institute, Columbia University, 2002.

———. "Europe in the Middle East." In *The Jews of the Middle East and North Africa in Modern Times*, edited by Simon, Michael Menachem Laskier and Sara Reguer, 19–28. New York: Columbia University Press, 2003.

———, Michael Menachem Laskier, and Sara Reguer, eds. *The Jews of the Middle East and North Africa in Modern Times*. New York: Columbia University Press, 2003.

———, Philip Mattar, and Richard W. Bulliet, eds. *Encyclopedia of the Modern Middle East*. 4 vols. New York: Macmillan, 1996.

Singer, Alan H. "Great Britain or Judea Nova? National Identity, Property, and the Jewish Naturalization Controversy of 1753." In *British Romanticism and the Jews: History, Culture, Literature*, edited by Sheila A. Spector, 19–36. New York: Palgrave/Macmillan, 2002.

Singerman, Robert. *Jewish Translation History: A Bibliography of Bibliographies and Studies*. Introduction by Gideon Toury. Benjamins Translation Library, vol. 44. Amsterdam and Philadelphia: John Benjamins Publishing Company, 2002.

Smith, Charlotte. *Elegiac Sonnets, and Other Poems*. London: Jones and Company, 1827.

Smith, Robert Michael. "The London Jews' Society and Patterns of Jewish Conversion in England, 1801–1859." *Jewish Social Studies* 43 (1981): 275–290.

Solomons, Israel. "Satirical and Political Prints on the Jews' Naturalization Bill, 1753." *Transactions of the Jewish Historical Society of England* 6 (1912): 205–233.

Southey, Robert, and Samuel Taylor Coleridge. *Omniana; or Horae otiosiores*. London: Longman, Hurst, Rees, Orme, and Brown, 1812.

Southgate, H. *Narrative of a Tour through Armenia, Kurdistan, Persia, and Mesopotamia*. London, 1840.

Spector, Sheila A. "Blake's Graphic Use of Hebrew." *Blake: An Illustrated Quarterly* 37 (2003): 75–79.

———. *"Glorious incomprehensible": The Development of Blake's Kabbalistic Language*. Lewisburg: Bucknell University Press, 2001.

———. *"Wonders Divine": The Development of Blake's Kabbalistic Myth*. Lewisburg: Bucknell University Press, 2001.

———, ed. *British Romanticism and the Jews: History, Culture, Literature*. New York: Palgrave/Macmillan, 2002.

Spenser, Edmund. *The Faerie Queene*. Edited by Thomas Roche, Jr. Assisted by C. Patrick O'Donnell, Jr. New Haven: Yale University Press, 1978.

Spielmann, M. H. *The History of "Punch."* London: Cassell & Co., 1895. Reprint, Detroit: Gale Research Company, 1969.

Spinoza, Benedict. *Ethics*. Included in his *Opera Posthuma*. Amsterdam, 1677.

——. *Ethics*. Translated by R. H. M. Elwes. New York: Dover, 1955.

Spirer, Ellen. "Candidates for Survival: A Talk with Harold Bloom." http://www.bostonreview.net/BR11.1/bloom.html. (March 13, 2004): 1–6.

Spolsky, Ellen, ed. *Summoning: Ideas of the Covenant and Interpretive Theory*. Albany: State University of New York Press, 1993.

Sprinchorn, Carl. "Sjuttonhundratalets Svenska Kolonisationsplaner." *Svensk Historisk Tidskrift* 43 (1923): 132–135.

Stafford, Barbara Maria. *Voyage into Substance: Art, Science, Nature, and the Illustrated Travel Account, 1760–1840*. Cambridge: The Massachusetts Institute of Technology Press, 1984.

Stanislawski, Michael. *Tsar Nicholas I and the Jews: The Transformation of Jewish Society in Russia 1825–1855*. Philadelphia: Jewish Publication Society of America, 1983.

Sternberg, Meir. *The Poetics of Biblical Narrative: Ideological Literature and the Drama of Reading*. Bloomington: Indiana University Press, 1985.

Stewart, R. W. *Disraeli's Novels Reviewed, 1826–1968*. Metuchen, NY: Scarecrow Press, 1975.

Sturzen-Becker, Oscar Patric. "Gustaf de Tredjes Guldmakere." *Månadsskrift* (October–December 1864): 730.

Swedenborg, Emanuel. *A Philosopher's Notebook*. Edited by Alfred Acton. Philadelphia: Swedenborg Scientific Association, 1931.

——. *The Spiritual Diary*. Translated by James Buss. London: Swedenborg Society, 1977.

——. *The True Christian Religion Containing the Universal Theology of the New Church*. Translated by W. C. Dick. London: Swedenborg Society, 1950.

Tafel, Rudolph. *Documents Concerning the Life and Character of Emanuel Swedenborg*. London: Swedenborg Society, 1875.

Targoff, Ramie. *Common Prayer: The Language of Public Devotion in Early Modern England*. Chicago and London: University of Chicago Press, 2001.

Temperley, Harold. *England and the Near East: The Crimea*. New York: Archon Books, 1965.

Tetreault, Ronald. "Shelley and Byron Encounter the Sublime: Switzerland, 1816." *Revue des Langues Vivantes* 41 (1975): 145–155.

Thackeray, William Makepeace. *Burlesques by William Makepeace Thackeray*. Pennsylvania State Electronic Classics Series. www.hn.psu.edu/faculty/jmanis/thackeray/burlesques.pdf, 15–26.

Tibawi, A. L. *British Interests in Palestine 1800–1901: A Study of Religious and Educational Enterprise*. London: Oxford University Press, 1961.

Trachtenberg, Joshua. *The Devil and the Jews: The Medieval Conception of the Jew and Its Relation to Modern Anti-Semitism*. New Haven: Yale University Press, 1943.

Trilling, Lionel. *Sincerity and Authenticity*. Cambridge: Harvard University Press, 1972.

Tuckett, J. E. S. "Savalette de Langes, Les Philaletes, and the Convent of Wilhelmsbad, 1782." *Ars Quatuor Coronatorum* 30 (1917): 131–171.

Valentin, Hugo. *Judarnas Historia i Sverige*. Stockholm: Albert Bonniers, 1924.

Vallins, David. *Coleridge and the Psychology of Romanticism: Feeling and Thought*. Basingstoke: Macmillan, and New York: St. Martin's Press, 2000.

Vereté, M. "The Restoration of the Jews in English Protestant Thought." *Middle East Studies* 8 (1972): 3–50.

Vermes, Geza. *Scripture and Tradition in Judaism*. Haggidic Studies. Second revised ed. Leiden: Brill, 1973.

Vital, David. *A People Apart: The Jews in Europe 1789–1939*. Oxford History of Modern Europe. General editor Lord Bullock and Sir William Deakin. Oxford: Oxford University Press, 1999.

Voght, Peter. "Zinzendorf's Theology of the Sabbath." In *The Distinctiveness of Moravian Culture: Essays and Documents in Moravian History in Honor of Vernon H. Nelson on his Seventieth Birthday*, edited by Craig Atwood and Peter Voght, 273–281. Nazareth, PA: Moravian Historical Society, 2003.

Voltaire [François-Marie Arouet]. *Candide, ou, L'optimisme*. Edited by Lester G. Crocker. London: University of London Press, 1958.

——. *Letters Concerning the English Nation*. Edited by Nicholas Cronk. Oxford and New York: Oxford University Press, 1994.

The Wandering Jew, or, The Shoemaker of Jerusalem: Who Lived When Our Lord and Savior Jesus Christ Was Crucified, and By Him Appointed to Wander Until He Comes Again: With His Discourse With Some Clergymen About the End of the World. In *A chap-book, containing the Hull version of the Wandering Jew legend*. Hull: John Pitts, 1769. Reprint, *Wandering Jew. A chap-book, containing The Hull Version of the Wandering Jew Legend*. London: John Pitts, 1800–1809?

Ward, Thomas. *Abelard to Eloisa: A Poetic Epistle, Newly Attempted*. London: J. Bew, 1782.

Watts, Isaac. *The Psalms, Hymns and Spiritual Songs of the Rev. Isaac Watts, D. D*. Boston: Samuel T. Armstrong, Crocker, and Brewster, 1823.

Weinreich, Max. *History of the Yiddish Language*. Translated by Shlomo Noble. 2 vols. Chicago: University of Chicago Press, 1980.

Wellek, René. "The Concept of Romanticism in Literary History." In *Concepts of Criticism*. 1963. New Haven: Yale University Press, 1973.

Westcott, Wynn. "The Rosicrucians Past and Present." In his *The Magical Mason: Forgotten Hermetic Writings of W. W. Westcott*, edited by Robert Gilbert. Wellingborough: Aquarian Press, 1983.

White, Hayden. *Metahistory: The Historical Imagination in Nineteenth-Century Europe*. Baltimore: The Johns Hopkins University Press, 1973.

Williams, C. Peter. "British Religion and the Wider World: Mission and Empire, 1800–1940." In *A History of Religion in Britain: Practice and Belief from Pre-Roman Times to the Present*, edited by Sheridan Gilley and W. J. Shiels, 381–405. Oxford: Blackwell, 1994.

Wilson, Andrew. *The Creation the Groundwork of Revelation, and Revelation the Attempt to Demonstrate that the Hebrew Language is Founded Upon Natural Ideas, and that the Hebrew Writings Transfer Them to Spiritual Objects*. Edinburgh, 1750.

Wilson, Richard and Alan Mackley. *Creating Paradise: The Building of the English Country House, 1660–1880*. New York and London: Hambledon, 2000.

Wohl, Anthony S. "'Ben JuJu': Representations of Disraeli's Jewishness in the Victorian Political Cartoon." In *Disraeli's Jewishness*, edited by Todd M. Endelman and Tony Kushner, 105–161. London: Valentine Mitchell, 2002.

Wolff, Joseph. *Travels and Adventures of the Rev. Joseph Wolff, Late Missionary to the Jews and Muhammadans in Persia, Bokhara, Cashmeer, etc*. London: Saunders, Otley, 1861.

Wolfson, Elliot. "Messianism in the Christian Kabbalism of Johann Kemper." In *Millenarianism and Messianism in Early Modern European Culture*, vol. 1, *Jewish Messianism in the Early Modern World*, edited by Matt Goldish and Richard Popkin, 139–187. Kluwer: Dordrecht Academic, 2001.

Wolfson, Harry. *The Philosophy of Spinoza*. Cambridge, MA: Harvard University Press, 1934. Reprint, New York: Meridian Books, 1958.

Wolfson, Susan J. "50–50? Phone a Friend? Ask the Audience?: Speculating on a Romantic Century, 1750–1850." *European Romantic Review* 11,1 (winter 2000): 1–11.

Wonnacott, William. "The Rite of Seven Degrees in London." *Ars Quatuor Coronatorum* 39 (1926): 63–98.

Wood, Alfred C. *A History of the Levant Company*. London: Oxford University Press, 1934. Reprint, New York: Barnes and Noble, 1964.

Wordsworth, William. *The Poetical Works of William Wordsworth*. Edited by Ernest de Selincourt and Helen Darbishire. 5 vols. Oxford: Clarendon Press, 1940–1949.

——. *The Prelude, 1799, 1805, 1850*. Edited by Jonathan Wordsworth, M. H. Abrams and Stephen Gill. New York: Norton, 1979.

——. *Prose Works*. Edited by Alexander Grosart, 3 vols. London: Edward Moxon, 1876. Reprint, New York: AMS Press, 1967.

Woulfe, Peter. "Experiments on Some Mineral Substances, Communicated by the Desire of William Hunter, FRS." *Philosophical Transactions of the Royal Society* 69 (1779): 13–23.

Wright, John. *A Revealed Knowledge of Some Things that Will Speedily Be Fulfilled in the World, Communicated to a Number of Christians, Brought Together at Avignon, by the Power of the Spirit of God, from all Nations*. London, 1794.

Wright, Thomas. *The Life of William Blake*. 1929. Reprint, New York: Burt Franklin, 1969.

Wu, Duncan. *Romantic Women Poets*. Oxford: Blackwell, 1997.

——, ed. *Romantic Women Poets: An Anthology*. Oxford, UK and Malden, MA: Blackwell, 1998.

Wunder, Richard P. *Hiram Powers: Vermont Sculptor*. Taftsville, VT: The Countryman Press in Cooperation with the Woodstock Historical Society, 1974.

Wyatt, Thomas. *Collected Poems*. Edited by Kenneth Muir and Patricia Thomson. Liverpool: Liverpool University Press, 1969.

Yerushalmi, Yosef Hayim. *Zakhor: Jewish History and Jewish Memory*. New York: Schocken Books, 1989.

Zim, Rivkah. *English Metrical Psalms: Poetry as Praise and Prayer, 1535–1601*. Cambridge: Cambridge University Press, 1987.

Zornberg, Aviva Gottlieb. *The Beginning of Desire: Reflections on Genesis*. New York: Doubleday, 1996.

INDEX